THE SYSTEMATIC DESIGN OF INSTRUCTION

FIFTH EDITION

THE SYSTEMATIC DESIGN OF INSTRUCTION

FIFTH EDITION

Walter Dick

Florida State University

Lou Carey

University of South Florida

James O. Carey

University of South Florida

New York   San Francisco   Boston
London   Toronto   Sydney   Tokyo   Singapore   Madrid
Mexico City   Munich   Paris   Cape Town   Hong Kong   Montreal

Acquisitions Editor: Arnis E. Burvikovs
Marketing Manager: Kathleen Morgan
Senior Production Manager: Valerie Zaborski
Project Coordination, Text Design, and Electronic Page Makeup: Elm Street Publishing Services, Inc.
Cover Designer/Manager: Nancy Danahy
Manufacturing Manager: Al Dorsey
Printer and Binder: Malloy Lithography
Cover Printer: Coral Graphic Services

Library of Congress Cataloging-in-Publication Data

Dick, Walter, 1937–
    The systematic design of instruction/ Walter Dick, Lou Carey, James O. Carey—5th ed.
        p. cm.
        Includes bibliographical references and index.
        ISBN 0-321-03780-4 (pbk.)
            1. Instructional systems—Design. 2. Training and development. 3. Organization effectiveness.
        4. Formative evaluation.
    I. Carey, Lou.   II. Carey, James O.   III. Title.
    LB 1028.38.D53   2001
    371.3'028—dc21   00-044977
                                                                            CIP

Please visit our website at http://www.awl.com

ISBN 0-321-03780-4

    5 6 7 8 9 10—ML—03

CONTENTS

Chapter 2
Assessing Needs to Identify Instructional Goal(s)   16

Chapter 3
Conducting a Goal Analysis   36

Chapter 6
Writing Performance Objectives 120

Chapter 7
Developing Assessment Instruments 144

**Chapter 8
Developing an Instructional Strategy**   **182**

Chapter 9
Developing Instructional Materials   240

Chapter 10
Designing and Conducting Formative
Evaluations   282

Chapter 11
Revising Instructional Materials   322

Chapter 12
Designing and Conducting Summative
Evaluations   348

PREFACE

During the many years since the original publication of *The Systematic Design of Instruction*, the field of instructional design has continued to grow, both as an area of study and as a profession. Increasing numbers of colleges and universities are offering courses in instructional design, and more companies are adding instructional designers to their staffs.

The natural tendency when preparing a new edition is to include the new trends and emerging ideas in the field. We have been confronted with a number of significant developments in the field of instructional design. For example, the term *performance technology* is now used as a superordinate concept that includes instructional design as a subset. We were faced with the decision to expand our coverage in this book to include all of performance technology. Similarly, a significant growth in the use of computers to deliver instruction has occurred during the last decade—quite a contrast to the almost obsolete mainframe-driven, computer-assisted instruction that represented the future when we published our first edition in 1978. Should we now orient the chapters on instructional strategies and developing instruction to computer-based multimedia instruction? In the area of theory, a challenge has been put forth by researchers who have adopted the constructivist view of learning. They have offered a variety of proposals about how learning occurs and have provided an array of interesting examples of instruction developed from the constructivist perspective. Should we attempt, in this edition, to present constructivist views and discuss how they reinforce or diverge from our own?

Issues related to performance technology, computers, and constructivism are important because they are influencing the field of instructional design. We have attempted to be responsive to these and other developments by relating them to the major components of the instructional design process. At the same time, we have chosen to stay, as nearly as possible, with the fundamental design process presented in the earlier editions of the book. We still think that this process works best as a starting point for learning instructional design. Furthermore, from our many years of teaching from this book, we have found that its current size and format are ideal for our students.

The changes we have made in recent editions of the text include a greater emphasis on these aspects:

- Analysis of the learner
- Analysis of the context in which skills will be learned
- Analysis of the context in which skills will be used
- Earlier and more frequent use of formative evaluation
- Concern for the transfer of learning to the ultimate site of performance
- Expanding formative evaluation to include assessment of newly learned skills and the impact of their use

We believe that these changes and additions will strengthen the fundamental process of instructional design without unduly complicating or confounding it for the novice.

The systems approach model used in this book was first taught in a course at Florida State University in 1968. Since that time, thousands of students have taken the course and have developed instructional materials that have had demonstrated effectiveness with learners. The model has been most heavily influenced by the work of Robert Gagné, Leslie Briggs, Robert Mager, Robert Glaser, and Lee Cronbach. It is a performance-oriented model stressing the identification of skills that students need to learn and the collection of data from students to revise instruction.

During the more than twenty years we have taught the instructional design course, we have had the valuable opportunity to observe our students' work and thus to refine our presentation of the concepts and procedures associated with each step in the model. This book is the culmination of a carefully conceived instructional strategy and of the many years of practical experience in implementing it. Since the publication of the first edition in 1978, we have obtained valuable feedback from instructors and students who have used the book, and we are most grateful for their helpful comments.

In the current edition we have retained the features that seem most important to readers of the previous editions. For example, theoretical descriptions of concepts are supplemented with numerous illustrations of their application. The examples have been carefully selected to represent a wide range of important skills. The examples and practice exercises have been designed to lead readers from an initial understanding of concepts to practical application, resulting eventually in their own instructional design project.

The reader will find that each of the chapters (after the first, which is an introduction to the overall instructional design model), is structured in a similar manner. We hope this structure will facilitate learning the concepts and procedures associated with the instructional design process. The description of the model's components in each of the chapters includes the following sections:

Objectives: The major objectives are listed for each chapter. They describe what the reader should be able to recall and apply after completing the chapter. They are stated in relatively general terms.

Background: This portion of each chapter provides the reader with a brief statement of the background, research and development, and/or problems that led to the development of the procedures associated with each particular component of the model.

Concepts: This section includes both definitions of critical concepts associated with the components as well as a description of "how to do it." It indicates how to carry out the procedures associated with each particular component. In some chapters, the concepts and procedures are covered in several sections rather than in one main Concepts section. This allows for a more thorough examination of detailed procedures.

Examples: In each chapter we provide examples of ways the processes described for each component can be applied. We use a variety of examples in the hope that readers will be able to apply each procedure to the content area in which they are interested.

Summary: This section is specifically provided for those readers who will be developing instructional materials as they study these chapters. It summarizes the concepts and procedures discussed in each chapter. By presenting the material in this manner, we hope to illustrate the interrelatedness of the various components of the model.

Practice and Feedback: We also provide a series of practice activities in which the reader is asked to apply a component of the instructional design process to a variety of examples. Readers will receive feedback to their responses to determine whether they understand the principles described in the chapter and to correct any misunderstandings they may be having. The examples used to illustrate procedures in the book have been purposefully kept simple. The reader should not have to learn the content related to an example to understand the procedure, which is the main focus.

References: A brief listing of the most relevant references appears at the end of each chapter. These are annotated to direct the reader to those resources that may help to amplify points made in the chapter.

The authors wish to extend their appreciation to Dennis C. Myers (deceased) of the University of Toledo for his assistance with various aspects of this book, and to James Russell, Donald Stepich, and their students at Purdue University for developing the first draft of the glossary. Bob Reiser, a Florida State colleague, has used the text in recent years to teach instructional design and has made many helpful suggestions for both teaching and revising the text.

In the spirit of constructive feedback, always an important component of the systematic design process, the authors welcome reactions from readers about ways in which the text may be strengthened to better meet their needs. Please send comments to the authors at the following e-mail addresses.

Walter Dick
wdick@mailer.fsu.edu
Lou Carey
CAREYL@typhoon.coedu.usf.edu
James O. Carey
JCAREY@chuma1.cas.usf.edu

TO THE INSTRUCTOR

We would like to share some of our experiences in teaching with this text. The fundamental decision that must be made by the instructor is to identify the instructional goal for the course. As in any instructional design effort, the nature of the goal will drive the instructional strategy and the evaluation.

The instructional goal can be expressed either as verbal information (i.e., list, describe, or recall various aspects of the instructional design process), or as an intellectual skill (i.e., apply the instructional design process in the creation of instruction). We refer to the first approach as the *knowledge approach* and the latter as the *product approach*.

When knowledge is the course goal, the text serves as a source of information. The role of the instructor is to amplify the principles presented in the materials, to provide examples, and to evaluate students' acquisition of the knowledge. *The Systematic Design of Instruction* is well suited to this type of instruction. It provides students with an instructional design model they can use to understand the major concepts in the field of education. Such ideas as "performance objectives" and "formative evaluation" can be presented and understood in terms of the overall design, delivery, and evaluation of instruction.

The product approach to teaching instructional design requires that students not only know about designing instruction but also develop instructional materials. It is this approach that we personally have found to be most successful in teaching instructional design. From our experience, students learn more through actually developing instruction. Concepts that appear to be academic in the text become very real to students as they grapple with such decisions as how many test items they need or what kind of practice exercises to use. The personal motivation and involvement of students also tend to increase with each succeeding assignment as they begin to produce instruction in their own content area. When students reach the one-to-one formative evaluation stage, they often become quite enthusiastic about observing learners as they interact with, and learn from, the materials the students have created. We believe that the product approach to teaching instructional design provides the greatest long-term return to students.

Instructional Strategy

The second major decision you, the instructor, must make in teaching instructional design is the instructional strategy you will use. First is the issue of the sequence of topics. The text presents the model components in the sequence typically followed when designing instruction. If the knowledge approach to the course is used, then it is likely that the components in the model will be presented as they appear in the text. If the product approach is used, then the component sequence and resulting instructional strategy may be different.

The first sequence we used was to have students learn about a component in the model and then complete the developmental assignment related to that component. For example, after students read the chapter on instructional goals, they develop a goal for the instruction they plan to write. Then, after reading about instructional analysis procedures, they would do an instructional analysis for their selected goal. This read–develop, read–develop process continued until they completed the model. Even though this approach seems quite rational, students often comment that they would have done things very differently in the beginning of the development of their instructional materials if they had been knowledgeable about the components at the end of the model. Many students also indicated that they needed more knowledge about the design process before making a significant commitment to developing instruction for a particular topic.

An alternative strategy, and one that we now use in our product approach to teaching the class, is best described as a *cluster approach*. In a semester course the students read several chapters in sequence each week. After several weeks, they identify their instructional goal and complete the first stage of analysis, the goal analysis. This demonstrates that they understand what they are going to teach, and the instructor can quickly remediate any who are having trouble.

The first report submitted by the students includes their goal statement, goal analysis, subordinate skills analysis, and learner and context analysis. (Our evaluation sheets are shown in Table 1.) While the reports are being graded, students continue with their study of objectives, assessments, and instructional strategies. These then become the major contents of the second report. The students in our courses typically create printed modules as the delivery mechanism for their instruction. They learn about this format and begin to write their instruction according to their instructional strategy. We have also taught instructional design in conjunction with a second course in computer-based instruction. The students who take both courses convert and present their instruction via computer.

While the students are writing their instruction, class time is spent learning about formative evaluation, and they begin, as soon as possible, to conduct their one-to-one evaluations. We require students to do three one-to-ones and a small group with at least eight learners. We do not require them to conduct the field-trial phase—there just is not enough time in the semester. (See Table 2 for our semester schedule for the course.) We are insistent that students complete the first two phases of the formative evaluation process. Their third and final report consists of their instruction and their formative evaluation.

Classroom Activities

The selection of the knowledge or product approach to instruction has significant implications for course management strategies and, particularly, for the use of class time. If the knowledge approach is chosen, then the course will focus primarily on the knowledge objectives that are stated at the beginning of each chapter in the text. The pace of classroom activities can be slow enough to allow for discussion time and the opportunity to talk about various examples and practice and feedback exercises. Students may learn the concepts best when they are required to provide their own examples.

If the product approach is used, the instructor must carefully monitor the weekly progress of the course to ensure that students have sufficient time to conduct the formative evaluation. In our experience talking with students who have used the text at other institutions, their greatest problem is moving through the course at a pace that allows time for the formative evaluation.

In our product approach to instruction, we provide some lectures to highlight important ideas, but we also use numerous class participation activities. Several sessions during the semester are considered workshops—students work in teams of three or four to review and critique the work of the other students in their group. This is excellent preparation for the group contexts in which most designers will work after graduation.

Evaluation of Student Products

We require students to prepare several reports that document their use of the systematic design process. We base our evaluation of students on these reports and on the instruction that the students create. Table 1 outlines the major components of these reports and shows the points allotted to each component. (The assignment of points is arbitrary; however, the points for the third report are approximately equivalent to those for the first two.) This distribution is proportional to the amount of work represented by the reports, and it keeps students motivated throughout the course (i.e., they can make up for early poor performance, or possibly detract from good performance, based on their performance on the final report).

For the instructor, the Report Checklists provide a convenient outline of the content that should be included in the documentation reports and the relative weighting of sections of the reports for evaluation purposes. If a component of a student's report fully meets a stated criterion, then the total points for the component should be assigned to the student. If some of the criteria are not met, then points should be deducted from the component accordingly. If the component is not included in the student's report, then no points should be given for it.

TABLE 1 | **Report Checklists**

Report 1	Points	Score
1. Goal statement	5	_____
2. Goal analysis	10	_____
3. Subskills analysis	10	_____
4. Identification of entry behaviors	3	_____
5. Description of learner interview	3	
6. General description of learners	2	_____
7. Description of performance context, implications for instruction	3	_____
Total	**34**	_____

Report 2	Points	Score
1. Comments on revisions made since Report 1	0	
2. Attach copy of revised instructional analysis and goal statement	0	
3. Performance objectives	10	_____
4. Sample assessments for each objective	8	_____
5. Describe instructional sequence	2	
6. Describe pre-instructional activities	2	
7. Information/example for each objective	10	_____
8. Practice/feedback for each objective	10	_____
9. Describe strategy for teaching terminal objective	2	_____
10. Describe student groupings and media selections	2	_____
11. Attach copies of pre- and posttests that will be used with the instruction.	4	_____
Total	**50**	_____

Report 3	Points	Score
1. Comments on revisions made since Report 2	0	
2. Attach copy of instructional analysis and Report 2	0	
3. Describe learners, materials, and procedures used in one-to-ones	5	_____
4. Describe results of one-to-ones, revisions	10	_____
5. Enclose copy of instructional materials and assessments used in small-group evaluation	20	_____
6. Describe characteristics of small-group learners	3	_____
7. Describe all the materials and instruments used in the small-group evaluation	3	_____
8. Describe the procedures in small-group evaluation	5	_____
9. Present the data from small-group evaluation	12	_____
10. Discuss the small-group data	10	_____
11. Describe revisions to instruction and assessment	12	_____
Total	**80**	_____

TABLE 2	Sample Semester Schedule

Week	Class Topic	Assignment Next Class
1	Course introduction	Chs. 1–3
2	Needs assessment and goal analysis	Ch. 4
3	Identify subskills, entry knowledge, and skills	Ch. 5
4	Learner and context analysis Report 1 due	Chs. 6 and 7
5	Objectives and assessments	Ch. 8
6	Developing an instructional strategy	Ch. 9
7	Developing instructional materials Report 2 due	Ch. 10
8	Formative evaluation procedures	Write instruction
9	Consulting session	Finish writing instruction Ch. 11
10	Formative evaluation: analyzing and reporting data	One-to-one evaluations
11	Discussion of projects	Small-group formative evaluation
12	Consulting session	Write report 3
13	Summative evaluation, course summary Report 3 due	Ch. 12
14	Report 3 returned	

THE SYSTEMATIC DESIGN OF INSTRUCTION

FIFTH EDITION

1 INTRODUCTION TO INSTRUCTIONAL DESIGN

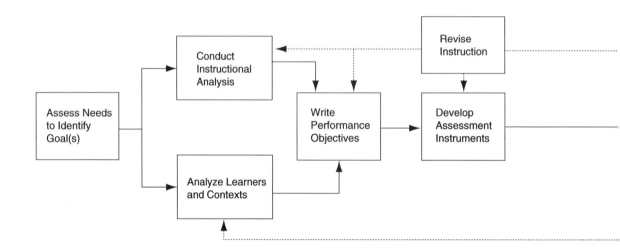

THE DICK AND CAREY SYSTEMS APPROACH MODEL FOR DESIGNING INSTRUCTION

The instructional process, or *teaching,* has traditionally involved instructors, learners, and textbooks. The content to be learned was contained in the text, and it was the instructor's responsibility to "teach" that content to the learners. Teaching could be interpreted as getting content from the text into the heads of learners in such a way that they could retrieve the information for a test. With this model, the way to improve instruction is to improve the instructor (i.e., to require the instructor to acquire more knowledge and to learn more methods for conveying it to learners).

A more contemporary view of instruction is that it is a systematic process in which every component (i.e., teacher, learners, materials, and learning environment) is crucial to successful learning. This perspective is usually referred to as the *systems point of view,* and advocates of this position typically use the systems approach to design instruction.

Let's consider what is meant by a system, and then consider the systems approach. The term *system* has become very popular as more and more of

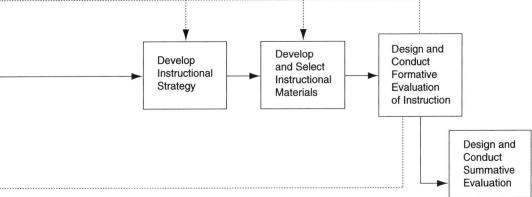

what we do is interrelated with what other people do. A system is technically a set of interrelated parts, all of which work together toward a defined goal. The parts of the system depend on each other for input and output, and the entire system uses feedback to determine if its desired goal has been reached. If it has not, then the system is modified until it does reach the goal. The most easily understood systems are those we create rather than those that occur naturally. For example, you probably have a heating or cooling system in your home that consists of various components that work together to produce warmth or coolness. The thermostat is the feedback mechanism through which the thermometer constantly checks the temperature and signals the system when more heat or cold is needed. When the desired temperature is reached, the system shuts itself off.

How is this related to instruction? First, the instructional process itself can be viewed as a system. The purpose of the system is to bring about learning. The components of the system are the learners, the instructor, the instructional materials, and the learning environment. These components interact in order to achieve the goal. For example, the instructor reviews sample problems in the textbook or manual with the learners in a quiet classroom. To determine whether learning is taking place, a test is administered. This is the instructional system thermostat. If learner performance is not satisfactory, then changes must be enacted to make the system more effective and to bring about the desired learning outcomes.

The result of using the systems view of instruction is to see the important role of all the components in the process. They must all interact effectively, just as the parts in a heating or cooling system must interact effectively in order to bring about the desired outcomes. There is not an overemphasis of any one component in the system, but a determination of the exact contribution of each one to the desired outcome. And it is clear that there must be both an assessment of the effectiveness of the system in bringing about learning and a mechanism to make changes if learning fails to occur.

Thus far, our discussion of the instructional process has focused on the interactive component of the process—namely, the time instructors and learners come together with the hope that learning will occur. But what about the preparation for the instructional process? How does the instructor decide what to do, and when? It is not surprising that someone with a systems view sees the preparation, implementation, evaluation, and revision of instruction as one integrated process. In the broadest systems sense, a variety of sources provide input to the preparation of the instruction. The output is some product or combination of products and procedures that are implemented. The results are used to determine whether the system should be changed, and, if so, how.

The purpose of this book is to describe a systems approach model for the design, development, implementation, and evaluation of instruction. This is not a physical system such as a furnace or air conditioner or heat pump (which will do both) but a procedural system. We will describe a series of steps, all of which will receive input from the preceding steps and will provide output for the next steps. All of the components work together in order for the user to produce effective instruction. The model includes an evaluation component that will help determine what, if anything, went wrong and how it can be improved.

While our model will be referred to as a systems approach model, we must emphasize that there is no single systems approach model for designing instruction. A number of models bear the label *systems approach,* and all of them share most of the same basic components. The systems approach model presented in this book is less complex than some but includes the major components included in other models. Collectively, these design models and the processes they represent are referred to as *Instructional Systems Development (ISD).*

Typically the major phases of ISD are analysis, design, development, implementation, and evaluation. Our particular model does not emphasize the first phase, analysis. Before instruction is created, it is necessary to determine the need for that instruction in terms of what problem within the organization will be solved through the use of new skills, or what opportunity can be seized because of new skills in the organization. This step *is* critically important to the success of the design process; however, there are excellent books that describe the performance analysis and needs assessment processes (see Kaufman, 1991, and Rossett, 1999). We will give only a brief description in Chapter 2 of the analysis process in order to create a context for the remainder of the model.

Note that the term *instructional design* is used as an umbrella term that includes all the phases of the ISD process. The term *design* is included in the general name of the process and is also the name for one of the major subprocesses. When we use the term *instructional design,* we will be referring to the entire ISD process. We will not belabor the issue of terminology further at this point. It will all become clear as you begin to use the instructional design process.

Instructional design models are based, in part, on many years of research on the learning process. Each component of the model is based on theory and, in most instances, on research that demonstrates the effectiveness of that component. The model brings together in one coherent whole many of the concepts that you may have already encountered in a variety of educational situations. For example, you undoubtedly have heard of performance objectives and may have already developed some yourself. Such terms as *criterion-referenced testing* and *instructional strategy* may also be familiar. The model will show how these terms, and the processes associated with them, are interrelated and how these procedures can be used to produce effective instruction.

The instructional strategy component of our model describes how the designer uses the information from the analysis of what is to be taught to formulate a plan for presenting instruction to learners. Our original approach to this component of the model was heavily influenced by the work of Robert Gagné as found in his book *The Conditions of Learning*, first published in 1965. Gagné's early work in the 1940s and 1950s was based on assumptions from behavioral psychology, where instruction is the reinforcement of appropriate learner responses to stimulus situations set up by the teacher. If students have learned, then it is more likely that they will exhibit a desired behavior in a given situation. Gagné's first edition of *The Conditions of Learning*, however, incorporated cognitive information-processing views of learning. In this view most behavior is assumed to be very complex and controlled primarily by a person's internal mental processes rather than external stimuli and reinforcements. Instruction is seen as organizing and providing sets of information and activities that guide, support, and augment students' internal mental processes. Learning has occurred when students have incorporated new information into their memories that enables them to master new knowledge and skills. Gagné further develops cognitive views of learning and instruction in later editions of *The Conditions of Learning* (1970, 1977, 1984).

Constructivism is a relatively recent branch of cognitive psychology that has had a major impact on the thinking of many instructional designers. Constructivist thinking varies broadly on many issues, but the central point is that learning is always a unique product "constructed" as each individual learner combines new information with existing knowledge and experiences. Individuals have learned when they have constructed new interpretations of the social, cultural, physical, and intellectual environments in which they live. Because learning in the constructivist view is so entwined with one's experiences, a primary role of the teacher is creating appropriate learning environments, sometimes called problem scenarios, in which students' learning experiences are authentic representations of real practices in applied settings.

Throughout this text, readers will find elements of behaviorist, cognitivist, and constructivist views adopted and adapted as appropriate for the varieties of learners, learning outcomes, learning contexts, and performance contexts that are discussed. The Dick and Carey Model incorporates an eclectic set of tools drawn from each of these three major theoretical positions of the past fifty years.

One additional comment may help clarify distinctions regarding the learning theories that underlie this instructional design model. As you read through the following chapters you will find the term *behavior* frequently used in all of its forms in a variety of different contexts. On finding repeated uses of the term, one might infer that the predominant theoretical foundation of the text is behaviorism. This would be a wrong assumption that arises from a confusion between the learning theory called behaviorism and the tools used by behaviorist psychologists and all other psychologists to study learning. The behaviorist views learning as a change in the probability of a response, but can only determine that a change in probability (i.e., learning) has occurred by observing the behavior. The tool used by the behaviorist (observation of behavior) is shared by all psychologists who study learning. Thus, the term *behavior* will be used frequently in this text, but it should not be concluded that we recommend either the classical conditioning models of early behaviorists or the operant conditioning models of later behaviorists as the primary theoretical foundations for designing and implementing instruction.

The model, as it is presented here, is based not only on theory and research but also on a considerable amount of practical experience in its application. We suggest that the novice instructional designer use the model principally in the sequence and manner presented in this chapter because students who have done so have been successful. On the other hand, we acknowledge that in particular circumstances and with increased design experience, you might need to change the model, or to perform the steps out of sequence. Also, we expect that more research and experience will help amplify the procedures associated with each component of the model.

In the section that follows, we will present the general systems approach model in much the same way as a cookbook recipe—you do this and then you do that. When you begin to use a recipe in your own kitchen, however, it takes on greater meaning, just as the model will when you begin to develop your own instruction: You select a topic for which instruction is needed, you develop your own instructional resources, you select your own set of learners, and so on. Your perspective on the model will probably change greatly. In essence, your use of your own kitchen, your own ingredients, and your own personal touch will result in a unique product.

The model that will be described in detail in succeeding chapters is presented on pages 2 and 3. The model includes ten interconnected boxes and a major line that shows feedback from the next-to-last box to the earlier boxes. The boxes refer to sets of procedures and techniques employed by the instructional designer to design, develop, evaluate, and revise instruction. The steps will be briefly described in sequence below and in much greater detail in subsequent chapters.

COMPONENTS OF THE SYSTEMS APPROACH MODEL

ASSESS NEEDS TO IDENTIFY GOAL(S)

The first step in the model is to determine what it is that you want learners to be able to do when they have completed your instruction. The instructional goal may be derived from a list of goals, from a needs assessment, from practical experience with learning difficulties of students, from the analysis of people who are doing a job, or from some other requirement for new instruction.

CONDUCT INSTRUCTIONAL ANALYSIS

After you have identified the instructional goal, you will determine step-by-step what people are doing when they perform that goal. The final step in the instructional analysis process is to determine what skills, knowledge, and attitudes, known as *entry behaviors,* are required of learners to be able to begin the instruction. A diagram will be produced that depicts the relationships among all of the skills that have been identified.

ANALYZE LEARNERS AND CONTEXTS

In addition to analyzing the instructional goal, there is a parallel analysis of the learners, the context in which they will learn the skills, and the context in which they will use them. Learners' current skills, preferences, and attitudes are determined along with the characteristics of the instructional setting and the setting in which the skills will eventually be used. This crucial information shapes a number of the succeeding steps in the model, especially the instructional strategy.

WRITE PERFORMANCE OBJECTIVES

Based on the instructional analysis and the statement of entry behaviors, you will write specific statements of what the learners will be able to do when they complete the instruction. These statements, which are derived from the skills identified in the instructional analysis, will identify the skills to be learned, the conditions under which the skills must be performed, and the criteria for successful performance.

DEVELOP ASSESSMENT INSTRUMENTS

Based on the objectives you have written, develop assessments that are parallel to and measure the learners' ability to perform what you described in the objectives. Major emphasis is placed on relating the kind of behavior described in the objectives to what the assessment requires.

DEVELOP INSTRUCTIONAL STRATEGY

Based on information from the five preceding steps, identify the strategy that you will use in your instruction to achieve the terminal objective. The strategy will include sections on preinstructional activities, presentation of information, practice and feedback, testing, and follow-through activities. The strategy will be based on current theories of learning and results of learning research, the characteristics of the medium that will be used to deliver the instruction, content to be taught, and the characteristics of the learners who will receive the instruction. These features are used to develop or select materials or to develop a strategy for interactive classroom instruction.

DEVELOP AND SELECT INSTRUCTIONAL MATERIALS

In this step you will use your instructional strategy to produce the instruction. This typically includes a learner's manual, instructional materials, and tests. (When we use the term *instructional materials* we are including all forms of instruction such as instructor's guides, student modules, overhead transparencies, videotapes, computer-based multimedia formats, and web pages for distance learning. We intend the term *materials* to have this broad connotation.) The decision to develop original materials will depend on the type of learning to be taught, the availability of existing relevant materials, and developmental resources available to you. Criteria for selecting from among existing materials are provided.

DESIGN AND CONDUCT THE FORMATIVE EVALUATION OF INSTRUCTION

Following the completion of a draft of the instruction, a series of evaluations is conducted to collect data that are used to identify how to improve the instruction. The three types of formative evaluation are referred to as *one-to-one evaluation, small-group evaluation,* and *field evaluation.* Each type of evaluation provides the designer with a different type of information that can be used to improve the instruction. Similar techniques can be applied to the formative evaluation of existing materials or classroom instruction.

REVISE INSTRUCTION

The final step (and the first step in a repeat cycle) is revising the instruction. Data from the formative evaluation are summarized and interpreted to attempt to identify difficulties experienced by learners in achieving the objectives and to relate these difficulties to specific deficiencies in the instruction. The line in the figure on pages 2 and 3 labeled "Revise Instruction" indicates that the data from a formative evaluation are not simply used to revise the instruction itself, but are used to reexamine the validity of the instructional analysis and the assumptions about the entry behaviors and characteristics of learners. It is necessary to reexamine statements of performance objectives and test items in light of collected data. The instructional strategy is reviewed and finally all this is incorporated into revisions of the instruction to make it a more effective instructional tool.

DESIGN AND CONDUCT SUMMATIVE EVALUATION

Although summative evaluation is the culminating evaluation of the effectiveness of instruction, it generally is not a part of the design process. It is an evaluation of the absolute and/or relative value or worth of the instruction and occurs only after the instruction has been formatively evaluated and sufficiently revised to meet the standards of the designer. Since the summative evaluation usually does not involve the designer of the instruction but instead involves an independent evaluator, this component is not considered an integral part of the instructional design process per se.

The nine basic steps represent the procedures that one employs when the systems approach is used to design instruction. This set of procedures is referred to as a systems approach because it is made up of interacting com-

FIGURE *1.1*

The Role of the Dick and Carey Model in the Broader Curriculum Development Process

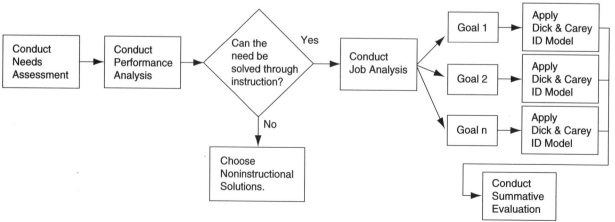

ponents, each having its own input and output, which together produce pre-determined products. Data are also collected about the system's effectiveness so that the final product can be modified until it reaches the desired quality level. When instructional materials are being developed, data are collected and the materials are revised in light of these data to make them as effective and efficient as possible.

Before concluding our discussion of the systems approach model, it should be made clear that, as it stands, this is not a curriculum design model. In order to design a curriculum many more steps would be required before identifying the instructional goals. Some of these techniques are known as needs assessment and job analysis. One should use the model in curriculum development projects after the instructional goals have been derived. Figure 1.1 illustrates how the Dick and Carey Model would fit into a broader curriculum development process.

USING THE SYSTEMS APPROACH MODEL

Now that you have read about this model, you should consider several very important questions about its use. These are discussed in the sections that follow.

WHAT ARE THE BASIC COMPONENTS OF SYSTEMATICALLY DESIGNED INSTRUCTION?

When the systems approach is used, some form of instructional materials is almost always created. These materials were initially referred to as programmed instruction. As the format changed, they became learning activity packages (LAPs) and modules. We will simply refer to *instruction*. A module is usually a self-instructional printed unit of instruction that has an integrated theme, provides students with information needed to acquire and assess specified knowledge and skills, and serves as one component of a total curriculum. While printed modules are still quite popular as a format for instruction, more and more designers are choosing to use computers, and specifically the Internet, as the mechanism for delivering selected modules, a complete unit of instruction, or a total curriculum.

Systematically designed instruction requires learners to interact actively with the instructional materials rather than simply allowing them to read the materials passively. The learners are asked to perform various types of learning tasks and receive feedback on that performance. Some type of testing strategy informs the learners whether they achieved mastery of the content and what they should do if they did not.

Based on the description of prior paragraphs, how would you recognize a module if you saw one? In its most simple form, a module might include a statement to students that says what it is they are about to learn and how they will be tested. It would provide printed instructional materials as well as some practice exercises. A self-test that might be used prior to taking a terminal test could also be included.

A more complex module might contain all of the items listed above, but might also incorporate a number of alternative sets of materials from which the learner could choose the one most appropriate. Alternative media forms such as a web site or videotapes could also be included. In addition, the learner might go to a laboratory to conduct an experiment or go outside the learning environment to gather information.

Keep in mind two important points. First, it is not possible to examine instructional materials and decide whether they contain all the components of systematically designed instruction. Many factors enter into the design decisions that determine what is and is not included. Second, you cannot determine by inspection whether instruction has been systematically designed. The systems approach is a process that is followed by designers, but it is not necessarily apparent by reviewing instructional materials. For example, simply inserting a set of objectives at the beginning of each chapter in a textbook does not mean that the textbook has been systematically designed!

FOR WHICH INSTRUCTIONAL DELIVERY SYSTEM IS THE SYSTEMS APPROACH APPROPRIATE?

The systems approach to the design of instruction includes the planning, development, implementation, and evaluation of instruction. As a part of this process, the delivery method of the instruction must be chosen. In some instances, it is most appropriate to have an instructor deliver the instruction, while in other situations, a variety of media may be employed. Most recently it seems that every new instructional effort tends to include a computer. In every instance, the systems approach is an invaluable tool for identifying what is to be taught, determining how it will be taught, and evaluating the instruction to find out whether it is effective.

The procedure described in this text for developing an instructional strategy is a generic one. It is applicable to the development of print instruction that is still favored in many instances for portability and production cost. The procedure can be easily used, however, to fit the requirements of any selected medium of instruction. Materials developers in video or multimedia, for example, could use the instructional strategy statements to create storyboards, screen displays, or flow charts for hyperlinking interactive sequences. The use of the systems approach prevents the designer from trying to create instruction for a medium prior to a complete analysis of what is to be taught and how. Most research suggests that it is the analysis process and the instructional strategies, rather than the delivery mode, that determine the success of the instruction. The systems approach is a generic planning process that ensures that instructional products developed for any delivery system are responsive to the needs of learners and effective in achieving the desired learning outcomes.

DOES THE USE OF THE SYSTEMS APPROACH IMPLY THAT ALL INSTRUCTION WILL BE INDIVIDUALIZED?

From our discussion of the development of printed modules and computer-based instruction, the reader might assume that systematically designed instruction is the same as individualized instruction; it is not. Let's assume, for the sake of discussion, that individualized instruction permits learners to progress at their own rate. (This is considered the minimal definition of individualized instruction!) A well-designed print module or computer-based lesson could certainly be used in this manner. So the systems approach can be used to design individualized instruction. However, it can also be used to design group-based instruction—if we may use this term in contrast with individualized instruction. The systems approach can be used, as already noted, to develop all types of instructor-led and interactive group activities. In fact, it is often the case that these are precisely the conditions that are most effective and efficient for bringing about the desired learning outcomes.

The reader should be careful to distinguish between the process of designing instruction and the delivery of that instruction. The systems approach is basically a design process, whereas instructors, modules, computers, and televisions are delivery mechanisms. These delivery mechanisms can be used with one or many learners at the same time. A major part of the design process is to determine how the instruction can be delivered most effectively.

The beneficiary of the application of the systems approach to the design of instruction is the individual learner. Careful attention is paid to determining what must be learned and what learners must already know in order to begin the instruction. The instruction is focused on the skills to be learned and is presented under the best conditions for learning. The learner is evaluated fairly with instruments that measure the skills and knowledge described in the objectives, and the results are used to revise the instruction so that it will be even more effective with succeeding learners. Following this process causes the designer to focus on the needs and skills of the learners and results in the creation of effective instruction.

WHY USE THE SYSTEMS APPROACH?

Few formal research studies address the question of the overall total effectiveness of the systems approach to designing instruction. Although much research has been done on various components of the model, rigorous studies that involve the total model are extremely rare because they are so difficult to conduct. The few studies that have been published tend to provide strong support for the approach. The primary support for the model, however, comes from designers who have used the process and have documented their success with learners.

It appears that there are a number of reasons that systematic approaches to instructional design are effective. The first is the focus, at the outset, on what learners are to know or be able to do when the instruction is concluded. Without this precise statement, subsequent planning and implementation steps can become unclear and ineffective.

A second reason for the success of the systems approach is the careful linkage between each component, especially the relationship between the instructional strategy and the desired learning outcomes. Instruction is specifically targeted on the skills and knowledge to be taught and supplies the appropriate conditions for the learning of these outcomes. Stated another way, instruction does not consist of a range of activities only some of which may be related to what is to be learned.

The third and perhaps most important reason for the success of the systems approach is that it is an empirical and replicable process. Instruction is designed not for one delivery, but for use on as many occasions as possible with as many learners as possible. Because it is reusable, it is worth the time and effort to evaluate and revise it. In the process of systematically designing instruction, data are collected to determine what part of the instruction is not working, and it is revised until it does work.

Because of these characteristics, the systems approach is valuable to instructors who are interested in successfully teaching basic and higher level competencies to learners. The competency-based approach has been widely adopted among educators; however, the most numerous applications of the systems approach may be found in industry and in military services. In these environments there is a premium on both efficiency of instruction and quality of student performance. The payoffs in both situations are quite obvious.

Who Should Use the Systems Approach?

As you study the instructional design model and, we hope, use it to design some instruction, you will find that it takes both time and effort. You will probably find yourself saying, "I could never use this process to prepare all my instruction," and you would probably be correct. The individual instructor who has day-to-day instructional responsibilities can use the process to develop only small amounts of written or mediated instruction at any given time. The process can also be used effectively and efficiently to select from among existing materials and to design instruction that is not materials based.

We have found that almost every instructor who has studied the process has come away with two reactions. The first is that they will certainly begin immediately to use some of the components in the model, if not all of them. The second reaction is that their approach to instruction will never be the same because of the insights they have gained from using the process. (The reader may be somewhat skeptical at this point; be sure to consider your own reactions *after* you have used this approach.)

A second group of users of the ISD approach is growing quite rapidly. They are typically referred to as *instructional designers,* since they are trained to use a systematic approach to designing new instructional systems or improving already existing systems. Their full-time job is to create replicable instructional programs that are effective with a particular learner population.

In contrast to the instructor who may be working alone, the instructional designer often works with a team of specialists to develop the instruction. The team would typically include a content specialist, a media production specialist, an evaluation specialist, and a manager. (When the instructor works alone, he or she usually must fill all of these roles.) The team approach draws on the expertise of specialists to produce a product that none could produce alone. In these settings there is a premium placed on interpersonal skills because seemingly everyone has ideas on how best to do what needs to be done.

This book has been written for both the instructor who would like to know more about the systems approach to instructional design and the beginning instructional designer who may pursue a career in this field. The book is also intended for the public school teacher, the university professor, the industrial trainer, and the military instructor. We are convinced that the model and procedures are equally applicable in both school and nonschool settings.

In our examples of various aspects of the application of the systematic design process, we have included instruction that is intended for all age groups, from young children to mature adults. We will use the terms *teacher, instructor,* and *designer* interchangeably throughout the book because we truly believe they are interchangeable.

As you read through the chapters that follow, you will find an instructional design example on training Neighborhood Crime Watch leaders. The example is carried through each step of the design model. You should also note that Appendices A through K contain an instructional design example for a school subject that is carried through each step of the model (using a variety of sentence types in writing paragraphs).

References and Recommended Readings

At the end of each chapter, several carefully selected references are listed. The books and articles supplement the description in the chapter or focus in more detail on an important concept that has been presented.

The references listed for this first chapter are somewhat different. These are books in the field of instructional design or ones that have direct implications for the practice of instructional design. Many of the topics in this book also appear in these references. The books vary in depth and breadth of coverage of topics, but they should all help to expand your knowledge and understanding of the instructional design field.

Anglin, G. J. (Ed.). (1991). *Instructional technology: Present, past, and future.* Englewood, CO: Libraries Unlimited. Wide range of informative chapters on the entire field of instructional technology.

Banathy, Bela H. (1968). *Instructional systems.* Palo Alto, CA: Fearon Publishers.

Banathy, Bela H. (1992). Comprehensive systems design in education. *Educational Technology, 32*(1), 33–35.

Briggs, L. J., Gustafson, K. L., & Tillman, M. H. (Eds.). (1991). *Instructional design: Principles and applications.* Englewood Cliffs, NJ: Educational Technology Publications. An update of an older classic. Many of our chapters parallel chapters in this book.

Dills, C. R., & Romiszowski, A. J. (1997). *Instructional development paradigms.* Englewood Cliffs, NJ: Educational Technology Publications. Presents various models and approaches to instructional design.

Driscoll, Marcy P. (1994). *Psychology of learning for instruction.* Boston: Allyn & Bacon. Contemporary approaches to learning that focus on instruction.

Duffy, T. M., & Jonassen, D. H. (Eds.). (1992). *Constructivism and the technology of instruction.* Hillsdale, NJ: Lawrence Earlbaum Associates. Comprehensive review of varying perspectives on constructivism.

Ertmer, P. A., & Newby, T. J. (1993). Behaviorism, cognitivism, constructivism: Comparing critical features from an instructional design perspective. *Performance Improvement Quarterly, (6)*4, 50–72. Useful comparisons of three theoretical bases with guidelines for instructional designers.

Ertmer, P. A., & Quinn, J. (1999). *The ID casebook: Case studies in instructional design.* Upper Saddle River, NJ: Prentice Hall. Wide array of examples of the application of instructional design processes to real world problems.

Fleming, Malcolm L., & Levie, W. Howard (1993). *Instructional message design.* (2nd ed.). Englewood Cliffs, NJ: Educational Technology Publications.

Gagné, Robert M. (1985). *The conditions of learning* (4th ed.). New York: Holt, Rinehart and Winston.

Gagné, Robert M. (Ed.). (1987). *Instructional technology: Foundations.* Hillsdale, NJ: Lawrence Erlbaum Associates.

Gagné, Robert M., Briggs, Leslie J., & Wager, Walter W. (1992). *Principles of instructional design* (4th ed.). New York: Holt, Rinehart and Winston.

Gagné, Robert M., & Medsker, Karen L. (1996). *The conditions of learning: training applications.* Fort Worth, TX: Harcourt Brace College Publishers. Same model as Gagné's original text by this name, but with the addition of examples from business and industry.

Gredler, Margaret E. (1997). *Learning and instruction: Theory into practice* (3rd ed.). Upper Saddle River, NJ: Prentice-Hall. A survey of learning theories that includes behaviorist, cognitivist, and constructivist views with applications for instruction.

Hannum, W., & Hansen, C. (1989). *Instructional systems development in large organizations.* Englewood Cliffs, NJ: Educational Technology Publications. An examination of the instructional design process as it is used with large projects.

Kaufman, R. (1991). *Strategic planning plus: An organizational guide.* Indianapolis, IN: Circle City Press.

Kemp, J. E., Morrison, G. R., & Ross, S. M. (1998). *Designing effective instruction* (2nd ed.). New York: Merrill Publishing. A revision of an older book, this edition covers many current instructional design concepts.

Knirk, Frederick G., & Gustafson, Kent L. (1986). *Instructional technology: A systematic approach to education.* New York: Holt, Rinehart and Winston.

Mager, Robert F. (1988). Making instruction work. Belmont, CA: Lake Publishing Co.

Mager, Robert F. (1992). *What every manager should know about training.* Belmont, CA: Lake Publishing Co.

Merrill, M. D., Drake, L., Lacy, M. J., & Pratt, J. (1996). Reclaiming instructional design. *Educational Technology, 36*(5), 5–7.

Reiser, R. A., & Dick, W. (1996). *Instructional planning: A guide for teachers* (2nd ed.). Boston, MA: Allyn and Bacon. A short book about the instructional design process for teachers and trainers.

Richey, R. (1992). *Designing instruction for the adult learner.* London: Kogan Page Limited. A theory of instruction based on an extensive review of the literature and empirical data from training studies.

Romiszowski, A. J. (1981). *Designing instructional systems.* London: Kogan Page.

Romiszowski, A. J. (1984). *Producing instructional systems.* London: Kogan Page.

Rossett, A. (1999). *First things fast.* San Francisco, CA: Jossey-Bass Pfeiffer. Performance analysis is contrasted with training needs assessment.

Rothwell, W. J., & Kazanas, H. C. (1997). *Mastering the instructional design process: A systematic approach.* (2nd ed.). San Francisco, CA: Jossey-Bass Publishers. A general text on the instructional design process.

Saettler, Paul (1990). *The evolution of American educational technology.* Englewood, CO: Libraries Unlimited. Very complete historical description of the development of the audiovisual field and the growth of instructional design.

Seels, Barbara, (Ed.). (1995). *Instructional design fundamentals: A reconsideration.* Englewood Cliffs, NJ: Educational Technology Publications. Perspectives on instructional design from theory, and implications for the design process.

Seels, B., & Glasgow, Z. (1990). *Exercises in instructional design.* Columbus, OH: Merrill. Fine set of practice activities for many of the skills taught in this text.

Seels, B., & Richey, R. (1994). *Instructional technology: The definition and domains of the field.* Washington, DC: Association for Educational Communications and Technology. Current thinking about the distinctive features of instructional technology that includes instructional design.

Smith, P. L., & Ragan, T. J. (1999). *Instructional design* (2nd ed.). New York: Wiley. Excellent chapters on instructional strategies for various learning outcomes.

2 ASSESSING NEEDS TO IDENTIFY INSTRUCTIONAL GOAL(S)

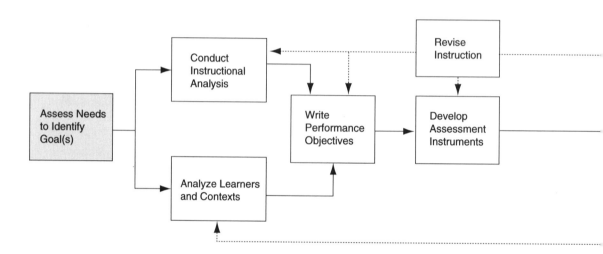

OBJECTIVES

- Define needs assessment, needs statements, and instructional goals.
- Identify an instructional goal that meets the criteria for initiating the design of effective instruction.
- Write an instructional goal that meets the criteria for initiating the development of instructional materials.

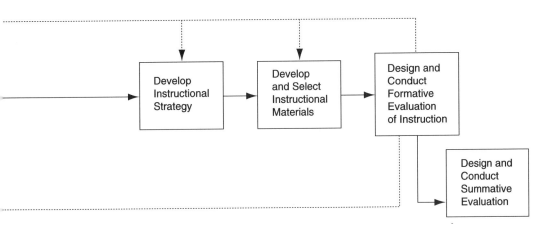

Perhaps the most critical event in the instructional design process is identifying the instructional goal. If done improperly, even elegant instruction may not serve the designer's real purpose. Two basic methods are used to identify instructional goals: the *subject-matter expert approach* and the *performance technology approach*.

Every reader of this book could be considered a subject-matter expert (SME, pronounced S-M-E or SMEE) in some area. You have completed, or will complete, an undergraduate degree in some field. Your knowledge of that field now greatly exceeds that of the general public, so you would be considered a SME.

When SMEs are asked to develop instruction in their areas of expertise, they will most likely consider what they were taught. Depending on their evaluation of that experience, they try either to replicate it or to improve it. The instructional goals established by SMEs often contain words like *know* and *understand* with regard to content information. This approach to the teaching–learning process emphasizes the communication of information from instructor to student in the instructional process.

Instructional designers favor the performance technology approach, where instructional goals are set in response to problems or opportunities. There is no preconceived notion of what will be included in an instructional package, or that, in fact, there is any need for instruction at all. Designers attempt to work with those who are responsible for ensuring that an organization is meeting its quality and productivity goals. These concerns apply to any organization, private or public. Organizations are constantly concerned with their ability to meet their clients' and customers' needs. To the extent they are not doing so, changes must be made.

But what changes? Designers engage in needs assessment and analysis processes to specifically identify the problem, which is not always an easy task. The real problem is not always what it initially appears to be. After the problem is identified, the designer attempts to identify the causes of the problem, and then identifies an array of solutions that could be implemented to solve the problem. Seldom is instruction the single answer to a problem. Usually a combination of changes is required to solve the problem effectively.

Designers derive instructional goals through the use of some type of needs assessment process. Goals are usually stated as skills, knowledge, and attributes that some group of learners must acquire to satisfy the identified need. This type of goal statement usually includes such verbs as *solve, apply,* and *manage.* They focus on *what learners will be able to do* when they complete the instruction, and *the real-world context in which they will have to use their new skills.* Consider two examples of ways to identify instructional goals.

A company acquired so many computers in the last two years that a management decision was made to terminate the use of outside service agents, and to establish twenty-five internal positions for computer technicians. From a performance technology perspective it can be implied that the equipment was malfunctioning sufficiently that the "need" for the technicians seemed warranted. (Other solutions might be to purchase more reliable computer equipment from another manufacturer, lease equipment, or include a long-term service contract as part of the purchase price.) The decision to use twenty-five technicians is only the beginning of the solution. If the decision is to hire already skilled technicians "from the outside," the training department may have no role in solving this problem. If, on the other hand, the decision is made to use current employees to fill these positions, then it is likely that some form of training will be required. If they currently do similar work on other equipment, then only minimal additional training may be required. If they have no related skills, then an entire curriculum may have to be developed by the training organization, or the employees could be enrolled in a nearby technical school.

The purpose of this description is to show that everyone wins when instruction provides learners with skills necessary to solve an organizational problem or to take advantage of an opportunity. Describing the problem or opportunity precisely and determining how it can be solved efficiently and effectively are important. Instruction is a costly solution, chosen only when other solutions are not satisfactory. Thinking of instruction as an expensive solution may not make sense, but within large organizations instruction can be very expensive compared to other alternatives.

As another example, a school board might want 95 percent of the students in the school district to pass the functional literacy examination; however, their records indicate that only 81 percent are passing the test. There is a gap of 14 percent between what is and what should be. An appropriate goal in this situation might be to increase the percentage of students passing the functional literacy examination by 14 percent, to a level of 95 percent passing.

It should be noted that the goal focuses on what learners will be able to do. Although it may not be clear exactly what skills make a person "functionally literate," at least we would have some idea of how we would proceed to derive more specific skills that would, altogether, represent this goal. Notice also that the goal describes the outcomes of instruction and not the process of instruction. A need statement should not refer to "a need to use computers in our instruction," or "a need for more third grade teachers." These are part of the process of achieving some goal, but do not represent good instructional design goal statements. The use of computers in a business and more teachers in a school is a means to an end and should not become ends in and of themselves.

Typically, the goals used by an instructional designer have been derived from some type of needs assessment, either formal or informal, and have been further refined by either a job or curriculum analysis. If we now consider the goal of raising the functional literacy scores, one set of information that should be obtained is the description of skills that are tested. With this list it is possible to determine where each skill is currently taught in the curriculum. Some skills may not be taught at all. Others may only be taught at the elementary level, and probably have been forgotten. It could be decided that in order to get 14 percent more of the students to pass the examination, a new course must be established to serve the needs of potentially low-performing students.

The goals for the new course would probably be in the areas of mathematics and language. These will be further broken down into topic areas, units, and ultimately into lessons. The process of identifying the topics to be included often seems to involve making sure that as much content as possible is covered, rather than determining exactly what it is that learners need to know. Data regarding student performance on each skill in the examination would be very useful for identifying which skills should receive special emphasis in the course.

In summary, instructional goals are ideally derived through a process of needs assessment that establishes rather broad indications of a problem that can be solved by providing instruction. Then an analysis of that goal is undertaken, either in the context of a curriculum or a job. As a result, more refined specific statements emerge that focus on what learners will be able to do and the context in which they will be able to do it.

CONCEPTS

PERFORMANCE ANALYSIS

Organizations, both public and private, are continually faced with problems that senior officers and managers must identify and solve. Problems reflect a failure to achieve certain organizational goals or to take advantage of opportunities. Those failures are often seen as resulting from the improper use of or a lack of skills. Thus, it is not unusual for an officer to identify a problem and assume that training is the solution. Such problems are often presented to the training department with the request that they develop some training to solve the problem. In these situations, the training department should undertake a performance analysis.

A performance analysis is a study conducted to determine the exact nature of an organizational performance problem and how it can be resolved. Quite often the original problem is only a symptom of a greater problem or is not really a problem at all. Robinson and Robinson (1995) have developed a general performance analysis model that is now widely used. The model is summarized briefly in the paragraphs that follow.

The Robinsons' model has several major components, and it is the responsibility of a performance analyst or team to collect information about each component. The model indicates that important performance problems are best identified in terms of the gap between the desired goals and mission of an organization and their current status. If a goal is being achieved, then no performance problem exists. On the other hand, if there is a significant difference between the *should* status of a goal and the *is* status, then further analysis is required.

For each goal within an organization, there should be a corresponding description of the behaviors that will be required of employees to reach the goal. For example, to achieve a particular sales goal, the required behaviors may include making at least fifty personal calls on former customers each month. These calls would represent the *should* level of performance in the Robinsons' model. A study of the actual performance of sales people regarding number of calls to former customers would represent the *is* status regarding this performance.

The analyst now compares the gaps in performance between the *should be* and *is*, and attempts to determine the causes. There may be causes that are external to the organization, such as changes in the economy or the introduction of a new product by a competitor, and there may be internal causes such as difficulties with an antiquated phone system or failure to hire sufficient sales people. Or, the causes for a gap may be that employees do not know how to perform the desired behaviors. When this is the case, training may be part of the solution to the problem.

The purpose of a performance analysis study is to acquire information on each of the components in the model in order to verify problems and identify possible solutions. If part of the solution is training on new skills or rejuvenating existing skills, then plans for an instructional design project are made. Experience has shown that under careful analysis, many organizational problems that previously were addressed by training now are solved via multicomponent solutions that may or may not include training.

It has been noted that managers or executives often describe problems in terms of the current situation, or the *is*, the way it is now. Examples would be, "Our deliveries are late," "None of our students got to the national spelling bee," "Our sales are down," and "Too many of our students are failing the basic skills test." In studying current results and performance, the designer would identify exactly *how* late the deliveries are or *what percentage* of the students are failing the basic skills test.

The *shoulds*, in contrast to the *ares*, are descriptions of what the situation ought to be. The word *should* is not used in the optimistic sense of "in the best of all worlds," but rather, in the realistic sense of the *required or mandated level of performance*, or a level that is the goal of the organization.

A *gap* is defined as *should* status minus *is* status. The gap of greatest consequence is that in organizational results. This gap is then associated with a gap in organizational performance (i.e., the behaviors that people in the organization are exhibiting). If it turns out that there is no gap, then no change is required, and obviously there is no requirement for new training. This is the situation whenever any organizational officer (including a school board member) surveys a situation and indicates that it is satisfactory—the *should* and *is* are the same, and there is no need for change.

When *should* and *is* differ, as they usually do, the gap between the two is often referred to as a *need*. In order to understand this need, it is useful to determine how people feel about it and how it is affecting them. Additionally, their views on possible causes for and solutions to the need can be illuminating. Readers familiar with total quality management will recognize a similarity between the performance analysis process and the techniques often used by groups of employees who identify problems and work in teams to identify and implement solutions.

The outcome of a performance analysis study is a clear description of a problem in terms of failure to achieve desired organizational results and the corresponding desired and actual employee behaviors, evidence of the causes of the problem, and suggested cost-effective solutions. Note that while an instructional designer may participate in a performance analysis study, there is no assumption that instruction will be a component of the solution. These studies are often team efforts, and the results reflect what is possible within the organization. An important consideration in selecting a solution is cost, and instruction is often one of the more expensive alternative solutions.

When designers use the Robinson and Robinson model for conducting a performance analysis, they review existing data and documentation regarding the problem and how "it ought to be." They collect additional data via interviews, surveys, observations, and small group discussions. This empirical process is rooted in the realities of the organization conducting the study. Any instruction resulting from such a study should be targeted to the identified need and should contribute ultimately to the satisfaction of the need.

Kaufman (1988, 1992, 1998) has provided many insights into the needs assessment process, including (1) the distinction between means and ends in terms of what organizations do, and (2) areas in which organizations have problems. Consider the following example from the public schools.

It is not unusual to hear principals say their teachers "need" to know more about computers. As a result, a workshop is provided so teachers can all become more competent. In this situation, teacher skills should be viewed as a means to an end, to turn out more competent *students*. The real needs assessment issue is what are the optimal and actual computer skills *of the students*, and, if there is a need here, what are the various solutions to upgrade those skills? A workshop for all teachers may or may not be the best solution. Kaufman urges us to examine gaps in organizational results rather than internal processes when we begin to identify needs and make plans for spending organizational resources to meet these needs.

Needs assessment is a critical component of the total design process. Trainers and educators must be aware of the tremendous cost of creating instruction for which there is no need; therefore, more emphasis is being placed on "front-end" analysis, performance analysis, and other approaches for identifying needs more accurately. In the past it was common for survey instruments to be the major means of identifying and documenting training needs. Today surveys are being supplemented or supplanted with more insightful interviews and direct observations of performers. The "performers" may be either the audience with the potential problem or experts who demonstrate how a particular task is to be performed on new equipment.

It is not our purpose in this book to explain or demonstrate how to conduct a complete needs assessment, because the books by Rossett (1987) and Kaufman (1988) provide the conceptual background and procedural details for performing this assessment. We therefore begin the instructional design process at the point following goal identification. We are in no way minimizing the importance of the process used to identify appropriate goals. Regardless of the procedure that is used to generate a goal, it is almost always necessary for the designer to clarify and sometimes amplify the goal in order for it to serve as a firm starting point for the instructional design process. Many goals are fuzzy, and designers must learn how to cope effectively with them.

CLARIFYING INSTRUCTIONAL GOALS

Mager (1972) has described a procedure that the designer can use when a vague, nonspecific goal is encountered. A fuzzy goal is generally some abstract statement about an internal state of the learner, such as "appreciating," "having an awareness of," "sensing," and so on. These kinds of terms often appear in goal statements, but the designer doesn't know what they mean because there is no indication of what learners would be doing if they achieved this goal. Designers assume that at the successful completion of their instruction, students should be able to demonstrate that they have achieved the goal. But if the goal is so unclear that it is not apparent what successful performance would be, then further analysis must be undertaken.

To analyze a vague goal, first write it down. Then indicate the things a person would do to demonstrate that he or she had achieved that goal or what they would be doing if they were performing the goal. Don't be too critical at first; just write everything down that occurs to you. Next, sort through the statements for those that best represent what is meant by your unclear goal. Now incorporate each of these indicators (there may be one or quite a few) into a statement that tells what the learner will do. As a last step, examine the goal statement and ask yourself this: If learners achieved or demonstrated each of the performances, would you agree that they had achieved your goal? If the answer is yes, then you have clarified the goal; you have developed one or more goal statements that collectively represent the achievement of an important goal. In the Examples section of this chapter we will demonstrate how this process can be used with vague goals.

The designer should be aware of this type of goal analysis procedure because many critical educational and training goals are not initially stated as clear, concise descriptions of performances of learners. They often are stated in terms that are quite meaningful (in general) to the originator, but have no specifics that the designer can use for developing instruction. Such goals should not be discarded as being useless. An analysis should be undertaken to identify specific performance outcomes that are implied by the goal. Often it will be helpful to use a number of knowledgeable people in the process so that you see the range of ideas that can emerge from the goal and the need for consensus on specific behaviors if truly successful instruction is to be developed.

LEARNERS, CONTEXT, AND TOOLS

Whereas the most important aspect of an instructional goal is the description of what learners will be able to do, that description is not complete without an indication of (1) who the learners are, (2) the context in which they will use the skills, and (3) the tools that will be available. A preliminary description of these aspects is important for two reasons. First, they require the designer to be clear about exactly who the learners will be rather than making vague statements or allusions to groups of learners. It is not unheard of for a design project to come to a halt when it is discovered that there are no learners available to receive the instruction. In essence, the instruction has no market.

Likewise, from the very beginning a project designer must be clear about the context in which the skills will be used and whether any aids or tools will be available. We will refer to this as the performance context. For example, if learners are going to be using computational skills, will they have access to calculators or computers? In the performance context, will they be working at a desk, or will they be on their feet talking to a customer? Must information be available from memory, or can a computer-based information retrieval system be used? Information about the performance context and the characteristics of the people who will be receiving the instruction is extremely important as the designer begins to analyze exactly what skills must be included in the instruction. Eventually, the information will be used to select instructional strategies to promote the use of the skills, not only in the learning context but also in the context in which they are eventually intended for application.

A complete goal statement should describe the following:

- The learners
- What learners will be able to do in the performance context
- The performance context in which the skills will be applied
- The tools that will be available to the learners in the performance context

An example of a complete goal statement would be the following: "The Acme call center operators will be able to use the Client Helper job aid to provide information to customers who contact the call center." All four components of a goal statement are included in this statement.

CRITERIA FOR ESTABLISHING INSTRUCTIONAL GOALS

Sometimes the goal-setting process is not totally rational; that is, it does not follow a systematic needs assessment process. The instructional designer must be aware that instructional design takes place in a specific context that includes a number of political and economic considerations, as well as technical or academic ones. Stated in another way, powerful people often determine priorities, and finances almost always determine the limitations of what can be done on an instructional design project. Any selection of instructional goals must be done in terms of the following concerns:

1. Will the development of this instruction solve the problem that led to the need for it?

2. Are these goals acceptable to those who must approve this instructional development effort?

3. Are there sufficient people and time to complete the development of instruction for this goal?

These questions are of great importance to the institution or organization that will undertake the development.

We cannot overly emphasize the importance of being able to relate logically and persuasively to the goals of instruction and to documented performance gaps within an organization. When instruction is developed for a client, the client must be convinced that if learners achieve the instructional goals, then a significant organizational problem will be solved or an opportunity will be realized through the use of the new skills. This kind of reasoning is as applicable to the development of instruction in public schools as it is to business, military, and public agencies.

The rationale for an instructional goal may help garner support from decision makers, but the designer (and managers) must be assured that there is sufficient time and resources for both the development of the instruction and its delivery. Most designers would agree that there is seldom sufficient time for either. One reason is that predicting the amount of time required to carry out a project is difficult. Another is that organizations often want something "yesterday"!

Not only is it difficult to predict how long it will take to develop instruction, but it is also difficult to predict how long learners will take to master the instructional goals (i.e., how long will the instruction last?). No readily accepted rules of thumb relate instructional (or learning) time to skills mastered. So many factors are involved that time estimates are difficult to make.

The most likely scenario is that the designer is told, "You have three weeks to develop a four-hour workshop." Until an organization has experience in making these decisions, they are made on the basis of immediate conditions in the work setting. Certainly the designer can shorten or lengthen instruction to fit the time available, but the primary instructional concern is to select the best possible instructional strategies for teaching the skills that must be mastered and then to determine how much time is required. Obviously, we can make more accurate learning-time estimates after several tryouts of the instruction.

The designer should examine additional questions when contemplating an individual project. Assuming that a need has been established and that time and resources are available, then the designer should determine whether the content is stable enough to warrant the cost of developing it. If it will be out of date in six months, then extensive instructional development is probably not warranted.

In addition, the instructional design process depends heavily upon the availability of learners to try out the instruction. If the designer cannot get access to appropriate learners, it will be impossible to implement the total design process. A small number of learners should be available to receive the instruction. If they are not, then the designer should reconsider the validity of the need.

The final concern is the designer's own expertise in the area in which the instruction will be developed. Experienced professional designers often work on teams in which, at least initially, the content area is totally foreign to them. The ability and willingness to work on teams is one of the most important characteristics of a successful designer.

A great deal of content learning must take place before the designer can work effectively. For those just learning the design process, it is preferable to begin with a content area in which they already have subject matter expertise. It is a lot easier to learn one new set of skills, namely, instructional design skills, than it is to learn two new sets of skills—both content and process—at the same time.

If you have chosen (or are required) to design an instructional package as you work through the chapters of this book, the process will consume many hours of your time. Before you select or identify an instructional goal, review the criteria listed in this chapter. It is particularly important (1) that you have the expertise to deal with the subject matter, (2) that learners are available to you to help evaluate and revise the instructional materials, and (3) that you have selected a goal that can be taught in a reasonable amount of time.

Two examples of the procedures used to develop instructional goals may help you formulate or evaluate your own goals. Both examples are based on an identified problem, needs assessment activities, and a prescribed solution to a problem. Each example has its own scenario to help clarify the context of the problem and the process used to identify the goals. For a third example from a school learning context, see Appendix A.

LEADING GROUP DISCUSSIONS

The first example is based on a common problem in community management. The following paragraphs describe planning decisions based on needs assessment, the instructional goal, information for clarifying instructional goals, and criteria for establishing instructional goals.

NEEDS ASSESSMENT   Following an extensive statewide needs assessment on neighborhood crime trends within their state, law enforcement officials noted the disparity between ideal community policing levels and the current level of community service that local police departments are able to provide. During the solutions phase of the needs assessment, one of the many possible solutions suggested for improving neighborhood service was increasing support for Neighborhood Crime Watch (NCW) organizations. It was noted that across the United States and in England, active NCW communities bolstered the effectiveness of local police, improved community–police communications, and reduced the amount of crimes committed (lost opportunities) within their neighborhoods. The panel studying this data called for finding ways to help neighborhoods better help themselves and targeted the Neighborhood Crime Watch Association as an organization worthy of further support.

A second task force was appointed to conduct a needs assessment study for Neighborhood Crime Watch organizations to determine how to increase the number of active NCW organizations within an area and improve the effectiveness of existing organizations. This panel concluded that (1) the NCW leader was the key person in determining the effectiveness of NCW groups, (2) leaders of the most effective groups had well-developed group discussion leadership skills, and (3) effective NCW leaders often entered local politics at the city and county level.

The state, upon the recommendation of the two task forces, decided to sponsor a grant to develop training for NCW leader volunteers throughout the state. The instruction was to focus on group discussion leadership skills, and training materials were to be provided to all counties within the state. Support would also be provided to local county government in-service training centers and staffs who would recruit, manage, and deliver the instruction. Training stipends were provided for one group of twenty NCW leaders per county for each of three years.

CLARIFYING THE INSTRUCTIONAL GOAL   The instructional goal is (1) a clear, general statement of learner outcomes, (2) related to an identified problem and needs assessment, and (3) achievable through instruction rather than some more efficient means such as enhancing motivation of employees.

What is the instructional goal? In this instance, the instructional goal is for NCW leaders to demonstrate in a neighborhood meeting, effective discussion group leadership skills. These discussions should be focused on encouraging neighbors to attend meetings, helping them identify crime problems in their community, and planning programs to help reduce identified problems.

What is the relationship between the goal and the needs assessment study? The instructional goal is directly linked to the law enforcement needs assessment study and to the task force recommendations about effective NCW leadership at the community level. It is also directly related to evidence that effective discussion group leadership was highly correlated with active NCW groups.

Does instruction appear to be the most effective way to achieve the goal? Developing effective discussion group leadership skills is directly related to instruction and practice, and these competencies are not likely to be developed through incentive programs for community volunteers.

Who are the learners? The learners are community volunteers who have agreed to provide leadership for their community NCW organization. They have varying education levels from high school graduates through advanced college degrees, and they have varying group leadership skills developed through community and church organizations, membership in quality teams at work, or formal employment as company owners, department chairs, managers, or supervisors. Most will have had no formal instruction in small group leadership. They are representative of the citizens living throughout the state who choose to become involved in improving the quality of life for their families and communities.

In what context will the skills be used? NCW leaders will use their group discussion skills in planning for neighborhood NCW meetings and in providing leadership for the discussions that occur during the meetings. These meetings may occur in members' homes or in community centers within the neighborhood.

What tools are available to aid learners' performance in the actual context? There are no formal tools available to the leaders. They do have access to neighborhood police officers, crime prevention experts with the police department, and national, state, and local neighborhood-level crime statistics. Books are available that describe NCW groups, programs, and activities. There is, however, no formal support for further developing and refining discussion group leadership skills other than practice, practice, practice.

CRITERIA FOR ESTABLISHING INSTRUCTIONAL GOALS

Instructional designers can use certain criteria to help ensure that instructional goals warrant the cost and effort of designing, developing, and field testing instruction. The group leadership instructional goal is examined in the following paragraphs using these criteria.

Is the instructional goal acceptable to administrators? In this instance, the design team interviewed local police agencies, county and state NCW association coordinators, and personnel in the county learning centers to determine their perceptions of the importance for and the feasibility of the training. They also interviewed several local NCW leaders concerning their desire to participate in the NCW leadership training sessions. Positive responses about the possibility of the instruction were received from all interviewees.

Are there sufficient resources (time, money, and personnel) to develop instruction? The state grant appears to provide sufficient resources for the instructional development team to develop and field test the materials. Resources are also available to support the county training centers for managing and delivering the instruction and for trainees to receive the instruction.

Is the content stable? The content and skills underlying effective group discussion leadership are very stable. In fact, traces of John Dewey's 1910 book, *How We Think,* can be seen interwoven in modern texts on problem-solving discussions for quality teams in business, education, government, service, and recreation organizations.

Are learners available? Learners are available for participating in both the development and implementation of the instruction. Most current NCW leaders have received no formal leadership training and would therefore provide good feedback to the designers on instructional effectiveness. NCW coordinators have agreed to identify and contact NCW leaders for formative evaluation activities. They will also contact and select the new volunteer members within a county area who will receive the instruction each year.

PROVIDING CUSTOMER SERVICE

An example of how to "defuzzy" an instructional goal will be helpful. Remember, simply because a goal is fuzzy does not mean it is not worthwhile. Just the opposite—it may be very worthwhile. For this example we have selected a goal common to many banks:

Personnel will know the value of courteous, friendly service.

Although we can all agree that the intentions of this goal are sound, it can be classified as fuzzy and should be clarified.

First, the phrase *will know the value of* can be changed to *will demonstrate* in order to communicate better what is expected of personnel. Second, we must determine exactly what personnel are expected to demonstrate. We can begin this task by dividing the comprehensive term *service* into more interpretable main parts. We chose to define service as (1) a greeting to the customer, (2) a business transaction, and (3) a conclusion. Even with these two relatively minor changes, the goal is much clearer.

Original Goal	Restated Goal
Personnel will know the value of courteous, friendly service.	Personnel will demonstrate courteous, friendly behavior while greeting customers, transacting business, and concluding transactions.

Although the goal is much better in the new form, there are still two terms, *courteous* and *friendly*, that remain to be clarified. By relating these two concepts to each of the three stages of service that have been identified, we can further clarify the goal.

Before we continue, remember the five steps included in making a fuzzy goal clearer are the following:

1. Write the goal on paper.
2. Brainstorm to identify the behaviors learners would demonstrate to reflect their achievement of the goal.
3. Sort through the stated behaviors and select those that best represent the goal.
4. Incorporate the behaviors into a statement that describes what the learner will be able to do.
5. Evaluate the resulting statement for its clarity and relationship to the original fuzzy notion.

To help with the brainstorming process to identify behaviors implied by *courteous* and *friendly*, we identified the behaviors specific to each of the three stages of service. We also decided to consider behaviors that could be classified as discourteous and unfriendly in a bank setting. The lists of behaviors bank personnel *could* demonstrate and *should not* demonstrate to be considered courteous and friendly are described in Table 2.1.

TABLE 2.1	Friendly and Courteous Behaviors During Business Transactions with Customers

GREETING THE CUSTOMER

Do	Don't
1. Initiate greeting to customer (e.g., "Hello" or "Good morning.").	1. Wait for customer to speak first.
2. Say something to customer to make service appear personal: (a) use customer's name whenever possible, (b) say, "It's good to see you again," or "We haven't seen you for a while."	2. Treat customer like a stranger or some one you have never seen before.
3. If you must complete a prior transaction before beginning work, smile, verbally excuse yourself, and say you will only need a moment to finish your current task.	3. Simply continue working on a task and fail to look up or acknowledge a customer until you are ready.
4. Inquire, "How may I help you today?"	4. Wait for customer to initiate conversation about service needed.

TRANSACTING BUSINESS

Do	Don't
1. Attend to the customers currently waiting in your line. If you must leave your station, simply inform *newly arriving* customers that your line is closing and invite them to *begin* waiting in an alternate line.	1. Shuffle customers to another line after they have waited in yours for a while.

| TABLE *2.1* | (Continued) |

Do (continued)	Don't (continued)
2. Listen attentively to customer as he or she explains problem or service desired.	2. Interrupt customers, even though you believe you know what they are going to say and can see by the paperwork the type of transaction they wish.
3. Keep customer's business as the primary focus of attention during transaction.	3. Chat with employees or other customers, thereby delaying current customer.
4. Complete any missing information on the form yourself, explaining to the customer what you have added and why.	4. Simply inform customers they have incorrectly or incompletely filled out a form, thereby making it their problem.
5. Give complete, clear instructions for additional forms that the customer should complete.	5. Simply say, "Complete these other forms and then come back."

CONCLUDING TRANSACTION

Do	Don't
1. Inquire whether they need any additional services today.	1. Dismiss a customer by focusing your eyes on the next customer in line.
2. Thank the customer for his or her business.	2. Act like you have done him or her a favor by completing the transaction.
3. Verbally respond to any comments that the customer may have initiated (e.g., the weather, a holiday or upcoming vacation, your outfit or haircut, new decorations, etc.).	3. Let customer-initiated comments drop as though unnoticed.
4. Conclude with a wish for their well-being (e.g., "Take care," "Have a nice trip," "Have a nice day," or "Hurry back.").	4. Allow customers to walk away without a final comment or wish for their well-being.

The lists of courteous and discourteous behaviors can be given to bank administrators for additions, deletions, and further clarification.

After the list of representative behaviors is as complete as you can make it, review the list at each stage of service to identify key behaviors that best represent the instructional goal. Based on the sample list, we would restate the instructional goal as follows. All three forms of the goal are included to enable you to compare them for completeness and clarity.

ORIGINAL GOAL
Personnel will know the value of courteous, friendly service.

REVISED VERSION
Personnel will demonstrate courteous, friendly behavior while greeting customers, transacting business, and concluding transactions.

- Personnel will demonstrate courteous, friendly behavior while greeting customers, transacting business, and concluding transactions by initiating conversation, personalizing comments, focusing attention, assisting with forms, and concluding with a "thanks" and a wish for the customer's well-being.
- *Learners, contexts, and tools:* The learners (personnel) are all bank employees who work directly with customers either in person, by telephone, or through written correspondence. The context is most typically the bank facility and spontaneous, interactive work with customers. Personnel will have no communication aids available to assist them in interacting with customers.

Although the final goal reflects only a subset of the behaviors generated during the brainstorming process, those selected convey the basic intention of the instructional goal. The complete list of courteous and discourteous behaviors that was generated should be saved as input for subsequent instructional analysis activities.

These two examples demonstrate that instructional goal definition and refinement can be a lengthy, complex process that incorporates many people in the identification of problems, needs assessment, performance analysis, and statements of clear instructional goals. In contrast, if instruction is to address real problems faced by a school or organization and reflect actual goals, then this process is necessary. The second example related to clarifying a fuzzy goal demonstrates that while a goal clarification process can result in a clearer instructional goal, it is still open to interpretation by instructional designers or instructors. It must be further clarified by defining the actual behaviors to be demonstrated within each of the general categories included in the instructional goal.

A final concern when identifying instructional goals is the context in which the behavior will be performed. In our first example, the group leadership goal would be achieved in a learning center with the hope that the behavior will transfer to community situations. The instructional goal for bank personnel implies that the ultimate performance will be with customers in a bank. The context of the performance of the goal will have important implications for the instructional strategy.

SUMMARY

Instructional goals are clear statements of behaviors that learners are to demonstrate as a result of instruction. They are typically derived through a needs assessment process and are intended to address problems that can be resolved most efficiently through instruction. They provide the foundation for all subsequent instructional design activities.

Instructional goals are selected and refined through a rational process that requires answering questions about a particular problem and need, about the clarity of the goal statement, and about the availability of resources to design and develop the instruction.

You should answer several questions about the problem and need:

1. Is the need clearly described and verified?
2. Is the need foreseeable in the future as well as currently?
3. Is the most effective solution to the problem instruction?

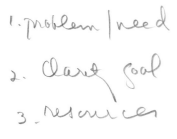

1. problem / need

2. Clarify goal

3. resources

4. Is there logical agreement between the solution to the problem and the proposed instructional goals?

5. Are the instructional goals acceptable to administrators and managers?

Questions you should answer related to the clarity of the instructional goal include the following:

1. Do the behaviors reflect clearly demonstrable, measurable behaviors?

2. Is the topic area clearly delineated?

3. Is the content relatively stable over time?

Questions to be answered related to resources include the following:

1. Do you have the expertise in the instructional goal area?

2. Are the time and resources required to complete the project available to you?

3. Is a group of learners available during the development process in order for you to evaluate and refine your instruction?

Frequently the instructional goal will be a very general statement of behaviors and content that must be clarified before some of the preceding questions can be answered. The procedure recommended for clarifying instructional goals includes the following steps:

1. Write down the instructional goal.

2. Generate a list of all the behaviors the learners should perform to demonstrate that they have achieved the goal.

3. Analyze the expanded list of behaviors and select those that best reflect achievement of the goal.

4. Incorporate the selected behaviors into a statement or statements that describe what the learners will demonstrate.

5. Examine the revised goal statement and judge whether learners who demonstrate the behaviors will have accomplished the initial broad goal.

An appropriate, feasible, and clearly stated instructional goal should be the product of these activities. Using this clarified statement of learner outcomes, you are ready to conduct a goal analysis, which is described in Chapter 3.

PRACTICE

1. The following list contains several instructional goals that may or may not be appropriate based on the criteria for writing acceptable instructional goals stated in this chapter. Read each goal and determine whether it is correct as written or should be revised. If you believe it can be revised given the information available, revise it and compare your work with the revisions provided in the Feedback section that follows.

   a. The district will provide in-service training for teachers prior to the administration and interpretation of standardized tests.

   b. Students will understand how to punctuate a variety of simple sentences.

    c. Salespersons will learn to use time management forms.

    d. Teachers will assign one theme each week.

    e. Customers will understand how to balance a checkbook.

2. The first step in developing a unit of instruction is to state the instructional goal. Several criteria can be used to help you select a suitable topic. From the following list of possible considerations for selection of an instructional goal, identify those that are relevant to a designer's selection of an instructional goal.

    _____ 1. Personal knowledge and skills in content area

    _____ 2. Stable content area

    _____ 3. Time required for writing instruction versus the importance of students possessing that knowledge or skill

    _____ 4. Students available to try out materials for clarity and revision purposes

    _____ 5. Areas in which students have difficulty learning

    _____ 6. Few materials available on the topic though instruction is considered important

    _____ 7. Content area is fairly logical

3. An instructional goal must be stated as clearly as possible. From the following lists of considerations select those within each section that are important for writing instructional goals.

    a. Behavioral versus nonbehavioral

        _____ 1. Behavior required of the student is obvious in the goal.

        _____ 2. Behavior in the goal can be observed.

        _____ 3. Behavior in the goal can be measured to determine whether students have reached the goal.

    b. Clear versus fuzzy goals

        _____ 1. Instructional goal includes a clearly stated behavior.

        _____ 2. Any limitations that will be imposed on the behavior are stated clearly.

    c. Time

        _____ 1. Approximate instructional time required for students to reach goal.

        _____ 2. Approximate time you can devote to developing and revising instruction.

4. Write an instructional goal for which you would like to develop a unit of instruction.

FEEDBACK

1. Following are suggestions for revising the instructional goals presented in the practice exercises:

    a. The first instructional goal, a, should be revised because it describes what the district is expected to accomplish rather than the teachers. The goal could be rewritten in the following way to reflect two units of instruction commonly provided by school districts. Notice the behavior to be exhibited by teachers has been clarified.

- Teachers will administer selected standardized tests according to the procedures described in the test manual.
- Teachers will interpret student performance on both individual and class profile sheets that are provided by the test maker.

b. Goal b should be revised since the words *will understand* are too general. The goal could be rewritten to clarify exactly the behavior students will use to demonstrate that they understand how to punctuate sentences. Additionally, the specific punctuation marks to be included in the lesson and used by students are included in the goal.

- Students will punctuate a variety of simple sentences using periods, question marks, and exclamation points.

c. In goal c, "learn to use" states the intended outcome of instruction, but behavior used to describe what sales personnel will actually do might be clarified as follows:

- Sales personnel will complete time management forms using a daily, weekly, and monthly schedule.

d. Goal d is not an instructional goal, but a description of the process teachers will use to enable students to practice composition skills; it totally ignores the nature of the skills students are expected to acquire during practice. Not enough information is included in the statement to enable the instructional goal to be rewritten.

e. The phrase *will understand* in goal e is imprecise. The instructional goal could be clarified as follows:

- Given canceled checks, a check register, and a monthly bank statement, customers will balance a checkbook.

2. If you answered yes to all of the criteria listed, you are correct. Each of these criteria is an important consideration in developing an instructional goal. With regard to personal knowledge of the topic, experienced instructional designers often work with SMEs from a variety of context areas in which the designer has no expertise.

3. All of the considerations listed in question 3 are important.

4. Refer back to the criteria listed in the answer to question 2. Evaluate your topic using each criterion statement.

- Does your goal meet each criterion?
- If it does not meet a particular criterion, can it be revised to do so?
- If it does not meet a particular criterion and cannot be revised to do so, you may want to write another instructional goal and try again.

You may need help in determining whether your goal meets some of the criteria for topic selection such as need or interest. You might discuss these issues relative to your goal with colleagues and students. Libraries and the Internet are good sources for determining whether materials on your topic are available and the nature of the available materials. Revise and rewrite your instructional goal as needed to meet the above criteria.

You may check the clarity of your goal by asking colleagues and intended learners to interpret verbally the instructional goal you have written. Do they interpret the goal and the required behavior exactly as you intended? You may need to revise.

If your goal is too big for the instructional time available (thirty minutes, one hour, two hours, etc.), you may want to divide the goal into its logical major parts, reword each part as an instructional goal, and then select the part most suited to your needs and time constraints.

If your goal is too small for the amount of time you desire, consider the skills the student will need to enter your instruction and the skills the student will be ready to learn as a result of completing it. By considering skills related to your goal in this fashion, you can identify the appropriate instruction to include for a specific period of time. Of course you will want to revise your instructional goal to include more skills or information as required.

Rewrite your instructional goal if necessary, and begin Chapter 3 after you have developed a clear, behaviorally stated instructional goal that you estimate will require the desired amount of instructional time.

REFERENCES AND RECOMMENDED READINGS

Burton, J. K., & Merrill, P. F. (1991). Needs assessment: goals, needs, and priorities. In Briggs, L. J., Gustafson, K. L., & Tillman, M. H. (Eds.). *Instructional design: Principles and applications.* Englewood Cliffs, NJ: Educational Technology Publications.

Gagné, R. M., Briggs, L. B., & Wager, W. W. (1992). *Principles of instructional design* (4th ed.). New York: Holt, Rinehart and Winston, 39–52. Educational goals are related to instructional outcomes, especially as they relate to different categories of learning.

Kaufman, R. (1988). *Planning educational systems.* Lancaster, PA: Technomic Publishing Co. This book describes a total educational planning process, which includes a detailed assessment of educational needs.

Kaufman, R. (1992). *Strategic planning plus.* Newbury Park, CA: Sage Publications. An emphasis on various analysis processes.

Kaufman, R. (1998). Strategic thinking: A guide to identifying and solving problems (revised). Arlington, VA & Washington, D.C.: American Society for Training & Development and the International Society for Performance Improvement.

Mager, R. F. (1972). *Goal analysis.* Belmont, CA: Fearon Publishers. This brief book describes a process used by the author to help groups clearly identify goals for their instruction.

Mager, R. M., & Pipe, P. (1997). *Analyzing performance problems* (3rd ed.). Belmont, CA: Lake Publishing Co. Describes an approach to determining if training is the solution to a performance problem, or if other solutions should be implemented.

Robinson, D. G., & Robinson, J. C. (1995). *Performance consulting: Moving beyond training.* San Francisco: Berrett-Koehler Publishers.

Rosenberg, M. (1990, January). Performance technology: Working the system. *Training,* 43–48. One of the defining articles on performance technology.

Rossett, A. (1987). *Training needs assessment.* Englewood Cliffs, NJ: Educational Technology Publications. An excellent description of various needs assessment techniques and supporting tools.

Rossett, A. (1992). Performance technology for instructional technologists: Comparisons and possibilities. *Performance and Instruction, 31* (10), 6–10.

Rossett, A. (1999). *First Things Fast.* San Francisco, CA: Jossey-Bass Pfeiffer. Approaches to determining if a performance problem exists in an organization.

Stolovitch, H., & Keeps, E. J. (1999). *Handbook of human performance technology* (2nd ed.) San Francisco: Jossey-Bass.

Watkins, R., Leigh, D., Platt, W., & Kaufman, R. (1998). Needs assessment—A digest, review, and comparison of needs assessment literature. *Performance Improvement, 37* (7), 40–53.

Zemke, R., & Kramlinger, T. (1982). *Figuring things out.* Reading, MA: Addison-Wesley. Describes a wide range of approaches to identifying performance problems.

3

CONDUCTING A GOAL ANALYSIS

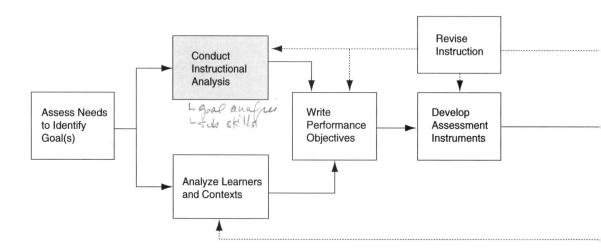

L goal anafiar
L sub skills

OBJECTIVES

- Classify instructional goals in the following domains: intellectual skill, verbal information, psychomotor skill, and attitude.
- Perform a goal analysis to identify the major steps required to accomplish an instructional goal.

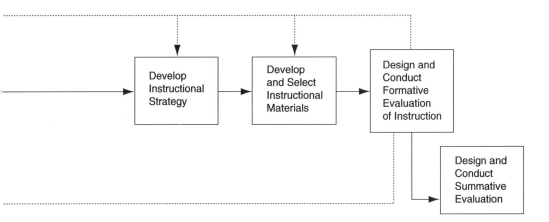

Develop
Instructional
Strategy

Develop
and Select
Instructional
Materials

Design and
Conduct
Formative
Evaluation
of Instruction

Design and
Conduct
Summative
Evaluation

*instructional
analysis*

=

skills

+

knowledge

↓

goals

+

sub. skills

BACKGROUND

As we move from chapter to chapter in describing the instructional design process, note that the step being discussed is highlighted in the diagram of the model.

The major purpose of instructional analysis is to identify the skills and knowledge that should be included in our instruction. Since this is a relatively complex process, we have separated it into two major substeps, each of which is addressed in a separate chapter in this book. In this chapter we will be discussing how the designer determines the major components of the instructional goal via the use of goal analysis. In the next chapter, we will describe how each step in the goal can be further analyzed to identify subordinate skills. The total process is referred to as instructional analysis.

The first question for the designer, following the identification of an instructional goal, is, "What exactly would learners be doing if they were demonstrating that they already could perform the goal?" Asking the question in this way is in sharp contrast to creating instruction by first identifying topics or content areas and then determining what information should be included for each topic based upon the current views of SMEs. The SME approach tends to stress *knowing,* whereas the instructional design approach stresses *doing.*

In recent years, researchers have tried to develop more effective procedures for identifying the appropriate skills and knowledge that should be included in instructional materials for students to efficiently and effectively achieve an instructional goal. For example, can you imagine the frustrations of a group of employees at a two-week training session on developing and maintaining a web site, who spend the first week studying the history and theory of the Internet? Not until the second week do they get to sit at a computer and begin to experience the excitement of learning to publish their own web page. This is an example of not only destroying learners' motivation but also of not having a procedure for identifying the skills that are *really* required to achieve the instructional goal.

Likewise, rather than describing the content of a course on Shakespeare in terms of ten plays that a student might read, instructional designers have attempted to identify precisely what it is that students will be able to do. Through the use of goal analysis, designers can move beyond simply stating what students will have read when they complete their course on Shakespeare. This chapter will focus on these goal analysis procedures.

It should be stressed that the goal analysis approach is not the only way to identify content that should be included in a set of instructional materials. The use of this approach, however, does result in the identification of skills that effectively lead to the achievement of an instructional goal.

CONCEPTS

An instructional analysis is a set of procedures that, when applied to an instructional goal, results in the identification of the relevant steps for performing a goal and the subordinate skills required for a student to achieve the goal. A subordinate skill is a skill that, while perhaps not important in and of itself as a learning outcome, must be achieved in order to learn some higher or superordinate skill. The acquisition of the subordinate skill facilitates or provides positive transfer for the learning of superordinate skills.

In this chapter we will discuss the analysis of the *goal statement* per se—that is, how to determine exactly what it is that the learner will be able to do. In Chapter 4 we will discuss the analysis process that is applied to identify the *subordinate* (or *prerequisite*) *skills* that must be learned in order to reach the goal. The overall process will be referred to as instructional analysis; it includes both a goal analysis and a subordinate skills analysis.

Goal analysis includes two fundamental steps. The first is to classify the goal statement according to the kind of learning that will occur. (The different categories of learning are referred to as *domains of learning.*) The second step is to identify and sequence the major steps required to perform the goal.

Review each of the following abbreviated goal statements:

1. Given a list of cities, name the state of which each is the capital.

2. Given a bank statement and a checkbook, balance the checkbook.

3. Set up and operate a videocamera.

4. Choose to make lifestyle decisions that reflect positive lifelong health concerns.

Each of these goals might serve as the starting point for an instructional program. The question is, "How do we determine what skills must be learned in order to achieve these goals?" The first step is to categorize the goal into one of Gagné's (1985) domains of learning. Each goal should be classified into one of the domains because of the implications for the goal analysis and the selection of the appropriate subordinate skills analysis techniques discussed in Chapter 4.

VERBAL INFORMATION

The first of our sample goals requires the learner to name the state for which each of the cities is the capital. There are many ways to teach such a skill and several ways the learner might try to learn it. But basically there is only one answer for each question and only one basic way to ask each question. There is no symbolic manipulation—no problem solving or rule applying. In essence, verbal information goals require the learners to provide specific responses to relatively specific questions.

You can usually spot a verbal information goal by the verb that is used. Often the learner must state, list, or describe something. It is assumed that the "something" that is to be stated or listed will be taught in the instruction; therefore, the learner is storing the information during the instruction and retrieving it for the test.

INTELLECTUAL SKILLS

Now let's consider goal number 2, which deals with balancing a checkbook. By nearly anyone's definition, this is a problem-solving task and therefore is classified as an intellectual skill. Intellectual skills are those that require the learner to do some unique cognitive activity—unique in the sense that the learner must be able to solve a problem or perform an activity with previously unencountered information or examples. The three most common types of intellectual skills are forming concepts, applying rules, and solving problems.

With these skills the learner can classify things according to labels and characteristics, can apply a rule, and can select and apply a variety of rules in order to solve problems. Any goal that requires a learner to manipulate symbolic information in some way will be an intellectual skill. So, in addition to our problem-solving goal, the following would also be classified as intellectual skills: being able to apply the rule for computing sales tax, and being able to classify a variety of creatures as either mammals or reptiles.

It is important to be able to identify the various levels of intellectual skills. Learning concepts essentially means being able to classify examples as being a part of the concept or not. If the concept is baseball equipment, then the learner would have to be able to determine whether various examples of equipment were baseball equipment. Note that the stimulus could be an object or even a picture or description of the object. The learner would have to have mastered the concept by learning the characteristics of baseball equipment that distinguishes it from all other sporting equipment, and from other objects as well.

Concepts are combined to produce rules. An example of a rule is "*a*-squared plus *b*-squared equals *c*-squared." In this rule, the learner has to have the concepts of *a*, *b*, and *c*, squaring, adding, and square root. The rule shows the relationship among these concepts. The knowledge of the rule is tested by giving the learner a variety of values for *a* and *b*, and asking for the value of *c*. The learner must follow a series of steps to produce the correct answer.

The highest level of intellectual skill is problem solving, and there are two types of problems: well-structured and ill-structured. The more typical is the well-structured problem that is usually considered to be an application problem. The learner is asked to apply a number of concepts and rules in order to solve a well-defined problem. Typically the learner (or problem solver) is given a lot of details about a situation, a suggestion of what rules and concepts might apply, and an indication of what the characteristics of the solution will be. There is a preferred way of going about determining what the solution should be. Algebra problems are a typical example of well-structured problems that have a preferred process, involve a variety of concepts and rules, and have a "correct" answer.

Researchers also classify some problems as ill-structured. These are problems in which not all the data required for a solution are readily available to the learner, and even the nature of the goal is not clear. Multiple processes can be used to reach a solution, and no one solution is considered the "correct" one. There is no better example of ill-structured problem solving than the instructional design process itself. Rarely do we know all the critical elements that relate to the formulation of the need for the instruction or the learners who will receive the instruction. There are various methods of analysis and strategies for presenting the instruction, and there are a variety of ways to assess the effectiveness of the instruction.

Most of the instruction created by instructional designers is in the domain of intellectual skills. It is important to be able to classify learning outcomes according to the various levels of skills, and to determine whether the instructional goal could be improved, or made more appropriate for learners, by elevating it to a higher level of intellectual skill outcome. This is especially true when the designer is presented with an instructional goal that is in the domain of verbal information.

PSYCHOMOTOR SKILLS

The third goal listed above involves setting up and operating a videocamera. This would be classified as a psychomotor goal because it involves the coordination of mental and physical activity. In this case equipment must be manipulated in a very specific way to successfully produce a video image.

The characteristics of a psychomotor skill are that the learner must execute muscular actions, with or without equipment, to achieve specified results. In certain situations there may be a lot of "psycho" in the psychomotor goal. That is, there may be a great deal of mental or cognitive activity that must accompany the motor activity. However, for purposes of instructional analysis, if the learner must learn to execute new, nontrivial motor skills, or performance depends on the skillful execution of a physical skill, we will refer to it as a psychomotor goal. Consider the following examples. Being able to throw a baseball is a psychomotor skill that requires repeated practice for mastery. Programming a VCR to automatically record a late-night program, in which the pushing of buttons is a trivial motor response for adults, is essentially an intellectual skill. Extended practice in the pushing of buttons is not required for mastery.

ATTITUDES

If we express a goal statement in terms of having learners choose to do something, as in the fourth example on choosing a healthy lifestyle, then that goal should be classified as an attitudinal goal. Attitudes are usually described as the tendency to make particular choices or decisions. For example, we would like individuals to choose to be good employees, choose to protect the environment, and choose to eat nourishing food. Goal number 4 stated that learners would choose to make lifestyle decisions that reflect a positive concern for their health. To identify an attitudinal goal, determine whether the learners will have a choice to make and whether the goal indicates the direction in which the decision is to be influenced.

Another characteristic of attitudinal goals is that they probably will not be achieved at the end of the instruction. They are quite often long-term goals that are extremely important but very difficult to evaluate in the short term.

As you examine an attitudinal goal, you will find that the only way we can determine whether learners have "achieved" an attitude is by having them do something. That *something* will be a psychomotor skill, intellectual skill, or verbal information; therefore, instructional goals that focus on attitudes can be viewed as influencing the learner to choose, under certain circumstances, to perform an intellectual skill or psychomotor skill, or to state certain verbal information.

Readers who are familiar with Gagné's work may be wondering what happened to his fifth domain of learning, cognitive strategies. We have deliberately omitted the terminology from the text because for our purposes cognitive strategies can be treated in a manner similar to ill-structured problem solving and taught as intellectual skills. Cognitive strategies are the metaprocesses that we use to manage the way that we think about things and ensure our own learning. Some strategies are as straightforward as mentally repeating the name of new acquaintances several times while visualizing their faces so that you can call them by name the next time that you meet them. A more complex cognitive strategy would be figuring out how to organize, cluster, remember, and apply new information from a chapter that will be included on a test. Now consider the very complex cognitive strategies that a civil engineer might use in laying out a section of farmland for housing development:

1. The engineer would need to have command of a vast array of physical and intellectual tools, such as computer-assisted design; geographic information system databases; land surveying; soil analysis; hydrology; and water, sewer, and electrical utilities systems.

2. The engineer would need to have command of a variety of "textbook" engineering strategies for the range of problems that would be encountered in a land development project.

3. For a large project, the engineer would have to manage cooperative team efforts for in-house and consulting specialists in environmental, legal, and architectural matters.

4. The engineer would have to organize, manage, and apply all of those tools, solution strategies, and collaboration skills in a formerly unencountered environment. Some tools would be useful; some would not. Some solutions would work; others would be rejected or modified. Some project team members would contribute quickly and reliably; others would require more direction and maintenance. In the end, the final site development would be a "one-of-a-kind" product of the engineer's ability to orchestrate a variety of resources toward the solution of a unique problem.

This description of a civil engineer's work can be compared directly with the description previously in this chapter of an instructional designer's work. Both are engaged in solving ill-structured problems. For the instructional design processes described in this text, we will place cognitive strategies with problem solving at the top of the intellectual skills grouping.

GOAL ANALYSIS PROCEDURES

It is important to recognize that the amount of instruction required to teach an instructional goal will vary tremendously from one goal to another. Some goals will represent skills that can be taught in less than an hour, while others will take many hours for students to achieve. The smaller the goal, the easier it is to do a precise analysis of what is to be learned. After we identify the domain of the goal, it is necessary to be more specific in indicating what the learner will be doing when performing the goal.

The best technique for the designer to use in analyzing a goal is to describe, in step-by-step fashion, exactly what a person would be doing when performing the goal. This is not as easy as it first may sound. The things that the person does may be physical activities that are easy to observe, as in a psychomotor skill. On the other hand, they may be "mental steps" that must be executed before there is any overt behavior, as in an intellectual skill. For example, it would be quite easy to observe the steps used to clean a paintbrush and spray equipment, but almost impossible to observe directly all the steps that a person might follow to determine how much paint would be required to cover a building.

As you go through the process of describing the exact steps that a person would take in performing your goal, you may find that one of the steps requires a decision followed by several alternate paths that can be pursued (and, therefore, must be learned). For example, with the cleaning of a paintbrush, you might find at one point in the cleaning process that the paint will not come out, so an alternative technique must be applied. Similarly, in attempting to solve the mathematics problems related to area and required paint, it may be necessary first to classify the problems as "type A"(smooth surface) or "type B" (rough surface). Based on that outcome, one of two very different techniques might be used to solve the problem. The point is that the learner has to be taught both how to make the decision and how to perform all of the alternative steps required to reach the goal.

Goal analysis is the visual display of the specific steps the learner would do when performing the instructional goal. Each step is stated in a box as shown in the flow diagram below:

What this diagram indicates is that if the learner had the tools available as described in the goal statement, then he or she could perform the goal by first doing step 1, which might be adding two numbers or it might be striking a particular key on a keyboard. After doing step 1, the learner would then perform step 2, then 3, 4, and 5. After doing step 5, the process would be complete, and, if done properly, would be considered a demonstration of the performance of the goal.

This sounds straightforward, and it is until you start doing an analysis of your own goal. Then questions arise about how large a step should be; how much can be included in one step? The answer depends primarily on the learner. If the instruction is for very young students, then the steps should be quite small. If the same topic were taught to older students, the same skills would be included, but they would likely be combined into larger steps.

The statement of each step must include a verb that describes an observable behavior. In our example, we used the verbs *adding* and *striking*. These are behaviors we can observe, or, in the case of *adding*, we can observe the answer that is written down. What we cannot see, for example, are people reading or listening; there is no direct result or product. If these are part of the goal, then the step should indicate what learners will identify from what they read or hear. Each step should have an observable outcome.

Another behavior that we cannot observe directly is decision making. Obviously it is a mental process based on a set of criteria. The decision-making steps are often critical to the performance of a goal, and depending on what decision is made, a different set of skills is used. If reaching the goal includes decision making, the decision step should be placed in a diamond with the alternate decision paths shown leading from the diamond.

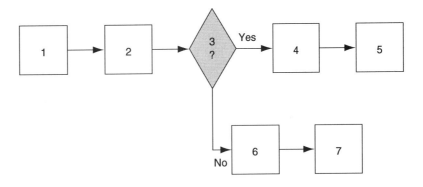

Let's walk through this diagram of the performance of a goal. The performer does step 1 and step 2 sequentially. Then a decision has to be made such as "Does the estimate exceed $300?" or "Is the word spelled correctly on the screen?" If, when performing the goal, the answer is yes, then the learner continues with steps 4 and 5. Alternatively, if the answer is no, then the learner would do steps 6 and 7.

Several important characteristics about decisions should be noted. First, a decision can be a step in the goal analysis process. The decision is written out with an appropriate verb and displayed in a diamond in the diagram. Second, there have to be at least two different skills to be learned and performed based on the outcome of the decision. A counter example would be one in which one step required the learner to "select an apple" and the next step to "peel the apple." The learner might be taught criteria to use for selecting an apple, but regardless of the apple that is selected, the next step is always to peel it. There are no alternative next steps, and no diamond would be used in the diagram.

If we alter the apple example, the step in the diamond might be to distinguish between red and yellow apples. After the distinction is made, the red apples might be treated in one manner, and the yellow in another. Clearly the learner would have to be able to distinguish between the two types of apples, and then be able to perform the appropriate procedure depending on the color of the apple. Note that the question that would appear in the diamond would be, "Is the apple yellow or red?" This implies that the learner would have to be able to make this distinction. If it is likely that students can already do this, then no teaching will be required; they will simply be told to do this at the appropriate point in the instruction. However, in some cases, it will be necessary to treat this as a skill—"The learner will be able to distinguish between red and yellow apples"—and eventually to provide instruction for this skill, just as you would for any other steps in the goal analysis process.

Notice also that the numbers in the boxes do not necessarily indicate the sequence in which all of the steps will be performed. In the example, if a person does steps 4 and 5 as a result of the decision made at 3, then the person would not do steps 6 and 7. The opposite would also be true. Also note that step 3, because it is in a diamond, *must* be a question. The answer to the question leads one to *different* steps or skills.

Several other conventions about diagramming a goal are useful to know. The first has to do with what you do if you run out of space. Suppose you are working across the page and need room for more boxes. Obviously, you can turn the page on its side. Another solution is shown in the following diagram. Use a circle after the last box on the line to indicate that this is the point at which the process breaks and will be reconnected to the boxes that begin with the same letter in the circle. The letter in the circle is arbitrary, but should not be the same as any other letter used elsewhere in your analysis diagram. In our example, we have used the letter *M*. You do not have to draw any connecting lines from one circle with an *M* to the other circle with an *M* because the reader can locate easily the next circle with the same letter in it.

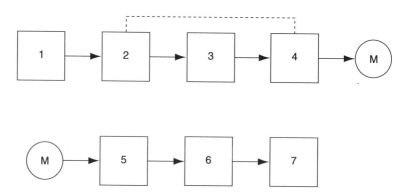

Another solution to the space problem is to drop down to the next line with your boxes and proceed backward from right to left with the description and numbering. As long as the line and arrows indicate the direction of flow, this is acceptable. The arrows are critical to the interpretation of the diagram. Also note the use of the dotted line. This means that when the goal is being performed, it is possible to go back to any number of earlier steps and come forward through the sequence again. Examine the diagram carefully to see the logic of the process that is being described.

As you analyze your goal, you may find that you have difficulty knowing exactly how much should be included in each step. As a general rule, at this stage, you would typically have at least five steps but not more than fifteen for one to two hours of instruction. If you have fewer than five, perhaps you have not been specific enough in describing the steps. If you have more than fifteen steps, then you have either taken too large a chunk to be analyzed, or you have listed the steps in too much detail. A very general rule-of-thumb is to review and revise the steps until you have five to fifteen steps for every one to two hours of instruction.

We have stated that the first step in the goal analysis process is to identify the learning domain of the goal. If it is either an intellectual skill or a psychomotor skill, the process just described is appropriate. If, however, it is verbal information, you would begin the analysis process by thinking, "Now let's see, what will the students be doing? I guess I will ask them to list the major bones in the body, to describe the major causes of bone injuries, and so forth. I'll just ask them on a test to do this, and they'll write down their answers." In a sense, there is no intellectual or psychomotor procedure other than the presentation of a test question and the retrieval of the answer. There is no problem solving with the information, nor any decision making required of the learner. Doing the goal analysis would be similar to preparing an outline of the topics contained in the goal, but there is no sequence of steps per se. Boxes could be used to indicate the major topics within the goal, but no arrows would be used to indicate that there is a sequence of steps to be performed. The best sequence for verbal information behaviors is chronological when a natural chronology can be identified. When there is no natural ordering among the topics, then they should be sequenced based on the inherent relationships among them; for example, spatial, easy to complex, familiar to unfamiliar, common content areas, and so forth.

One special note should be made about the goal analysis of an attitudinal goal. If the goal is an attitude, then it is necessary to identify the behavior that will be exhibited when the attitude is demonstrated. Is it an intellectual skill or a psychomotor skill? If so, use the procedural flow chart process described previously. On the other hand, if the attitude demonstration constitutes verbal information, then your goal analysis will be a list of the major topics contained in the information.

In summary, goal analysis for intellectual and psychomotor skills is an analysis of the steps to be performed; for a verbal information goal, it is a list of the major topics to be learned; and either approach is used depending on the nature of an attitudinal goal.

ANALYSIS OF SUBSTEPS

The goal analysis process has one more step, which is to examine each of the key steps in the goal and imagine performing the step or explaining it to a learner. Is it a single, unitary process or a skill that requires two or more steps? This is analogous to doing a goal analysis for each step just as you originally did for the goal itself.

Consider the following examples of steps in an instructional goal. The first is "Place jack under bumper of car." While this could be described as a series of steps for an adult population, it is probably best represented as one step in the process of changing a tire on a car. But what about a step like "Conduct needs assessment"? This is a step in a goal of designing instruction that surely is too large to be a single step for any audience. It should be broken down into steps such as "Design needs assessment instruments," "Meet with focus group," and "Summarize data."

Suppose one of the steps in a goal is "boil water." Most adults should know what to do, or they could be taught quickly. For learners who are young children (or an adult who has managed to avoid the kitchen), you might want to list the substeps as "Obtain pan," "Fill with water," "Place pan on burner," "Turn on burner," "Is water bubbling?" and "Remove pan." This is an extreme example, but it illustrates how substeps are identified.

The appropriate diagramming of substeps is shown in the generic diagram that follows:

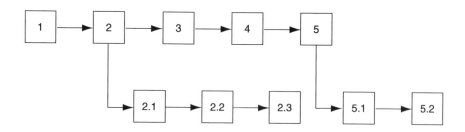

This analysis indicates that a hypothetical goal has five major steps. Step 2 can be best represented by three substeps, 2.1, 2.2, and 2.3. These three substeps are *equivalent to* step 2. If you do steps 2.1, 2.2, and 2.3, you have done 2! The diagram also shows that step 5 can best be described by substeps 5.1 and 5.2. There is no need to identify substeps separately unless there are at least two substeps. This further analysis of the steps in the goal can be used to re-diagram the goal as follows:

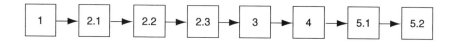

These two analyses are exactly equivalent in terms of their instructional design implications.

How do you know if you should break down a step into substeps? There is no exact answer to this question, but you should think about the complexity of the step for the learners who were identified in the goal statement and how you would explain or demonstrate this step to a learner. Does the explanation naturally follow a step-by-step pattern? At this stage of the design process, it is better to identify too many steps rather than too few. The greater detail tends to ensure that the instruction will include all the skills that are required by the learner. It is also possible to omit some of the information later in the design process if the steps appear to be too detailed. If, on the other hand, this additional analysis leads to what the designer considers minutia, then in all likelihood, it is not required, and you should stay with the more general statement of the step in the goal.

MORE SUGGESTIONS FOR IDENTIFYING STEPS WITHIN A GOAL

If you cannot state your goal in terms of sequential steps, perhaps it has not been clearly stated in terms of the outcome behavior required. If it has, and you still have difficulty, there are several procedures you can use to help identify the steps. First, describe for yourself the kind of test item or assessment you would use to determine whether the learners could perform your goal. Next, think about the steps that the learner would have to go through to respond to your assessment or test. Another suggestion is to "test" yourself;

that is, observe yourself, both in the physical and mental sense, performing the goal. Note each of the steps you go through and the decisions you have to make. These are the steps you would record as the goal analysis. Although these procedures may produce a series of steps that seem very simple to you, remember that you are the SME; they probably will not be so simple or obvious to the uninformed learner.

There are several other ways to conduct a goal analysis. In addition to recording your own steps in performing the goal, find others who you know can do it, and ask them the steps they would follow. How do their steps compare with yours? Often there will be differences that you should consider in the final representation of the goal. It is sometimes possible to observe others performing your goal. What steps do they follow? It is also a good idea to consult written materials such as textbooks, technical manuals, or policies and procedures manuals to determine how the skills in your goal are described.

In order to do a goal analysis, it is apparent that the designer must either have extensive knowledge about the goal or be working with someone who does. This need for knowledge may have a down side if the designer has already taught the topic or goal in a regular classroom setting. We have routinely observed that novice designers tend to list the steps they would follow in *teaching* a goal rather than the steps that a learner would use in *performing* the goal. Teaching and performing are somewhat different. Verbs to watch for in your description of the steps in your goal analysis are *describe, list, say,* and so forth. These are almost never part of performing psychomotor, intellectual, or attitude goals, but rather are words that we would use to describe how we would teach something. We will reach that point later in the instructional design process. For now we only want to portray, in graphic form, the steps that someone would follow if they were performing your goal.

Another problem in conducting a goal analysis is the inclusion of skills and information that are "near and dear" to the designer but are not really required for the performance of the goal. Designers with a lot of experience in a topic area may be subject to this problem or, more likely, it will arise when the designer is working with a SME. The SME insists on including a certain topic, skill, or information. This becomes a political issue, which can be resolved only through negotiation.

The main purpose of the goal analysis is to provide an unambiguous description of exactly what the learner will be doing when performing the goal. Once the goal analysis has been completed, the designer can identify the exact nature of each skill, and any prerequisite skills, that must be mastered.

EXAMPLES

The first phase of performing an instructional analysis involves two major steps: (1) classifying the goal into a domain of learning, and (2) performing a goal analysis by identifying and sequencing the major steps required to perform the goal. Table 3.1 includes five sample instructional goals and a list of the four learning domains previously described. First, we will classify each goal into one of the domains and then identify and sequence the major steps required to perform the goal. The letter of the corresponding learning domain is written in the space provided to the left of each goal statement.

TABLE *3.1* **Sample Instructional Goals and Learning Domains**

Domain Letter	Sample Goals	Learning Domain
B	1. Determine the distance between two specified places on a state map.	A. Verbal information—stating facts, providing specific information (e.g., naming objects)
C	2. Putt a golf ball.	B. Intellectual skills—making discriminations, learning concepts, using rules, and solving problems
D	3. Choose to maximize personal safety while staying in a hotel.	
		C. Psychomotor skills—physical activity, which usually includes mental activity as well
A	4. Describe the five parts of a materials safety data sheet (MSDS) that are most important for job-site safety.	D. Attitudes—making particular choices or behaving in a manner that implies an underlying belief or preference
B	5. Lead group discussions aimed at solving given problems.	

INTELLECTUAL SKILLS GOALS

Examine the first goal listed in Table 3.1, determining distances between specified places on a state map. This goal is classified as an intellectual skill because learners will be required to learn concepts, follow rules, and solve problems in performing the goal. With the goal classified, we should identify the major steps required to perform the goal and the best sequence for the steps. A good way for the designer to proceed is to identify the type of test item that would be used to determine if a student could perform this skill. You could obtain a copy of a state map and review how this task can be accomplished using the map as a reference. Checking the map, one sees that there are obviously three separate and distinct ways to determine distance between specified places. One is to use a mileage table, another is to use a mileage scale, and yet another is to add miles printed along highways between the cities. If the student is to be able to use all three methods, then there will be three main methods included in the goal analysis.

Another task would be to decide which of the three identified methods is most appropriate to use in a particular situation. This task implies that there is a decision to be made; therefore, the criteria necessary to make the decision must be learned. Figure 3.1 contains the major steps required to perform the goal. If learners need to determine the distance between major cities within a state, they will perform tasks 1, 2, 3, and 4. If they need to determine the distance between distant towns or a city and a town, they will use tasks 1, 2, 3, 5, and 6. Similarly, if they need to determine the distance between relatively close cities and towns, which would be the situation if the answer to the first two questions were no, they will do steps 1, 2, 3, 5, and 7. When a choice or decision must be made in order to perform a goal, then when and how to make the decision must be learned together with the other steps. Simply teaching learners to use each of the three procedures would not be adequate for this goal. At this point we have the instructional goal analyzed to provide a framework that will enable us to identify the subordinate skills required to accomplish each major task.

FIGURE 3.1

Goal Analysis for an
Intellectual Skill
Goal:
Determine distance between speci-
fied cities and towns on a state map.
Type of Learning:
Intellectual skill

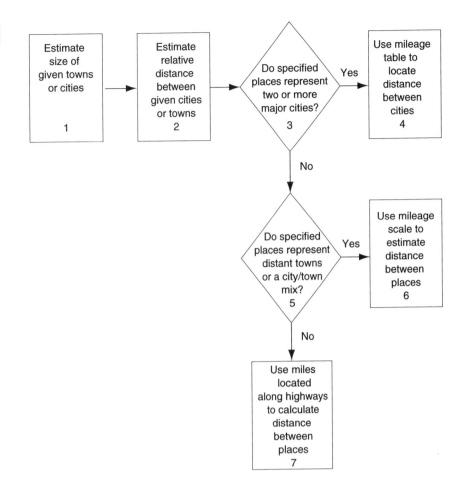

PSYCHOMOTOR SKILLS GOALS

The second instructional goal presented in Table 3.1, putting a golf ball, should be classified as a psychomotor skill since both mental planning and physical execution of the plan are required to putt the ball into the cup. Neither banging the ball around the green nor simply "willing" the ball into the cup will accomplish the task. Rather, mental planning and calculating, combined with accurately executing the stroke based on mental calculations, are required.

Now that we have the putting goal classified by domain, we should proceed to identify and sequence the major steps learners would take to execute the goal. Figure 3.2 contains the major steps, in sequence, required to accomplish the goal. As we watch a golfer preparing to putt the ball, we notice some mental planning activities appear to occur. The steps identified that follow planning simply provide a broad overview of the complete task from beginning to end. Note that the substeps were identified for step 4 and could be identified for several of the other steps. The sequence we have at this point provides us with the framework we will need to identify the subordinate skills required to perform each of the steps already identified.

ATTITUDINAL GOALS

The third goal listed in Table 3.1, choosing to maximize personal safety while staying in a hotel, is classified as an attitudinal goal because it implies

FIGURE 3.2

Goal Analysis for an Intellectual Skill

Goal:
Putt a golf ball.
Type of Learning:
Psychomotor

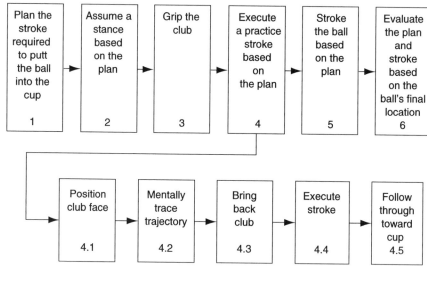

FIGURE 3.3

Goal Analysis for an Intellectual Skill

Goal:
Choose to maximize personal safety while staying in a hotel.
Type of Learning:
Attitude

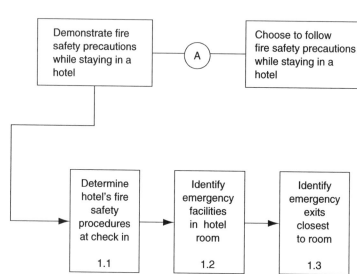

behavior based on an underlying attitude or belief. What would learners be doing if they were exhibiting behavior that showed they were safety conscious while staying in a hotel? The first step to building a framework for this goal would be to visit several hotels and inquire about safety features provided by them. This activity would probably result in identifying the three main areas of concern:

1. Hotel fires
2. Personal safety while in hotel room
3. Protection of valuable possessions

Figure 3.3 shows the major steps for maximizing personal safety as it relates to hotel fires. This series of steps reflects the actual behaviors that a person would perform if he or she *chooses* to maximize fire safety precautions while at a hotel. Each of these major steps could be broken down further, but, for now, they indicate what a person would be doing if he or she performs the first part of this goal. A similar analysis would be done for the second and third components of the goal related to personal safety and protecting valuable possessions.

VERBAL INFORMATION GOALS

The fourth instructional goal in Table 3.1, describing the five parts of a materials safety data sheet (MSDS) that are most important for job-site safety, is classified as a verbal information goal, because learners are required to recall specific information about the contents of a document. A MSDS is a federally mandated information sheet provided to customers by chemical manufacturers. Knowledge of five topics is required to perform this goal; they are illustrated in Figure 3.4. There is no mandated order inherent in the information. Note that for a verbal information goal these are not "steps" in the sense that one goes from one activity to the next. Thus, the goal analysis simply indicates the major topics of information that must be covered in the instruction.

Now turn your attention to the fifth instructional goal in Table 3.1, leading group discussions aimed at solving given problems. This goal is classified as an intellectual skill since it requires learning concepts and rules as well as solving problems. The seven steps identified to perform this goal and the planned sequence are included in Figure 3.5. There is a natural flow of tasks from left to right because the product developed at each step becomes input for the subsequent one. This step-by-step explanation of the general instructional goal will make subsequent instructional analysis activities much easier.

TYPICAL FIRST APPROACH TO GOAL ANALYSIS

When reading a text such as this, the instructional goal diagrams may appear to have simply flowed from the word processors of the authors. When the reader initially applies the process, however, it does not always seem to work as smoothly and easily. It might be useful to show a typical "first pass" at goal analysis and to point out some of the problems that can be avoided.

F I G U R E *3.4*

Goal Analysis for an Intellectual Skill

Goal:
Describe the five parts of a materials safety data sheet.
Type of Learning:
Verbal information

Describe fire and explosion hazard data	Describe reactivity data	Describe health hazard data	Describe precautions for safe handling and use	Describe control measures
1	2	3	4	5

F I G U R E *3.5*

Goal Analysis for an Intellectual Skill

Goal:
Participate as leader in group discussions aimed at solving given problems.
Type of Learning:
Intellectual skill

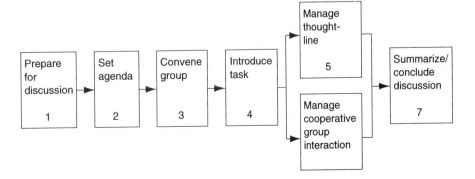

Examine Figure 3.6, which shows the analysis of a wordy goal related to the initial use of a word processing program. It appears that the analyst did not say, "How would I perform this goal?" but seemed to ask, "How would I teach this goal?" We might want to explain some background information to begin the instruction. However, at this point we only want to list the steps in actually performing the goal. So if the designer were performing the goal in Figure 3.6, he or she would not start with an explanation of operating systems; thus, step 1 should be eliminated.

Step 2 appears to be a general step related to getting the system up and running. It should be revised to express what the learner would be doing—namely, turn on power and locate start menu. Step 3 should be eliminated because it is a general process for first-time users that would only appear as a substep.

In step 4, the expert who was performing the goal would never stop to explain what an application program is. This may be a subordinate skill somewhere in the instruction, but it doesn't belong here; thus, it too should be eliminated. All we want to do is note the steps in getting the word processing application working.

Moving on to step 5 puts us back on track, but what is meant by "use toolbars "? It should be dropped because the substance of the goal is included in step 6.

The final step, step 6, includes writing, editing, and printing a document. This is much too large a step for a goal analysis. It should be broken down into the following separate steps: create a file, enter a paragraph of prose, edit a paragraph, and print a paragraph.

Given this analysis, we would rewrite the goal as follows: Operate a word-processing application by entering, editing, and printing a brief document. The revised steps are shown in Figure 3.7. It looks considerably different from the initial one in Figure 3.6. Also note, as you review the steps

FIGURE 3.6

Faulty Goal Analysis of an Intellectual Skill Related to Word Processing

Goal:

Students will be able to boot up PCs, describe operating systems, and create, edit, and print a document using a word-processing application.

Type of Learning:

Intellectual skill

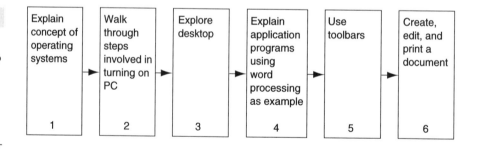

FIGURE 3.7

Revised Goal Analysis for Word Processing Goal

Goal:

Students will be able to operate a word-processing application by entering, editing, and printing a brief document.

Type of Learning:

Intellectual skill

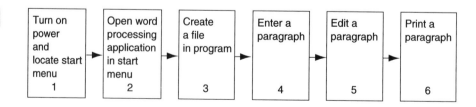

necessary to carry out the goal, that no one step is equivalent to performing the goal; *all* the steps must be performed in sequence in order to demonstrate the ability to perform the goal.

Readers interested in a school curriculum example should view the goal analysis in Appendix B.

SUMMARY

The goal analysis process is begun only after you have a clear statement of the instructional goal. The first step in the goal analysis process is to classify the goal into one of the four domains of learning. It will either be an attitude, an intellectual skill, verbal information, or a psychomotor skill.

The second step in goal analysis is to identify the major steps that learners must perform to demonstrate they have achieved the goal. These major steps should include both the behavior and relevant content, and they should be sequenced in the most efficient order. For intellectual skill and psychomotor goals, as well as most attitudes, a sequential diagram of the steps to be taken is appropriate. An analysis of verbal information will usually result in a set of topics that can be organized by chronology or by other inherent relationships such as parts of a whole, simple to complex, or familiar to unfamiliar. Remember that perfect frameworks of skills required for a goal are rarely created on the first attempt. Your initial product should be viewed as a draft and should be subjected to evaluation and refinement. Specific problems to look for during the evaluation include steps that are unnatural in the process, too small or too large, and misplaced in the sequence.

The final product of your goal analysis should be a diagram of skills, which provides an overview of what learners will be doing when they perform the instructional goal. This framework is the foundation for the subordinate skills analysis described in Chapter 4.

PRACTICE

1. Table 3.2 contains a list of learning domains and instructional goals. Read each goal in column two and classify it using the learning

TABLE 3.2 | **Classify Instructional Goals by Learning Domain**

Learning Domain	Sample Instructional Goal	Rationale
A. Psychomotor Skill	_____ 1. Open and maintain a checking account.	
B. Intellectual Skill	_____ 2. Label parts of the human body using common terminology.	
C. Verbal Information	_____ 3. Separate an egg yolk from the egg white, using the shell as a tool.	
D. Attitude	_____ 4. Choose to behave safely while flying on airplanes.	

domains listed in column one. Space is provided in column three for you to write the rationale that you need to classify each goal. Check your work with the examples provided in Table 3.3 in the Feedback section.

2. On separate sheets of paper, identify and sequence the major areas of activity implied by each of the instructional goals shown in the first practice activity. Check your analysis with those provided in Figures 3.8 through 3.11. Your analysis will be slightly different from ours because there usually is no one way to analyze the steps in a goal.

FEEDBACK

1. Compare your work in Table 3.3

2. Compare your decisions about what constitutes the major steps and sequences for each of the four instructional goals listed in Figures 3.8 through 3.11.

In deciding the major steps and sequence for the tasks related to opening and maintaining a checking account, a simple chronological order for main events was used. You cannot deposit money into an account that has not been opened, you cannot keep a register of activities if none has occurred, and you cannot withdraw money from an account if none has been deposited. These major steps and the order identified using the instructional goal would provide the framework necessary for you to identify subordinate skills required to accomplish each step.

The second goal, locating and labeling parts of the human body, did not have a chronology of events that could be used to develop a logical framework. An organizing method needed to be identified that would enable us to

(Text continues on page 56.)

TABLE 3.3	**Feedback for Classifying Instructional Goals**

Learning Domain	Sample Instructional Goal	Rationale
A. Psychomotor Skill B. Intellectual Skill C. Verbal Information	**B** 1. Open and maintain a checking account.	Requires a complex set of discriminations, concepts, and rules to make decisions and solve problems.
D. Attitude	**C** 2. Label parts of the human body using common terminology.	Requires associating a name with a part of the body. Each part of the body has one name. It does not require anything but recalling labels or names.
	A 3. Separate an egg yolk from egg white, using the shell as a tool.	Requires mental planning and accurate translation of mental plans into physical actions.
	D 4. Choose to behave safely while flying on airplanes.	Behavior implies an underlying attitude about safety.

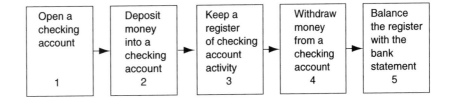

FIGURE 3.8

Goal Analysis for an
Intellectual Skill

Goal:
Open and maintain a checking
account.

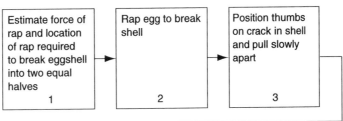

FIGURE 3.9

Goal Analysis for an
Intellectual Skill

Goal:
Locate and label various parts of the
human body.

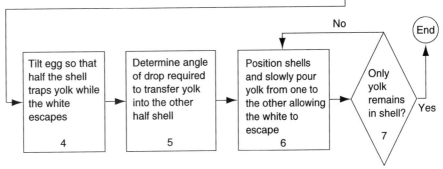

FIGURE 3.10

Goal Analysis for a
Psychomotor Skill Goal

Goal:
Using the shell as a tool, separate an
egg yolk from the egg white.

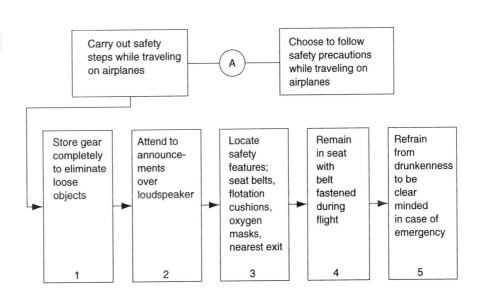

FIGURE 3.11

Goal Analysis for an
Attitudinal Goal

Goal:
Choose to follow safety precautions
while traveling on airplanes.

cluster or group information in a logical manner. We chose to organize the content using a "parts of a whole" plan (i.e., main areas of the body). We then selected a sequence for the areas by moving from the top to the bottom—for example, head, arms, hands, trunk, legs, and feet. Note that the words are not connected with arrows because these are not sequential steps that must be performed.

The psychomotor skill required to crack an egg and separate the yolk from the white also had a natural sequence of events. The shell could not be pulled apart until it was broken, and the egg white could not be separated until the shell was pulled apart. Like most psychomotor tasks, this one requires practice. The only way your mind can tell your hands how hard to tap the shell or how fast to pour the yolk is to practice the skill. Incorrect estimations and translations result in squashed shells and broken yolks.

The instructional goal on airplane safety has a sequence of sorts that does help with this goal. Carry-on items are stored and then attention is given to safety announcements. The announcements will help in locating safety features on the plane. Then it is necessary to keep the seat belt on and to limit one's alcoholic intake.

REFERENCES AND RECOMMENDED READINGS

Gagné, R. M. (1985). *Conditions of learning* (4th ed.). New York: Holt, Rinehart and Winston. This book is a classic in regard to many aspects of instructional design, including the domains of learning and hierarchical analysis.

Gagné, R. M., Briggs, L. J., & Wager, W. W. (1992). *Principles of instructional design* (4th ed.). New York: Holt, Rinehart and Winston. Provides a number of examples of the application of hierarchical analysis to intellectual skills.

Jonassen, D. H. (1997). Instructional design models for well-structured and ill-structured problem-solving learning outcomes. *Educational Technology Research and Development, 45* (1), 65–94. Provides examples and procedures for designing and developing both well-structured and ill-structured problem-solving instruction.

Jonassen, D. H., Tessmer, M., & Hannum, W. (1999). *Handbook of task analysis procedures.* Mahwah, NJ: Lawrence Erlbaum.

Levine, E. R. (1983). *Everything you always wanted to know about job analysis.* Tampa, FL: Mariner Publishing Co. This is a paperback introductory text on job analysis.

Loughner, P., & Moller, L. (1998). The use of task analysis procedures by instructional designers. *Performance Improvement Quarterly, 11* (3), 79–101.

Mager, R. F. (1988). *Making instruction work.* Belmont, CA: David S. Lake Publishers. Discusses goal analysis and shows the use of a flow diagram to clarify a goal.

Merrill, P. F. (1980). Analysis of a procedural task. *NSPI Journal, 19* (2), 11–15. Merrill uses flow-charting methods to identify the subordinate skills of a complex intellectual skill.

4 IDENTIFYING SUBORDINATE SKILLS AND ENTRY BEHAVIORS

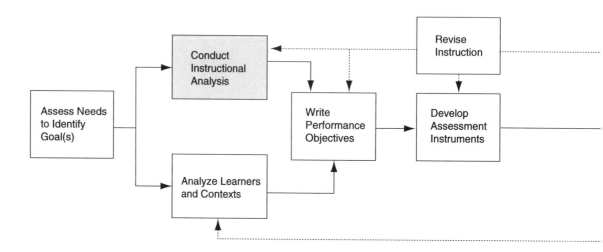

OBJECTIVES

- Describe approaches to subordinate skills analysis including hierarchical, cluster, and combination techniques.
- Describe the relationship among the subordinate skills identified through subordinate skills analysis, including entry behaviors.
- Apply subordinate skills analysis techniques to steps in the goal analysis, and identify entry behaviors as are appropriate.

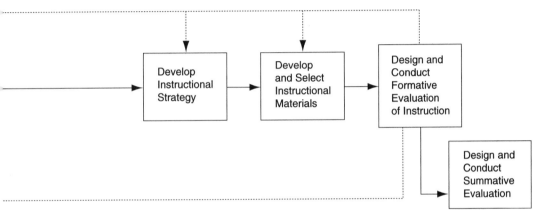

BACKGROUND

This is the second chapter on the instructional analysis process. In the prior chapter, the procedures for carrying out a goal analysis were described. After the steps in the goal have been identified, it is necessary to examine each step to determine what learners must already know or be able to do before they can learn to perform that step in the goal. This second step in the instructional analysis process is referred to as subordinate skills analysis.

The purpose is to identify the appropriate set of subordinate skills for each step. If required skills are omitted from the instruction, and many students do not already have them, then the instruction will be ineffective. On the other hand, if superfluous skills are included, the instruction will take more time than it should, and the unnecessary skills may actually interfere with learning the required skills. The identification of either too many or too few skills can be a problem.

Several processes are used to identify subordinate skills. We will describe each of the techniques and indicate how they can be applied to various types of goals. We will begin with "pure" goals—that is, goals in which the steps are only intellectual or psychomotor skills. Complex goals, however, often involve several domains. A combination approach that can be used with complex goals will also be described.

Concepts

HIERARCHICAL APPROACH

The hierarchical approach is used to analyze individual steps in the goal analysis that are classified as intellectual or psychomotor skills. To understand the hierarchical approach, consider an instructional goal that requires the student to justify the recommendation that a particular piece of real estate should be purchased at a particular time. This is an intellectual skill goal, and it requires students to learn a number of rules and concepts related to the assessment of property values, the effect of inflation on property values, the financial status of the buyer, and the buyer's short- and long-term investment goals. The skills in each of these areas would depend on knowledge of the basic concepts used in the financial and real estate fields. In this example, it would be extremely important to identify and teach each of the critical rules and concepts prior to teaching the steps for analyzing a particular situation and making a recommendation.

How does the designer go about identifying the subordinate skills a student must learn in order to achieve a higher-level intellectual skill? The hierarchical analysis technique suggested by Gagné consists of asking the question, "What must the student already know so that, with a minimal amount of instruction, this task can be learned?" By asking this question, the designer can identify one or more critical subordinate skills that will be required of the learner prior to attempting instruction on the step itself. After these subordinate skills have been identified, the designer then asks the same question with regard to each of them; namely, "What is it that the student must already know how to do, the absence of which would make it impossible to learn this subordinate skill?" This will result in the identification of one or more additional subordinate skills. If this process is continued with lower and lower levels of subordinate skills, one quickly reaches a very basic level of performance, such as being able to recognize whole numbers or being able to recognize letters.

To get a visual understanding of how the designer "builds" the hierarchical analysis, consider the generic hierarchy shown in Figure 4.1. Here a "rule" serves as the immediate subordinate skill required to learn a particular problem-solving skill. It is important to understand that box 2 represents one step in performing the goal. After the rule has been identified (box 2.4), the designer then asks, "What must the student know how to do in order to learn the rule?" The answer is that the student must learn two *concepts*, which are represented in boxes 2.2 and 2.3. When asked, "What must the student know how to do to learn the concept in box 2.2?" the answer is nothing, so no additional skills are listed. For box 2.3, the question results in the identification of a relevant discrimination, which is shown in box 2.1. Figure 4.1 represents how the analysis would appear when laid out in a diagram.

Figure 4.1 is consistent with Gagné's hierarchy of intellectual skills. Gagné has noted that in order to learn how to perform problem-solving skills, learners must first know how to apply the rules that are required to solve the problem. Thus, the immediate subskills to the instructional goal are the rules that must be applied in the problem situation.

Further, Gagné has noted that rules are based on recognizing the components or concepts that are combined in the rules. In other words, in order to learn the relationship among "things," you must be able to classify them. The subordinate skills required for any given rule are typically classifying the concepts that are used in the rules. Finally, the learner must be able to discriminate whether a particular example is relevant to the concept.

Hypothetical Hierarchical
Analysis of a Step from a
Problem-Solving Goal

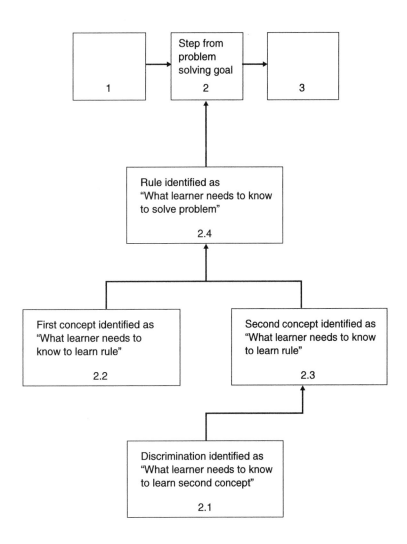

This hierarchy of skills is helpful to the designer because it can be used to suggest the type of specific subordinate skills that will be required to support any particular step in the goal. If the step is a problem-solving skill (or selecting and using a number of rules), then the subskills should include the relevant rules, concepts, and discriminations. On the other hand, if the application of a single rule is being taught, then only the subordinate concepts and discriminations would be taught.

To apply the hierarchical approach to the steps in the goal analysis, the designer applies it to *each step* in the goal, including any decision steps. The question is asked, "What would the learner have to know in order to learn to do the *first step* in performing the goal?" The question is repeated for each of the subskills for the first step and then for each of the remaining steps in the goal. If this approach were used with the hypothetical problem-solving goal that was shown in Figure 4.1, the result might resemble that shown in Figure 4.2.

Observe in Figure 4.2 that the same subskills have been identified as in the original methodology suggested by Gagné. The fact that there are no subskills listed for steps 1, 3, and 4 indicates that the designer has determined that there are no relevant skills that the learner must master before being taught these steps. This is often a perfectly reasonable assumption.

An example of the result of using the hierarchical instructional analysis technique appears in Figure 4.3. In the diagram it can be seen that step 8

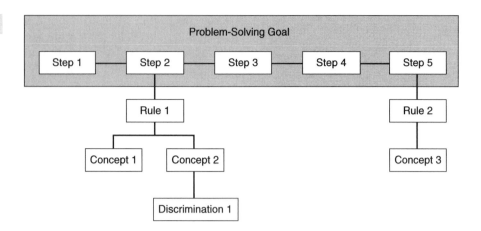

from the goal analysis requires students to estimate to the nearest one-hundredth of a unit (plus or minus one one-hundredth) a designated point on a linear scale marked only in tenths. Three subordinate skills have been identified for step 8. These are related to estimating a point to the nearest hundredth on a scale marked only in tenths units, dividing that scale into subunits, and identifying a designated point on a particular scale. Each of these skills has subordinate skills that are identified.

The use of hierarchical analysis is also illustrated in Figure 4.4. Notice that the cognitive task performed by the learner is shown in the four successive substeps labeled 1, 2, 3, and 4 from the goal analysis. In this particular example, the subordinate skills are the same as those identified for the same skill in Figure 4.3; however, it should be noted that they are organized somewhat differently.

These particular analyses were not devised on the basis of one attempt at the process, or even two or three. It takes a number of attempts at identifying the vertical subordinate skills and their interrelationships before you can be satisfied that all the relevant skills are identified and stated appropriately. It is almost impossible to know when an appropriate and valid hierarchical analysis of an instructional goal has been achieved.

After you are satisfied that you have identified all the subskills required for students to master your instructional goal, you will want to diagram your analysis. The following conventions are used when diagramming a hierarchical analysis:

1. The instructional goal is stated at the top. All the steps in the goal appear in numbered boxes at the top of the hierarchy.

2. All subordinate intellectual skills appear in boxes that are attached via lines coming from the tops and bottoms of boxes.

3. Verbal information and attitudinal skills are attached to intellectual and motor skills via horizontal lines, as will be shown in subsequent sections.

4. Arrows should indicate that the flow of skills is upward toward the goal.

5. If two lines should not intersect, then use an arch as shown for the line between box 2 and box 7 in Figure 4.3. The interpretation is that the skill in step 2 is required for steps 5 and 7, but not step 6.

6. Statements of all subordinate skills, including decisions, should include verbs that indicate what the student must be able to do. Avoid boxes that include only nouns.

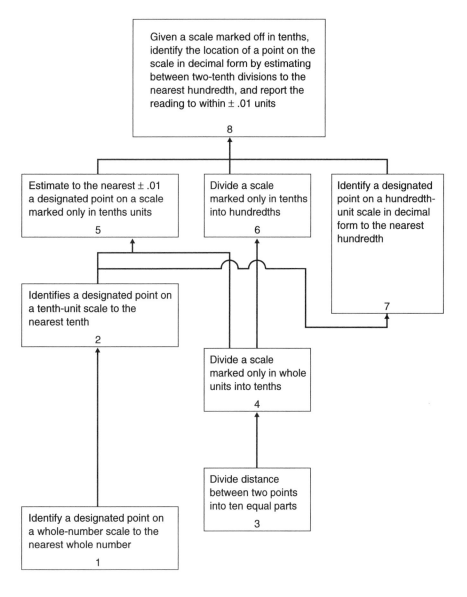

7. Hierarchies, in the real world, are not necessarily symmetrical, and they can take on all kinds of shapes. There is no one correct appearance for a hierarchy.

8. If one of the steps in the goal analysis is a question and is represented by a decision diamond, it is necessary to determine whether there are subordinate skills required to make that decision.

Doing a hierarchical analysis for each step is not an easy task because we are not accustomed to thinking about the content of instruction from this point of view. One way to proceed is to ask, "What mistake might students make if they were learning this particular skill?" Often the answer to this question is the key to identifying the appropriate subordinate skills for the skill in question. The kinds of *misunderstandings* that students might have will indicate the *understandings*, also known as *skills*, which they must have. For example, if students might err because they become confused between stalactites and stalagmites, then an important subordinate skill would be the ability to classify examples of these two entities.

FIGURE 4.4

Hierarchical Analysis of
Steps in a Goal Analysis

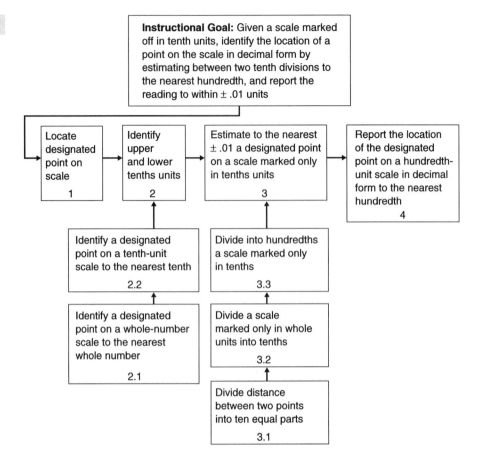

It is important to review your analysis several times, making sure that you have identified all the subskills required for students to master the instructional goal. At this point you should again use the backward-stepping procedure, from the highest, most complex skill in your hierarchy to the lowest, simplest skills required by your learners. This will allow you to determine whether you have included all the necessary subskills. It may be possible to check the adequacy of your back-stepping analysis by starting with the simplest skills in your hierarchy, and working upward through the subskills to the most complex skills. You should also ask the following questions:

1. Have I included subskills that relate to the identification of basic concepts, such as objects or object qualities? (Example: Can a tetrahedron be identified?)

2. Have I included subskills that enable students to identify abstractions by means of a definition? (Example: Can the student explain what a city is, or show what an emulsion is?)

3. Have I included subskills that will enable students to apply rules? (Example: Can the student make sentence verbs agree with subjects, or simplify mixed fractions?)

4. Have I included subskills in the analysis that will enable students to learn how to solve problems required to demonstrate mastery of the instructional goal?

You may be able to identify subskills you have omitted by using these questions to evaluate your instructional analysis. You may also make another type of interesting discovery, namely, that your instructional goal is limited to having students learn how to make discriminations or identify concepts. While these skills are obviously important, you may want to modify the goal statement by requiring students to use a rule or to solve problems that require the use of the concepts and discriminations that you originally stated in your goal.

You may also find that you have included skills that are "nice to know" but are not *really* required in order to achieve your goal. Many designers begin with the attitude that these skills are important and should be included. In the end, superfluous tasks often confuse learners or unnecessarily increase the length of the instruction, which can cause the instruction for more important tasks to be rushed or omitted due to time constraints. You do not need to include everything you know about a topic in a hierarchy. The whole point of using the hierarchical approach is to identify just what the learner must know to be successful—nothing more and nothing less. Although it is sometimes tempting not to do so, our best advice is to let the analysis identify the skills for you. It is absolutely the best starting point.

As you proceed with the instructional analysis, it is important to have a clear idea of the distinction between the steps and substeps of performing a goal, and subordinate skills. The steps and substeps are the activities that an expert or competent person would describe as the steps in the performance. The subordinate skills would not necessarily be identified by a competent person when describing the process. These are the skills and knowledge that learners will have to learn before they can perform the steps in the goal. For example, if you were teaching someone to boil water, one of the steps would be "Turn on the burner." One of the subordinate skills for that step would be "Identify examples of *burners*." If you were actually boiling water, you would never say, "This is the burner"; you would simply put the pan with the water on the burner. Obviously you must recognize a burner, but verbally identifying it is not a step in the process of boiling water.

CLUSTER ANALYSIS

We demonstrated previously that it makes little sense to try to do a goal analysis of a verbal information goal because no logical procedure is inherent in the goal. Instead, you move directly to the identification of information needed to achieve the goal.

How do you identify the subordinate skills that should be taught? The answer is almost always apparent from the statement of the goal itself. If the student must be able to identify the states associated with each capital city, then there are fifty subskills, one associated with each state and its capital. It would be useless to write those out as part of the analysis. They could easily be reproduced from a text. In contrast, the subskills are sometimes not as apparent, as in the goal, "List five major causes of inflation." The answer may depend on a particular economic theory. In this case, it might be worth listing the five major reasons as part of what we will refer to as a cluster analysis.

The most meaningful analysis of a verbal information goal is to identify the major categories of information that are implied by the goal. Are there ways that the information can be clustered best? The state capitals might be clustered according to geographic regions; the bones of the body might be clustered by major parts of the body such as head, arms, legs, and trunk. If the goal were to be able to list all the major league baseball cities, they might be clustered by American and National Leagues and then by divisions.

How do you diagram a cluster analysis? One way is to use the hierarchical technique with the goal at the top and each major cluster as a subskill. If this is done, it should be clearly labeled as a verbal information cluster analysis, and not a hierarchy. It would be just as easy to use an outline format and simply list each of the clusters.

It is sometimes embarrassing for teacher-designers to find that when instructional analysis techniques are used, an instructional goal that they have often taught and for which they would like to develop systematically designed instruction is, in fact, simply verbal information. They can feel guilty that they are not teaching rules and problem solving, but this guilt is sometimes misplaced.

There are times when the acquisition of verbal information is critically important. For example, learning vocabulary in a foreign language is verbal information that is the foundation of learning a very complex set of communication skills. The verbal information we must learn as children or as adults is the vehicle we use to develop much more complex concepts and rules. Verbal information goals should not be automatically discarded upon discovery, but considered for their relevance to other important educational goals. Verbal information is the knowledge base called upon when we execute our how-to intellectual skills.

SUBORDINATE SKILLS ANALYSIS TECHNIQUES FOR ATTITUDE GOALS

In order to determine the subordinate skills for an attitudinal goal, the designer should ask, "What must learners do when exhibiting this attitude?" and, "Why should they exhibit this attitude?" The answer to the first question is almost always a psychomotor skill or an intellectual skill. The purpose of the goal is to get the learner to choose to do either a psychomotor or an intellectual skill; therefore, the first half of the analysis for an attitudinal goal requires hierarchical analysis techniques. This aids in identifying the subskills that will be required *if* the learner chooses to do them. If the learner is to choose to jog, then it is necessary to teach the learner to jog. If the learner is to choose to appreciate a certain body of literature, then the student must learn to comprehend and analyze it.

The second part of the analysis is, "Why should the learner make a particular choice?" The answer to this question is usually verbal information. The verbal information may either be analyzed using a separate cluster analysis, or it may be integrated, as verbal information, into the basic hierarchical analysis that was done for the first half of the analysis. The verbal information constitutes the persuasive part of attitude shaping, along with modeling and reinforcement, and it should be included as an integral part of the instructional analysis.

In order to represent an attitude on an instructional analysis chart, simply write the attitude goal in a box *beside* the psychomotor or intellectual skill goal that will be analyzed. Connect the two main boxes with a line like this:

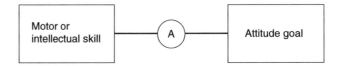

This connecting line shows that the motor or intellectual skill is supporting the attitudinal goal. At this point it is obvious that we are beginning to combine the various analysis techniques. These combinations, which are sometimes called information maps, are described in the following section.

Combining Instructional Analysis Techniques

We have just described how an attitudinal goal can be analyzed using a hierarchical analysis. It is quite common to find that the instructional analysis process results in identifying a combination of subordinate skills from several domains for a goal that was classified as belonging to only one domain.

Consider, for example, the combination of intellectual skills and verbal information. It is not unusual when doing a hierarchical analysis to identify knowledge that the learner should "know." Just "knowing something" is not an intellectual skill as we have defined it here and therefore would not, by the rules, appear on an intellectual skills hierarchy. But often it is important that this knowledge, which is verbal information, appear as a part of the analysis of what must be learned to achieve the instructional goal. Briggs and Wager (1981) therefore suggest that the verbal information be shown in a box with a connecting line like this:

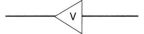

This indicates that the verbal information in the right-hand box is used in support of the intellectual skill in the left-hand box. In a hierarchy, it might look like this:

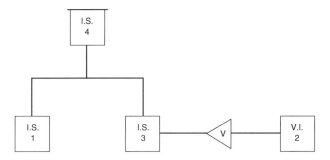

Boxes 1, 3, and 4 represent intellectual skills, while box 2 is verbal information.

What happens if you put all the diagramming techniques together? It is conceivable that an attitude goal with a psychomotor component might require subordinate intellectual skills and verbal information! It would look something like this:

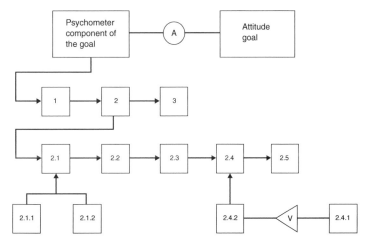

The diagram indicates that the primary goal is for learners to develop an attitude that will be demonstrated by the execution of some psychomotor behavior. The psychomotor skill is composed of three steps, 1, 2, and 3. A subskill analysis of skill 2 indicates that it includes five steps, 2.1 through 2.5. Two intellectual skills, 2.1.1 and 2.1.2, are subordinate to step 2.1. The intellectual skill 2.4.2 requires verbal information, 2.4.1, in order to support step 2.4.

INSTRUCTIONAL ANALYSIS DIAGRAMS

At this point we will review the diagramming procedures for doing an instructional analysis. The first step, of course, is to classify your instructional goal and perform a goal analysis. Then select the appropriate technique(s) for identifying the subordinate skills.

Type of Goal or Step	Type of Analysis
Intellectual skill	Hierarchical
Psychomotor skill	Hierarchical
Verbal information	Cluster
Attitude	Hierarchical and/or cluster

As the designer proceeds with the analysis, the subordinate skills are visually displayed in diagrams. The following diagram illustrates the basic appearance of a hierarchical analysis. When diagrammed, any particular set of subskills required to reach a terminal objective can have a variety of structural appearances. The following diagram is generally used to represent a goal analysis. There are no subordinate skills, so all the skills are diagrammed in one continuous line.

It is also traditional to place superordinate skills above the skills upon which they are dependent. In this way, the reader will automatically recognize the implied learning relationship of the subskills. This is illustrated in the following diagram. Notice that subskills 1.1, 1.2, and 1.3 do not depend on each other, but that learning skill 1 requires the previous learning of 1.1, 1.2, and 1.3. Objectives 2, 3, and 4 are not interdependent; 4.1 and 4.2 must be learned prior to 4.

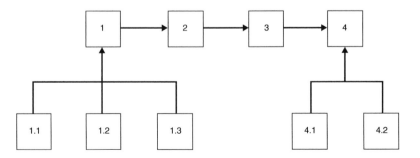

The following diagram illustrates the dependence of subsequent skills upon those preceding them.

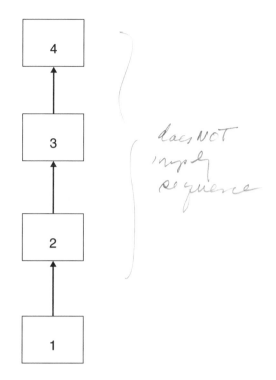

does NOT imply sequence

The student must learn subskill 1 in order to be able to learn to perform subskill 2. Likewise, before subskill 4 can be learned, subskills 1, 2, and 3 must be mastered; thus, these skills form a hierarchy. Note, this does not mean that 1, 2, 3, and 4 are performed in sequence. If they were, then they would be the substeps of a superordinate skill, and would be diagrammed as follows:

implies sequence

In addition, we noted that attitudinal goals can be indicated by the following:

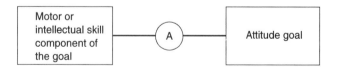

Verbal information is indicated by connecting it to an intellectual skill via a line and a triangle containing the letter V.

Skill in using these diagramming conventions should help you grasp the implied relationship of subskills in an instructional analysis diagram. The order for learning each skill is also implied through the sequencing of skills.

Take note of the numbers that have appeared in the various diagrams of subordinate skills. Do not interpret them to mean more than they do. At this point in the instructional design process, the numbers in the boxes are used simply as a shorthand method for referring to the box; they *do not* represent the sequence in which the skills will be taught. Using these numbers, we can discuss the relationship between box 7 and box 5 without describing the skills that are involved. We should not be thinking about how we will teach these skills, but rather, ensuring that we have the correct skills included in our analysis. At a later point in the design process, it will be necessary to decide on the instructional sequence for the skills, and you may wish to renumber the skills at that time.

Why is the instructional analysis process so critical to the design of instruction? It is a process the instructional designer can use to identify those skills really needed by the student to achieve the terminal objective, and to help exclude unnecessary skills. This may not appear to be a terribly strong argument when considered in light of a particular instructional goal that you might select. You might feel that you are so thoroughly familiar with the content and skills required of the student that this type of analysis is superfluous. You may be assured, however, that as you become involved in a variety of instructional design projects you cannot be a subject-matter expert in all areas. It will be necessary to engage in analytic processes of this type with a variety of subject matter specialists to identify the critical skills that will result in efficient and effective instruction.

ENTRY BEHAVIORS

The instructional analysis process serves another important function that we have not yet discussed. It helps the designer identify exactly what learners will already have to know or be able to do *before* they begin the instruction. These skills are referred to as entry behaviors because learners must already have mastered them in order to learn the new skills included in the instruction. We will describe how the designer identifies entry behaviors and indicate why this is so important. We will use some of the analyses presented earlier in this chapter to show how they can be extended to include entry behaviors.

The procedure used to identify entry behaviors is directly related to the subordinate skills analysis process. You know that with the hierarchical analysis you ask, "What does the learner need to know in order to learn this skill?" The answer to this question is one or more subordinate skills. If you continue this process with each successive set of subordinate skills, the bottom of the hierarchy will contain very basic skills.

Assume you have such a highly developed hierarchy. It represents the array of skills required to take a learner from the most basic level of understanding up to your instructional goal. It is likely, however, that your learners already have some of these skills, and therefore it will not be necessary to teach all the skills in the extended hierarchy. In order to identify the entry behaviors for your instruction, examine the hierarchy or cluster analysis and identify those skills that a majority of the learners will have already mastered before beginning your instruction. Draw a dotted line above these skills in the analysis chart. The skills that appear above the dotted line will be those you must teach in your instruction. Those that fall below the line are called entry behaviors.

Why are entry behaviors so important? They are defined as the skills that fall directly below the skills you plan to teach; therefore, they are the initial building blocks for your instruction. Given these skills, learners can begin to acquire the skills presented in your instruction. Without these skills, a learner will have a very difficult time trying to learn from your instruction. Entry behaviors are a key component in the design process. An example of how entry behaviors can be identified through the use of a hierarchy appears in Figure 4.5. This is basically the same hierarchy that appeared in Figure 4.3; however, three more skills have been added to the analysis chart. A dotted line has been drawn across the page indicating that all skills above the line will be taught in the instructional materials. All the skills listed below the line will be assumed to be skills already attained by students before beginning the instruction.

Each skill below the line was derived directly from a superordinate skill that already appeared on the instructional analysis chart. Each was derived by asking the question, "What does the learner have to be able to do in order to learn this skill?" Note that even the entry behaviors identified in Figure 4.5 have a hierarchical relationship to each other. The skills that have been derived include the ability to interpret whole and decimal numbers. These are skills that *must* be mastered in order to learn skills 1 and 7, but they will not be taught in this instruction. Students will have to have mastered these skills *before* they begin the instruction on reading a scale.

Instructional designers should identify expected entry behaviors of learners by continuing the instructional analysis to the point that skills identified become basic for their learners. The designer must assume that most, if not all, of the learners will have these skills. It is then a matter of simply drawing a dotted line through the instructional analysis chart to separate those skills to be included in the instruction from those skills that learners in the target population are assumed to have already mastered.

The description thus far has related entry behaviors to a hierarchical instructional analysis. This same approach can be taken with the cluster and combination analyses. If a cluster or combination approach is used in which subordinate skills and knowledge are identified, then the identification process can be continued until basic skills are identified, and so indicated by the dotted line.

You should be aware that the examples we have used have been rather clear-cut in that they describe specific skills related to specific instructional goals. There are some descriptors of learners that may be considered as either entry skills for a particular instructional unit or as descriptive of the general target population. Consider the question of students' reading levels.

It is apparent that instructional materials typically depend heavily on the reading ability of students; students must have some minimum level of reading ability to become involved with the materials. Is the specification of reading level a description of a general characteristic of the learners or is it a specific entry behavior that students must possess before beginning instruction? Clear arguments could be made on either side of this issue. You may be able to identify other skills that would produce similar problems.

A technique you might employ to identify the appropriate classification for such an ability is to determine whether you think it would be worthwhile or feasible for an instructor to test a learner for that particular skill prior to permitting the learner to begin the instruction. If the answer to that question is "yes, it would be worth the time to test the learner," then you have probably defined a specific entry behavior. If, on the other hand, it would seem to be inappropriate to test the skill of the learner (such as giving a reading test) before instruction, then the factor you have identified is probably better classified as a general characteristic of the learners for whom the unit is intended.

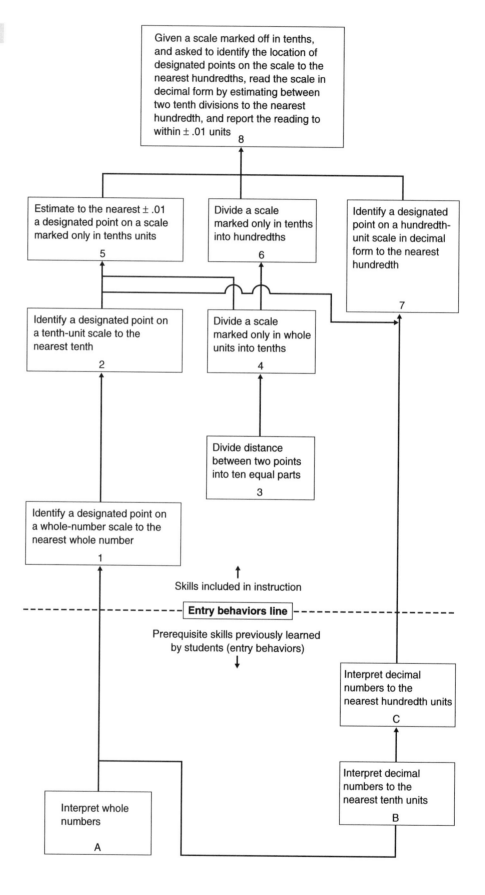

Given a scale marked off in tenths, and asked to identify the location of designated points on the scale to the nearest hundredths, read the scale in decimal form by estimating between two tenth divisions to the nearest hundredth, and report the reading to within ± .01 units   8

Estimate to the nearest ± .01 a designated point on a scale marked only in tenths units   5

Divide a scale marked only in tenths into hundredths   6

Identify a designated point on a hundredth-unit scale in decimal form to the nearest hundredth   7

Identify a designated point on a tenth-unit scale to the nearest tenth   2

Divide a scale marked only in whole units into tenths   4

Divide distance between two points into ten equal parts   3

Identify a designated point on a whole-number scale to the nearest whole number   1

Skills included in instruction ↑

Entry behaviors line

Prerequisite skills previously learned by students (entry behaviors) ↓

Interpret decimal numbers to the nearest hundredth units   C

Interpret decimal numbers to the nearest tenth units   B

Interpret whole numbers   A

How you go about identifying the specific entry behaviors for your materials will depend on where you stopped when you conducted your instructional analysis. If you identified only those tasks and skills that you plan to include in the instructional materials, then you will need to take each of the lowest skills in the hierarchy and determine the subordinate skills associated with them. These would be listed on your instructional analysis chart beneath a line that clearly differentiates them from subordinate skills that will be included in the instructional materials.

If your subordinate skills analysis were carried out to the point of identifying basic, low-level skills, then it should be possible for you simply to draw a dotted line through the chart above those skills that you assume most learners have already acquired.

Also note that when developing instructional materials about topics of general interest that emphasize information objectives, there sometimes are apparently no required entry skills other than the ability to read the materials and to use appropriate reasoning skills to reach the instructional goal. If you find that you have identified such an area, then it is perfectly legitimate to indicate that, while the materials are intended for a certain group of learners, there are no specific entry behaviors required to begin the instruction.

THE TENTATIVENESS OF ENTRY BEHAVIORS

As one of our colleagues has indicated to us, the identification of entry behaviors is one of the real danger spots in the instructional design process. His point is that the designer is making assumptions about both what the learners must know and should already know. Obviously, the designer can err in one of two directions, and each has consequences. For example, some curriculum materials are designed for only the brightest students. This situation would be reflected in a subordinate skills analysis in which the dotted line separating skills to be taught from skills assumed to be known is placed relatively high on the chart, which suggests that learners already have mastered most of the skills described on the chart. When the assumed entry behaviors are not already mastered by the majority of the target population, the instructional materials lose their effectiveness with a large number of learners. Without adequate preparation in the entry skills, learners' efforts are inefficient and the materials are ineffective.

The second error occurs when the dotted line is drawn too low on the instructional analysis. In this situation it is presumed that learners have few or none of the skills required to achieve the instructional goal. An error of this type is costly both in terms of developing instructional materials that are not really needed by learners, and in terms of the time required for learners to study skills they have already mastered.

It should be noted that the designer is making a set of assumptions at this early point about the learners who will use the instruction. If time is available, a try-out sample of group members should be tested and interviewed to determine if most of them have the entry behaviors derived from the subskills analysis. Procedures for doing this will be discussed in later chapters. If time does not permit this, then the assumptions will have to be tested at a later time in the development process. Delaying this verification of the entry behaviors, however, can lead to a situation in which a lot of development has taken place improperly because of a mismatch between the learner and the instruction.

If it is discovered that there is not a good alignment between the entry skills of the learners, and the skills planned for inclusion in the instruction, then a fundamental question must be answered. Is specific content being taught, or is the target population being taught? If it is the former, then little or no change is required in entry behaviors. One simply keeps looking until a group of learners with the right entry behaviors is found. Your instruction is for them! If your purpose is to teach a specific group of learners, however, then the instruction must be modified by the addition or subtraction of instruction to match the entry behaviors that do exist within the group. There is no one correct answer to this dilemma. Each situation must be considered in light of the needs assessment that resulted in the creation of the instructional goal.

In the same manner, it is often found that only a portion of the intended learners has the entry behaviors. What accommodation can be made for this situation? It may be possible to have several "starting points" within the instruction, and learners' scores on entry behavior tests can be used to place them at the appropriate starting point. Or the solution may again be that the instruction was designed for learners with certain entry behaviors. Those who do not have these skills must master them somewhere else before beginning the instruction. There are usually no easy answers to this all-too-common situation.

EXAMPLES

HIERARCHICAL ANALYSIS OF AN INTELLECTUAL SKILL

TOPIC Problem-solving group discussions.

INSTRUCTIONAL GOAL Lead group discussions aimed at solving problems.

The hierarchical approach was selected to continue the analysis of step 6 as shown in Figure 3.5. Three main discussion leader actions were identified as behaviors that would aid in managing cooperative group interaction. These behaviors are engendering cooperative member behaviors, defusing blocking behaviors, and alleviating group stress during a meeting. These three actions are illustrated and sequenced in the following diagram. Since they are not hierarchically related, there is some latitude in how they are sequenced. Engendering cooperative action is listed first because it is the most straightforward and positive of the three actions. Defusing blocking behaviors is listed second because it is a complement to positive actions, and alleviating group stress is listed last. In the superordinate skill, skill 6, the learner will integrate the use of the three subordinate skills in order to manage cooperative group interaction.

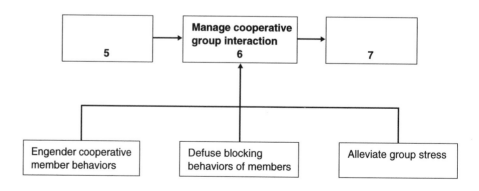

We can continue the hierarchical analysis by identifying the skills that are subordinate to each of the management skills. For this we focus on one task at a time, so we begin with engendering cooperative member behaviors. In order for leaders to engender cooperative behaviors, they will need to be able to recognize strategies for engendering cooperative behavior and to recognize group members' cooperative actions. Finally, they will need to be able to name strategies for encouraging cooperative interaction and name member actions that facilitate cooperative interaction. These latter tasks are verbal information, so they are connected to their respective classification tasks using verbal information symbols. These skills could be diagrammed as follows:

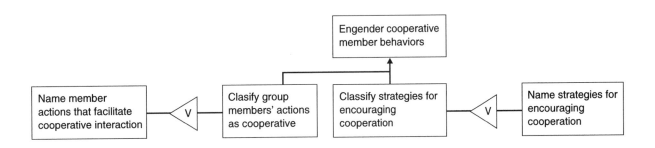

Now let's turn our attention to the second task in the diagram: defusing blocking behaviors of group discussion members. To demonstrate this skill, leaders would need to classify strategies for defusing blocking behaviors as well as group member actions that block cooperative interaction. Each of these behaviors has a verbal information component consisting of naming defusing strategies and naming member actions that block cooperative interaction. The following diagram illustrates these tasks:

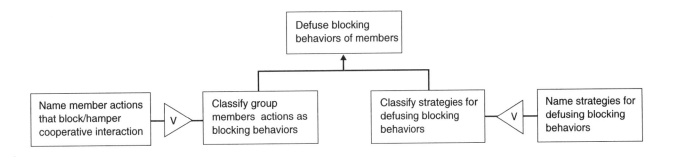

We are now ready for the third skill: alleviating group stress. Similar to the first two tasks, leaders need to classify leader actions for alleviating group stress and symptoms of group stress. These two tasks are supported by verbal information tasks related to naming the strategies and naming the symptoms. These tasks can be diagrammed as follows:

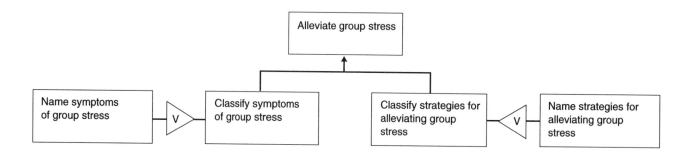

A completed draft of the analysis thus far is included in Figure 4.6 to demonstrate the relationship among subtasks in the hierarchy. First, notice that the original seven steps provide an overview and step-by-step sequence for the instructional goal that is written at the top of the diagram. Second, notice the hierarchical substructure beneath step 6. The substructure identifies the subordinate skills in the hierarchy for only step 6. Third, notice that the three group-management steps have been arranged horizontally (subordinate skills 6.5, 6.10, and 6.15), which implies that they are not hierarchically related. To complete the instructional analysis for the instructional goal, you would identify the information to be included in the remaining verbal information tasks and the subordinate skills for the other major steps identified in the instructional goal. As you can see from this example, a thorough analysis of an intellectual skill can become quite elaborate.

CLUSTER ANALYSIS FOR VERBAL INFORMATION SUBORDINATE SKILLS

TOPIC Cooperative group discussion.

SUBORDINATE SKILLS Name member actions that facilitate cooperative interaction and name member actions that block or hamper cooperative interaction.

Although some instructional goals are verbal information tasks, more often we need to perform an analysis of verbal information subordinate skills that are embedded within an intellectual skills hierarchy. Figure 4.7 contains a cluster analysis for two of the verbal information subordinate skills tasks in the managing cooperative group discussion analysis depicted in Figure 4.6. Verbal information for subskill 6.1, name member actions that facilitate cooperative interaction, and subskill 6.6, name member actions that block or hamper cooperative interaction, are included. Task 6.1 contains one cluster of information: spontaneous actions when introducing and reacting to new ideas. Task 6.6 contains two clusters of information: spontaneous, unplanned actions and planned, purposeful actions. Each of the three clusters has its own column in Figure 4.7.

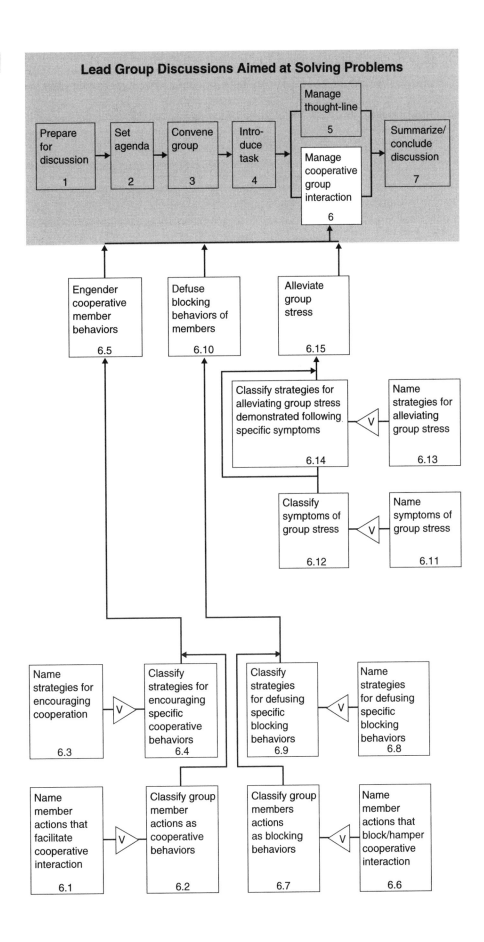

Cluster Analysis of Verbal Information Tasks for Goal on Leading Group Discussion

Name member actions that facilitate cooperative interaction 6.1	Name member actions that block or hamper cooperative interaction 6.6	
Spontaneous, unplanned actions:	**Spontaneous, unplanned actions:**	**Planned/purposeful actions:**

Spontaneous, unplanned actions: (6.1)

6.1.1 When introducing and reacting to new ideas:

1. treats all members' **ideas** fairly (impartiality) and with due consideration
2. comes with open mind
3. listens and considers others' comments
4. volunteers information and ideas
5. expects others to have sincere motives
6. invites others to participate
7. demonstrates good will constantly
8. resists pressures to conform
9. appreciates loyalties members feel toward others and other groups

6.1.2 When *ideas* are questioned by group members:

1. admits personal errors in ideas, judgment
2. resists tendency to abandon ideas too quickly
3. explains ideas further to enable fair examination
4. helps modify ideas for group acceptance

Spontaneous, unplanned actions: (6.6)

6.6.1 When introducing and reacting to new ideas

1. neglects comments made by colleagues who:
   a. rarely speak
   b. lack influence
2. neglects comments because they:
   a. are poorly phrased
   b. are unpopular
   c. lack immediate appeal
3. accepts ideas too quickly due to:
   a. desire to make quick progress
   b. advocacy by popular, articulate, experienced member (favoritism)
   c. desire to be considered cooperative
   d. novelty
4. comes with fully formed conclusions
5. proposes and exhorts
6. only remarks when invited
7. misconstrues others' motives
8. neglects others comments, ideas
7. rewards/punishes others for ideas
8. pressures others to conform
9. demeans members' loyalties to others

6.6.2 When *ideas* are questioned by group members:

1. refuses to admit personal error
2. shows dogmatic commitment to own ideas
3. views questions as personal attack (oversensitive)
4. reacts to questions defensively

6.6.3 Attempts to control others by building a personal image through:

1. adopting a sage role ("I've been here longer and I know."); remains quiet early, then saves the group with reasonable recommendations
2. dropping names, places, experiences
3. collusion (feeding cues to colleagues, opening opportunities for each other)
4. moving faster than others, suggests solutions before others get started
5. taking extreme position, then moving to center to appear cooperative
6. over-responding (listening and responding to feint cooperativeness)
7. showing specious earnestness ("That's such a **gooood** idea **yooou** have.")
8. using trendy language for popular appeal

Planned/purposeful actions:

6.6.4 Attempts to control others by inducing feelings of inadequacy in them through

1. using technical language unnecessarily
2. demanding definitions repetitively
3. displaying studied disregard of another's comments (going back to previous speaker as though nothing was said)
4. usurping leader's functions repeatedly

6.6.5 Attempts to control others by delaying work of group through:

1. summarizing unnecessarily at short intervals
2. cautioning against moving too fast
3. deceptively showing deliberation and adjustment (posture/gestures)

6.6.6 Attempts to control others by putting them off balance through:

1. inappropriately changing pace, tone, volume
2. distorting another's ideas to make them appear contradictory, extreme, unreasonable
3. abruptly switching from logic to sentimentality
4. disparaging important matters with overcasual reaction or verbal minimization
5. studied misrepresentation

Subordinate Skills Analysis of an Additional Goal That Requires Both Intellectual Skills and Verbal Information

Topic Banking.

Instructional Goal Open and maintain a checking account.

The major steps identified for opening and maintaining a checking account were illustrated in Chapter 3 in Figure 3.8. Step 2, deposit money into a checking account, was selected to demonstrate the analysis required to identify subskills for this task. They are included in Figure 4.8. Note in the figure that another goal analysis has been carried out because the step is so large. Steps 2.1 through 2.8 are the steps to perform if one were depositing money in a checking account.

The tasks were identified and sequenced using a chronological approach. After obtaining a sample deposit slip for reference, we identified what should be done first, second, third, and so forth to complete the form. Steps 2.1 through 2.8 illustrate the process of depositing money into a checking account. Steps 2.3 and 2.4 show that a decision must be made based on the type of transaction that is desired. An individual may wish to deposit (a) cash only, (b) checks only, (c) cash and checks, or (d) checks only, and have a portion of the total returned as cash during the transaction. The exact steps to take will be determined by the nature of the money to be deposited.

Next, we further analyzed the steps a student would have to take to deposit cash (2.3) and checks (2.4). This analysis appears in Figure 4.9. Notice in these analyses that a combination of goal and hierarchical approaches are used. For example, a student cannot possibly total the amount of cash to be deposited without learning the subordinate skill of addition. Similarly, the learner cannot determine the total amount of the deposit after subtracting the amount of cash to be returned without first learning to subtract. Students can, however, learn where to enter checks on a deposit slip without first learning that they should sign each check and record their account number on it.

Analysis of a Psychomotor Skill

Topic Putting a golf ball.

Instructional Goal Putt a golf ball into the cup.

Psychomotor skills usually require a combination of intellectual and motor skills, and the intellectual skills often require supporting verbal information. The chronological procedure to follow in putting a golf ball was illustrated in Figure 3.2. At this point we need to continue the instructional analysis to identify the subordinate skills and information required to perform each step previously identified. As an illustration, we will first analyze the subordinate skills required to perform step one: Plan the stroke required to putt the ball into the cup. The analysis appears in Figure 4.10.

Note in the diagram that the subordinate skills required to plan the stroke are all intellectual skills, or the *psycho* component of the psychomotor skill. The *motor* component occurs when the golfer translates the plan into action. As an observer of someone putting, the designer can readily see the motor part of the skill, whereas the mental part remains hidden. All of the mental activity required to plan the stroke should be completed prior to moving to step 2: Assume a stance based on the plan.

F I G U R E *4.8*

Additional Goal Analysis for Single Step in Checking Account Goal

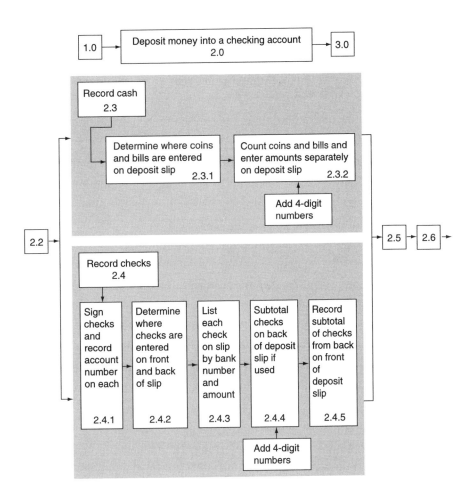

The first step in this psychomotor skill is an intellectual skill, so we apply the hierarchical analysis procedure. In response to the question, "What would the student need to be able to do in order to learn how to plan the stroke?", we determine that the plan consists of predictions on the direction the ball should be hit and the force with which it should be hit. In turn, direction of the putt depends on knowledge of the required trajectory of the ball, which in turn depends on knowledge of the "lay of the land." A similar analysis has been used to identify the subordinate skills associated with determining how hard to hit the ball.

Two items are of importance in this example. The first is that step 1 in the goal, namely, making a plan about how to hit the ball, is a step that must be taught. It cannot be taught, however, until students have learned about direction and force and their accompanying subordinate skills. These skills can then be combined into the step of making a plan.

Now examine the four subskills beneath step 4. You should again go through the process of determining whether each is an intellectual skill, and, if so, whether further hierarchical analysis is required. Steps 4.1, 4.3, 4.4, and 4.5 are motor skills that should require no further analysis. Step 4.2 is an intellectual skill, however, and it requires the use of the plan as well as all the accompanying subordinate skills listed for step 1. It is not necessary to repeat all these skills in the chart. This dependency can be noted by simply putting

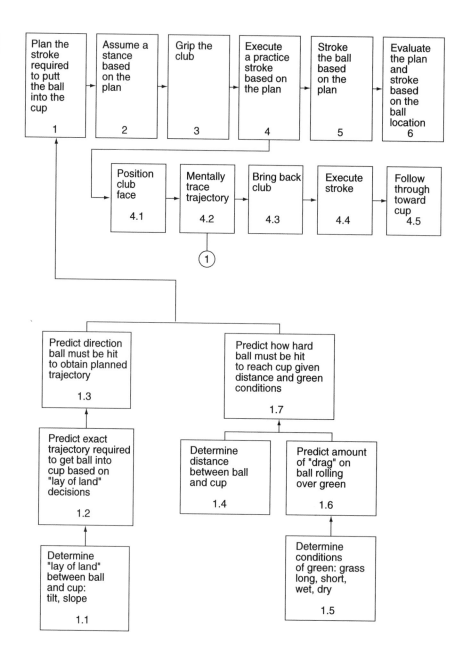

FIGURE 4.10

Hierarchical Analysis of First Step in Psychomotor Skill of Putting a Golf Ball

Goal:
Putt a golf ball
Type of Learning:
Psychomotor

1 in a circle under step 4.2 to indicate that all of step 1 must be learned *before* this step.

Each of the other steps in the putting procedure would need to be analyzed to identify the subordinate skills required to perform it. Skill is acquired through both accurate mental predictions and practice at translating the predictions into physical actions. Much practice is required for accurate translations.

SUBORDINATE SKILLS ANALYSIS FOR AN ATTITUDINAL GOAL

The attitudinal goal analysis example that follows will illustrate one technique you could use to develop an instructional analysis for such a goal.

Starting with the goal statement, the necessary skills and information are identified in a step-by-step sequence.

TOPIC Personal safety while staying in a hotel.

INSTRUCTIONAL GOAL The learner will choose to maximize personal safety while staying in a hotel.

The choice to follow safety precautions while registered in a hotel requires that learners know about potential dangers to themselves, know the procedures to follow, and then actually follow the procedures. The attitudinal instructional goal was introduced in Chapter 3 and preliminary analysis and sequence decisions were illustrated in Figure 3.3.

To continue the analysis, we focus only on fire hazards. What procedures should a hotel occupant follow to minimize the risk of being harmed during a hotel fire? We identified a procedure that contains three basic steps:

1. Inquire about hotel's fire safety rules, procedures, and precautions when checking into the hotel.

2. Check emergency facilities in assigned room.

3. Check emergency exits closest to room.

They have been placed in this sequence because it fits the natural order of events.

The next step is to analyze the information and skills an individual would need in order to accomplish each step. Remember that one important component of shaping an attitude, and thereby increasing the chances that people will demonstrate the desired behavior, is to provide them with information about why they should act in a certain way. In your analysis of these tasks, be sure to include information about why each should be accomplished.

Begin with the first task. Why should someone request fire safety information? Information to help them choose to do this would include facts about death and injury due to fires in hotels. Facts about the frequency of hotel fires, additional hazards in high-rise hotels, or perhaps the number of persons killed or injured annually in hotel fires could be included. The purpose of this information is to get their attention and help them realize that they, too, are at risk while registered in hotels.

They would require other information for the first task as well. They must be able to judge whether the hotel's reported safety precautions and procedures are adequate. To make this judgment, they will need information about routine fire safety precautions that they can expect to find in hotels. So, the first task in our procedure includes supporting information about why patrons should gather fire safety information about hotels and what they should expect to find. The first subordinate skill and the supporting information could be diagrammed as follows:

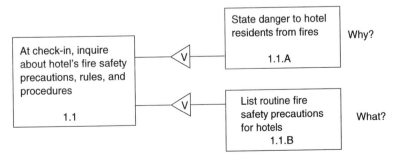

If we were to observe hotel patrons inquiring about fire safety procedures while checking into the hotel, we could correctly infer that they were choosing to maximize their personal safety while staying in the hotel (our original attitudinal goal).

From here, move to the second subordinate skill: check emergency facilities in assigned room. Again, they will need to know why they should do this and what they could expect to find. This information is diagrammed in the following manner:

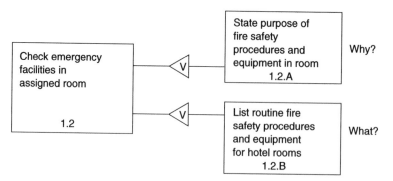

The third subordinate skill is related to why hotel guests should check emergency exits close to their assigned rooms, and what they should expect to see. This information appears in the next illustration.

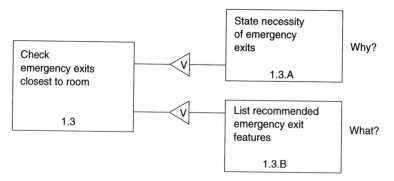

A completed analysis for the fire precaution skill appears in Figure 4.11. Notice in the diagram that the main subordinate skills are placed horizontally. Blocks of information required to perform each step in the procedure are connected to the appropriate box using this symbol:

After completing the analysis of skills 2 and 3, it would be wise to check each set of subordinate skills to determine whether they are related to the original attitudinal goal. If patrons were performing the tasks as specified, could we infer that they were demonstrating an attitude toward maximizing their personal safety while staying in a hotel? If the answer is yes, then we have not strayed from our original goal.

IDENTIFICATION OF ENTRY BEHAVIORS

Examine again the instructional analysis on banking skills included in Figures 4.8 and 4.9. Suppose you were asked to identify the entry points for the following target groups: (a) eighth-grade students, (b) college-bound seniors, and (c) the general population who uses banking services. Which of the tasks in the procedures do you believe should be entry behaviors for eighth-grade students? Go back and review each of the steps in the procedure. We would include all the steps in the procedure in our instruction and label the addition skills in Figure 4.9 as entry behaviors. Now consider the second target population, college-bound seniors. Which tasks would you cite as entry behaviors and which would you include in the instruction? We would keep the same pattern: all steps in the procedure would be included in instruction, and the arithmetic intellectual skills would be considered entry behaviors. We would maintain the same strategy for the population at large. It would be impossible to teach an individual to open and accurately maintain a checking account before he or she had mastered addition of decimal numbers in multiple columns. This is an example of the type of skill described earlier in which the students, regardless of age, location, or motivation, all need the same entry skills prior to learning the banking procedure.

FIGURE *4.11*

Subordinate Skills Analysis of Selected Component of an Attitudinal Instructional Goal

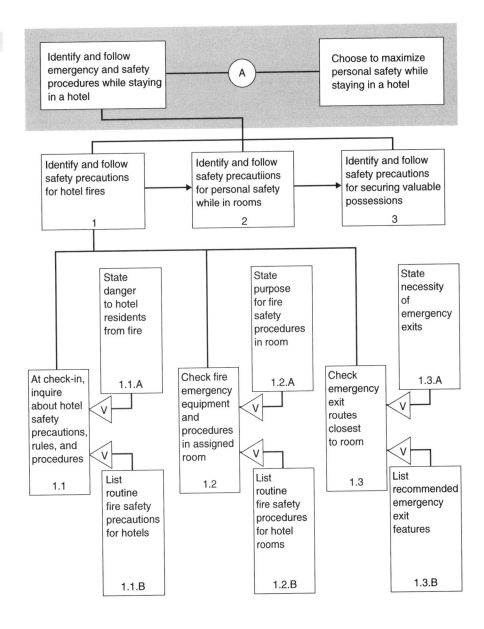

Figure 4.12 repeats the subordinate skills analysis from Figure 4.9. Notice in the new diagram that broken lines have been added to indicate that addition is considered an entry behavior and, as such, it will not be taught during instruction.

Next consider the hierarchical instructional analysis in leading group discussions in Figure 4.6. Which tasks do you believe should be labeled as entry behaviors for the Neighborhood Crime Watch leaders? For this very heterogeneous group, we label two skills as entry behaviors. See Figure 4.13. Suppose the target population were instead college graduates who had prior training in group discussion skills and several years of experience serving as chairs for various committees at work and in the community. For this group, all skills beneath 6.5, 6.10, and 6.15 would possibly be classified as entry behaviors. The instruction for this group could focus on practicing these three leadership skills in interactive groups with detailed feedback on their verbal and nonverbal management actions during the meetings.

Now, review the attitude instructional analysis on personal safety in a hotel that is included in Figure 4.11. Where would you place the entry behaviors line? We would assume that all steps in the procedures, and the information required for each step, were needed; therefore, no entry behaviors line needs to be included in the diagram.

Readers interested in a public school example should review the sample subordinate skills and entry behaviors included in Appendix C.

SUMMARY

In order to begin a subordinate skills analysis, it is necessary to have a clear description of the main tasks learners need to perform in order to accomplish

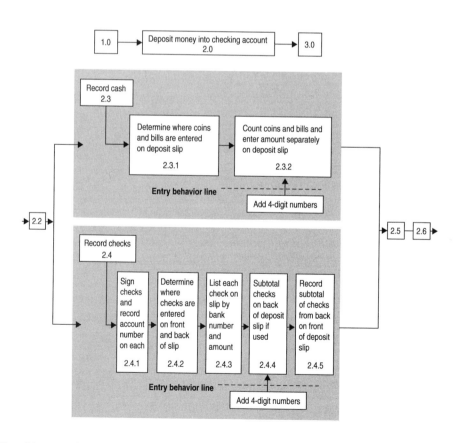

FIGURE 4.12

Entry Behavior Lines Added to Instructional Analysis on Depositing Money into a Checking Account

the instructional goal. The derivation of these major steps was described in Chapter 3. To conduct a subordinate skills analysis, you must analyze each of the major steps in a goal. If a step is verbal information, a cluster analysis would be done. Hierarchical analysis should be used with intellectual and psychomotor skills.

Goal analysis of an attitude identifies the behaviors that would be exhibited if someone held that attitude. During the subordinate skills analysis phase, each of the behaviors would need to be analyzed.

Verbal information required to perform either the intellectual or psychomotor skill would be placed within the framework to support the related steps in the hierarchy. This information might include what to expect and why a particular action should be performed.

For each of the skills identified during this subordinate skills analysis, the process is repeated. That is, each of the identified subordinate skills is analyzed to identify its respective subordinate skills. This step-down process is used until you believe that no further subordinate skills remain to be identified. At this point, the designer identifies the entry behaviors that will be required of learners by drawing a dotted line below those skills that will be taught and above those that will not. The skills that are identified in the analysis that will not be taught are referred to as *entry behaviors*.

The final product of the subordinate skills analysis is a framework of the subordinate skills required to perform each main step of the instructional goal. The total instructional analysis includes the instructional goal, the main steps required to accomplish the goal, the subordinate skills required to accomplish each main step, and the entry behaviors. This framework of skills is the foundation for all subsequent instructional design activities.

It is important to evaluate the analysis of learning tasks before proceeding to the next phase of design activities, because many hours of work remain to be completed. The quality of the analysis will directly affect the ease with which succeeding design activities can be performed and the quality of the eventual instruction. Specific criteria to use in evaluating the analysis include whether all relevant tasks are identified, superfluous tasks are eliminated, and the relationships among the tasks are clearly designated through the configuration of tasks on the chart and the placement of lines used to connect the tasks. Producing an accurate, clear analysis of tasks typically requires several iterations and refinements.

Figure 4.14 summarizes the major concepts from the last two chapters. The goal is translated into a diagram of steps and substeps via the goal analysis process. Those steps, in turn, are used to derive the subordinate skills and the entry behaviors for the goal. The overall process is referred to as an instructional analysis.

PRACTICE

In the exercises that follow, you will be asked to complete a subordinate skills analysis for psychomotor, intellectual, and verbal information goals. The topics and goals used in the examples are purposely different from those used in previous examples. Working with new goals at this point will provide you with a broader base of experience that should be beneficial when you select a topic and goal of your own.

Work through each example, and then compare your analysis with the sample one in the Feedback section. If your analysis is different, locate the differences and determine whether you would like to make any revisions in yours. You may like your analysis better than the sample provided, but you should be able to explain and justify the differences.

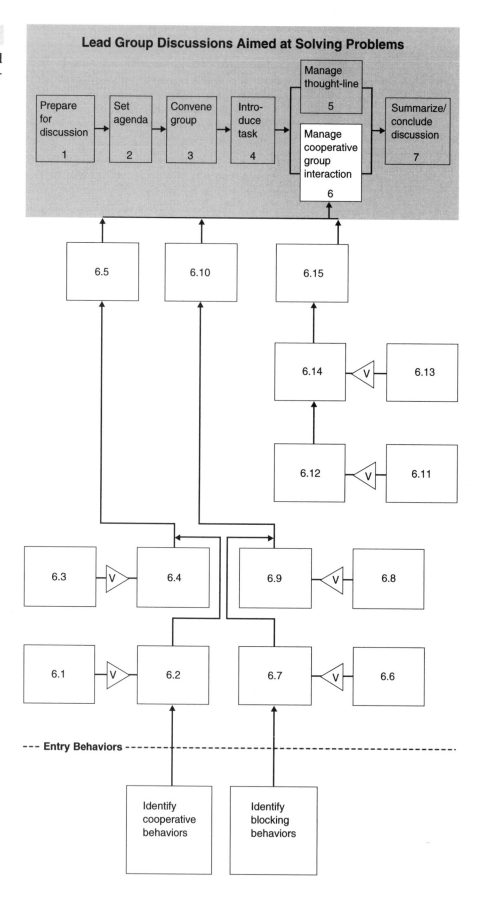

FIGURE 4.14

Components of the
Instructional Analysis
Process

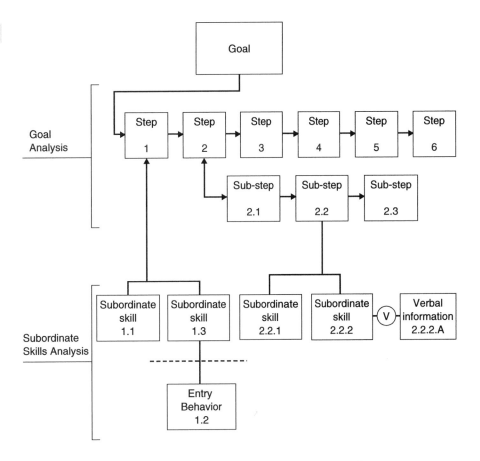

I. HIERARCHICAL ANALYSIS FOR AN INTELLECTUAL SKILL

TOPIC Map skills.

Demonstrate your ability to do a hierarchical analysis by identifying the subordinate skills required to perform each of the four main steps for the following instructional goal on map reading.

INSTRUCTIONAL GOAL Use a map of your town to locate specific places and determine the distances between them.

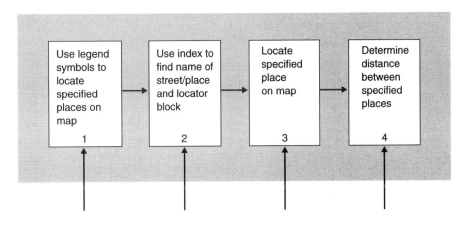

To aid your analysis, you may want to obtain a copy of a local city map and use it to perform each of these main steps. As you work, note what tasks you must perform and what information and skills you need to perform each one.

When you complete your hierarchical analysis, compare your hierarchy with the one in Figure 4.16 in the Feedback section. Analyze and explain any differences.

II. CLUSTER ANALYSIS FOR VERBAL INFORMATION

TOPIC Parts of the body.

INSTRUCTIONAL GOAL Label the parts of the body using common terminology.

One strategy for this analysis might be to proceed from the top to the bottom, or head to feet. Another format consideration might be to use a combination task box and outline format to avoid repeating the word *label* many times. Compare your cluster analysis with the one in Figure 4.17 in the Feedback section.

III. ENTRY BEHAVIORS

a. Review the psychomotor goal analysis on changing a tire in Figure 4.15. Assume that your target population is high school juniors with a temporary driver's license. Identify any steps in the procedure for the entry behaviors that you believe are relevant for this analysis. Modify the procedural analysis in the diagram to reflect your work.

b. Review the hierarchical analysis on reading a map located in Figure 4.16 (Feedback). Assume that your target population is sixth-grade students who are below average, average, and above average in reading and arithmetic skills. Which tasks in the analysis would you predict are entry behaviors and which do you believe should be included in instruction for the sixth-grade group? Modify the diagram in Figure 4.16 to reflect your work.

c. Consider the verbal information on locating and labeling parts of the human body in Figure 4.17 (Feedback). Assume that your target population is third-grade students. Which tasks do you believe should be considered entry behaviors? Remember that the task requires students not only to locate, but also to label parts, which requires spelling. Modify Figure 4.17 to show your work.

FEEDBACK

I. Compare your hierarchical analysis with the one shown in Figure 4.16.

II. Compare your verbal information cluster analysis with the one shown in Figure 4.17.

III. a. No subordinate skills are included in the instructional analysis on changing a tire that should be designated as entry behavior skills for this high school learner group.

b. Probably only two subordinate skills in the instructional analysis for the map reading goal would be considered entry behaviors; these are subordinate skill 4.8, multiply by whole numbers, and skill 4.10, multiply by fractions. Students who cannot multiply by whole numbers or fractions would need either to have step 4 excluded from their instruction or receive modified instruction where they calculate distance using only addition.

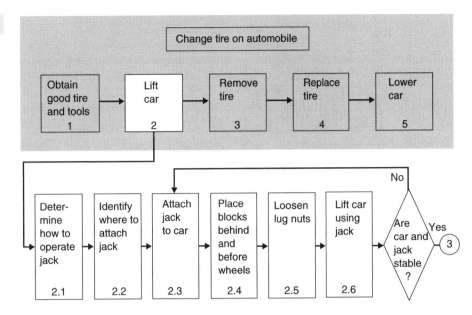

FIGURE 4.15

Goal Analysis for Changing an Automobile Tire

c. Entry behaviors identified for the verbal information cluster analysis include the ability to discriminate among the head, arms, hands, trunk, leg, and foot. Correct spelling of terms will be covered in the instruction; thus, it is not included as an entry behavior.

REFERENCES AND RECOMMENDED READINGS

Gagné, R. M. (1985). *Conditions of learning* (4th ed.). New York: Holt, Rinehart and Winston. This book is a classic in regard to many aspects of instructional design, including the domains of learning and hierarchical analysis.

Gagné, R. M., Briggs, L. J., & Wager, W. W. (1992). *Principles of instructional design* (4th ed.). New York: Holt, Rinehart and Winston. Provides a number of examples of the application of hierarchical analysis to intellectual skills.

Jonassen, D. H. (1997). Instructional design models for well-structured and ill-structured problem-solving learning outcomes. *Educational Technology Research and Development, 45* (1), 65–94. Provides examples and procedures for designing and developing both well-structured and ill-structured problem-solving instruction.

Jonassen, D. H., Tessmer, M., & Hannum, W. (1999). *Handbook of task analysis procedures.* Mahwah, NJ: Lawrence Erlbaum.

Levine, E. R. (1983). *Everything you always wanted to know about job analysis.* Tampa, FL: Mariner Publishing Co. This is a paperback introductory text on job analysis.

Loughner, P., & Moller, L. (1998). The use of task analysis procedures by instructional designers. *Performance Improvement Quarterly, 11* (3), 79–101.

Mager, R. F. (1988). *Making instruction work.* Belmont, CA: David S. Lake Publishers. Discusses goal analysis and shows the use of a flow diagram to clarify a goal.

Merrill, P. F. (1980). Analysis of a procedural task. *NSPI Journal, 19* (2), 11–15. Merrill uses flow-charting methods to identify the subordinate skills of a complex intellectual skill.

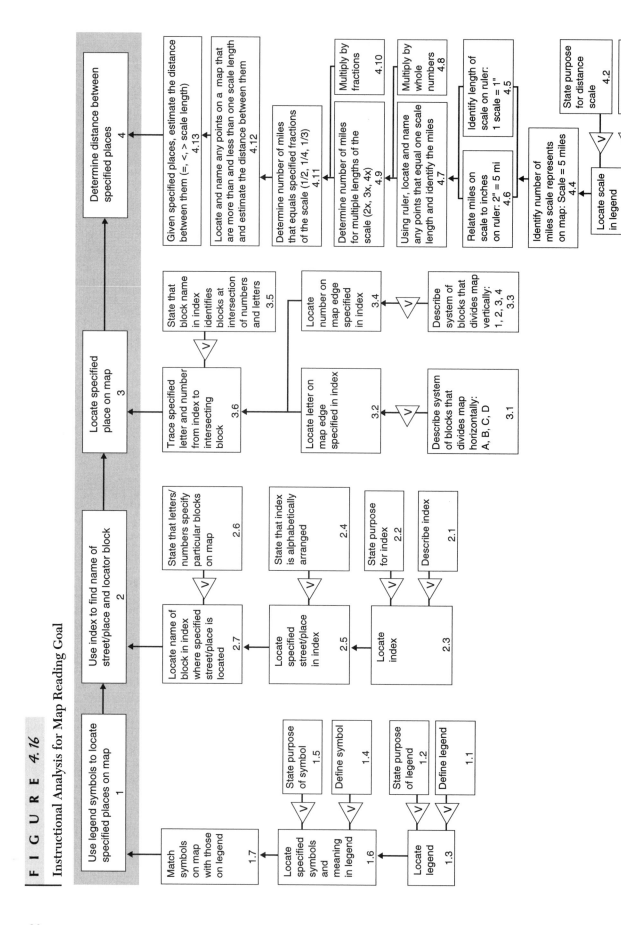

F I G U R E *4.16*

Instructional Analysis for Map Reading Goal

FIGURE 4.17

Cluster Analysis of a Verbal Information Task

Goal:
Locate and label various parts of the human body.
Type of Learning:
Verbal Information

Locate and label parts of the head	Locate and label parts of the arm	Locate and label parts of the hand	Locate and label parts of the trunk	Locate and label parts of the leg	Locate and label parts of the foot
1.0	2.0	3.0	4.0	5.0	6.0

Locate and label:	Locate and label:	Locate and label:	Locate and label:	Locate and label:	Locate and label:
			Front		
1.1 scalp	2.1 armpit	3.1 back	4.1 shoulder	5.1 thigh	6.1 heel
1.2 hair	2.2 upper arm	3.2 palm	4.2 collarbone	5.2 knee	6.2 arch
1.3 ear	2.3 elbow	3.3 finger	4.3 chest	5.3 calf	6.3 sole
1.4 forehead	2.4 forearm	3.4 thumb	4.4 breast	5.4 shin	6.4 toe
1.5 eyebrows	2.5 wrist	3.5 knuckle	4.5 rib cage	5.5 ankle	6.5 toe joint
1.6 eyes		3.6 fingertip	4.6 ribs		6.6 toe nail
1.7 eyelids		3.7 fingernail	4.7 waist		
1.8 cheeks		3.8 identifying pattern (print)	4.8 navel		
1.9 nose			4.9 hip bones		
1.10 nostrils			4.10 hip joint		
1.11 mouth			Back		
1.12 lips			4.11 shoulder blades		
1.13 teeth			4.12 rib cage		
1.14 tongue			4.13 waist		
1.15 jaw			4.14 hips		
1.16 neck					
1.17 Adam's apple					

CHAPTER

5 ANALYZING LEARNERS AND CONTEXTS

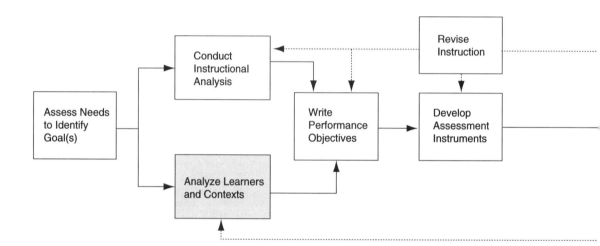

OBJECTIVES

- Name the general characteristics of a target population that are important to consider when developing instruction.
- Name contextual characteristics of the eventual setting where acquired skills will be performed.
- Name contextual characteristics of the instructional setting.
- For a given instructional goal and context, describe methods and sources for obtaining information about the target population, performances setting, and learning setting.
- Analyze and describe the general characteristics of a target population.
- Analyze and describe the contextual characteristics of the eventual performance and instructional settings.

94

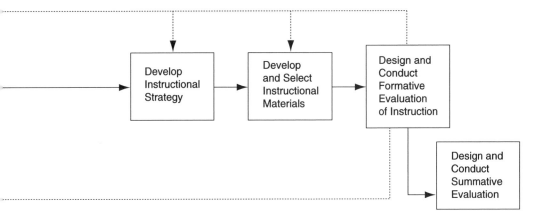

The previous chapters have focused on identifying the skills and knowledge to be taught. From a needs assessment a goal was identified that, in turn, was analyzed to determine the specific steps included in the goal. Additional analysis was used to identify (1) the subordinate skills that must be included in the instruction and (2) the entry skills that learners must have to begin the instruction.

Not only must the designer determine what is to be taught, but also the characteristics of the learners, the contexts in which the instruction will be delivered, and the contexts in which the skills will eventually be used. We refer to these types of analyses as learner analysis and context analysis. They provide the details that help shape both what is taught and, especially, how it is taught.

What do we need to know about the people we are instructing? Answers vary greatly on this question. One approach is to learn as much as possible in order to design instruction that is most appropriate for the learners. Data collection can be expensive and time consuming, and it may yield information that is not very useful. Another approach is to assume that as designers we already know enough about the learners to forgo collecting information about them. For some designers, this may be true, but for others who are designing for new learner populations, assumptions about the learners may be inaccurate and cause significant problems when the instruction is delivered.

Historically, educational psychologists have examined an array of individual difference variables and their relationship to learning. Studies of intelligence and personality traits fill the literature. From an instructional design perspective, we want to know which variables significantly affect the achievement of the group of learners we will instruct, since designers create instruction for groups of learners who have common characteristics. In this chapter we identify a set of variables that research has indicated affects learning. If you describe your learners in terms of these variables, you can modify your instructional strategy to enhance learning.

Of equal importance at this point in the design process are the analyses of the context in which learning will occur and the context in which learners will use their newly acquired skills. In some instances, a learner is taught a skill in a classroom, demonstrates mastery on a posttest, and that is the end of the matter. Likewise, a student may use the mathematics skill learned this year in a mathematics class next year. In these situations, the context for learning and the context for using the skill are essentially the same.

In contrast, consider a course on interpersonal skills for managers. These skills may be taught and practiced in a training center, yet used in a variety of corporate settings. These different contexts should be reflected in the media selected for instruction, in the instructional strategy, and in evaluations of the learners.

Another reason for the designer to analyze the learners and contexts is that these analyses cannot be done in one's office. Designers should talk with learners, instructors, and managers; they should visit classrooms, training facilities, and the learners' workplace to determine the circumstances in which learners will be acquiring and using their new skills. All of these experiences significantly enhance designers' understanding of what is being taught and how it will be used.

CONCEPTS

LEARNER ANALYSIS

Let's begin by considering who the learners are for any given set of instruction. We will refer to these learners as the *target population*—they are the ones you want to "hit" with the appropriate instruction.

Sometimes the target population is also referred to as the target audience or target group. It is referred to using descriptors such as age, grade level, topic being studied, job experience, or job position. For example, a set of materials might be intended for systems programmers, fifth-grade reading classes, middle managers, or high school principals. These examples are typical of the descriptions usually available for instructional materials. But the instructional designer must go beyond these general descriptions and be much more specific about the skills required of the learners for whom the materials are intended.

It is important to make a distinction between the target population and what we will refer to as *try-out learners*. The target population is an abstract representation of the widest possible range of users, such as college students, fifth graders, or adults. Try-out learners, on the other hand, are those learners who are available to the designer while the instruction is being developed. It is assumed that these try-out learners are members of the target population—that is, they are college students, fifth graders, and adults, respectively. But the try-out learners are *specific* college students, fifth graders, or adults. While the designer is preparing the instruction for the target population, the try-out learners will serve as representatives of that group in order to plan the instruction and to determine how well the instruction works after it is developed.

What information do designers need to know about their target population? Useful information includes (1) entry behaviors, (2) prior knowledge of the topic area, (3) attitudes toward content and potential delivery system, (4) academic motivation, (5) educational and ability levels, (6) general learning preferences, (7) attitudes toward the organization giving the instruction, and (8) group characteristics. The following paragraphs elaborate each of these categories.

ENTRY BEHAVIORS Target population members must have already mastered certain skills (i.e., entry behaviors) associated with learning the goal prior to beginning instruction. The research literature also discusses other characteristics of learners, categorized as either specific or general in nature, that relate to learners' knowledge, experience, and attitudes. These also influence the outcome of instruction. Interested readers may want to consult the work of Richey (1992) for a detailed review of this research.

PRIOR KNOWLEDGE OF TOPIC AREA Much of the current learning research emphasizes the importance of determining what learners already know about the topic that will be taught; rarely are they completely unaware or lacking in at least some knowledge of the subject. Further, they often have partial knowledge or misconceptions about the topic. When we teach, learners may try to interpret what is being said in light of the associations they can make with their prior learning. They construct new knowledge by building on their prior understanding; therefore, it is extremely important for the designer to determine the range and nature of prior knowledge.

ATTITUDES TOWARD CONTENT AND POTENTIAL DELIVERY SYSTEM Learners may have impressions or attitudes about the topic that will be taught and perhaps even how it might be delivered. For example, the target population may have mastered the rules for scoring a bowling game but have no interest in learning how to bowl. Or, they might be interested in learning how to bowl if they can do it at a bowling alley, but would not be interested if they have to simulate it on a computer or in a gymnasium. The designer should determine, from a sample set of learners, the range of prior experience, knowledge, and attitudes toward the content area that will be covered in the instruction. Designers also should determine learners' expectations regarding how the instruction might be delivered.

ACADEMIC MOTIVATION (ARCS) Many instructors consider the motivation level of learners the most important factor in successful instruction. Teachers report that when learners have little motivation or interest in the topic, learning is almost impossible. Keller (1987) developed a model of the different types of motivation necessary for successful learning, and he suggested how to use this information to design effective instruction. Keller's model is called the ARCS model (attention, relevance, confidence, and satisfaction). The model will be discussed in detail in the chapter on instructional strategies; it will be used here to show how to obtain information from learners during the learner analysis.

Keller suggests asking learners questions such as these: How relevant is this instructional goal to you? What aspects of the goal interest you most? How confident are you that you could successfully learn to perform the goal? How satisfying would it be to you to be able to perform the goal? The answers to these questions will provide insight into the target population and into potential problem areas in the design of instruction. Do not *assume* that learners are very interested in the topic, find it relevant to their interests or job, feel confident that they can learn it, and will be satisfied when they do. These assumptions are almost never valid. It is important to find out how learners feel *before* you design the instruction rather than while it is being delivered. We will discuss the implications of learners' academic motivation and describe procedures for collecting motivational data after considering more general characteristics of the learners.

EDUCATIONAL AND ABILITY LEVELS Determine the achievement and general ability levels of the learners. This information will provide insight into the kinds of instructional experiences they may have had and perhaps their ability to cope with new and different approaches to instruction.

GENERAL LEARNING PREFERENCES Find out about the target population's learning skills and preferences and their willingness to explore new modes of learning. In other words, are these learners seemingly fixated on the lecture/discussion approach to learning, or have they experienced success with seminar-style classes, case study, small-group problem-based learning, or independent Web-based courses?

ATTITUDES TOWARD TRAINING ORGANIZATION Determine the target population's attitudes toward the organization providing the instruction. Do they have a positive, constructive view of both management and their peers, or are they somewhat cynical about senior leadership and their ability to provide appropriate training? Researchers have indicated that such attitudes are substantial predictors of the success of instruction in terms of the likelihood of newly learned skills being used on the job. Those with positive attitudes about the organization and their peers are more likely to use the skills.

GROUP CHARACTERISTICS A careful analysis of the learners will provide two additional kinds of information that can be influential in the design of instruction. The first is the degree of heterogeneity within the target population on important variables. Obviously, finding ways to accommodate diversity is important. The second kind of information is an overall impression of the target population based on direct interactions with them. This is not simply accepting a stereotypical description or a management description of the learners; this requires interaction with them in order to develop an impression of what they know and how they feel.

These learner variables will be used to select and develop the objectives for instruction, and they will especially influence various components of the instructional strategy. They will help the designer develop a motivational strategy for the instruction and will suggest various types of examples that can be used to illustrate points, ways in which the instruction may (or may not) be delivered, and ways to make the practice of skills relevant for learners.

COLLECTING DATA FOR LEARNER ANALYSIS

There are various ways to collect data about learners. One method would involve a site visit for structured interviews with managers, instructors, and learners. These interviews might yield valuable information about learners' entry behaviors, personal goals, attitudes about the content and training organization, and self-report skill levels. During the site visit, the designer could also observe learners in the performance and instructional contexts. Either on site or using distance technology, designers could administer surveys and questionnaires to obtain similar information about learners' interests, goals, attitudes, and self-report skills. In addition to self-report and supervisor judgment, designers could administer pretests in order to identify learners' actual entry behaviors and prior knowledge and skills.

OUTPUT The results of a learner analysis include a description of the learners' (1) entry behaviors and prior knowledge of the topic, (2) attitudes toward the content and potential delivery system, (3) academic motivation, (4) prior achievement and ability levels, (5) learning preferences, (6) general attitudes toward the organization providing training, and (7) group characteristics.

CONTEXT ANALYSIS OF PERFORMANCE SETTING

The designer must be concerned about the characteristics of the setting in which the skills and knowledge will be used. Instruction should be part of satisfying a need that has been derived from a needs assessment. The needs assessment should be based on the identification of failures in results or opportunities for an organization. The instruction must contribute to meeting an identified need by providing learners with skills and attitudes that will be used, if not in the workplace, certainly somewhere other than the classroom. Seldom is something learned simply for the purpose of demonstrating mastery on a test at the end of the instruction; therefore, as designers it is important for us to know the environment in which our learners will be using their new skills. From a constructivist perspective, a careful context analysis is critical for aiding the learner in making appropriate constructions. Accurate analysis of the performance context should enhance the learners' motivation, sense of instructional relevance, and transfer of new knowledge and skills to the work setting.

MANAGERIAL OR SUPERVISOR SUPPORT We must learn about the organizational support that learners can expect to receive when using the new skills. Research indicates that one of the strongest predictors of use of new skills in a new setting (called *transfer of training*) is the support received by the learner. If managers, supervisors, or peers ignore or punish those using new skills, then the use of the new skills will cease. If personnel recognize and praise those using new skills, then skills will be used, and hopefully their use will address the problem identified in the original needs assessment.

If management support is not present, then the designer (or the training organization) has an added problem associated with this project, namely recruiting their support. It is often helpful to include managers in project planning, ask them to serve as subject-matter experts, and perhaps ask them to serve as mentors or coaches for the learners when they return to the workplace.

PHYSICAL ASPECTS OF THE SITE The second aspect of the context analysis is to assess the physical context in which the skills will be used. Will their use depend on equipment, facilities, tools, timing, or other resources? This information can be used to design the training so that skills can be practiced in conditions as similar as possible to those in the workplace.

Social Aspects of the Site Understanding the social context in which skills are to be applied is critical for designing effective instruction. In analyzing social aspects, some relevant questions to ask include the following. Will learners work alone or as team members? Will they work independently in the field, or will they be presenting ideas in staff meetings or supervising employees? Are the skills to be learned already used proficiently by others in the organization, or will these learners be the first?

Relevance of Skills to Workplace To ensure that new skills meet the identified needs, we should assess the relevance of the skills to be learned by employees currently working in the performance site. Designers should assess whether physical, social, or motivational constraints to the use of the new skills exist. Physical constraints might include lack of work space, outdated equipment, inadequate time or scheduling, or too few personnel. For example, it would do little good to provide customer service training for a receptionist who has a constant stream of customers, all four telephone lines lit, and a thirty-minute delay for customers with appointments. Likewise, training in instructional uses for computers is irrelevant for teachers who have no computers in their classrooms.

COLLECTING DATA FOR CONTEXT ANALYSIS IN THE PERFORMANCE SETTING

Although some instructional analyses can be done in the office, context analyses require designers to observe in the appropriate setting. These observations influence the entire future course of the project because they provide critical information not only for direct input to the project but also for enhancing the skills and knowledge of designers.

On-site visits for purposes of context analysis should be planned well in advance, and one or more visits should be made. These sites will be situation specific, and some may have been identified in the needs assessment.

The purpose for the visits is to gather data from potential learners and managers and to observe the work environment where the new skills will be used. The basic data-gathering procedures include interviews and observations. The interviews should be conducted using written questions that focus on the issues presented in this chapter. Answers to the questions are situation or project specific and depend on the unique nature of each setting.

Output The major outputs of this phase of the study are (1) a description of the physical and organizational environment where the skills will be used, and (2) a list of any special factors that may facilitate or interfere with the learners' use of the new skills.

CONTEXT ANALYSIS OF LEARNING ENVIRONMENT

There are two aspects to the analysis of the learning environment: determining what is and what should be. The *what is* is a review of the setting in which instruction will take place. This might be only one site, such as a corporate training center, or it could be one of many sites that a client has available. The *what should be* is facilities, equipment, and resources that adequately support the intended instruction.

In the learning context analysis, the focus is on the following elements: (1) the compatibility of the site with instructional requirements, (2) the adaptability of the site for simulating aspects of the workplace or performance site, (3) the adaptability of the site for using a variety of instructional strategies and training delivery approaches, and (4) the constraints present that may affect the design and delivery of instruction. The following paragraphs briefly elaborate each of these areas.

COMPATIBILITY OF SITE WITH INSTRUCTIONAL REQUIREMENTS In the instructional goal statement prepared in the first step of the model, the tools and other support items required to perform the goal were listed. Does the learning environment that you are visiting include these tools? Can it accommodate them if they are provided? The most common "tool" today is probably a computer. Are computers available? Are they compatible with the computers in the training organization? And, of great importance, are they compatible with those in other training sites that may be used for the instruction?

ADAPTABILITY OF SITE TO SIMULATE WORKPLACE Another issue is the compatibility of the training environment with the work environment. In training, an attempt must be made to simulate those factors from the work environment that are critical to performance. Will it be possible to do so in the designated training context? What would have to be changed or added?

ADAPTABILITY FOR DELIVERY APPROACHES The list of tool requirements from the goal statement indicates the *what should be* with regard to the learning context and, obviously, for the performance context as well. There may be other limitations or requirements that should be noted at this point in the analysis. These relate to organizational mandates that have been placed on your instruction. The organization may have decided that the instruction must be deliverable in typical corporate training centers in the United States or throughout the world, or that the instruction is intended for the "typical" fourth-grade classroom. Determine what delivery approach can be used in the proposed instructional sites.

LEARNING-SITE CONSTRAINTS AFFECTING DESIGN AND DELIVERY For whatever reason, an upfront decision may have been made that this instruction will be computer-based and self-instructional. The decision may not have been made on the basis of an analysis of the capability of a computer system to deliver the desired instruction. In these types of cases, the context analysis of the learning environment becomes critically important. The designer may find that the computers in various training sites or on employees' desks are incompatible, and it will triple the cost of the project to provide compatible computers. Or, the organization may recognize the benefit of compatible delivery systems and use this opportunity to conform. The major point is that the development of the instruction should *never* be initiated before addressing these kinds of matters. Most experienced designers have, at one time or another, regretted the omission of constraints analysis in the design process.

In an ideal situation, the location of the training and the means of delivering it would be decided on the basis of an analysis of the requirements for teaching the instructional goal. In the extreme, some argue that training should not be delivered until the individual has need of it. It would be delivered, just in time, in the workplace, not in a group setting in a classroom.

We are a long way from that vision. An instructor who teaches twenty to twenty-four learners leads nearly all corporate training. Public education is teacher-led with typically twenty to forty students. However, more self-instructional approaches and facilities are becoming available, and more instruction is being delivered at a workstation computer that includes an electronic performance support system. As these systems become both more complex and more available for training use, systematic design principles will be even more applicable for the development of efficient, effective instruction for such systems.

COLLECTING DATA FOR CONTEXT ANALYSIS IN THE LEARNING ENVIRONMENT

The analysis of the learning context is similar, in many ways, to that of the workplace. The major purpose of the analysis is to identify available facilities and limitations of the setting.

The procedure to follow in analyzing the learning context is to schedule visits to one or more training sites and schedule interviews with instructors, managers of the sites, and learners, if appropriate. As with performance context analysis, have interview questions prepared in advance. If the learners are similar to those who will be taking your instruction, they may be able to provide valuable information about their use of the site. It is also important to observe the site in use and to imagine its use for your instruction. Additionally, determine any limitations on your use of the site and the potential impact on your project.

OUTPUT The major outputs of the learning context analysis are: (1) a description of the extent to which the site can be used to deliver training on skills that will be required for transfer to the workplace, and (2) a list of any limitations that may have serious implications for the project.

PUBLIC SCHOOL CONTEXTS

Before summarizing this section, it is worth reviewing learner and context analysis from the perspective of the designer who will be developing instruction for public schools. Designers who support learner and learning environment analyses may believe they are already familiar with them in the public school sector, and no further analysis is necessary. We encourage you to renew your experience base by doing the proposed analyses with learners, teachers, and typical classrooms. We also encourage you to think beyond the accepted textbook and curriculum guide approach to public schooling. That approach has led to the criticism that much of public education emphasizes factual recall over conceptual understanding and textbook problems over authentic application. Constructivist theorists have been justifiably sharp in their criticism of teaching/learning activities that are abstracted from, and thus not relevant to, authentic physical, social, and problem contexts. This leads not only to diminution of students' motivation, but also to inability to transfer learning for application in meaningful, real-life problem situations outside the school walls.

The importance cannot be overemphasized of analyzing the context in which skills learned in school classrooms will ultimately be used. Those who work in vocational education see the immediate relevance of this step to their design efforts. They want to provide vocational graduates with skills that can be used and supported in the workplace. However, consider something like fifth-grade science instruction. What is the "performance site" for skills learned in such a course? One way to answer the question is to identify where the skills will be used next in the curriculum and talk with those teachers about the contexts in which the skills are used and about how well prepared students have been in these skills in the past.

Another analysis of the performance context relates to the use of the skills and knowledge outside the school. Why are the students learning these skills? Do they have any application in the home or the community, in hobby or recreational interests, or in vocational or higher educational pursuits? If so, carefully note performance context applications and bring them to the instructional strategy stage of design. These applications are exactly what is needed to boost motivation, provide context for new content and examples, and design practice activities that are seen as relevant by students. In essence, we believe the learner and context analysis step in the instructional design model is just as important to the public school designer as it is to one who will be working with adult populations in diverse training and work environments.

EVALUATION AND REVISION OF THE INSTRUCTIONAL ANALYSIS

Most designers review and revise design analyses *before* the first draft of instruction is created. One component of the design process for which a preliminary tryout can be made is the instructional analysis. The reason we are discussing the tryout in this chapter, rather than in the last one, is that the tryout can occur at the same time the designer is conducting the learner and context analyses. Those analyses bring the designer into contact with potential learners, or recent learners, who can review the instructional analysis with the designer.

The instructional analysis diagram indicates the goal, the steps required to perform the goal, the subordinate skills, and the required entry behaviors. In order to review the reasonableness of your analysis, select several people who have the characteristics of the target population. Sit with each person and explain what the analysis means. State the goal and explain what someone would do if he or she were able to do it. You might provide an example in which you go through the steps. Then explain how each of the sets of subskills supports one or more of the steps in the goal. Explain what is meant by entry behaviors, and ask if the person knows or can do each of the entry behaviors you have listed for your instruction.

What is the purpose of this explanation? You hear yourself explaining your ideas as you have represented them in the analysis. Sometimes just the act of explaining the analysis will lead to insights about duplications, omissions, or unneeded information. Almost without regard to what the learner says during the explanation, you may find changes you want to make.

In addition to your personal reactions, you need to see how a learner from the target population reacts to the skills you will be teaching. You will be "explaining" and not "teaching," but you will want to stop occasionally to ask questions of the learner. Does the learner understand what you are talking about? How would the learner describe it in his or her own words? Can the learner perform the entry behaviors? These questions focus on the task, but you can include learner analysis questions as well. What better time to ask if he or she understands the relevance of the skills, has knowledge of the topic area, or sees how learning and using the skills will alleviate a problem or need.

If you do this review with several learners, perhaps ones who are somewhat divergent in their backgrounds and experiences but still members of the target population, you will gain information to refine the instructional analysis.

You might also explain your materials to supervisors in the work setting to obtain their input. Supervisors can provide insights from both content-expert and context-feasibility perspectives. Input from target learners and supervisors will aid revising the instructional analysis before you begin the next phase of the design process, writing performance objectives and assessments, which depend entirely on information from the instructional analysis.

EXAMPLES

Identifying learner characteristics and the contextual characteristics of the performance and learning settings is an important early step in designing instruction. In this section we illustrate how learner characteristics, the performance context, and the learning context are described for the instructional goal of leading group discussions. In performing these analyses, using a two-dimensional matrix format may be helpful. This format allows designers to record a lot of information in a limited amount of space and to find it readily as they work on various aspects of the instruction.

LEARNER ANALYSIS

Table 5.1 contains an example of a learner analysis for new Neighborhood Crime Watch leaders. The first column of the table names the categories of information considered, the second column names data sources for obtaining the information, and the third column contains information specific to the NCW leaders as they enter the group leadership instruction. Notice, as you read through the categories, how you begin to form a picture of the group of NCW leaders.

TABLE 5.1 | **Description of Learner Characteristics for Newly Appointed Neighborhood Crime Watch (NCW) Leaders**

Information Categories	Data Sources	Learner Characteristics
1. Entry behaviors	**Interviews and Observations:** Three current and three newly elected NCW chairs; the county NCW supervisor; three police liaison officers **Test Data:** Posttest performance from group membership training	**Performance Setting:** Learners have no prior experience as Neighborhood Crime Watch chairpersons, and most have no prior experience in serving as the leader in problem-solving discussions. Learners have served as members in work- or community-related committee meetings; however, most have had no formal training in problem solving through interactive discussions. **Learning Setting:** Learners have successfully completed our training for group members in problem-solving, interactive discussions.

TABLE *5.1* | (Continued)

Information Categories	Data Sources	Learner Characteristics
2. Prior knowledge of topic area	**Interviews and Observations:** Same as above	Learners have general knowledge of the group leadership area from participating as members in group discussions and from observing different leaders they have had through the years. As adults who have interacted more-or-less successfully with colleagues, they possess, at least at an awareness level, many of the skills required to be effective discussion leaders.
3. Attitudes toward content	**Interviews and Observations:** Same as above	Learners believe the group problem-solving skills they will learn are beneficial and will help them become good, contributing members of team efforts. They also believe that acquiring the upcoming group leadership skills will help them ensure that their committee meetings will be effective and productive.
4. Attitudes toward potential delivery system	**Interviews and Observations:** Same as above	Learners have experience learning through live lectures, web-based instruction, and live group problem-solving simulations as a result of the prior instruction. They liked the convenience of the web-based instruction, and they believe that the simulations were helpful.
5. Motivation for instruction (ARCS)	**Interviews and Observations:** Same as above **Questionnaires:** Sent to all current NCW chairpersons in the county	Learners are positive about their selection of leaders, and are anxious to develop/refine their leadership skills. They believe the leadership skills are *relevant* to their jobs as Neighborhood Crime Watch chairpersons, and they are *confident* they can become effective group discussion leaders. These factors, along with the interactive nature of the instruction, should help ensure that learners are *attentive* during instruction.
6. Educational and ability levels	**Interviews and Observations:** Same as above **Records:** Biographical data from NCW Chairperson Application Form **Test Data:** Posttest performance from group membership training	**Education Levels:** Learners vary in their formal education with some completing high school, some college, and some graduate degrees. **Ability Levels:** Besides academic progress, learners' interpersonal skills are a concern. Based on experiences in the prior "group member" training, it seems that learners are heterogeneous with some high in interpersonal skills, some moderate, and some low.

TABLE *5.1* | (Continued)

Information Categories	Data Sources	Learner Characteristics
7. General learning preferences	**Attitude Data:** Questionnaire from group membership training **Interviews and Observations:** All 16 learners in group membership training session	Learners are experienced with a variety of learning formats; however, they prefer not to be publicly "put on the spot" until they are completely clear about trainer and group expectations and the skills they are to demonstrate in a group setting. In workshop settings, they prefer a short cycle of (1) presentation (What do you expect of me?) (2) private rehearsal (How can I best accomplish this?), and then (3) interactive "on the spot" simulations (Can I manage group interaction/progress with real people and problems?). They like simulations and like to be involved.
8. Attitudes toward training organization	**Interviews:** NCW supervisor, police liaison officers, current NCW leaders	Respondents have positive feelings about the organization developing the materials, about web-based instruction delivered via the Internet, and about the county learning center they used during prior group leadership training. All think the training is a good idea for helping new NCW leaders plan and manage their organizations. They also believe the training is helping them become acquainted with other NCW leaders from across the county and that these relationships will help them build an interpersonal network of support.
9. General group characteristics a. Heterogeneity b. Size c. Overall impressions	**Interviews:** NCW supervisor, police liaison officer **NCW Records:** Needs assessment, history with NCW leaders, training program, biographical forms for leaders **Observations:** 3 current NCW leaders conducting neighborhood meetings	**Heterogeneity:** Learners are extremely heterogeneous in that they come from various neighborhoods throughout a county; come from a wide variety of work settings and areas of expertise; have varying years of work experience; and represent a mix of age, gender, and cultural backgrounds. **Size:** There will be a total of twenty learners per training site to maximize learning efficiency for live group interactive work. **Overall impressions:** Instruction will need to be efficient, effective, and convenient or "volunteer" participants may choose not to read materials, complete computer-based activities independently, or attend all group sessions.

PERFORMANCE CONTEXT ANALYSIS

A performance context analysis is shown in Table 5.2. Again, information categories are listed in column 1, data sources are included in column 2, and per-

TABLE 5.2

Description of Performance Context for Neighborhood Crime Watch (NCW) Leaders

Information Categories	Data Sources	Performance Site Characteristics
1. Managerial/ supervisory support	**Interviews:** 3 current Neighborhood Crime Watch (NCW) chairpersons; 3 police support/liaison persons; and the county NCW program administrator **Records:** Studied NCW charter and literature; studied records for NCW leaders (function, duties, etc.)	Supervision of NCW chairpersons is minimal. Supervision mainly takes the form of providing current information. For example, they receive organizational bulletins, materials, and information from NCW Web site. They receive immediate notification of current crimes committed in their neighborhoods, details of those crimes, and statistical summaries of local and area crimes on NCW Web site from assigned police liaison person. Police liaison person also serves as on-call resource person for chairpersons seeking information, and attends NCW meetings as resource person for total group questions.
2. Physical aspects of site	**Interviews:** Same as above **Observations:** Attended 3 NCW meetings in different regions of the county	**Facilities:** There are no facilities provided by NCW Association or police for scheduled NCW meetings. Meetings typically occur within the neighborhood in a committee member's home or in a neighborhood association facility. **Resources:** No money is provided for NCW member meetings. Any resources required (meeting announcements, materials distributed to attendees, refreshments, etc.) for operating the meetings are sponsored by participating NCW members. **Equipment:** No particular equipment is required for the NCW meetings. **Timing:** Meetings are typically scheduled by the chairperson two to three times per year and at additional times if a particular situation warrants it.

formance site characteristics are described in column 3. Gathering such information about the arena in which NCW leaders work will aid designers in choosing the best instructional strategies to use for maximizing the transfer of skills to the performance site. In this case, the leaders will be working in a public arena gathering information, organizing meetings and programs, and performing group-management tasks during formal and informal meetings. They are unsupervised and receive little support except for the county NCW coordinator and the assigned local police support person. Providing these support individuals with information and strategies for supporting the NCW leaders in their communities could prove very beneficial for enhancing each leader's effectiveness in the community.

TABLE 5.2 | (Continued)

Information Categories	Data Sources	Performance Site Characteristics
3. Social aspects of site	**Interviews:** Same as above **Observations:** Same as above	**Supervision:** The chairperson has no supervision during the conduct of the meeting. **Interaction:** The chairperson is actively interacting with community members who attend the NCW meetings. This interaction is as a leader to manage the work of the group. The chairperson has a police officer at meetings to serve as a content expert on crime and the law, and can invite other experts to meetings as the topic to be discussed warrants. **Others effectively using skills:** There are no others effectively using discussion leadership skills in the meetings because the chairperson is the single designated NCW leader for the community. Others in the group may have discussion leadership skills developed in the workplace or in other community settings.
4. Relevance of skills to workplace	**Interviews:** Same as above **Observations:** Same as above **Records:** Reviewed needs assessment study describing characteristics of effective/ineffective NCW leaders	**Meet identified needs:** The leadership training should meet NCW's identified needs of improving the effectiveness of NCW chairpersons in the problem solving/solutions meetings. New chairpersons will be able to use the skills for their first neighborhood meeting session, and the skills will serve them well in the future meetings.

LEARNING CONTEXT ANALYSIS

Table 5.3 contains a learning context analysis for the group leadership instructional goal. A list of the information categories appears in the first column, the data sources in the second column, and learning context characteristics in the third column. From this information, we can infer that the design team has a very good instructional situation. The importance of the neighborhood crime problem and the political/social priority currently attached to it has created the financial and professional resources, facilities, equipment, and personnel to provide quality instructional products and training sessions. The only apparent limitations placed on the designers are those related to balancing learning efficiency and cost effectiveness.

TABLE 5.3	Description of Learning Context for Neighborhood Crime Watch (NCW) Chairpersons

Information Categories	Data Sources	Learning Site Characteristics
1. Number/nature of sites	**Interviews:** Managers **Site Visits:** **Observations:**	**Number:** One site per county in each of fifty counties across state. **Facilities:** The web-based instruction will occur over the Internet and be delivered directly into the new NCW leaders' homes. The group instruction is to occur in each county's government training facility. Typical facilities across the state contain one lecture hall for eighty to one hundred persons, three to five classrooms for twenty to twenty-five persons, one conference room for sixteen to twenty persons, one learning center open 8:00 a.m. until 8:00 p.m. with one to two managers available for materials distribution, equipment assistance, and learner guidance, one administrative office. Depending on scheduling conflicts, all facilities are available for the NCW chairperson training. **Equipment:** Typical centers contain chalkboards; overhead projection screens and projectors; LCD projector for computer display projection onto screens; newsprint pads and stands; five to six multi-media computer workstations. **Resources:** A state grant is provided to create centrally the web-based instruction that will be distributed statewide. In addition, the grant will fund for each county a group instructor, instructional materials, mailings, and secretarial assistance (scheduling/communication). **Constraints:** 1. The learning center is busy. Scheduling instruction may be difficult; however, there is less use evenings and weekends when planned training will occur for community volunteers. 2. The regular instructors available in each site are not content experts in group discussion leadership. Instructor training will need to be developed and implemented. One expert trainer may need to be available for trouble-shooting across the sites.

TABLE *5.3* | (Continued)

Information Categories	Data Sources	Learning Site Characteristics
2. Site compatibility with instructional needs	**Interviews:** Managers, Instructors **Site Visits:** **Observations:**	**Instructional strategies:** A variety of instructional strategies can be employed including self-study print materials, computer-based instruction, classroom presentations and discussion, and simulated, small group discussion sessions in conference rooms. **Delivery approaches:** Support is available for production and use of all typical print and nonprint materials. Support is also available for newer technologies such as WWW and other computer based, multi-media formats. The training center is also wired and equipped for local area and wide area telecommunications and teleconferencing. **Time:** Instructional time in the center is limited to fifteen hours for project due to constraints placed by volunteer NCW chairpersons. This time is typically divided into ten weekly, ninety-minute periods. Independent study time is possible off site between these scheduled sessions. **Personnel:** Each site has an administrator, several trainers, technicians, and secretaries. There are no trainers present who have provided small group leadership instruction for NCW volunteers, although they have provided leadership training for city and county government employees.
3. Site compatibility with learner needs	**Interviews:** Managers, Instructors, Learners **Site Visits:** **Observations:**	**Location (distance):** The learning centers are located centrally within each county area, making transportation for group sessions convenient. **Conveniences:** Restaurants are located in the areas, and there is a coffee shop within most of the centers. **Space:** The conference room can be used for group simulations and the classrooms for smaller group "meeting" rehearsals. **Equipment:** If needed, the five to eight computer workstations can be scheduled to avoid time conflicts with NCW leaders.

TABLE 5.3 | (Continued)

Information Categories	Data Sources	Learning Site Characteristics
4. Feasibility for simulating work-place	**Interviews:** Managers, Instructors, Learners **Site Visits:** **Observations:**	**Supervisory characteristics:** This cannot be simulated since leaders will have no supervision and little support in their neighborhoods (county NCW coordinator and local police officer). **Physical characteristics:** The physical characteristics can be simulated since volunteers typically meet in neighborhood homes and community centers. **Social characteristics:** Within the neighborhood, learners will work as the leaders of Neighborhood Crime Watch interactive group discussions. These discussions with learners as leaders can readily be simulated in the centers.

SUMMARY

To begin this stage of instructional design, you should have completed the goal analysis and the subordinate skills analysis including the identification of entry behaviors. You should also have general ideas about the target population for which instruction will be developed. These ideas usually include general descriptions such as kindergarten children, seventh graders, college freshmen, ambulance drivers, or automobile operators convicted of reckless driving following a serious accident.

The first task is to identify the general characteristics that members of the target population bring to the instruction. These characteristics include descriptions such as reading levels, attention span, previous experience, motivation levels, attitudes toward school or work, and performance levels in previous instructional situations. Another important characteristic is the extent and context of related knowledge and skills that members of the target population already possess. One outcome from these target group analysis activities is a description of the learners' characteristics that will facilitate later design considerations such as appropriate contexts, motivational information and activities, materials formatting, and the amount of material to be presented at one time.

The second task is to describe the performance context, or environment, where learners will assume their natural roles as students, employees, citizens, or clients and actually use the information and skills prescribed in the instructional goal. Categories of information about the performance site that are important to describe include whether the learner will receive managerial or supervisory support in the performance context, the physical and social aspects of the performance site, and the relevance of the information and skills to be learned to the performance site.

TABLE *5.4* | **Sample Form for Analyzing Learner Characteristics**

Information Categories	Data Sources	Learner Characteristics
1. Entry behaviors	Interview target learners, supervisors; Pretest	
2. Prior knowledge of topic area	Interview target learners, supervisors; Observe in performance setting; Pretest	
3. Attitudes toward content	Interviews Questionnaires Observations	
4. Attitudes toward potential delivery system	Interviews Questionnaires Observations	
5. Motivation for instruction (ARCS)	Interviews Questionnaires Observations	
6. Educational and ability levels	Interviews Questionnaires Observations	
7. General learning preferences	Interviews Questionnaires Observations	
8. Attitudes toward training organization	Interviews Questionnaires Observations	
9. General group characteristics a. Heterogeneity b. Size c. Overall impressions	Interviews Questionnaires Records	

The final task in this section is to describe the learning context. Critical issues in the learning context are discovered through a review of resources that could support instruction and constraints that could inhibit instruction or limit instructional options. Both resources and constraints are usually analyzed in categories such as finances, personnel, time, facilities, equipment, and local culture. In addition, you should describe the compatibility of the learning site with your instructional needs and the learners' needs. Finally, you should describe the feasibility of simulating the performance site within the learning site. The closer you can simulate the performance site, the more likely learners will be able to transfer and implement newly acquired skills.

With the analyses of learners, performance context, and learning context complete, you are ready to begin the next design phase: writing performance objectives appropriate for the prescribed skills, learners, and contexts.

TABLE 5.5 **Sample Form for Analyzing Performance Context**

Information Categories	Data Sources	Performance Site Characteristics
1. Managerial/supervisory support	**Interviews:** Current persons holding position, supervisors, administrators **Organization Records:**	Reward system (intrinsic—personal growth opportunities; extrinsic—financial, promotion, recognition) Amount (time) and nature of direct supervision Evidence of supervisor commitment (time, resources)
2. Physical aspects of site	**Interviews:** Current persons holding position, supervisors, administrators **Observations:** Observe one to three sites considered typical	Facilities: Resources: Equipment: Timing:
3. Social aspects of site	**Interviews:** Current persons holding position, supervisors, administrators **Observations:** Observe typical person performing skills at sites selected	Supervision: Interaction: Others effectively using skills:
4. Relevance of skills to workplace	**Interviews:** Current persons holding position, supervisors, administrators **Observations:** Observe typical person performing skills at sites selected	Meet identified needs: Current applications: Future applications:

PRACTICE

1. Examine the instructional goal analysis on opening and maintaining a checking account in Figures 4.8 and 4.9. Assume that your learners are people entering a bank and opening their *first* personal checking account. Imagine the characteristics of this group and complete the learner characteristics analysis in Table 5.4 for your imagined group. (You may want to photocopy the analysis form in Table 5.4 before you write on it, and use it to analyze learner characteristics for instruction you are designing.) Naturally your learner analysis will differ from the one we constructed, but you can use ours in Table 5.7 to examine the types of information we cover.

TABLE *5.6*   **Sample Form for Analyzing the Learning Context**

Information Categories	Data Sources	Learning Site Characteristics
1. Number/nature of sites	**Interviews:** Managers **Site visits: Observations:**	Number: Facilities: Equipment: Resources: Constraints: Other:
2. Site compatibility with instructional needs	**Interviews:** Managers, instructors **Site visits: Observations:**	Instructional strategies: Delivery approaches: Time: Personnel: Other:
3. Site compatibility with learner needs	**Interviews:** Managers, instructors, learners **Site visits: Observations:**	Location (distance): Conveniences: Space: Equipment: Other:
4. Feasibility for simulating workplace	**Interviews:** Managers, instructors, learners **Site visits: Observations:**	Supervisory characteristics: Physical characteristics: Social characteristics: Other:

2. Using Table 5.5, analyze the performance site characteristics for the instructional goal "open and maintain a checking account." (Again, you may want to use the table as a template for analyzing performance site characteristics for instruction you are developing.) Compare your performance site analysis for the banking instruction with the example we created in Table 5.8 in the Feedback section.

3. Perform a learning context analysis for the instructional goal "open and maintain a checking account" using the categories provided in Table 5.6. Compare your learning context analysis for the banking instruction with the example we created in Table 5.9 in the Feedback section.

TABLE *5.7* **Learner Characteristics of Any Persons Entering a Bank and Opening Their First Personal Checking Account**

Information Categories	Data Sources	Learner Characteristics
1. Entry behaviors	**Interviews:** Target learners, bank tellers, checking account managers; pretest	Learners have adequate arithmetic skills to begin the instruction.
2. Prior knowledge of topic area	**Interviews:** Target learners, bank tellers, checking account managers; pretest	Since learners have voluntarily come to the bank to open their first checking account, they obviously know about checking accounts and what they are for. The pretest demonstrated that most learners already possess the procedural logic required for opening and maintaining a checking account. All that remains is for them to learn to use the forms correctly (deposits, withdrawals, statements, check register, etc.).
3. Attitudes toward content	**Interviews:** Target learners, bank tellers	Learners are positive about learning the new skills to help ensure that they use forms and procedures correctly to minimize money mistakes on their part and ensure that the bank does not "lose their money."
4. Attitudes toward potential delivery system	**Interviews:** Target learners, bank tellers, checking account managers	It appears that the most cost effective and instructionally efficient instruction will be a booklet that learners obtain when they open a checking account with the bank. They can take the booklet home and use it as a guide when they need to deposit, withdraw, understand a statement, or balance an account. Learners and bank employees believe that the booklet will

(continued)

FEEDBACK

1. See Table 5.7 for a sample learner analysis.
2. See Table 5.8 for a sample performance site analysis.
3. See Table 5.9 for a sample learning context analysis.

TABLE *5.7* | (Continued)

Information Categories	Data Sources	Learner Characteristics
4. (continued)		provide efficient instruction for those who can read and add. Others will need to obtain assistance from family members, friends, or bank personnel.
5. Motivation for instruction (ARCS)	**Interviews:** Target learners, bank tellers, checking account managers	Learners are highly motivated. They want to acquire skills to protect their money (losing money by bouncing checks or receiving financial penalties), and it will be very satisfying to them to be able to have their own accounts.
6. Educational and ability levels	**Interviews:** Target learners, bank tellers, checking account managers; pretest; records	**Educational:** Learners are typically high school seniors, college freshmen, or newly employed persons who are managing their finances for the first time. Other customers are immigrants new to the area. **Ability (achievement/aptitude):** Learners are extremely heterogeneous in their achievement/ability levels. While most have the basic language and math skills required, some do not.
7. General learning preferences	**Interviews:** Target learners	Learners prefer pictorial diagrams, examples, and illustrations. They also want the bank to provide ongoing assistance.
8. Attitudes toward training organization	**Interviews:** Target learners	Learners have no prior experience with the bank or the training organization; thus, their only expectations are positive ones.
9. General group characteristics	**Interviews:** Target learners, bank tellers, checking account managers; pretest; records	**a. Heterogeneity:** High **b. Size:** Individualized **c. Overall impressions:** Motivated, capable

TABLE *5.8*

Performance Context for Instructional Goal: Opening and Maintaining Your First Personal Checking Account

Information Categories	Data Sources	Performance Site Characteristics
1. Managerial/ supervisory support	**Interviews:** Target learners, bank tellers, checking account managers	**Reward system:** Intrinsic—independence; extrinsic—managing checking account without financial penalties or cancellations.
		Amount (time) and nature of direct supervision: Customers are independent and receive no supervision.
		Evidence of supervisor commitment (time, resources): Bank tellers assist customers with their deposits and withdrawals when requested and when errors appear in forms. Checking account officers provide assistance when problems occur with overdrafts.
2. Physical aspects of site	**Interviews:** Target learners, bank tellers, checking account managers	**Facilities:** Although most checking account work is performed off the bank premises, desks are provided in bank lobbies that contain the date, generic bank forms, and a pen. At the automatic teller site, instructions for depositing and withdrawing money and envelopes to hold deposits are provided.
		Resources: N/A (not applicable)
		Equipment: N/A
		Timing: N/A
3. Social aspects of site	**Interviews:** Bank tellers, checking account managers	**Supervision:** None
		Interaction: N/A
		Others effectively using skills: Other family members or friends typically hold and effectively use checking accounts

TABLE 5.8	(Continued)

Information Categories	Data Sources	Performance Site Characteristics
4. Relevance of skills to workplace	**Interviews:** Target learners, bank tellers, checking account managers	**Meet identified needs:** Yes. Most checking account errors committed by new users are based on inadequate information about bank rules and procedures governing checking account use. **Current applications:** Appropriate for current policy and technology. **Future applications:** Appropriate for remote banking technology (automatic teller machines and bank cards allowing automatic withdrawal from other commercial sites).

TABLE 5.9	The Learning Context for Instructional Goal: Opening and Maintaining Your First Personal Checking Account

Information Categories	Data Sources	Learning Site Characteristics
1. Number/nature of sites	**Interviews:** Checking account managers **Site visits:** **Observations:**	**Number:** Multiple sites throughout state. **Facilities:** None, independent learning with print materials. **Equipment:** None required. **Resources:** None required. Materials will be distributed by tellers and account officers when customers open accounts. **Constraints:** None
2. Site compatibility with instructional needs	**Interviews:** Checking account managers **Site visits:** **Observations:**	**Instructional strategies:** Print materials carrying all instruction. **Delivery approaches:** Independently use print materials (customers who need additional assistance can receive it from bank personnel by request). **Time:** Learners study materials independently away from bank, thus learning time will vary. **Personnel:** No additional personnel are required. Current checking account officers and tellers will answer additional questions customers may have.

TABLE *5.9* | (Continued)

Information Categories	Data Sources	Learning Site Characteristics
3. Site compatibility with learner needs	**Interviews:** Checking account managers	**Location (distance):** N/A; learners study instructional booklets independently at home. **Conveniences:** N/A
	Site visits: Observations:	**Space:** N/A **Equipment:** N/A
4. Feasibility for simulating workplace	**Interviews:** Checking account managers	**Supervisory characteristics:** N/A **Physical characteristics:** N/A **Social characteristics:** N/A The learning site and the performance site are the same for this instruction. Learners will use the instructional booklets at home as they prepare actual deposit or withdrawal forms and while they balance their accounts. They will use the materials *while they use their checking accounts.*
	Site visits: Observations:	

REFERENCES AND RECOMMENDED READINGS

Gagné, Robert M., & Driscoll, M. P. (1988). *Essentials of learning for instruction* (2nd ed.). Englewood Cliffs, NJ: Prentice-Hall. This book discusses the cognitive psychology approach to understanding the learner.

McCombs, B. L. (1982). Transitioning learning strategies research and practice: Focus on the student in technical training. *Journal of Instructional Development, 5* (2), 10–17. This research stresses the importance of considering the entry knowledge and learning skills that learners bring to the instructional setting.

Richey, R. (1992). *Designing instruction for the adult learner.* London: Kogan Page. Excellent analysis of the impact of motivation on instructional effectiveness.

Rothwell, W., & Kazanas, H. C. (1992). *Mastering the instructional design process.* San Francisco: Jossey-Bass Publisher, 83–95. Excellent set of questions to ask about delivery and application environments.

Tessmer, M., & Harris, D. (1993). *Analyzing the instructional setting.* London: Kogan Page. A complete process for examining the environment in which learning will take place.

6

Writing Performance Objectives

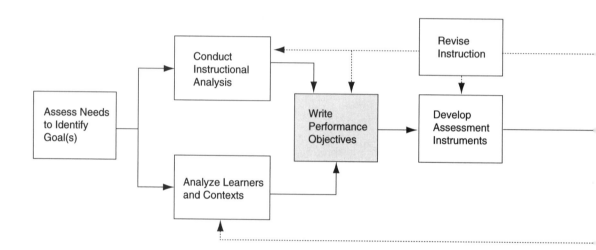

Objectives

- Differentiate among the terms *instructional goal, terminal objective, subordinate skill, subordinate objective, behavioral objective, performance objective,* and *instructional objective.*
- Name and describe the components of a properly written performance objective.
- Elaborate an instructional goal to describe the performance context.
- Write a terminal objective that includes relevant information about the instructional context.
- Write performance objectives for skills that have been identified in an instructional analysis. These objectives should include the conditions under which the skill will be performed, the skill to be performed, and the criteria to be used to assess learner performance.

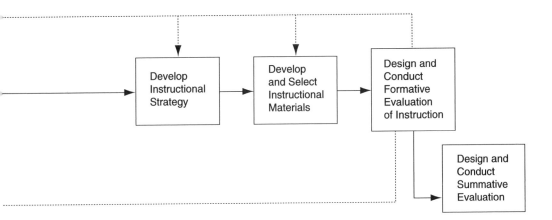

BACKGROUND

Perhaps the best-known component of the instructional design model is the writing of performance objectives, or, as they are more commonly called, *behavioral objectives*. Since publication of his book on objectives in 1962, Robert Mager has influenced the total educational community through his emphasis on the need for clear, precise statements of what students should be able to do when they complete their instruction. The term *behavioral objective* became familiar to many educators in the 1960s.

During that time, workshops were set up for public school teachers throughout the country. Thousands of teachers were trained to write behavioral objectives in order to become accountable for their instruction. However, two major difficulties emerged when the process of defining objectives was not included as an integral component of a total instructional design model.

First, without such a model it was difficult for instructors to determine how to derive objectives. Although instructors could master the mechanics of writing an objective, there was no conceptual base for guiding the derivation of objectives. As a result, many teachers reverted to the tables of content in textbooks to identify topics for which they would write behavioral objectives.

The second and perhaps more critical concern was what to do with the objectives after they were written. Many instructors were simply told to incorporate objectives into their instruction in order to become better teachers. In reality, most objectives were written and then placed in desk drawers, never to affect the instructional process.

Researchers have investigated whether using objectives makes any difference in learning outcomes. In almost all the research studies, this question has been asked in the context of an operational instructional setting. In a typical experiment, one group of students receives a sequence of instruction preceded by statements of what they should be able to do when they complete the instruction. A control group receives the same instructional materials, but without the statements of the instructional objectives. The results of this type of research have been ambiguous. Some studies have shown significant differences in learning for those students who receive objectives; other studies have shown no differences. Summary analyses of the research findings indicate a slight but significant advantage for students who are informed of the objectives for their instruction.

Although these investigations are of interest, they do not address the importance of objectives in the process of designing instruction. Objectives guide the designer in selecting content and developing the instructional strategy and assessment process. Objectives are critical to the design of instruction, regardless of whether they are presented to learners during instruction.

Statements of what learners should be able to do when they complete instruction are useful not only to designers but also to students, instructors, curriculum supervisors, and administrators. If objectives for a unit or course are made available to students, they have clear-cut guidelines for what is to be learned during the course and tested afterward. Few students are likely to be lost for long periods of time, and more are likely to master the instruction when they know what they are supposed to be learning. Informing students of the purpose for instruction from the outset is congruent with current notions of learner-centered instruction and constructivist viewpoints. Knowledge of intended outcomes aids students in linking new knowledge and skills to their current knowledge and experiences.

Objections to the use of behavioral objectives have been raised. For example, detractors can point to the seemingly trivial objectives in some instructional materials. However, these objectives typically are not based on a carefully conducted instructional analysis illustrating the relationship of each new skill to ones previously acquired. Similarly, many educators acknowledge that writing objectives in areas such as humanities or interpersonal relations is more difficult than in other disciplines. Instructors in these areas, however, often are required to assess learner performance and communicate acceptability (e.g., grades, and personnel evaluations). The development of objectives supports the work of instructors in these disciplines by taking them through the following tasks: (1) specifying the skills, knowledge, and attitudes they will teach, (2) determining the strategy for instruction, and (3) establishing criteria for evaluating student performance when instruction ends.

Although some instructors might see objectives as detrimental to free-flowing classroom discussion, they actually serve as a check on the relevance of discussion. Objectives also can increase the accuracy of communication among instructors who must coordinate their instruction. Statements describing what learners should be able to do when they complete their instruction provide a clear description of what should be covered, thus helping to prevent instructional gaps or duplication. Objectives can also indicate to parents or supervisors what students or employees are being taught. General course goals, which are often used for this purpose, may sound interesting and challenging, but seldom indicate what it is that learners will know or be able to do when instruction is completed.

CONCEPTS

PERFORMANCE OBJECTIVE

The most important concept associated with this chapter is that of a performance objective. A performance objective is a detailed description of what students will be able to do when they complete a unit of instruction. First, it should be pointed out that three terms are often used synonymously when describing learners' performance. Mager first used the term *behavioral objective* to emphasize that it is a statement that describes what the student will be able to do. Some educators have strongly objected to this orientation. Other, perhaps more acceptable, terms have been substituted for *behavioral*. You will therefore see in the literature the terms *performance objective* and *instructional objective*. When you see these you can assume that they are synonymous with behavioral objective. You should not be misled to think that an instructional objective describes what an instructor will be doing. It describes instead the kinds of knowledge, skills, or attitudes that the instructor will be attempting to produce in learners.

We have said previously that the instructional goal describes what learners will be able to do when they complete a set of instructional materials. It describes the real-world context, outside the learning situation, where the learner will use the skills and knowledge. When the instructional goal is converted to a behavioral objective, it is referred to as the *terminal objective*. The terminal objective describes exactly what the student will be able to do when he or she completes a unit of instruction. The context for performing the terminal behavior is created within the learning situation, not the real world. Similarly, the skills derived through an analysis of the steps in a goal are called *subordinate skills*. The objectives that describe the skills that pave the way to the achievement of the terminal objective are referred to as *subordinate objectives*. Though this paragraph may seem to be filled with jargon, these terms will become meaningful as you use the instructional design model. In summary, the goal is a statement of what students will be able to do in the performance context that you described in Chapter 5. The goal is rephrased as a terminal objective describing what students will be able to do in the learning context, and subordinate objectives describe the building-block skills that students must master on their way to achieving the terminal objective.

Performance objectives are derived from the skills in the instructional analysis. One or more objectives should be written for each of the skills identified in the instructional analysis. Sometimes, this includes writing objectives for the skills identified as entry behaviors.

Why should objectives be written for entry behaviors if they are not included in instruction? The most important reason for having objectives for entry behaviors is that the objective is the basis for developing test items to determine whether students actually have the entry behaviors you assumed they would have. To help ensure the appropriateness of given instruction for particular students, items should be written to assess the skills stated in the performance objectives for your entry behaviors. In addition, it will be useful for the designer to have these objectives should it be determined that learners in the target population do not have the entry behaviors, and it becomes necessary to develop instruction for these behaviors.

COMPONENTS OF AN OBJECTIVE

How are objectives written for the goal statement, steps in the goal, subordinate skills, and entry behaviors? The work of Mager continues to be the standard for the development of objectives. His model for an objective is a statement that includes three major components. The first component describes the skill or behavior identified in the instructional analysis. The objective must describe what the learner will be able to do. This component contains both the *action* and the *content* or *concept*. In the distance estimation problem described in Figure 4.3, the skill or behavior is to "identify the location of a point on the scale in decimal form by estimating between two-tenth divisions to the nearest hundredth."

The second component of an objective describes the conditions that will prevail while a learner carries out the task. Will learners be allowed to use a computer? Will they be given a paragraph to analyze? These are questions about what will be available to learners when they perform the desired behavior. In the distance estimation problem, the conditions are "given a scale marked off in tenths."

The third component of an objective describes the criteria that will be used to evaluate learner performance. The criterion is often stated in terms of the limits, or range, of acceptable answers or responses. The criterion answers the question, "Does an answer have to be exactly correct?" The criterion indicates the tolerance limits for the response. The criterion may also be expressed in terms of a qualitative judgment, such as the inclusion of certain facts in a definition or a physical performance judged to be acceptable by an expert. In the distance estimation problem, the criterion for an acceptable answer is "report the reading to within +.01 units.

The following statement contains all three components of the objective: "Given a scale marked off in tenths, identify the location of a point on the scale in decimal form by estimating between two-tenth divisions to the nearest hundredth, and report the reading to within +.01 units."

Gagné (1989) has described both a four- and a five-part objective. The four-part objective contains the following four elements: (1) the stimulus situation that initiates the performance (i.e., the conditions), (2) an action word or verb (e.g., *writes*), (3) a word denoting the object acted upon (e.g., *research paper*), and (4) a phrase that indicates the characteristics of a performance that determine its correctness (i.e., criteria). This definition differs from Mager's three-part objective in that the behavior element is divided into individual parts containing the verb and the object or content. His five-part objective (1992) contains: (1) situation (the circumstances of the performance), (2) tools and constraints (the means for operating and the limits to performance), (3) action, (4) object, and (5) capability (the link between the objective and the goal). Situation and tools and constraints are used to further define the conditions element.

One problem that sometimes occurs is that an objective may not convey any real information, even though it may meet the formatting criteria for being an objective. For example, consider the following objective: "Given a multiple-choice test, complete the test and achieve a score of at least nine out of ten correct." While this may be a slightly exaggerated example, it can be referred to as a universal objective in the sense that it appears to meet all the criteria for being an objective and is applicable to almost any cognitive learning situation. It says nothing, however, in terms of the actual conditions or the behavior that is to be learned and evaluated. You should always make sure that your objectives are not universal objectives.

DERIVATION OF BEHAVIORS

It has been stated that objectives are derived directly from the instructional analysis; thus, they must express precisely the types of behavior already identified in the analysis. If the subskill in the instructional analysis includes, as it should, a clearly identifiable behavior, then the task of writing an objective becomes simply the adding of criteria for behavioral assessment and describing the conditions under which the behavior must be performed. For example, if the subskill is "divides a scale into tenths," then a suitable objective might be stated thus: "Given a scale divided into whole units, divide one unit into tenths. The number of subunits must be ten, and the size of all units must be approximately the same."

Sometimes, however, the designer may find that subskill statements are too vague to write a matching objective. In this circumstance, the designer should carefully consider the verbs that may be used to describe behavior. Most intellectual skills can be described by such verbs as *identify, classify, demonstrate,* or *generate.* These verbs, as described by Gagné, Briggs, and Wager (1992), refer to such specific activities as grouping similar objects, distinguishing one thing from another, or solving problems. Note that Gagné et al. have not used the verbs *know, understand,* or *appreciate* because they are too vague. When these words are used (inappropriately) in objectives, *know* usually refers to verbal information, *understand* to intellectual skills, and *appreciate* to attitudes. These vague terms should be replaced by more specific behavioral verbs.

The instructor must review each objective and ask, "Could I observe a learner doing this?" It is impossible to observe a learner "knowing" or "understanding." Often these verbs are associated with information that the instructor wants the students to learn. To make it clear to students that they are supposed to learn certain skills, it is preferable to state in the objective exactly how students are to demonstrate that they *know* or *understand* the skills. For example, the learner might be required to state that New York and California are approximately three thousand miles apart. If students are able to state (or write) this fact, it may be inferred that they know it.

Gagné, Briggs, and Wager (1992) have suggested that intellectual skill and verbal information objectives describe not only the actual behavior to be observed, but also the intent of the behavior, a distinction also made by Mager (1975). For example, students might demonstrate their ability to identify Latin words by circling such words in a mixed list of English and Latin words. This statement of an objective not only describes what the students will be doing, namely, "circling words," but it also describes the capability that will be demonstrated, namely, "identifying." In other words, the intent of the objective is not to have the students demonstrate their ability to draw circles, but to demonstrate their ability to identify examples of Latin words.

Objectives that relate to psychomotor skills usually are easily expressed in terms of a behavior (e.g., running, jumping, or driving). When objectives involve attitudes, the learner is usually expected to choose a particular alternative or sets of alternatives. On the other hand, it may involve the learner making a choice from among a variety of activities.

Derivation of Conditions

With the knowledge, skill, or attitudinal component of the objective clearly identified, you are ready to specify the conditions part of the objective. Conditions refer to the exact set of circumstances and resources that will be available to the learner when the objective is performed. In selecting appropriate conditions you need to consider both the behavior to be demonstrated and the characteristics of the target population. You should also distinguish among the functions that the conditions component serves. These functions include specifying (1) the cue or stimulus that learners will use to search the information stored in memory, (2) the characteristics of any resource material required to perform the task, and (3) the scope and complexity of the task, and relevant or authentic contexts for the real-world performance setting.

Consider first the cue or stimulus provided for learners. This is an especially important consideration for testing verbal information tasks. Suppose you wanted to ensure that learners could associate a particular concept with its definition, or vice versa. It is common to find the conditions for this type of task simply written as, "From memory, define . . . ," or as, "Given a paper and pencil test, define . . . ." Neither of these examples identifies the cue or stimulus the learners will use to search their memory or schema for the related information.

There are several conditions that could be used to describe the stimuli learners will be given to aid their recall of verbal information. Consider the following list of stimuli (conditions) and behaviors, each of which could enable learners to demonstrate that they know or can associate the concept with the definition.

Condition	Behavior
Given the term, $\longrightarrow$	write the definition.
Given the definition, $\longrightarrow$	name the term.
Given the term and a set of alternative definitions, $\longrightarrow$	select the most precise definition.
Given an illustration of the concept, $\longrightarrow$	name and define the concept illustrated.
Given the term, $\longrightarrow$	list its unique physical characteristics.
Given the term, $\longrightarrow$	list its functions or roles.

Although each of these conditions is "from memory," it more clearly specifies the nature of the stimulus material or information that learners will be given in order to search their memory for the desired response. Each condition also implies a paper and pencil test, but merely specifying a paper and pencil test as the condition leaves the issue of an appropriate stimulus undefined.

The second function of the conditions component of an objective is to specify any resource materials that are needed to perform a given task. Such resource materials might include the following: (1) illustrations such as tables, charts, or graphs; (2) written materials such as reports, stories, or newspaper articles; (3) physical objects such as rocks, leaves, slides, machines, or tools; and (4) reference materials such as dictionaries, manuals, databases, textbooks, or the Web. Besides naming the resources required, the conditions should specify any unique characteristics the resources should possess.

The third function of the conditions component is to control the complexity of a task in order to tailor it to the abilities and experiences of the target population. Consider how the following conditions control the complexity of a map-reading objective.

1. Given a neighborhood map containing no more than six designated places, . . .

2. Given a neighborhood map containing no more than twelve designated places that are spaced one inch apart, a locator grid and index, and a scale with one inch equal to one mile, . . .

3. Given a commercial map of a city, . . .

Such conditions limit the complexity of the same task to make it appropriate for a given target group.

The fourth function is aiding the transfer of knowledge and skill from the instructional setting to the performance setting. The conditions element is used to specify the most real-world, authentic, or relevant materials and contexts possible given the resources in the instructional setting.

In deciding the conditions that should be specified, the primary considerations should be the performance and instructional contexts, the nature of the stimulus material, and the characteristics of the target population. Special resources required in either of the two contexts and limitations on task complexity are both conditions that are directly related to the nature of appropriate stimuli and the capabilities of the group.

Although the preceding examples have focused on intellectual skills and verbal information, conditions appropriate for demonstrating psychomotor skills and attitudinal choices should also be considered carefully. Related to psychomotor tasks, you will need to consider the nature of the context in which the skill will be performed and the availability of any required equipment for performing the task. For example, if learners are to demonstrate that they can drive an automobile, you need to consider whether automatic or standard transmissions should be required. You also need to consider whether the driving demonstration will involve inner-city freeways, interstate highways, downtown streets, two-lane country roads, or all of these. Such decisions will influence the equipment required, the nature of instruction, the time required for practicing the skills, and the nature of the driving test.

Specifying the conditions under which learners will demonstrate that they possess a certain attitude also requires careful consideration. Three important issues are the context in which the choice will be made, the nature of the alternatives from which the learner will choose, and the maturity of the target population. These considerations are important because choices may be situation specific. For example, choosing to demonstrate good sportsmanship during a tennis match may depend on the importance of the match in terms of the consequences for winning or losing. It may also depend on the player's sense of freedom to "act out" feelings of frustration and anger without negative repercussions. It will also depend on the age and corresponding emotional control of the players. Demonstrating the true acquisition of a sportsmanlike attitude would require a competitive match where attitudes could be expressed without fear of reprisal. Simply stating the appropriate behavior on a pencil and paper test or demonstrating it under the watchful eye of the coach will not suffice.

Specifying conditions for both psychomotor skills and attitudinal choices can be tricky. An appropriate set of conditions may be difficult to implement in the instructional and testing setting. For this reason, simulations are sometimes required. When they are, the designer must remember that the actual demonstration of the attitude has been compromised.

The conditions associated with an objective will shape the instruction every bit as much as the behavior in the objective. For example, does the learner have to memorize the information in the objective? Why does it have to be memorized? Can the information be looked up in a reference manual, or will there not be time for that? In this particular example, if learners only need to be able to find the information, then the instruction will consist of opportunities, with feedback, to look for various bits of information related to the objective. If information must be immediately available, however, then the focus of the practice will be on ways to store and quickly retrieve the information from memory.

How does the designer decide exactly what the conditions should be? Sometimes it is simply a matter of SME judgment. Often the designer can use the context analysis as the basis for describing conditions of performance. After all, the context analysis describes the situations under which the desired behavior will occur, and that is what we want to describe in the conditions of an objective.

Derivation of Criteria

The final part of the objective is the criterion for judging acceptable performance of the skill. In specifying logical criteria, you must consider the nature of the task to be performed. Some intellectual skill and verbal information tasks have only one response that would be considered correct. Examples include balancing a ledger sheet, matching the tense or number of subjects and verbs, and stating a company safety policy. In such instances, the criteria are that learners can produce the precise response. Some designers add the word *correctly* to this type of objective, whereas others state no criterion and assume that it is implicit in the conditions and behavior. However you choose to treat such objectives, you should keep in mind that specifying the number of times that learners are to perform the task (e.g., two out of three times or correctly 80 percent of the time) does not indicate the objective criterion. The question of "how many times" or "how many items correct" and similar statements are questions of mastery. The designer must determine how many times a behavior must be demonstrated in order to be sure that learners have mastered it. This decision is usually made when test items are developed. The important point is that the criterion in the objective describes what behavior will be acceptable or the limits within which a behavior must fall.

Some intellectual skills and verbal information tasks do not result in a single answer, and learners' responses can be expected to vary. Examples include dividing a line into equal parts and estimating distance using a scale. In these types of instances the criteria should specify the tolerance allowed for an acceptable response. Other tasks that result in a variety of responses include designing a solution to a business problem, writing paragraphs, answering essay questions on any topic, or producing a research report. The criteria for such objectives should specify any information or features that must be present in a response for it to be considered accurate enough. For complex responses, a checklist of response features may be necessary to indicate the criteria for judging the acceptability of a response.

The criteria for judging the acceptability of a psychomotor skill performance may also need to be specified using a checklist to indicate the expected behaviors. Frequency counts or time limits might also be necessary. A description of the body's appearance as the skill is performed may need to be included (e.g., the position of the hands on a piano keyboard).

Specifying criteria for attitudinal goals can also be complex. Appropriate criteria will depend on such factors as the nature of the behavior observed, the context within which it is observed, and the age of members of the target population. It might include a tally of the number of times a desirable behavior is observed in a given situation. It could also include the number of times an undesirable behavior is observed. You may find that a checklist of anticipated behaviors is the most efficient way to specify criteria for judging the acquisition of an attitude. A frequent problem with criteria for attitude measurement is the evaluator's ability to observe the response within a given time period and circumstance; thus, compromise may be necessary.

One problem that can arise in certain instructional settings is a statement that expert judgment or instructor judgment is the criterion for judging learner performance. It is wise to begin with a determination to avoid listing expert judgment as the criterion for an objective since it is not helpful to you or to the learners. It only says that someone else will judge the learner's performance. In situations in which a judge must be used, try to consider the types of things you would look for if you were the expert who was judging the performance. Develop a checklist of the types of behaviors and include these in the statement of the objective to ensure a clear understanding of the criteria.

A second problem is that criteria for an answer, product, or performance can be complex and specified in a variety of categories. Examples of the different categories include (1) adequate form of a response (i.e., the physical structure of a response); (2) adequate function of the response (i.e., meeting the specified purpose or intention for the response); and (3) adequate qualities, or aesthetics. Let's consider two examples using these three categories of criteria to clarify the idea of complex criteria. Suppose that learners were to produce chairs upon which one could sit. The chair can be judged by its features and strength (physical structure), by whether it is comfortable (function or purpose), and by its aesthetic appearance (color, balance, coordination, etc.).

Now consider the criteria in these categories that might be applied to a written paragraph. Related to form, criteria might include whether it is indented and formatted according to structural rules. For function or purpose, criteria such as conveying information on one topic, persuading a reader, or providing adequate directions might be appropriate. Related to qualities or aesthetics, criteria might include clarity, interest value, logical chronology and transition, and creativity.

Many other different categories of criteria can be applied to learners' answers, products, and performances. Other examples include categories such as social acceptability, environmental soundness, economic viability, parsimony, and so forth. Designers will need to analyze the complexity of the task to be performed and, during this analysis, derive appropriate categories of criteria that should be considered in judging a learner's response. Mastery should be judged based on whether learners' responses adequately meet the criteria categories and qualities within each category. Many instructional designers use rubrics or checklists to define complex criteria for acceptable responses.

PROCESS FOR WRITING OBJECTIVES

In order to make objectives, and subsequent instruction, consistent with the context analysis, designers should review the goal statement before writing objectives. Does it include a description of the ultimate context in which the goal will be used? If not, the first step should be to edit the goal to reflect that context.

The second step is to write a terminal objective. For every unit of instruction that has a goal, there is a terminal objective. The terminal objective has all three components of a behavioral objective, and its conditions reflect the context that will be available in the *learning environment.* In other words, the goal statement describes the context in which the learner will ultimately use the new skills while the terminal objective describes the conditions for performing the goal at the end of the instruction. Ideally these two sets of conditions would be the same, but, by necessity, they may be quite different.

After the terminal objective has been established, the designer writes objectives for the skills and subskills included in the instructional analysis. If, in your goal analysis, you broke down one or more of your major steps into substeps, you have a decision to make. Will you have only one objective that describes the substeps that must be performed, or will you write an objective for each of the substeps? If you broke down a step into four substeps, the choice would be between having one objective and four objectives. You will find in later chapters that for each objective you write you will have a specific assessment of that behavior, and you will have a component of the instruction that will teach that behavior. We give examples of both alternatives in the section that follows.

The next step is to write objectives for the subordinate skills on the instructional analysis chart. This will include intellectual skills, verbal information, and, in some cases, psychomotor skills.

But, what do you do when you get to the entry behavior line? You have to make another decision. If the entry behaviors consist of such basic skills and information that you think almost all members of the target population know them and would be insulted to be tested on them, then no objectives are required. On the other hand, if the entry behaviors reflect skills and information that may not be known to all learners, then write objectives for these skills.

The steps in writing objectives are as follows:

- Edit goal to reflect eventual performance context.
- Write terminal objective to reflect context of learning environment.
- Write objectives for each step in goal analysis for which there are no substeps shown.
- Write an objective for each grouping of substeps under a major step of the goal analysis, or write objectives for each substep.
- Write objectives for all subordinate skills.
- Write objectives for entry behaviors if some students are likely not to possess them.

EVALUATION OF OBJECTIVES

A good way to evaluate the clarity and feasibility of an objective you have written is to construct a test item that will be used to measure the learners' accomplishment of the task. If you cannot produce a logical item yourself, then the objective should be reconsidered. Another way to evaluate the clarity of an objective is to ask a colleague to construct a test item that is congruent with the behavior and conditions specified. If the item produced does not closely resemble the one you have in mind, then the objective is not clear enough to communicate your intentions.

You should also evaluate the criteria you have specified in the objective. This may be done by using the criteria to evaluate existing samples of the desired performance or response. These may be samples produced by you, by colleagues, or by anyone who has performed the task. You should specifically attend to whether each criterion named is observable within the specified conditions and time frame. Determining the observability of criteria usually is easier for verbal information and intellectual skill tasks than it is for psychomotor skill and attitudinal objectives, as you might suspect.

While writing objectives, the designer must be aware that these statements of criteria will be used to develop assessments for the instruction. The designer might again check the clarity and feasibility of objectives by asking, "Could I design an item or task that indicates whether a learner can successfully do what is described in the objective?" If it is difficult to imagine how this could be done in the existing facilities and environment, then the objective should be reconsidered.

Another helpful suggestion is that you should not be reluctant to use two or even three sentences to adequately describe your objective. There is no requirement to limit objectives to one sentence. You should also avoid using the phrase "after completing this instruction" as part of the conditions under which a student will perform a skill as described in an objective. It is assumed that the student will study the materials prior to performing the skill. Objectives do not specify *how* a behavior will be learned.

One final word: Do not allow yourself to become deeply involved in the semantics of objective writing. Many debates have been held over the exact word that must be used in order to make an objective "correct." The point is that objectives have been found to be useful as statements of instructional intent. They should convey to the designer or subject matter specialist in the field what it is that the student will be able to do; however, objectives have no meaning in and of themselves. They are only one component in the total instructional design process, and only as they contribute to that process do they take on meaning. The best advice at this point is to write objectives in a meaningful way and then move on to the next step in the instructional design process.

THE FUNCTION OF OBJECTIVES

It is worth noting that objectives serve a variety of functions, not just as statements from which test items and tasks are derived. Objectives have quite different functions for designers, instructors, and learners, and it is important to keep these distinctions in mind. For the designer, objectives are an integral part of the design process. They are the means by which the skills in the instructional analysis are translated into complete descriptions of what students will be able to do after completing instruction. Objectives serve as the input documentation for the designer or test construction specialist as they prepare the test and the instructional strategy. It is important that designers have as much detail as possible for these activities.

After the instruction has been prepared for general use, the objectives are used to communicate to both the instructor and learners what it is that may be learned from the materials. To accomplish this, it is sometimes desirable to either shorten or reword the objectives so that they express ideas that can be understood by the learners based on their knowledge of the content. Designers should be aware of this shift in the use of objectives, and reflect this distinction in the materials they create.

Consider how a comprehensive list of objectives created during the design process can be modified for inclusion in instructional materials. How do these modified objectives differ from those used by designers? First, few of the objectives for subordinate skills that were used during the development of materials are used. Generally only the major objectives are included in the publication, Web page, or instructional module. Second, the wording of those objectives appearing in the materials is modified. The conditions and criteria are often omitted in order to focus learners' attention on the specific behaviors to be learned, resulting in better communication of this information. Finally, students are more likely to attend to three to five major objectives than to a lengthy list of subordinate objectives.

EXAMPLES

This section contains examples of performance objectives for verbal information, intellectual skills, psychomotor skills, and attitudes. To aid your analysis of each example, the conditions are highlighted using the letters *CN*, the behaviors are identified with a *B*, and the criteria are indicated using the letters *CR*. You would not include these letters in your own objectives. Following each set of examples is a discussion that should also aid your analysis.

VERBAL INFORMATION AND INTELLECTUAL SKILLS

The verbal information tasks in Table 6.2 and the intellectual skills in Tables 6.1 and 6.2 are taken from Figure 4.6, which illustrated the instructional analysis for the instructional goal "Lead group discussions aimed at problem solv-

TABLE 6.1

Sample Instructional Goal with Performance Context, and Terminal Objective with Learning Context for the Goal: Lead Group Discussions Aimed at Solving Problems

Instructional Goal	Instructional Goal with Performance Context Added
Lead group discussions aimed at solving problems.	During actual Neighborhood Crime Watch (NCW) meetings held at a designated neighborhood site (e.g., member home, neighborhood social/meeting facility) (CN), successfully lead group discussions aimed at solving crime problems currently existing in the neighborhood (B). Member cooperation will be used to judge achievement of this goal (CR).
	Terminal Objective with Learning Context Added
	During simulated Neighborhood Crime Watch (NCW) meetings attended by new NCW leadership trainees and held at a county government training facility (CN), successfully lead group discussions aimed at solving given problems (B). Member cooperation will be used to judge the achievement of this goal (CR).

TABLE *6.2*	Sample Performance Objectives for Verbal Information and Intellectual Skills Tasks for the Instructional Goal "Lead Group Discussions Aimed at Solving Problems"

Main Step in Instructional Goal	Performance Objective for Main Step
6. Manage cooperative group interaction.	6.1 During simulated Neighborhood Crime Watch (NCW) meetings comprised of new NCW leadership trainees and held at a county government training facility (CN), manage cooperative group interaction (B). Discussion members should participate freely, volunteer ideas, cooperate fully with leader and other members (CR).

Subordinate Skills	Sample Subordinate Objectives for Main Step
6.1 Name member actions that facilitate cooperative interaction.	6.1.1 When requested either orally or in writing (CN) to name group member actions that facilitate cooperative interaction, name those actions (B). At least six facilitating actions should be named (CR).
	6.1.2 When asked either orally or in writing (CN) to indicate what members should do when their ideas are questioned by the group, name positive reactions that help ensure cooperative group interaction (B). Learner should name at least three possible reactions (CR).
6.2 Classify member actions as cooperative behaviors.	6.2.1 Given written descriptions of a group member's actions during a meeting (CN), indicate whether the actions are cooperative behaviors (B). Learner should classify correctly at least 80 percent of the actions demonstrated.
	6.2.2 Given videos of staged NCW meetings depicting members actions (CN), indicate whether the actions are cooperative (B). Learner should classify correctly at least 80 percent of the actions demonstrated.
6.3 Name strategies for encouraging member cooperation.	6.3.1 When asked in writing to name leader actions that encourage and stifle member discussion and cooperation (CN), name these actions (B). Learner should name at least ten encouraging and corresponding stifling actions (CR).
6.4 Classify strategies for encouraging cooperation.	6.4.1 Given written descriptions of group leader's actions during a meeting (CN), indicate whether the actions are likely to encourage or stifle cooperative group interaction (B). Learner should correctly classify at least 80 percent of the actions depicted (CR).
	6.4.2 Given videos of staged NCW meetings depicting staged leader's actions (CN), indicate whether the leader's actions are likely to encourage or stifle member cooperation (B). Learner should classify correctly at least 80 percent of both the encouraging and corresponding stifling actions demonstrated (CR).

| TABLE 6.2 | (Continued) |

Subordinate Skills	Sample Subordinate Objectives for Main Step
6.5 Engender cooperative member behaviors.	6.5.1 In simulated NCW problem-solving meetings with learner acting as group leader (CN), initiate actions to engender cooperative behavior among members (B). Group members cooperate with each other and with leader during discussion (CR).

ing." Table 6.1 includes the instructional goal and the terminal objective for the performance and instructional contexts. Table 6.2 contains the objectives for a sample of subordinate intellectual skills and verbal information tasks depicted in Figure 4.6.

VERBAL INFORMATION In the example of verbal information objectives in Table 6.2, notice that the conditions specify key terms that must be used in test items presented to learners. For example, in subordinate objectives 6.1.1 and 6.1.2 for skill 6.1, key terms prescribed are *group member actions that facilitate cooperative interaction* and *what members should do when their ideas are questioned.* These key terms will function as cues the learner will use to locate related information stored in memory. Although there are many different ways that corresponding test items could be formatted (e.g., as complete questions or statements), the key terms must be presented to the learner. Notice also that the manner in which the key terms will be presented to learners is made clear, *in writing.* Notice, also, that the behaviors used in the subskill and the objective are the same. Even in cases when they are not exactly the same, the behaviors used should reflect ones that enable learners to demonstrate the same covert skill (e.g., name versus list). Finally, consider the criterion in each objective. Because the number of actions named by learners will undoubtedly vary, the number of actions that should be named by learners is prescribed.

INTELLECTUAL SKILLS In the intellectual skills examples (e.g., 6.2.1 and 6.2.2 for skill 6.2) notice that the conditions part of the objective is similar to that used in the verbal information objectives. Not only is key terminology included (e.g., *group members' facilitating actions during a meeting and facilitating actions*), but the manner in which these actions will be presented is prescribed as well (e.g., *written descriptions of members' actions and videos of staged NCW meetings depicting facilitating actions*). In objective 6.5.1, there are no key terms stated in the conditions; however, the examination will take place in *simulated NCW problem-solving meetings with learner acting as group leader.* Notice that the conditions in these three intellectual skills help prescribe the complexity of the task. Detecting positive member actions is probably easier in a written script than in a video of interactive member dialogue, which is probably easier than detecting the same actions when you are "ego involved" leading the meeting yourself and processing the verbal and nonverbal behaviors of colleagues you are actively facilitating. Notice that the behaviors in the subordinate skills and corresponding objectives are congruent. Even when alternative terms are used, the skill demonstrated will be the one prescribed in the

TABLE 6.3

Sample Psychomotor Skills and Matching Performance Objectives

Steps		Matching Behavioral Objectives
2.1 Determine how to operate jack.	2.1	Given a standard scissors jack and detached jack handle (that is not placed beneath a car) (CN), operate the jack (B). Attach the handle securely, pump the handle so the jack lifts, release the safety catch, and lower the jack to its closed position (CR).
2.2 Identify where to attach jack to car.	2.2	Given an unattached scissors jack and a car to be lifted that is perched precariously on the brim of the road (CN), prepare for attaching the jack (B). Relocate the car to a flat, stable location; locate the best place on the frame of the car in proximity to the wheel to be removed; then position the jack squarely beneath the frame at that location (CR).
2.3 Attach jack to car.	2.3	Given a scissors jack placed squarely beneath the frame at the appropriate spot (CN), attach the handle and raise the jack (B). Jack is squarely beneath frame at appropriate spot and raised just to meet car frame. Contact between jack and car is evaluated for balance and adjusted if necessary. Car is NOT lifted and lug nuts are NOT loosened (CR).
2.4 Place blocks behind and before wheels that remain on ground.	2.4	Without being given blocks and without being told to locate appropriate blocks (CN), locate blocks and place behind wheels to remain on ground (B). Locate enough brick-size blocks of a sturdy composition and place one before and behind each wheel that is away from jack (CR).
Goal: Change tire on an automobile.	T.O.	Given an automobile with a flat tire, all tools required to change the tire secured in their normal positions in the trunk, and an inflated spare tire secured normally in the wheel well (CN), replace the flat tire with the spare tire (B). Each step in the procedure will be performed in sequence and according to criteria specified for each step (CR).

subordinate skill. Notice the criteria included in these objectives. In subordinate objectives 6.2.1 and 6.2.2, the learner is required to locate 80 percent of the cooperative behaviors demonstrated in the scenarios and videos. On the other hand, the criterion for objective 6.5.1 is that members within the leader's interactive groups need to cooperate with each other and the leader. In other words, the behavior of members within the group will provide evidence of the leader's success.

PSYCHOMOTOR SKILLS

Figure 4.15 contains an abbreviated goal analysis for changing an automobile tire. The subordinate objectives in Table 6.3 are based on the substeps included in the analysis.

As noted previously, writing performance objectives for psychomotor skills is more complex than writing objectives for verbal information and for many intellectual skills. In this abbreviated list of examples, notice the increased specificity in the conditions. Any special circumstances must be prescribed. Notice in objective 2.4 that the designer does not want the learner to be given blocks or to be reminded to obtain them. Obviously part of the demonstration will be for the learner to recall as well as to perform this step.

The verbs are also important and may require some translation to ensure that the behaviors are observable. Notice the shifts in 2.1 from "determine how to" to "operate the." To measure whether the learner has "determined how to," observable behaviors needed to be identified, thus the shift in the verb.

Notice, also, how the criteria differ from those in the previous examples. Specifying the criteria for steps in a psychomotor skill typically requires listing the substeps that must be accomplished. The criteria for each of these objectives contain such a list.

Another interesting feature about objectives for psychomotor skills should be noted. Although each objective has its own conditions, the conditions, behaviors, and criteria in preceding examples are often conditions for performing any given step. For example, an implied condition for objective 2.2 is the successful completion of objective 2.1. Similarly, an implied condition for objective 2.3 is the successful completion of objective 2.2.

Finally, notice the criteria listed for the terminal objective. Actually listing all the criteria for performing this objective would require listing again all of the specific criteria for each step in the process, because completing all the steps constitutes performing the terminal objective. For this reason, the criteria listed for each objective should be placed on a checklist that could be used to guide the evaluation of the learner's performance.

ATTITUDES

Developing objectives for the acquisition of attitudes can also be complex in terms of the conditions, behaviors, and criteria. The examples listed in Table 6.4 are taken from the attitudinal goal on hotel safety included in Figure 4.11, and they serve as good illustrations of problems the designer could encounter.

The first thing you should notice about the conditions in these objectives is that they would be very difficult to implement, for several reasons. Individual rights and privacy are two problems, and gaining access to rooms to observe whether doors were bolted and jewelry and money were put away is another. In such instances the designer would undoubtedly need to compromise. The best compromise would probably be to ensure that individuals know what to do should they choose to maximize their personal safety while in a hotel. A pencil and paper test on related verbal information or problem-solving scenarios may be the best the designer can do.

Consider another attitude example that is more manageable. Recall the courteous, friendly bank tellers in Chapter 2. The attitude goal and objectives

TABLE 6.4 | **Example Attitudes and Matching Performance Objectives**

Attitudes	Matching Behavioral Objectives
1. Choose to maximize safety from fires while registered in a hotel.	1.1 Unaware that they are being observed during hotel check-in (CN), travelers (always (CR)): (1) request a room on a lower floor, and (2) inquire about safety features in and near their assigned room such as smoke alarms, sprinkler systems, and stairwells (B).
2. Choose to maximize safety from intrusion while registered in a hotel.	2.1 Unaware they are being observed as they prepare to leave the hotel room for a time (CN), travelers (always (CR)): (1) leave radio or television playing audibly and lights burning, and (2) they check to ensure the door locks securely as it closes behind them (B).
	2.2 Unaware that they are being observed upon reentering their hotel rooms (CN), travelers (always (CR)) check to see that the room is as they left it and that no one is in the room. They also keep the door bolted and chained (B) at all times (CR).
3. Choose to maximize the safety of valuables while staying in a hotel room.	3.1 Unaware that they are being observed during check-in (CN), always (CR) inquire about lockboxes and insurance for valuables. They place valuable documents, extra cash, and unworn jewelry in a secured lockbox (B).
	3.2 Unaware that they are being observed upon leaving the room for a time (CN), travelers do not leave jewelry or money lying about on hotel furniture (B).

included in Table 6.5 for teller attitudes appear to be observable and measurable. This particular example will enable us to illustrate some important points. First, the conditions are exactly the same for all four of the selected behaviors; thus, they are written once before the behaviors to avoid redundancy. Recall that the measurement of attitudes requires that the tellers know how to act while greeting a customer and why they should act in this manner. They also must believe they are free to act in the manner they choose, which means that they cannot know that they are being observed. Another condition is that they choose to be courteous even when they are very busy. The designer could infer that a teller who chooses to greet customers in a friendly manner under these conditions possesses the desired attitude.

The criterion for acceptable performance (always) is also the same for all four objectives, so it too is placed preceding the list of behaviors.

The expected behaviors are listed separately beneath the conditions and criteria. This brief list of behaviors could be expanded to include those behaviors that tellers are never (CR) to exhibit while greeting a customer (e.g., wait

TABLE 6.5	Manageable Attitude and Matching Performance Objectives

Attitude	Matching Performance Objective
Tellers will choose to treat customers in a friendly, courteous manner.	Unaware they are being observed during transactions with customers on a busy day (CN), tellers will always (CR): 1. Initiate a transaction with a customer by: (a) smiling, (b) initiating a verbal greeting, (c) saying something to make the service appear personalized, (d) verbally excusing themselves if they must complete a prior transaction, and (e) inquiring how they can be of service (B). 2. Conduct a customer's transaction by: (a) listening attentively to the customer's explanation, (b) requesting any clarifying information required, (c) providing any additional forms required, (d) completing or amending forms as needed, (e) explaining any changes made to the customer, and (f) explaining all materials returned to the customer (B). 3. Conclude each transaction by: (a) inquiring about any other services needed, (b) verbally saying, "Thank you," (c) responding to any comments made by the customer, and (d) ending with a verbal wish (e.g., "Have a nice day," "Hurry back," or "See you soon").

for the customer to speak first and fail to look up or acknowledge a customer until ready).

With these objectives a supervisor could develop a checklist for tallying the frequency with which each behavior occurs. From such tallies, the supervisor could infer whether the teller possessed the prescribed attitude.

SUMMARY

Before beginning to write performance objectives, you should have a completed instructional analysis. You should also have completed your learner and context analysis. With these products as a foundation, you are ready to write performance objectives for your goal, all steps and substeps in that goal, and subordinate skills.

To create each objective, you should begin with the behaviors that are described in the skill statements. You will need to add both conditions and criteria to each skill to transform it into a performance objective. In selecting appropriate conditions, you should consider: (1) appropriate stimuli and cues to aid the learners' search of their memories for associated information, (2) appropriate characteristics for any required resource materials, (3) appropriate levels of task complexity for the target population, and (4) the relevance or authenticity of the context in which the skill will be performed. For attitudinal objectives, you will also need to consider circumstances in which the learners are free to make choices without reprisal.

The final task is to specify a criterion or criteria appropriate for the conditions and behavior described, and appropriate for the developmental level of the target group. When there is only one correct response possible, many designers omit criteria as they are clearly implied, whereas other designers choose to insert the term *correctly*. When the learners' responses can vary, as they can for tasks in all four domains, criteria that set the limits for an acceptable response must be added. Deriving criteria for psychomotor skills and attitudes typically is more complex in that several observable behaviors generally need to be listed. These behaviors, however, are very useful for developing required checklists or rating scales. In specifying criteria, designers must be careful *not* to rely on imprecise criteria such as "expert judgment." There are a variety of categories of criteria that designers can consider in selecting those most appropriate for a given learner response. Examples of such categories include structure, function, aesthetics, social acceptability, environmental soundness, economic viability, and so forth.

Your complete list of performance objectives becomes the foundation for the next phase of the design process. The next step is to develop criterion-referenced test items for each objective, and the required information and procedures are described in Chapter 7.

PRACTICE

I. Judge the completeness of given performance objectives. Read each of the objectives listed below, and judge whether each objective includes conditions, behaviors, and a criterion. If any element is missing choose the part(s) omitted.

1. Given a list of activities carried on by the early settlers of North America, understand what goods they produced, what product resources they used, and what trading they did. The following is/are missing from the objective:
   a. important conditions and criterion
   b. observable behavior and important conditions
   c. observable behavior and criterion
   d. nothing

2. Given a mimeographed list of states and capitals, match at least 35 of the 50 states with their capitals without the use of maps, charts, or lists. What is missing from this objective?
   a. observable response
   b. important conditions
   c. criterion performance
   d. nothing

3. During daily business transactions with customers, know company policies for delivering friendly, courteous service. Which of the following is missing from this objective?
   a. observable behavior
   b. important conditions
   c. criterion performance
   d. a and b
   e. a and c

4. Students will be able to play the piano. Which of the following is missing from this objective?
   a. important conditions
   b. important conditions and criterion performance
   c. observable behavior and criterion performance
   d. nothing

TABLE *6.6*

Performance Objectives for Main Steps in the Banking Goal Illustrated in Figure 4.8

Instructional Goal: Open and maintain a checking account. (1) Obtain information about the costs and benefits of checking accounts at two to three banks convenient to your work or home, (2) assess the costs and benefits for your particular financial circumstances and needs, (3) choose a particular account for your needs, (4) open a checking account, and (5) maintain a checking account.

Terminal Objective: Given written descriptions (brochures and advertisements) of various checking accounts along with their purpose, costs, and benefits; and given descriptions of several bank customers along with their financial circumstances and checking needs: (1) recommend and justify a particular account for each customer, (2) complete the initial application for the customer, and (3) demonstrate how to use the account forms including the (a) signature cards, (b) deposit slips, (c) checks, (d) check register, and (e) bank statement.

Performance Objectives:

1.0 Given written descriptions (brochures and advertisements) of various checking accounts along with their purpose, costs, and benefits; and given descriptions of several bank customers along with their financial circumstances and checking needs: (1) recommend and justify a particular account for each customer, (2) complete the initial application form for the customer, and (3) make an initial deposit.

2.0 Using in-bank lobby, an automatic teller machine, and electronic deposit procedures, complete the necessary forms to deposit money into the account.

3.0 Using a computer-based accounting program such as Quicken, establish accounts, enter credits and debits, including regular deposits and withdrawals, automatic deposits and withdrawals, bank charges, and interest earned to balance the register and produce account reports of income and expenditures.

4.0 Using a bank check, ATM, and automatic withdrawal forms, withdraw money from a given checking account.

5.0 Given a monthly checking account statement and given a computer-based record (e.g., Quicken) balance the two records. Discrepancies between the two records should be located, explained, and resolved.

5. Given daily access to music in the office, choose to listen to classical music at least half the time. Which of the following is missing from this objective?
   a. important conditions
   b. observable behavior
   c. criterion performance
   d. nothing

II. Convert instructional goals, main steps, and subordinate skills into terminal and subordinate objectives. It is important to remember that objectives are derived from the instructional goal and subordinate skills analyses. For this reason, these practice tasks ask you to create objectives for goal and subordinate skills analyses that you completed in prior chapters.

1. Examine the instructional goal and main steps 1.0 to 5.0 in Figure 4.8 for opening and maintaining a checking account. Demonstrate conversion of the goal and main steps (subordinate skills) in the goal analysis by doing the following:

   • Elaborate the instructional goal for a real-world, community setting.

| TABLE 6.7 | Checklist of Criteria for Evaluating Elaborated Goals, Terminal Objectives, and Performance Objectives |

Yes	No	**I. Goal Statement**
___	___	1. Ultimate performance context described?
___	___	2. Context as described. Authentic and realistic?

Yes	No	**II. Terminal Objective**
___	___	1. Conditions reflect the context of the learning environment?
___	___	2. Behavior and criteria congruent with those in the goal statement?

Yes	No	**III. Conditions**
___	___	1. Included?
___	___	2. Describe what learners will be given as stimulus to solicit the desired behavior (e.g., key terms, definitions, illustrations, figures, graphs, written passages, particular tools or equipment, etc.)?
___		3. Clearly communicated to enable colleagues to produce congruent assessment items/situations that contain the prescribed conditions?
___	___	4. Describe/imply the context in which learners must demonstrate their knowledge/skill?

Yes	No	**IV. Skills**
___	___	1. Congruent with the level or type of learning prescribed in the enabling skill (i.e., behaviors are same or synonyms; e.g., state, tell, name or classify, locate, differentiate among)?
___	___	2. Observable (i.e., can watch learner perform or see results of performance)?
___	___	3. Measurable (i.e., can imagine ways to rate how well learner performs behavior)?
___	___	4. Congruent with the content (concepts, rules, procedures, etc.) prescribed in the subordinate skill?
___	___	5. Clearly expressed so that a colleague could produce an assessment item/procedure that matches the content intended by the author of the objective?

Yes	No	**V. Criteria/standards**
___	___	1. Included when learners' responses can vary in quality (e.g., estimate mileage *correct to within 10 miles* or create a classroom test *with an internal consistency reliability index* $\geq.65$)?
___	___	2. At appropriate level for successfully performing the skill in the performance setting?

- Create a terminal objective.
- Write performance objectives for the main steps.

Create a table such as the one in Table 6.6 to aid your work. Compare your context description, terminal objective, and performance objectives with those presented in Table 6.6.

III. Evaluate performance objectives.

1. Use the checklist in Table 6.7 as an aid to developing and evaluating your own objectives.
2. Indicate your perceptions of the quality of your objectives by inserting the number of the objective in either the *yes* or *no* column of the checklist to reflect your judgment.

3. Examine those objectives receiving *no* ratings and plan ways the objectives should be revised.
4. Based on your analysis, revise your objectives to correct ambiguities and omissions.

FEEDBACK

I. 1. c
    2. d
    3. e
    4. b
    5. d

II. 1. Compare your instructional goal elaboration, terminal objective, and main step performance objectives with the examples in Table 6.6.

III. Evaluate the goal elaborations, terminal objectives, and your performance objectives using the rubric in Table 6.7. If you want further feedback on the clarity and completeness of performance objectives you have written, ask a colleague for a critique.

REFERENCES AND RECOMMENDED READINGS

Caviler, J. C., & Klein, J. D. (1998). Effects of cooperative versus individual learning and orienting activities during computer-based instruction. *Educational Technology Research and Development, 46*(1), 5–17. Demonstrates the effectiveness of providing objectives to learners.

Gagné, R. M. (1989). *Studies of learning: 59 years of research.* Tallahassee, FL: Learning Systems Institute, 260–261.

Gagné, R. M., Briggs, L. J., & Wager, W. W. (1992). *Principles of instructional design.* (4th ed.). New York: Holt, Rinehart, and Winston. The authors describe a five-component behavioral objective, and relate objectives to the various domains of learning.

Gronlund, N. E. (2000). *How to write and use instructional objectives.* (6th ed.). Columbus, OH: Merrill. Gronlund describes the derivation of objectives for various types and levels of learning and their use in both teaching and classroom assessment.

Kibler, R. J., Cegala, D. J., Barker, L. L., & Miles, D. T. (1974). *Objectives for instruction and evaluation.* Boston, MA: Allyn and Bacon, 29–64. Kibler et al. propose a five-component model for behavioral objectives. Attention is given to common difficulties that arise when writing objectives.

Mager, R. F. (1975). *Preparing instructional objectives.* Palo Alto, CA: Fearon Publishers. This is the original text of Mager's 1962 book on objectives. Mager's humor is well served by the branching programmed-instruction format.

Mager, R. F. (1988). *Making instruction work.* Belmont, CA: David S. Lake Publishers. More recent description of Mager's position on objectives.

Roberts, W. K. (1982). Preparing instructional objectives: usefulness revisited. *Educational Technology, 22* (7), 15–19. The varied approaches to writing objectives are presented and evaluated in this article.

Yelon, S. L. (1991). Writing and using instructional objectives. In Briggs, L. J., Gustafson, K. L., & Tillman, M. H. (eds.). *Instructional design: Principles and applications.* Englewood Cliffs, NJ: Educational Technology Publications.

CHAPTER

7   DEVELOPING ASSESSMENT INSTRUMENTS

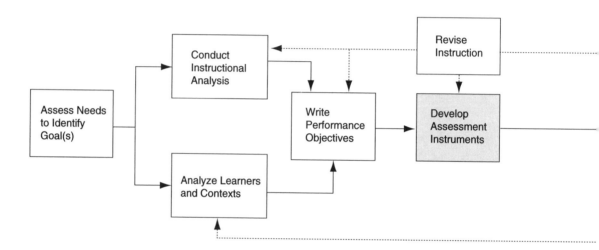

OBJECTIVES

- Describe the purpose for criterion-referenced tests.
- Describe how entry behaviors tests, pretests, and posttests are used by instructional designers.
- Name four categories of criteria for developing criterion-referenced tests and list several considerations within each criterion category.
- Given a variety of objectives, write criterion-referenced, objective-style test items that meet quality criteria in all four categories.
- Develop instructions for product development, live performance, and attitude assessments, and develop a rubric for evaluating learners' work.
- Evaluate instructional goals, subordinate skills, learner and context analyses, performance objectives, and criterion-referenced test items for congruence.

144

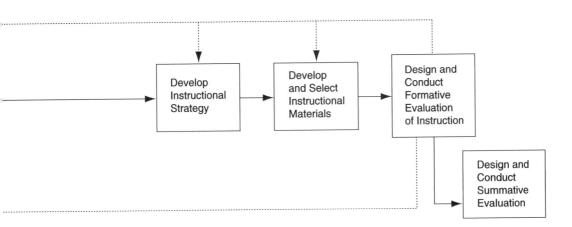

BACKGROUND

Achievement testing is currently at the forefront of the school-reform movement in the United States. One new concept, *learner-centered assessment*, permeates the school-reform literature, and is defined by Baron (1998) as assessment that enhances student learning. Learning-centered assessment tasks are expected to function as learning events, and in this model, learners are encouraged to engage in self-assessment on their path to assuming responsibility for the quality of their own work.

The definitions of learner-centered assessment are congruent with traditional definitions of criterion-referenced testing, a central element of systematically designed instruction. Learner-centered assessments are to be criterion-referenced (i.e., linked to instructional goals and an explicit set of performance objectives derived from the goals). This type of testing is important for evaluating both learners' progress and instructional quality. The results of criterion-referenced tests indicate to the instructor exactly how well learners were able to achieve each instructional objective, and they indicate to the designer exactly what components of the instruction worked well, and which ones need to be revised. Moreover, criterion-referenced tests enable

145

learners to reflect on their own performances by applying established criteria to judge their own work. Such reflection aids learners in becoming ultimately responsible for the quality of their work.

You may wonder why test development appears at this point in the instructional design process rather than after instruction has been developed. The major reason is that the test items must correspond one-to-one with the performance objectives. The performance required in the objective must match the performance required in the test item or performance task. Likewise, the nature of the test items that will be given to learners serves as a key to the development of the instructional strategy.

In this chapter we discuss how designers construct various types of assessment instruments. We use the term *assessment* because "testing" often implies paper-and-pencil, multiple-choice tests. *Assessment* is used as a broader term that includes all types of activities that can be used to have learners demonstrate whether they have mastered new skills. At this point in the design process, it is necessary to construct sample assessments for each objective.

CONCEPTS

The major concept in this chapter is criterion-referenced assessment. A criterion-referenced assessment is composed of items or performance tasks that directly measure skills described in one or more behavioral objectives. The term *criterion* is used because assessment items serve as a benchmark to determine the adequacy of a learner's performance in meeting the objectives; that is, success on these assessments determines whether a learner has achieved the objectives in the instructional unit. More and more often the term *objective-referenced* is being used rather than *criterion-referenced*. The purpose for this shift is to be more explicit in indicating the relationship between assessments and performance objectives. Assessment items or tasks are referenced directly to the performance described in the objective for the instructional materials. You may therefore consider these two terms essentially synonymous.

Another use of the word *criterion* relates to the specification of the adequacy of performance required for mastery. Examples of this second type of criterion include such benchmarks as "the student will answer all the items correctly," "the student will follow all six steps in the safe storage of flammable liquids," and "the student will cut an angle with an accuracy level of five degrees." This type of criterion specification may be established for one test item written for one behavioral objective, several test items written for one objective, or several test items written for many objectives. Clarity in specifying objectives and criteria for adequate performance is necessary as a guide to adequate test construction. Based on a particular behavioral objective and established criteria, a posttest may require only one test item or it may require many.

FOUR TYPES OF CRITERION-REFERENCED TESTS AND THEIR USES

There are basically four types of tests the designer may create, including the entry behaviors test, the pretest, practice or rehearsal tests, and posttests. Each of these test types has a unique function in designing and delivering instruction. Let's look at each type of test from the viewpoint of the person who is designing instruction. What purposes do they serve within the instructional design process?

ENTRY BEHAVIORS TEST The first type of test, an entry behaviors test, is given to learners before they begin instruction. These criterion-referenced tests assess learners' mastery of prerequisite skills, or skills that learners must have already mastered before beginning instruction. Prerequisite skills appear below the dotted line on the instructional analysis chart. If there are entry behaviors for an instructional unit, test items should be developed and used with learners during the formative evaluation.

It may be found that, as the theory suggests, learners lacking these skills will have great difficulty with the instruction. In contrast, it may be found that for some reason the entry behaviors are not critical to success in the instruction. It should be noted that if there are no significant entry behaviors identified during the instructional analysis, then there would be no need to develop corresponding objectives and test items. Also, if some skills are more questionable than others in terms of being already mastered by the target population, then it is these questionable skills that should be tested on the entry behaviors test.

PRETEST The purpose of a pretest is not necessarily to show a gain in learning after instruction by comparison with a posttest, but rather to profile the learners with regard to the instructional analysis. The pretest is administered to learners before they begin instruction to determine whether they have previously mastered some or all of the skills that are to be included in the instruction. The reason for determining whether learners have mastered part or all of the skills is efficiency. If all the skills have been mastered, then the instruction is not needed. On the other hand, if only a part of the skills have been mastered, then pretest data enable the designer to be most efficient in the creation of instruction. Perhaps only a review or a reminder is needed for part of the skills, while time consuming, direct instruction with examples and rehearsal is required for others.

Designers have some latitude in determining which enabling skills to include on a pretest, and they must use their judgment in selecting the objectives that are most important to test. Deciding the exact skills to include and the number of skills is probably unique to each instructional goal and particular context. The pretest typically includes one or more items for key skills identified in the instructional analysis, including the instructional goal.

Since both entry behaviors tests and pretests are administered prior to instruction, they are often combined into one instrument. Appearing on one instrument, however, does not make them one and the same test. Different items assess different skills from the instructional goal diagram, and the designer will make different decisions based on learners' scores from the two sets of items. From entry behaviors test scores designers decide whether learners are ready to begin the instruction. From pretest scores they decide whether the instruction would be too elementary for the learners and, if not too elementary, how to develop instruction most efficiently for a particular group.

Should you always administer a pretest over the skills to be taught? Sometimes it is not necessary. If you are teaching a topic that you know is new to your target population, and if their performance on a pretest would only result in random guessing, it is probably not advisable to have a pretest. A pretest is valuable only when it is likely that some of the learners will have partial knowledge of the content. If time for testing is a problem, it is possible to design an abbreviated pretest that assesses the terminal objective and several key subordinate objectives.

PRACTICE TESTS The purpose for practice tests is to provide active learner participation during instruction. Practice tests enable learners to rehearse new knowledge and skills and to judge for themselves their level of understanding and skill. Instructors use students' responses to practice tests to provide corrective feedback and to monitor the pace of instruction. Practice tests contain fewer skills than either the pretest or posttest, and they are typically focused at the lesson rather than the unit level.

POSTTESTS Posttests are administered following instruction, and they are parallel to pretests, except they do not include items on entry behaviors. Similar to the pretest, the posttest measures objectives included in the instruction. As for all the tests that are described here, the designer should be able to link the skill (or skills) being tested with its corresponding item on the posttest.

Related to selecting skills from the instructional goal analysis, the posttest should assess all of the objectives, and especially focus on the terminal objective. Again, as with the pretest, the posttest may be quite long if it measures all the subordinate skills, and it may be more comprehensive in terms of having more items on more of the skills in the instructional goal analysis. If time is a factor and a briefer test must be developed, then the terminal objective and important subskills should be tested. Items should be included to test those subskills that are most likely to give learners problems on the terminal objective.

Eventually the posttest may be used for assessing learner performance and assigning credit for successful completion of a program or course; however, the initial purpose for the posttest is to help the designer identify the areas of the instruction that are not working. If a student fails to perform the terminal objective, the designer should be able to identify where in the learning process the student began not to understand the instruction. By examining whether each item is answered correctly and linking the correct and incorrect responses to the anchor subordinate skill, the designer should be able to do exactly that.

All four types of tests are intended for use during the instructional design process. After the formative evaluation of the instruction has been completed, however, it may be desirable to drop part or all of the entry behaviors test and the pretest. It would also be appropriate to modify the posttest to measure only the terminal objective. In essence, much less time would be spent on testing when the design and development of the instruction is complete. A summary of the test types, design decisions, and the objectives typically included on each type of test follows.

Test Type	Designer's Decision	Objectives Typically Tested
Entry behaviors test	• Are target learners ready to enter instruction? • Do learners possess the required prerequisite skills?	• Prerequisite skills or those skills below the dotted line in the instructional analysis
Pretests	• Have learners previously mastered the enabling skills? • Which particular skills have they previously mastered? • How can I most efficiently develop this instruction?	• Terminal objectives • Main steps from the goal analysis

Test Type	Designer's Decision	Objectives Typically Tested
Practice tests	• Are students acquiring the intended knowledge and skills? • What errors and misconceptions are they forming? • Is instruction clustered appropriately? • Is the pace of instruction appropriate for the learners?	• Knowledge and skills for a subset of objectives within the goal • Scope typically at the lesson rather than the unit level
Posttests	• Have learners achieved the terminal objective? • Is the instruction more or less effective for each main step and for each subordinate skill? • Where should instruction be revised? • Have learners mastered the intended information, skills, and attitudes?	• The terminal objective • Main steps and their subordinate skills

DESIGNING A TEST

How does one go about designing and developing a criterion-referenced test? A primary consideration is matching the learning domain with an item or assessment task type. Objectives in the verbal information domain typically require objective-style test items. Objective-style test items include formats such as short-answer, alternative response, matching, and multiple-choice items. It is relatively easy to examine learners' verbal information responses, whether written or oral, and judge whether they have mastered a verbal information objective. Learners either recall the appropriate information or they do not.

Objectives in the intellectual skills domain are more complex, and they generally require either objective-style test items, the creation of a product (e.g., musical score, research paper, widget), or a live performance of some type (e.g., conduct an orchestra, act in a play, or conduct a business meeting). At higher levels of intellectual skills, it is more difficult to create an assessment item or task, and it is more difficult to judge the adequacy of a response. What if an objective requires the learner to create a unique solution or product? It would be necessary to write directions for the learner to follow, establish a set of criteria for judging response quality, and convert the criteria into a checklist or rating scale, often called a rubric, that can be used to assess those products.

Assessment in the attitudinal domain can also be complex. Affective objectives are generally concerned with the learner's attitudes or preferences. Usually there is no direct way to measure a person's attitudes (e.g., whether they support diversity within the organization). Items for attitudinal objectives generally require that either the learners state their preferences or that the instructor observes the learners' behavior and infers their attitudes from their actions. For example, if learners voluntarily engage in advocacy for the promotion of minority employees on three different occasions, the instructor may infer that they support diversity. From these stated preferences or observed behaviors, inferences about attitudes can be made.

Test items for objectives in the psychomotor domain are usually sets of directions on how to demonstrate the tasks, and they typically require the learner to perform a sequence of steps that collectively represents the instructional goal. Moreover, criteria for acceptable performances need to be identified and converted into a checklist or rating scale that the instructor uses to indicate whether each step is executed properly. The checklist can be developed directly from the skills and execution qualities identified in the instructional analysis. The designer may also wish to test the subordinate skills for the motor skills. Often these are intellectual skills or verbal information that can be tested using an objective-item format before having the student perform the psychomotor skill. On occasion the performance of a psychomotor skill, such as making a ceramic pot, results in the creation of a product. It is possible to develop a list of criteria for judging the adequacy of this product.

DETERMINING MASTERY LEVELS

For each behavioral objective you write there must be a criterion level specified, which indicates how well the student must perform the skill described in the objective on the assessments you provide. In essence, the criterion indicates the mastery level required of the student. The concept of mastery level, as opposed to criterion level, is more often applied to a test for an entire unit of instruction or an entire course. An instructor may state that, in order for learners to "master" this unit, they must achieve a certain level of performance. The question remains, "How do you determine what the mastery level should be?"

Researchers who work with mastery learning systems suggest that mastery is equivalent to the level of performance normally expected from the best learners. This method of defining mastery is clearly norm-referenced (i.e., a group comparison method), but sometimes it may be the only standard that can reasonably be used.

A second approach to mastery is one that is primarily statistical. If designers want to make sure that learners "really know" a skill before they go on to the next instructional unit, then sufficient opportunities should be provided to perform the skill so that it is nearly impossible for correct performance to be the result of chance alone. When multiple-choice test items are used, it is fairly simple to compute the probability that any given number of correct answers to a set of items could be due to chance. With other types of test items it is more difficult to compute the probability of chance performance, but easier to convince others that performance is not just a matter of chance. Simply exceeding the chance level of performance, however, may not be a very demanding mastery level. Setting it higher than chance often is a rather arbitrary decision.

An ideal situation for setting a mastery level is one in which there is an exact, explicit level of performance that defines mastery. It might be argued that in order for soldiers to learn to send encoded messages, they must be able to spell standard military terms. In this circumstance, a mastery level of 100 percent for a unit on spelling military terms is not entirely arbitrary. It is based on the criticality of the skill in question to the learning of subsequent skills. The greater the relationship between the two, the higher the mastery level should be set. As a general principle, mastery level for any performance should be considered with respect to both evaluating the performance at that point in time and enhancing the learning of subsequent, related skills in the unit or in the rest of the course.

In some situations, the best definition of mastery is the level required in order to be successful on the job. With many complex skills there is a continuum of performance, with the novice or beginner at one end and the experienced expert at the other. What level is required in the workplace or on the transfer task that the learner will eventually be expected to perform? The context analysis can yield useful information regarding the expected level of performance, and can be used in the design of the criterion-referenced assessment process. If no one is currently using the skills, then managers or subject-matter experts must use their professional judgment to estimate mastery levels. If the levels prove to be unrealistic, they can be adjusted in the future.

WRITING TEST ITEMS

Regardless of the type of learning involved in the objective, appropriate test item writing techniques should be applied to the development of criterion-referenced tests. There are four categories of test item qualities that should be considered during the creation of test items and assessment tasks. These categories are goal-centered criteria, learner-centered criteria, context-centered criteria, and assessment-centered criteria. Each category of quality is described in the following paragraphs.

GOAL-CENTERED CRITERIA Test items and tasks should be congruent with the terminal and performance objectives. They should match the behavior, including the action and concepts, prescribed. To match the response required in a test item to the behavior specified in the objective, the designer should consider the learning task or verb prescribed in the objective. Objectives that ask the student to *state* or *define, perform with guidance,* or *perform independently* will all require a different format for questions and responses.

It is critical that test items measure the exact behavior described in the objective. For example, if an objective indicates that a student will be able to match descriptions of certain concepts with certain labels, then the test items must include descriptions of concepts and a set of labels, which the student will be asked to match.

Let's look at an example. Given a scale marked off in tenths and asked to identify designated points on the scale, label the designated points in decimal form in units of tenths. Corresponding test items for this objective follow:

_____ 1. In tenths of units, what point on the scale is indicated at the letter A?

_____ 2. In tenths of units, what point on the scale is indicated at the letter B?

You can see in this example that the objective requires the learner to read exact points on a scale that is divided into units of one tenth. The test item provides the learner with such a scale and two letters that lie at specified points on the scale. The learner must indicate the value of each point in tenths.

You will encounter more illustrations similar to this in the Examples and Practice sections. It is important to note carefully the behavior described by the verb of the objective. If the verb is *to match, to list, to select,* or *to describe,* then you must provide a test item that allows a student to match, list, select, or describe. The objective will determine the nature of the item. You do not arbitrarily decide to use a particular item format such as multiple choice. Test and item format will depend on the wording of your objectives.

Test items and tasks should meet the conditions specified in the objective. If a special item format, equipment, simulations, or resources are prescribed, they should be created for the assessment. An open-book examination differs greatly from an examination in which reference material is forbidden. The expected conditions of performance included in the performance objective serve as a guide to the test-item writer.

Test items and tasks should provide learners with the opportunity to meet the criteria necessary to demonstrate mastery of an objective. One must determine the number of items that is required for judging mastery of each objective assessed, and whether all the required criteria are included on the checklist or rating scale.

The behavioral objective also includes the criteria used to judge mastery of a skill. No absolute rule states that performance criteria should or should not be provided to learners. Sometimes it is necessary for them to know performance criteria and sometimes it is not. Learners usually assume that, in order to receive credit for a question, they must answer it correctly.

LEARNER-CENTERED CRITERIA Test items and assessment tasks must be tailored to the characteristics and needs of the learners. Criteria in this area include considerations such as learners' vocabulary and language levels, developmental levels for setting appropriate task complexity, motivational and interest levels, experiences and backgrounds, and special needs.

The vocabulary used in the directions for completing a question and in the question itself should be appropriate for the intended learners. Test items should not be written at the vocabulary level of the designer unless that level is the same as that expected for the target learners. Learners should not miss questions because of unfamiliar terms. If the definition of certain terms is a prerequisite for performing the skill, then such definitions should have been included in the instruction. The omission of necessary terms and definitions is a common error.

Another consideration relative to familiarity of contexts and experiences is that learners should not miss an item or task because they are asked to perform it in an unfamiliar context, or using an unfamiliar assessment format. Items can be made unnecessarily difficult by placing the desired performance in an unfamiliar setting. When this is done, the designer is not only testing the desired behavior, but is also testing additional, unrelated behaviors as well. Though this is a common practice, it is an inappropriate item-writing technique. The more unfamiliar the examples, question types, response formats, and test-administration procedures, the more difficult successful completion of the test becomes. One example of this "staged" difficulty is creating problems using contrived, unfamiliar situations. The setting of the problem, whether at the beach, at the store, at school or at the office, should be familiar to the target group. Learners can demonstrate skills better using a familiar topic rather than an unfamiliar one. If an item is made unnecessarily difficult, it may hamper accurate assessment of the behavior in question.

Designers must also be sensitive to issues of gender and diversity in creating items and tasks. Items that are biased either on the surface or statistically against any particular group are not only inappropriate, but unethical as well. Finally, they should consider how to aid learners in becoming evaluators of their own work and performances. Self-evaluation and self-refinement are two of the main goals of all instruction since they can lead to independent learning.

CONTEXT-CENTERED CRITERIA In creating test items and assessment tasks, designers must consider the eventual performance setting as well as the learning or classroom environment. Test items and tasks must be as realistic, or authentic to the actual performance setting as possible. This criterion helps to ensure transfer of the knowledge and skills from the learning to the performance environment.

Feasibility and resources in the learning environment are often a consideration as well. Sometimes the learning setting fails to contain the equipment necessary to reproduce exact performance conditions. Designers must sometimes be creative in their attempts to provide conditions as close to reality as possible. The more realistic the testing environment, the more valid the learners' responses will be. For example, if the behavior is to be performed in front of an audience, then an audience should be present for the exam.

ASSESSMENT-CENTERED CRITERIA Learners can be nervous during assessment, and well-constructed, professional-looking items and assessment tasks can make the assessment more palatable to them. Test-writing qualities include correct grammar, spelling, and punctuation. They also include clearly written and parsimonious directions, resource materials, and questions.

To help ensure item and task clarity and to minimize learners' test anxiety, learners should be given all the necessary information to answer a question before they are asked to respond. Ideally, the learners should read a question or directions, mentally formulate the answer, and then either supply the answer or select it from a given set of alternatives.

Items written to "trick" learners often result in testing behaviors other than the one specified in the objective. Designers should spend their time constructing good simulation items rather than inventing tricky questions. If the object is to determine how well learners can perform a skill, then a series of questions ranging from very easy to extremely difficult would provide a better indication of their performance levels than one or two tricky questions (e.g., double negatives, misleading information, compound questions, incomplete information, etc.).

There are also many rules for formatting each type of objective test item, product and performance directions, and rubrics. These rules are most often related to producing the most clear item and assessment tasks possible. Ideally, learners should err because they do not possess the skill and not because the test item or assessment is convoluted and confusing. Designers who are unfamiliar with formatting rules for items and directions should consult criterion-referenced measurement texts that elaborate formatting rules for assessments.

SETTING MASTERY CRITERIA

In constructing the test, a major question that always arises is, "What is the proper number of items needed to determine mastery of an objective?" How many items must learners answer correctly to be judged successful on a particular objective? If learners answer one item correctly, can you assume they have achieved the objective? Or, if they miss a single item, are you sure they have not mastered the concept? Perhaps if you gave the learners ten items per objective and they answered them all correctly or missed them all, you would have more confidence in your assessment. There are some practical suggestions that may help you determine how many test items an objective will require. If the item or test requires a response format that will enable the student to guess the answer correctly, then you may want to include several parallel test items for the same objective. If the likelihood of guessing the correct answer is slim, however, then you may decide that one or two items are sufficient to determine the student's ability to perform the skill.

If you examine the question of the number of items in terms of the learning domain of the objective, it is easier to be more specific. To assess intellectual skills it is usually necessary to provide three or more opportunities to demonstrate the skill. With verbal information, however, only one item is needed to retrieve the specific information from memory. If the information objective covers a wide range of knowledge (e.g., identify state capitals), then the designer must select a random sample of the instances, and assume that student performance represents the proportion of the verbal information objective that has been mastered. In the case of psychomotor skills, there also is typically only one way to test the skill, namely, to ask the student to perform the skill for the evaluator. The goal may require the student to perform the skill under several different conditions. These should be represented in repeated performances of the psychomotor skill.

TYPES OF ITEMS

Another important question to consider is, "What type of test item or assessment task will best assess learners' performance?" The behavior specified in the objective provides clues to the type of item or task that can be used to test the behavior. In Table 7.1 the column on the far left lists the types of behavior prescribed in the behavioral objective. Across the top are the types of test items that can be used to evaluate student performance for each type of

TABLE 7.1 | **Type of Behavior and Related Item Types**

Type of Behavior Stated in Objective	Essay	Fill-in-the-Blank	Completion	Multiple-Choice	Matching	Product Checklist	Live Performance Checklist
State	X		X				
Identify		X	X	X	X		
Discuss	X		X				
Define	X		X				
Select				X	X		
Discriminate				X	X		
Solve	X	X	X	X		X	
Develop	X		X			X	
Locate	X	X	X	X	X	X	
Construct	X	X	X			X	X
Generate	X		X			X	X
Operate/Perform							X
Choose (attitude)	X			X			X

behavior. The table includes only suggestions. The "sense" of the objective should suggest what type of assessment is most appropriate.

As the chart indicates, certain types of behavior can be tested in several different ways, and some test item formats can assess specified behavior better than others. For example, if it is important for learners to remember a fact, asking them to state that fact is better than requesting reactions to multiple-choice questions. Using the objective as a guide, select the type of test item that gives learners the best opportunity to demonstrate the performance specified in the objective. There are other factors to consider when selecting the best test-item format. Each type of test item has its strengths and its limitations. To select the best type of item from among those that are adequate, consider such factors as the response time required by learners, the scoring time required to analyze and judge answers, the testing environment, and the probability of guessing the correct answer.

Certain item formats would be inappropriate even when they speed up the testing process. It would be inappropriate to use a true/false question to determine whether a student knows the correct definition of a term. Given such a choice, the student does not define, but discriminates between the definition presented in the test item and the one learned during instruction. In addition to being an inappropriate response format for the behavior specified in the objective, the true/false question provides learners with a fifty-fifty chance of guessing the correct response.

Test items can be altered from the "best possible" response format to one that will save testing time or scoring time, but the alternate type of question used should still provide learners with a reasonable opportunity to demonstrate the behavior prescribed in the objective. When the instruction is implemented, it is important that instructors be able to use the evaluation procedures. The designer might use one type of item during the development of the instruction, and then offer a wider range of item formats when the instruction is ready for wide-scale use.

The testing environment is also an important factor in item format selection. What equipment and facilities are available for the test situation? Can learners actually perform a skill given the conditions specified in an objective? If equipment or facilities are not available, can realistic simulations, either paper and pencil or other formats, be constructed? If simulations are not possible, will such questions as "List the steps you would take to _____" be appropriate or adequate for your situation? The farther removed the behavior in the assessment is from the behavior specified in the objective, the less accurate is the prediction that learners either can or cannot perform the behavior prescribed. Sometimes the exact performance as described in the objective is impossible to assess, and thus other, less desirable ways must be used. This will also be an important consideration when the instructional strategy is developed.

SEQUENCING ITEMS

There are no hard and fast rules that guide the order of item placement on a test of intellectual skills or verbal information, but there are suggestions that can guide placement. Final decisions are usually based on the specific testing situation and the performance to be tested.

A typical sequencing strategy for designers, who need to hand-score constructed responses and to analyze responses within objectives, is to cluster items for one objective together, regardless of item format. The only type of item that would be an exception to this strategy is the lengthy essay question.

Such questions typically are located at the end of a test to aid learners in managing their time during the test. A test organized in this fashion is not as attractive as one organized by item format, but it is far more functional for both the learner and the instructor. It enables the learner to concentrate on one area of information and skill at a time, and it enables the instructor to analyze individual and group performance by objective without first reordering the data.

WRITING DIRECTIONS

Tests should include clear, concise directions. Beginning a test usually causes anxiety among learners who will be judged according to their performance on the test. There should be no doubt in their minds about what they are to do to perform correctly on the test. There are usually introductory directions to an entire test and subsection directions when the item format changes.

The nature of test directions changes according to the testing situation, but the following kinds of information are usually found in test directions:

1. The test title suggests the content to be covered, rather than simply saying pretest or "Test I."

2. A brief statement explains the objectives or performance to be demonstrated, and the amount of credit that will be given for a partially correct answer.

3. Learners are told whether they should guess if they are unsure of the answer.

4. Instructions specify whether words must be spelled correctly to receive full credit.

5. Learners are told whether they should use their names or simply identify themselves as members of a group.

6. Time limits, word limits, or space limits are spelled out. In addition, learners should be informed about whether they need anything special to respond to the test such as number 2 pencils, machine-scored answer sheets, a special text, or special equipment such as calculators or maps.

It is difficult to write clear and concise test directions. What is clear to you may be confusing to others. Write and review directions carefully to ensure that learners have all the information they need to respond correctly to the test.

EVALUATING TESTS AND TEST ITEMS

Test directions and test items for objective tests should undergo formative evaluation tryout before they are actually used to assess student performance. A test item may seem perfectly clear to the person who wrote it but thoroughly confusing to the individual required to respond to it. Many things can go wrong with a test. The designer should ensure the following: (1) test directions are clear, simple, and easy to follow; (2) each test item is clear and conveys to learners the intended information or stimulus; (3) conditions under which responses are made are realistic; (4) the response methods are clear to learners; and (5) appropriate space, time, and equipment are available for learners to respond appropriately.

After writing a test, the designer should administer it to a student or individual (not one from the actual target group) who will read and explain aloud what is meant by both the directions and questions, and respond to each question in the intended response format. In constructing a test, the designer can unknowingly make errors, and this preliminary evaluation of the test can prevent many anxious moments and wasted time for learners and instructors, or even invalid test results. Even something as simple as incorrectly numbered items will result in scrambled answers on response sheets and difficulty in interpreting results. The same applies to unclear directions, confusing examples or questions, and vocabulary that is too advanced for the learners being tested. A preliminary evaluation of the test with at least one person, and preferably several persons, will help pinpoint weaknesses in the test or individual test items that can be corrected.

After an exam is given, the designer should assess the results for item clarity. Test items that are missed by most of the learners should be analyzed. Instead of measuring their performance, such questions might point to some inadequacy in the test items, the directions for completing the items, or the instruction. Items that are suspect should be analyzed and possibly revised before the test is administered again.

A practical testing problem exists for designers who must test several different groups of learners on the same objectives at the same time or within a short time span of a day or week. To guarantee the integrity of their answers, designers may need to construct several different versions of a posttest. In addition to the pretest, as many as five or six versions of a posttest may be required.

When constructing test items, and tests in general, the designer should keep in mind that tests measure the adequacy of (1) the test itself, (2) the response form, (3) the instructional materials, (4) the instructional environment and situation, and (5) the achievement of learners.

All the suggestions included in this discussion should be helpful in the development of criterion-referenced tests. If you are an inexperienced test writer, you may wish to consult additional references on test construction. Several references on testing techniques are included at the end of this chapter.

DEVELOPING INSTRUMENTS TO MEASURE PERFORMANCES, PRODUCTS, AND ATTITUDES

Developing instruments used to measure performance and products does not involve writing test items per se. Instead, it requires writing directions to guide the learners' activities and constructing a rubric to guide the evaluation of the performances or products.

Many complex intellectual skills have both process and product goals. For example, consider a course in which this textbook might be used. The instructional goal could be, "Use the instructional design process to design, develop, and evaluate one hour of self-instructional materials." Students would be required to document each step in the process and produce a set of instructional materials. The instructor could assess the process by examining the students' descriptions of their use of the process and their intermediate products such as an instructional analysis and behavioral objectives. A rating scale would be used to evaluate each step in the process. A separate scale would be used to evaluate the instruction that is produced.

Clearly, there are situations in which the process is the major outcome, with little concern for the product. The belief is that with repeated use of the process, the products will continue to improve. In other situations, the product or result is all important, and the process used by the learner is not critical. As the designer, you must have the skills to develop both traditional tests and novel approaches that employ other forms of observation and rating-scale types of assessments. In this section, the methods to use when developing such instruments are described.

WRITING DIRECTIONS Directions to learners for performances and products should clearly describe what is to be done and how. Any special conditions such as resources or time limits should be described. In writing your directions, you also need to consider the amount of guidance that should be provided. It may be desirable to remind learners to perform certain steps and to inform them of the criteria that will be used in evaluating their work. In such instances (e.g., developing a research paper or making a speech), examinees can be given a copy of the evaluation checklist or rating scale that will be used to judge their work as a part of the directions. In other circumstances (e.g., answering an essay question or changing a tire), providing such guidance would defeat the purpose of the test. Factors you can use in determining the appropriate amount of guidance are the nature of the skill tested, including its complexity, the sophistication level of the target learners, and the natural situations to which learners are to transfer the skills as determined in your context analysis.

Instructions to examinees related to the measurement of attitudes differ from those given for measuring performances and products. For accurate evaluation of attitudes, it is important for examinees to feel free to "choose" to behave according to their attitudes. Examinees who are aware that they are being observed by a supervisor or instructor may not exhibit behaviors that reflect their true attitudes.

Covertly observing employees, however, can be problematic in many work settings. Agreements are often made between employees and employers about who can be evaluated, who can conduct the evaluation, what can be evaluated, whether the employee is informed in advance, and how the data can be used. Even with these understandable limitations, it is sometimes possible through planning and prior agreements to create a situation where reasonable assessment of attitudes can occur.

DEVELOPING THE INSTRUMENT In addition to writing instructions for learners, you will need to develop a rubric to guide your evaluation of performances, products, or attitudes. There are five steps in developing the instrument:

1. Identify the elements to be evaluated.
2. Paraphrase each element.
3. Sequence the elements on the instrument.
4. Select the type of judgment to be made by the evaluator.
5. Determine how the instrument will be scored.

IDENTIFY, PARAPHRASE, AND SEQUENCE ELEMENTS Similar to test items, the elements to be judged are taken directly from the behaviors included in the behavioral objectives. Recall that categories of elements typically include aspects of the physical form of the object or performance, the utility of the product or performance, and the aesthetic qualities of the product or performance. You should ensure that the elements selected can actually be observed during the performance or in the product.

Each element should be paraphrased for inclusion on the instrument. The time available for observing and rating, especially for an active performance, is limited, and lengthy descriptions such as those included in the objectives will hamper the process. Often only one or two words are necessary to communicate the step or facet of a product or performance to the evaluator. In paraphrasing, it is also important to word each item such that a yes response from the evaluator reflects a positive outcome and a no response reflects a negative outcome. Consider the following examples for an oral speech:

Incorrect	Yes	No	Correct	Yes	No
1. Loses eye contact	___	___	1. Maintains eye contact	___	___
2. Pauses with "and, uh"	___	___	2. Avoids "and, uh" pauses	___	___
3. Loses thought, idea	___	___	3. Maintains thought, idea	___	___

In the incorrect example the paraphrased list of behaviors mixes positive and negative outcomes that would be very difficult to score. In the correctly paraphrased list, items are phrased such that a yes response is a positive judgment and a no response is a negative one. This consistency will enable you to sum the yes ratings to obtain an overall score that indicates the quality of the performance or product.

After elements are paraphrased, they should be sequenced on the instrument. The order in which they are included should be congruent with the natural order of events, if there is one. For example, an essay or paragraph evaluation checklist would include features related to the introduction first, to the supporting ideas second, and to the conclusions last. The chronological steps required to change a tire should guide the order of steps on the checklist. The most efficient order for bank tellers' behaviors would undoubtedly be greeting the customer, conducting the business, and concluding the transaction. In general, the goal analysis sequence is useful for suggesting the sequence of elements.

DEVELOPING THE RESPONSE FORMAT The fourth activity in developing an instrument to measure performances, products, or attitudes is to determine how the evaluator will make and record the judgments. There are at least three evaluator response formats including a checklist (e.g., yes or no); a rating scale that requires levels of quality differentiation (e.g., poor, adequate, and good); a frequency count of the occurrence of each element considered; or some combination of these formats. The best evaluator response mode depends on several factors including the following: (1) the nature and complexity of the elements observed; (2) the time available for observing, making the judgment, and recording the judgment; (3) the accuracy or consistency with which the evaluator can make the judgments; and (4) the quality of feedback to be provided to the examinee.

Checklist The most basic of the three judgment formats is the checklist. If you choose the checklist, you can easily complete your instrument by including two columns beside each of the paraphrased, sequenced elements to be observed. One column is for checking yes to indicate that each element was present. The other is for checking no to indicate either the absence or inadequacy of an element. Benefits of the checklist include the number of different elements that can be observed in a given amount of time, the speed with which it can be completed by the evaluator, the consistency or reliability with which judgments can be made, and the ease with which an overall performance score can be obtained. One limitation of the checklist is the absence of information provided to examinees about why a no judgment was assigned.

Rating Scale A checklist can be converted to a rating scale by expanding the number of quality level judgments for each element where quality differentiation is possible. Instead of using two columns for rating an element, at least three are used. These three columns can include either not present (0), present (1), and good (2); or poor (1), adequate (2), and good (3). Including either a (0) or (1) as the lowest rating depends on whether the element judged can be completely missing from a product or a performance. For example, some level of eye contact will be present in an oral report, and the lowest rating should be a 1. A paragraph, however, may have no concluding sentence at all; thus a score of 0 would be most appropriate in this instance. The particular ratings selected depend on the nature of the element to be judged.

Similar to checklists, rating scales have both positive and negative features. On the positive side, they enable analytical evaluation of the subcomponents of a performance or product, and they provide better feedback to the examinee about the quality of a performance than can be provided through a checklist. On the negative side, they require more time to use because finer distinctions must be made about the quality of each element evaluated. They also can yield less reliable scores than checklists, especially when more quality levels are included than can be differentiated in the time available or than can be consistently rated. Imagine a rating scale that contains 10 different quality levels on each element scale. What precisely are the differences between a rating of 3 and 4 and a rating of 6 and 7? Too much latitude in making the evaluations will lead to inconsistencies both within and across evaluators.

Two strategies for developing scales can help ensure more reliable ratings. The first is to provide a clear verbal description of each quality level. Instead of simply using number categories and general terms such as (1) inadequate, (2) adequate, and (3) good, you should use more exact verbal descriptors that represent specific criteria for each quality level. Consider the following example related to topic sentences in a paragraph.

	General			
	Missing	**Poor**	**Adequate**	**Good**
1. Topic sentence …	0	1	2	3

	Improved			
	Missing	**Too broad/ specific**	**Correct specificity**	**Correct specificity & interest value**
1. Topic sentence …	0	1	2	3

Both response scales have four decision levels. The example on the top contains verbal descriptors for each rating, but the question of what constitutes a poor, adequate, and good topic sentence remains unclear. In the response format on the bottom, the criterion for selecting each rating is more clearly defined. The more specific you can be in naming the criterion that corresponds to each quality level, the more reliable you can be in quantifying the quality of the element judged.

The second strategy you can use for developing scales is to limit the number of quality levels included in each scale. There is no rule stating that all elements judged should have the same number of quality levels, say a four- or five-point scale. The number of levels included should be determined by the complexity of the element judged and the time available for judging it. Consider the following two elements from a paragraph example.

	Yes (1)	No (0)					
1. Indented	____	____	1. Indented	0	1	2	3
2. Topic sentence	____	____	2. Topic sentence	0	1	2	3

In the checklist on the left, the elements could each reliably be judged using this list. Considering the rating scales on the right, you can see an immediate problem. Indenting a paragraph and writing a topic sentence differ drastically in skill complexity. Imagine trying to differentiate consistently four different levels of how well a paragraph is indented! Yet, as indicated in the preceding example, four different levels of the quality of a topic sentence would be reasonable.

A good rule for determining the size of the scale for each element is to ensure that each number or level included corresponds to a specific criterion for making the judgment. When you exhaust the criteria, you have all the levels that you can consistently judge.

Frequency Count The third response format the evaluator can use in rating products, performances, and attitudes is the frequency count. A frequency count is needed when an element to be observed, whether positive or negative, can be repeated several times by the examinee during the performance or in the product. For example, in a product such as a written report, the same type of outstanding feature or error can occur several times. During a performance such as a tennis match, the service is repeated many times, sometimes effectively and sometimes not. In rating behaviors such as those exhibited by bank tellers, the teller can be observed during transactions with many different customers and on different days. The instances of positive and negative behaviors exhibited by the teller should be tallied across customers and days.

A frequency count instrument can be created by simply providing adequate space beside each element in order to tally the number of instances that occur. Similar to the checklist, the most difficult part of constructing a frequency count instrument is in identifying and sequencing the elements to be observed.

SCORING PROCEDURE The final activity in creating an instrument to measure products, performances, and attitudes is to determine how the instrument will be scored. Just as with a paper-and-pencil test, you will undoubtedly need objective-level scores as well as overall performance scores. The checklist is the easiest of the three instrument formats to score. Yes responses for all elements related to one objective can be summed to obtain an objective-level score, and yes responses can be summed across the total instrument to obtain an overall rating for the examinee on the goal.

Objective-level scores can be obtained from a rating scale by adding together the numbers assigned for each element rated within an objective. A score indicating the examinee's overall performance on the goals can be obtained by summing the individual ratings across all elements included in the instrument.

Unlike objective tests, checklists, and rating scales, determining an appropriate scoring procedure for a frequency count instrument can be challenging. The best procedure to use must be determined on a situation-specific basis, and it depends on the nature of the skills or attitudes measured and on the setting. For example, when rating the interactive performance of classroom teachers or sales personnel, some instances of the behaviors you want to observe will occur during the evaluation, whereas others will not. In such cases you must consider whether a lack of occurrence is a negative or neutral outcome. In another situation such as tennis, you will have many opportunities to observe an element such as the service and to readily count the number of strategically placed first serves, foot faults, or let serves. It is quite easy to tally the total number of serves made by a player and to calculate the proportion of overall serves that were strategically placed first serves, foot faults, let services, and so forth. Yet, once these calculations are made, you must still decide how to combine this information to create a score on the instructional goal related to serving a tennis ball.

Regardless of how you decide to score a frequency count instrument, it is important that you consider during the developmental process how it will be done and compare the consequences of scoring it one way versus an alternative way. The manner in which you need to score an instrument may require modifications to the list of elements you wish to observe; therefore, scoring procedures should be planned prior to beginning to rate learner performances. When no feasible scoring procedure can be found for a frequency count instrument, you might reconsider using either a checklist, a rating scale, or a combination format instead.

USING PORTFOLIO ASSESSMENTS

Portfolios are collections of criterion-referenced assessments that illustrate learners' work. These assessments might include objective-style tests that demonstrate progress from the pretest to the posttest, products that learners developed during instruction, or live performances. Portfolios might also include assessments of learner's attitudes about the domain studied or the instruction.

Portfolio *assessment* is defined as the process of meta-evaluating the collection of work samples for observable change or development. Objective tests are assessed for learner change or growth from pretests through posttests, and products and performances are tracked and compared for evidence of learner progress.

There are several features of quality portfolio assessment. First, the work samples must be anchored to specific instructional goals and performance objectives. Second, the work samples should be the criterion-referenced assessments that are collected during the process of instruction. They are the regular pretests and posttests, regardless of test format, and typically no special tests are created for portfolio assessment. Third, each regular assessment is accompanied by its rubric with a student's responses evaluated and scored, indicating the strengths and problems within a performance. With the set of work samples collected and sequenced, the evaluator is ready to begin the process of assessing growth.

The assessment of growth is often accomplished at two levels. The first level is learner self-assessment, which is one of the tenets of the learner-centered assessment movement. Learners examine their own materials, including test scores, products, performances, and scored rubrics, and they record their judgments about the strengths and problems in the materials. They also describe what they might do to improve the materials. Instructors then examine the materials set, without first examining the evaluations by the learner, and record their judgments. Following the completion of the instructor's evaluation, the instructor and the learner compare their evaluations, discussing any discrepancies between the two evaluations. As a result of this interview, they plan together next steps the learner should undertake to improve the quality of his or her work.

Portfolio assessment is not appropriate for all instruction since it is very time consuming and expensive. The instruction would need to span time so that the learner has time to develop and refine skills. The instruction should also yield the required products or performances for the assessment.

A course in instructional design would be an appropriate situation for portfolio assessment since many products are developed and refined over a span of several months. The products created by the learner include an instructional goal, an instructional analysis, an analysis of learners and contexts, performance objectives, assessment instruments and procedures, an instructional strategy, a set of instructional materials, often a formative evaluation of the materials, and a description of the strengths in the instruction as well as refinement prescriptions for identified problems. During the design and development process, a rubric would be used to score each element in the process. At the conclusion of the course, a meta-evaluation of all the materials and initial rubrics would be undertaken. This is often the point where learners say, "If only I knew then what I know now."

EVALUATING CONGRUENCE IN THE DESIGN PROCESS

In the systems approach to instructional design, the output from one step is the input to the next. Since this is the case, it is important to stop periodically to determine whether products being created are consistent from step to step in the process.

At this point in the design process, the goal has been analyzed, subordinate skills identified, learners and contexts analyzed, objectives written, and assessments developed. It is imperative that the skills, objectives, and assessments all refer to the same skills, so careful review is required in order to ensure this congruence.

How can you best organize and present your materials so that you can evaluate them at this point in the instructional design process? One criterion is that each component builds on the product from the previous one and, therefore, the materials should be presented in a way that enables comparison among the various components of your design. The designer should, at a glance, be able to see whether the components are parallel and adequate. One way to achieve this is to organize the materials such that related components are together. Consider the structure in Table 7.2. Each segment of the table contains skills from the instructional analysis, objectives, and sample assessments. The last line should contain the instructional goal, the terminal objective, and the test item(s) for the terminal objective. The evaluator can, at a glance, determine if test items have been included that will enable them to demonstrate whether they have mastered the objective.

Note that you must create an assessment for the terminal objective. Consider how you would respond if someone asked how learners would demonstrate that they had achieved your instructional goal. What would you ask learners to do to demonstrate that they had reached mastery? The answer should describe an assessment that requires the learner to use the major steps in the goal successfully. Typically there would also be separate

TABLE *7.2*

Structure of the Design Evaluation Chart

Subskill	Performance Objective	Sample Assessment
1	Objective 1	Test item
2	Objective 2	Test item
3	Objective 3	Test item
Instructional Goal	Terminal Objective	Test item

TABLE *7.3*

Example of a Design Evaluation Chart

Skill	Performance Objective	Test Item(s)
1. Write the formula for converting yards to meters.	1. From memory, correctly write the formula for converting yards to meters.	1. In the space provided below, write the formula used to convert yards to meters.
2. Convert measures in yards to comparable meters.	2. Given different lengths in yards, convert the yards to meters, correct to one decimal place.	2. 5 yds = _____ meters 7. 5 yds = _____ meters 15 yds = _____ meters

assessments for each of the steps in the process so that it will be possible to determine, as the instruction proceeds, whether learners are mastering each step as it is taught.

Table 7.3 contains an example of the type of material that would be included in each section of Table 7.2. Check the performance required in all three components in Table 7.3 to ensure that each is parallel. In addition, check the criteria stated in the objective to determine whether the nature of the assessment enables learners to meet the criteria.

The sequence of subskills presented on your chart is important. If you place them in the order you believe they should be taught, then you will be able to receive additional feedback from a reviewer concerning the logic you have used for sequencing skills and presenting instruction. This additional feedback may save steps in rewriting or reorganizing your materials at a later point. The topic of sequencing skills will be addressed in greater detail in the next chapter.

One additional way to show content experts and other evaluators the relationship among subskills that you have identified is to provide them with a copy of the instructional analysis chart. All items should be keyed to the numbering of the subskills in the analysis chart. This diagram can be used with your design evaluation table to present a clearer representation of your content analysis and design.

After you have received feedback concerning the adequacy of your design and made appropriate revisions in your framework, you will have the input required to begin work on the next component of the model, namely developing an instructional strategy. Having a good, carefully analyzed design at this point will facilitate your work on the remaining steps in the process.

EXAMPLES

When you examine test items, you can use the four categories of criteria discussed previously in this chapter to help focus your attention on particular aspects of the item. These categories include (1) goal-centered criteria, or the congruence between the test item and the conditions, behavior, and performance criteria stated in the performance objective; (2) learner-centered criteria, including areas such as their vocabulary, interests, experiences, and needs; (3) context-centered criteria that include characteristics of the eventual performance and learning contexts; and (4) assessment-centered criteria that include the general clarity of the item. Table 7.4 contains a checklist of these criteria. You will want to use the checklist as you review the example items in this section, create your own test items, and critique the items you develop.

TEST ITEMS FOR VERBAL INFORMATION AND INTELLECTUAL SKILLS

The behavioral objectives from Table 6.2 (Instructional goal, "Lead group discussions aimed at solving problems": Step 6, "Manage cooperative group interaction") are repeated in Table 7.5. Due to space constraints, only objectives 6.1.1 through 6.5.1 are included. A test item or set of items is illustrated for each of the objectives. As you examine the test items, notice first the congruence between the performance objective and the item relative to objective conditions, behavior, and criteria. Note that key terms are highlighted in the items to direct learners' attention. Second, examine the items for their appropriateness for the NCW leaders who were described in Chapter 5. Third,

TABLE 7.4 | **Sample Checklist of Criteria for Evaluating Test Items**

Yes	No	Criteria
		I. Objective-item congruence: Is material present in the test item congruent with:
___	___	1. Conditions specified in objective?
___	___	2. Behavior specified in objective?
___	___	3. Concepts or content in objective?
___	___	4. Criteria specified in objective?
		II. Learner-item congruence: For designated learners, is the item appropriate relative to:
___	___	1. Complexity of vocabulary and sentence structure?
___	___	2. Familiarity of contexts, examples, and scenarios?
___	___	3. Familiarity of assessment format and/or any equipment required?
___	___	4. Absence of biasing material (e.g., gender, cultural, political)?
		III. Site context-item congruence: Is performance required in test item authentic for:
___	___	1. The learning context?
___	___	2. The performance context?
		IV. Clarity: Is material presented in the test item:
___	___	1. Free from grammatical and spelling errors?
___	___	2. Expressed clearly?
___	___	3. Precise in wording relative to key terms and concepts?
___	___	4. Direct and straightforward?

TABLE *7.5*

Parallel Test Items for the Verbal Information and Intellectual Skills Performance Objectives in Table 6.2 for the Instructional Goal: Lead Group Discussions Aimed at Solving Problems

Performance Objectives for Subordinate Skills	Parallel Test Items
6.1.1 When requested in writing to name group member actions that facilitate cooperative interaction, name those actions. At least six facilitating actions should be named.	1. List positive actions you and committee members should take to *facilitate* cooperative group interaction during NCW meetings. (Create response lines for nine responses.)
6.1.2 When asked in writing to indicate what members should do when their ideas are questioned by the group, name positive reactions that help ensure cooperative group interaction. Learner should name at least three possible reactions.	1. Suppose you introduce a new idea during a NCW meeting and the value of your idea is questioned by one or more committee members. What positive reactions might you have to *facilitate* cooperative group interaction? (Create response lines for four responses.)
6.2.1 Given written descriptions of a group member's facilitating actions during a meeting (CN), indicate whether the actions are cooperative behaviors(B). Learner should correctly classify at least 80 percent of the actions described.	1. Read the script of the NCW meeting illustrated in Figure 1. Each time the leader or a member of the NCW group exhibits a cooperative behavior, place a checkmark beside that line in the script.
6.2.2 Given videos of staged NCW meetings depicting member's actions (CN), indicate whether the actions are cooperative. Learner should classify correctly at least 80 percent of the actions demonstrated.	(*Reader note:* This video and response sheet are both located in the practice test section on the NCW web-based training site.) **DIRECTIONS** **Skill:** Classify Cooperative NCW Leader and Member Actions. Click on the Videos button on the left of your screen and select Video 1 from the video table of contents that appears. Then: (a) Highlight and print the Leader Response Form for Video 1 (b) Study the response form, reading the directions for marking your responses. (c) Locate the Video 1 title button on your screen and click on the Video 1 title when you are ready to complete the assessment. (d) When you are finished (you may view the video twice in the process of completing your ratings), click on the Feedback-Video 1 title in the video menu. (e) Compare your ratings with those provided in the Feedback-Video 1 and note any discrepancies. (f) Keep your response form and notes about discrepancies, and bring them to the next instructional session at the center.
6.3.1 When asked in writing to name leader actions that encourage and stifle member discussion and cooperation (CN), name these actions (B). Learner should name at least ten encouraging and corresponding stifling actions(CR).	List twelve positive actions and their corresponding stifling actions that you as an NCW leader can take to affect member interaction during NCW meetings. (Create double response lines for twelve responses with headings of Positive Actions and Stifling Actions.)

examine the items for appropriateness in the learning and performance sites described in Chapter 5. The last section of Table 7.5 contains the learning site and performance site assessment for main step 6 to aid your assessment for

TABLE 7.5 | (Continued)

Performance Objectives for Subordinate Skills	Parallel Test Items
6.4.1 Given written descriptions of group leader's actions during a meeting(CN), indicate whether the actions are likely to encourage or stifle cooperative group interaction(B). Learner should correctly classify at least 80 percent of the actions depicted(CR).	1. Read the script of an NCW meeting illustrated in Figure 2. Each the leader or a member of the NCW group exhibits a behavior that is likely to encourage member cooperation, place a checkmark (✔) on the left side of the script in the corresponding script line. In contrast, each time the leader exhibits a behavior likely to stifle member cooperation, place a checkmark on the right side of the script beside that line.
6.4.2 Given videos of staged NCW meetings depicting staged leader's actions, indicate whether the leader's actions are likely to encourage or stifle member cooperation(B). Learner should classify correctly at least 80 percent of the encouraging and stifling actions demonstrated(CR).	(*Reader note:* This video and response sheet are both located in the practice test section on the NCW Web-based training site.)
	Directions: **Skill:** Classify NCW Leader Actions Likely to Encourage and Stifle Member Cooperation. (a) Highlight and print the Leader Response Form 2 (b) Study the sheet, reading the directions for marking your responses. (c) Locate Video 2 in the videos menu on your screen and click on the Video 2 title when you are ready to complete the assessment. (d) When you are finished (you may view the video twice in the process of completing your ratings), click on the Feedback-Video 2 title in the video menu. (e) Compare your ratings of the leader's actions with those provided in the Web site and note any discrepancies. (f) Keep Response Form 2 and notes about discrepancies, and bring them to the next instructional session at the center.
6.5.1 In simulated NCW problem-solving meetings with learner acting as group leader (CN), initiate actions to engender cooperative behavior among members(B). Group members cooperate with each other and with leader during discussion(CR).	**Directions:** **Skill:** Engender cooperative behavior among members. During the NCW meeting today, you will serve as NCW leader for 30 minutes. During your meeting, a member (staff) will introduce a problem not previously discussed in the group. You will lead the group discussion as the problem is discussed and demonstrate personal actions before the group that you believe will engender members' cooperative participation. If you have questions about your actions or the actions of others, do not raise them with staff or members of your group until the 30 minutes has passed.

(continued)

this criterion. At the posttest point, learners will be observed as they lead group discussions and the evaluator will use an observation form to note the behaviors exhibited by leaders in each site and tally the frequency with which each occurs. Finally, examine the items for their general clarity. Notice the differences in performance complexity between the verbal information and intellectual skills items.

TABLE 7.5 | (Continued)

Performance Objective for Main Step	Prescription for Frequency Count Observation Instrument (used by evaluator during simulations and actual meetings)
6. During simulated NCW meetings comprised of new NCW leadership trainees and held at a county government training facility, manage cooperative group interaction. Discussion members should participate freely, volunteer ideas, cooperate fully with leader and other members.	The following categories will be used relative to main step 6: Manage cooperative group interaction in both the learning and performance contexts. A. Engendering actions demonstrated Frequency 1. _____ _____ 2. _____ _____ (etc.)
During actual NCW meetings held at a designated neighborhood site (e.g., member home, neighborhood social/meeting facility), lead group discussions aimed at solving crime problems currently existing in the neighborhood.	B. Defusing actions demonstrated Frequency 1. _____ _____ 2. _____ _____ (etc.) C. Stress-alleviating actions Frequency demonstrated 1. _____ _____ 2. _____ _____ (etc.) D. Rating of overall quality of cooperative group interaction (circle one) Mild 1 2 3 4 5 Excellent

A CHECKLIST FOR EVALUATING MOTOR SKILLS

In measuring the performance of motor skills, you will need instructions for the performance and a rubric that you can use to record your evaluations of the performance. The examples provided are based on the automobile tire changing performance objectives included in Table 6.3.

The directions for the examinee are contained in Table 7.6. The directions differ slightly from the terminal objective in Table 6.3. For the examination, the car will not have the specified flat tire. Instead, the learner is to replace any tire designated by the examiner. Imagine the logistical problems of having to evaluate fifteen or twenty learners on these skills and having to begin each test with a flat tire on the car. Other information included in the instructions also is based on the practicality of administering the test. Notice that the student is required to return and secure all tools, equipment, and parts to their proper place. While helping to ensure that the examinee knows how to perform these tasks, it also ensures that the equipment and car are ready for the next examinee.

Information is also provided for the examinee about how the performance will be judged. These instructions tell examinees that in order to receive credit, they must: (1) recall each step, (2) perform it using the appropriate tool, (3) use each tool properly, and (4) always be safety conscious in performing each step. Given this information, they will understand that fail-

TABLE 7.6	Directions for a Psychomotor Skill Test (Changing a Tire)

Using the equipment provided in the trunk of the car, remove from the car any one of the tires designated by the instructor. Replace that tire with the spare tire secured in the trunk. The test will be complete when you have (1) returned the car to a safe-driving condition, (2) secured all tools in their proper place in the trunk, (3) secured the removed tire in the spare tire compartment in the trunk, and (4) replaced any lids or coverings on the wheel or in the trunk that were disturbed during the test.

Your performance on each step will be judged using three basic criteria. The first is that you remember to perform each step. The second is that you execute each one using the *appropriate* tools in the *proper* manner. The third is that you perform each step with safety in mind. For safety reasons, the examiner may stop you at any point in the exam and request that you (1) perform a step that you have forgotten, (2) change the manner in which you are using a tool or ask that you change to another tool, or (3) repeat a step that was not performed safely. If this occurs, you will not receive credit for that step. However, you will receive credit for correctly executed steps performed after that point.

TABLE 7.7	Partial Checklist for Evaluating a Psychomotor Skill (Changing a Tire)

Name _Karen Haeuser_   Date __6–12__   Score_____
                                                  (   )

_____ 1. Obtains spare and tools
      (   )

      11   2. Lifts car   Yes   No
    (13)

              2.1 Checks jack operation
                  a. Attaches jack handle securely   X   _____
                  b. Pumps handle to lift jack   X   _____
                  c. Releases and lowers jack   X   _____

              2.2 Positions jack
                  a. Checks car location, stability   X   _____
                  b. Relocates car, if needed   X   _____
                  c. Locates spot on frame to attach jack   X   _____
                  d. Positions jack in appropriate spot   X   _____

              2.3 Attaches jack to car
                  a. Raises jack to meet frame   X   _____
                  b. Evaluates contact between jack/car   _____   X
                  c. Adjusts jack location, if needed   _____   X

              2.4 Places blocks beside wheels
                  a. Locates appropriate blocks   X   _____
                  b. Places block before wheels   X   _____
                  c. Places block behind wheels   X   _____

_____ 3. Removes tire
      (   )
_____ 4. Replaces tire
      (   )
              Etc.

ure to comply with any one of these four criteria will mean a loss of credit for that step. They are also told that they can be stopped at any point during the test. Knowing that this can happen, why it can happen, and the consequences of it happening will lessen their anxiety if they are stopped during the exam.

A partial checklist that can be used to evaluate performance is included in Table 7.7. Only main step 2, lifts car, is illustrated. Notice that the main headings within step 2 are numbered consistently with the steps in the goal analysis (Figure 4.15) and the performance objectives in Table 6.3. The criteria listed in each objective in Table 6.3 are paraphrased and assigned letters (e.g., a, b, c, etc.) for the checklist. Related to the evaluator's response format, two columns are provided.

The next step in developing the instrument was to determine how learners' scores would be summarized. It was decided to obtain both main step scores (e.g., lifts car) as well as a total score for the test. To facilitate this scoring plan, blanks are placed to the left of each main step. The total number of points possible in step 2 is recorded in parentheses beneath the space. The number of points earned by each student can be determined by counting the number of Xs in the "Yes" column. This value can be recorded in the blank beside main step 2. In the example, you can see that the examinee earned eleven of the possible thirteen points. Summing the points recorded for each main step in the left-hand column will yield a total score for the test. This score can be recorded at the top of the form beside the name. The total possible points for the test can be recorded in the parentheses beneath the total earned score.

One final observation should be made. The evaluator needs to determine how to score items 2.2.b and 2.3.c when no adjustment to the car or jack is needed. One strategy would be to place an X in the column for each of these steps even when they are not needed. Simply leaving them blank or checking the "No" column would indicate that the student committed an error, which is not the case.

INSTRUMENT FOR EVALUATING BEHAVIORS RELATED TO ATTITUDES

For rating behaviors from which attitudes can be inferred, you will need either a checklist, rating scale, or frequency count. Our example is based on the courteous bank teller illustrations in Chapter 2 and Table 6.5. Because a teller should be evaluated in the performance site using several example transactions with a customer, a frequency count response format will undoubtedly work best. A sample instrument is contained in Table 7.8.

Notice that at the top of the instrument there is space for identifying the teller and the date or dates of the observations. There is also space for tallying the number of transactions observed. This information will be needed later to interpret the data. There is also space to record the total number of positive and negative behaviors exhibited by the teller during the observations.

The particular behaviors sought are paraphrased in the far left column. Similar to the checklist, there are two response columns for the evaluator. The only difference is that space is provided in this example for tallying many behaviors during several different transactions.

In determining how to score the instrument, the number of behaviors perceived as positive (186) was tallied, and the number perceived as negative (19) was also tallied. Reviewing the summary of this simulated data, it appears that the teller behaved in a courteous manner toward customers in

TABLE *7.8*

A Frequency Count Instrument for Evaluating Behaviors from which Attitudes Will Be Inferred (Courteous Service)

Name _Robert Jones_   Date(s) _4/10, 17, 24_

Total Transactions Observed _HHt HHt HHt_ Total + _186_   Total _−19_

A. Customer Approaches and Teller:	Yes	No
1. Smiles	HHt HHt	HHt
2. Initiates verbal greeting	HHt HHt HHt	
3. Personalizes comments	HHt HHt HHt	
4. Excuses self when delayed	////	//
5. Inquires about services	HHt HHt ////	/
6. Attends to all in line	HHt HHt	///
7. Other:		

B. During Transaction, Teller:	Yes	No
1. Listens attentively	HHt HHt HHt	
2. Requests clarifying information	HHt ////	
3. Provides forms required	HHt ////	
4. Completes/amends forms	HHt ////	
5. Explains changes made	HHt ////	
6. Explains materials returned	HHt HHt //	///
7. Other:		

C. Concluding Transaction, Teller:	Yes	No
1. Inquires about other services	HHt HHt HHt	
2. Says, "Thank you"	HHt HHt HHt	
3. Responds to customer comments	HHt HHt	HHt
4. Makes concluding wish	HHt HHt HHt	
5. Other:		

the vast majority of the instances. This information can be interpreted in two ways, depending on the teller's knowledge of the observations. If the teller was unaware of the observations and chose to behave in this manner, then the evaluator could infer that the teller indeed displayed a positive attitude in providing courteous, friendly service. Conversely, if the teller was aware of the examination, then the evaluator could infer that the teller knew how to behave courteously during transactions with customers and chose to do so while under observation.

MATERIALS FOR EVALUATING THE DESIGN

After completing the test items for your behavioral objectives, it is time to evaluate the congruence among elements in the design process. The three products you should evaluate are the major skills and subordinate skills in the instructional analysis, behavioral objectives based on the skills, and test items based on the objectives. Table 7.9 contains a partial design evaluation

TABLE *7.9*

A Section of a Design Evaluation Chart for the Instructional Goal: "Lead Group Discussions Aimed at Solving Problems," Step 6, "Manage Cooperative Group Interaction"

Skill	Behavioral Objectives	Test Items
6.3 Name actions for encouraging cooperation.	6.3.1 When asked in writing to name actions for encouraging and stifling discussion member cooperation, name these actions. Learner should name at least ten ways.	1. There are several strategies you can use as a NCW leader to *encourage and stifle cooperative discussion* during your meetings. What direct actions might you take as the leader to encourage member participation and cooperation? (Create response lines for ten responses.)
6.4 Classify strategies for encouraging and stifling cooperation.	6.4.1 Given written descriptions of group leader's actions during a meeting, indicate whether the actions are likely to encourage or stifle cooperative group interaction. Learner should correctly classify at least 80 percent of the actions depicted.	Place a plus (+) before those group leader actions most likely *to encourage* and a minus (–) before those actions likely *to stifle* cooperative group interaction. ____ 1. Introduces all members who attend the meeting. ____ 2. Emphasizes status differences among group members. ____ 3. Glances around the group welcomingly. ____ 4. Names a particular group member to start discussions. ____ 5. Comments positively after each person as commented. (etc.)
6.5 Engender cooperative member behaviors.	6.5.1 In simulated NCW problem-solving meetings with learner acting as group leader, initiate actions to engender cooperative behavior among members. Group members cooperate with each other and with leader during discussion.	As you observe ____ (name) ____ manage the meeting, what actions did he/she take *to engender* or encourage cooperative group behavior? Actions to Engender Cooperation Frequency 1. _____ _____ 2. _____ _____ 3. _____ _____ (etc.)

chart for the instructional goal on leading group discussions. The first column contains selected subordinate skills for step 6, "Manage cooperative group interaction," the second column contains the behavioral objectives for the selected skills, and the third column includes matching test items for each of the objectives. In addition to the chart, you should have a copy of your analysis of the goal (Figure 4.6), learner characteristics (Table 5.1), performance-site characteristics (Table 5.2), and learning-site characteristics (Table 5.3).

In evaluating the congruence among the various design elements, you might use the following procedure:

1. Compare each of the skill statements in the goal analysis in Figure 4.6 with its counterpart in Table 7.9. The wording of the subordinate skills should be the same.

2. Contrast the wording of each skill in column 1 with the behavioral objectives in column 2. The behavior described in the skill should be included in its corresponding behavioral objective. Your skills and behavioral objectives should differ only in that conditions and perhaps criteria have been added.

3. Determine whether your behavioral objectives are reasonable given the prescribed context and objectives development criteria. Review (a) your description of the learner characteristics, performance-site characteristics, and learning-site characteristics; and (b) the checklist for evaluating behavioral objectives. Using these documents as developmental standards, you can not only judge congruence but perhaps you will also identify revisions that will improve your intended linkages.

4. Judge the congruence between your behavioral objectives and test items based on the objectives. Again you will not only need the design evaluation chart but also learner and site descriptions to judge the congruence among items, objectives, learners, and contexts. You will also want to use the test item criteria checklist. With these design elements in hand, you will be able to judge better your design congruence and quality.

Readers interested in a school-based example may refer to the materials included in Appendix D.

SUMMARY

In order to develop criterion-referenced tests, you will need the list of performance objectives that are based on the instructional analysis. The conditions, behavior, and criteria contained in each objective will help you determine the best format for your assessment instrument.

An objective test format will be best for many of the verbal information and intellectual skill objectives; however, you still must decide what objective-style item format would be most congruent with the prescribed conditions and behaviors. Objective items should be written to minimize the possibility of correctly guessing the answer, and they should be clearly written so that all stimuli or cues prescribed in the objective are present in the item or instructions. You must also decide how many items you will need to measure adequately student performance on each objective. In determining the number of items to produce, you need to consider how many times the information or skill will be tested. Enough items to support the construction of pretests and posttests should be produced. Whenever possible, learners should be presented with a different item each time an objective is measured.

Some intellectual skills cannot be measured using objective test items. Examples include writing a paragraph, making a persuasive speech, and analyzing and contrasting certain features of two different methods for predicting economic trends. Intellectual skills that result in a product or a performance, psychomotor skills, and behaviors related to attitudes should be measured using tests that consist of instructions for the learner and an observation instrument for the evaluator. In creating these instruments you must identify, paraphrase, and sequence the observable elements of the product, performance, or behavior. You will also need to select a reasonable judgment format for the evaluator and determine how the instrument will be scored.

The quality of your items and instruments depends on the quality of your objectives, which in turn depends on the quality of your instructional analysis and goal statement. After reviewing the items you have developed for your objectives, you should stop forward progress in the design process and evaluate your overall design to this point.

Following this overall design evaluation, you can proceed to the next chapter on instructional strategies. During this phase of the design process, you will determine what tests to include in your instructional package and how they will be used. In the subsequent chapter on developing instructional materials, you will use your sample objective items and test plan to construct the objective tests you will need. If you have developed rating instruments instead of objective items, you will plan how and when to use these instruments related to the instructional strategy and materials.

PRACTICE

I. Judge whether each of the following statements about criterion-referenced tests is correct. If it is, place a C in the space before the item. If it is incorrect, state briefly why it is incorrect. Check your answers in section I of the Feedback.

_____ 1. A criterion-referenced test is composed of items that measure behavior.

_____ 2. A criterion-referenced test is the same as an objective-referenced test.

_____ 3. Test items in criterion-referenced tests need not measure the exact type of behavior described in a behavioral objective.

_____ 4. Test items for criterion-referenced tests are developed directly from skills identified in the instructional analysis.

_____ 5. It is always a good idea to construct entry behavior test items for the pretest.

_____ 6. Entry behavior test items are developed to measure skills learners should possess before beginning instruction.

_____ 7. Pretests are used prior to instruction to indicate students' prior knowledge about what is to be taught as well as their knowledge of prerequisite entry skills.

_____ 8. Criterion-referenced test items are written directly from behavioral objectives, which in turn are written directly from the skills in an instructional analysis.

II. Using the instructional analysis diagram that follows, indicate by box number(s) the skills that should be used to develop test items for:

1. Entry behaviors test: _____

2. Pretest: _____

3. Posttest: _____

III. Write parallel assessments for performance objectives. Examine the performance objectives on depositing money into a checking account illustrated in Table 7.10. On a separate sheet of paper, write a test item or other assessment that is congruent with the conditions, behavior, and content prescribed in each of the objectives. Assume the following:

• Your target group consists of college-bound high school seniors, all of whom have the required arithmetic entry behaviors for beginning your unit.

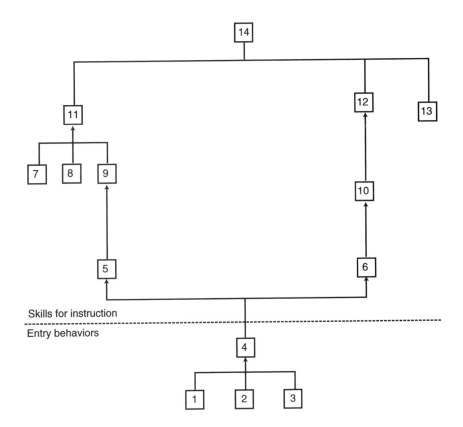

Skills for instruction

Entry behaviors

- The performance context is a local bank chosen by the students and their parents. At the conclusion of the instruction, all students in the class will actually open a checking account, with their parents' permission.
- The instructional context is a high school classroom. Local banks have all willingly provided banking materials to aid authenticating the instruction. As an aid to your work, you may wish to review the format and requirements of your own deposit slips.

You can use the checklist in Table 7.4 as an aid to constructing your items and for evaluating those you create. Compare the assessments you write with those in Table 7.11. Your items will undoubtedly differ from those provided since ours reflect only a few of many that could have been written.

IV. Develop a test that includes instructions for the learner and evaluation forms for the psychomotor skill of putting a golf ball. The following behavioral objectives are based on the instructional analysis in Figure 4.6. The test should have two parts, including putting form and putting accuracy. Compare the instructions you write with the ones included in section IV of the Feedback. Compare the evaluation form you design with the one contained in Table 7.12 of the Feedback section.

Objectives: On a putting green and using a regulation ball and putter:

5.1 Demonstrate good form while putting the golf ball. The body must be relaxed and aligned with the target, and the club must

TABLE *7.10*

Performance Objectives for Subskills in the Banking Goal Illustrated in Figures 4.8 and 4.9

Step 2.0 Deposit money into a checking account (Table 6.6)

Step	Objectives
2.1	When asked to name sources for obtaining deposit slips, name two sources.
2.2	Given a sample generic deposit slip, enter name, address, account number, and date.
2.3.1	Given a sample deposit slip, locate spaces where currency and coins are recorded.
2.3.2	Given specified amounts of bills and coins, count money and enter the totals on the deposit slip.
2.4.1	Given a set of sample checks, sign each as name appears on account, and enter account number beneath name.
2.4.2	Given a sample deposit slip, locate spaces where checks should be entered including space provided for bank number and for amount of check.
2.4.3.1	Given sample checks, locate bank number on checks.
2.4.3.2	Given sample checks, enter the checks on the deposit slip.
2.4.4	Given the back side of a deposit slip with the checks entered, total the amount to be deposited.
2.4.5	Given a total of checks to be deposited from the back side of the deposit slip, record the total on the front side in the appropriate space.
2.5	Given a deposit slip with the total amount of cash and checks entered on the front of the slip, determine the total amount of money to be deposited.
2.6	When asked how to submit a completed deposit form, cash and checks, name two ways to submit the deposit.
2.7	Given a completed deposit slip and a bank receipt for the deposit, determine whether the amount of money on the receipt matches the deposit.
2.8.1	Given a bank transaction register and a completed deposit form, record the date, transaction nature (deposit), and amount of deposit; then adjust the account balance.
2.8.2	When asked how to ensure that you have been given credit for a deposit you have made, state that deposit receipts are stored for safety in a personal bank file.

be comfortably gripped at the correct height. The stroke must be the appropriate height, speed, and direction for the target and smoothly executed. The face of the putter should be square throughout the stroke.

6.1 Putt uphill, downhill, and across hill on a sloped putting green; from distances of ten, fifteen, and twenty-five feet; putt accurately enough for the balls to reach a distance of no less than three feet from the cup.

TABLE 7.11

Sample Test Items for the Verbal Information and Intellectual Skills Performance Objectives for the Instructional Goal, "Opening and Maintaining a Checking Account," Step 2, "Deposit Money Into a Checking Account" (Steps 2.1 Through 2.8)

Objectives		Test Items
2.1	When asked to name sources for obtaining deposit slips, name two sources.	List two sources where you can obtain deposit slips. 1. _____ 2. _____
2.2	Given a sample generic deposit slip, enter name, address, account number, and date.	Review the sample deposit slip. Enter the information required to identify you as the depositor.
2.3.1	Given a sample deposit slip, locate spaces where currency and coins are recorded.	Look at the sample deposit slip. 1. Place a B for bills beside the space where bills should be recorded. 2. Place a C for coins beside the space where coins should be entered.
2.3.2	Given specified amounts of bills and coins, count money and enter the totals on the deposit slip.	Sum the following amounts of money and enter the total on your deposit slip. Coins Bills 3 quarters 4 20-dollar bills 4 dimes 5 10-dollar bills 2 nickels 3 1-dollar bills 3 pennies
2.4.1	Given a set of sample checks, sign each as name appears on account, and enter account number beneath name.	Review the sample checks provided for deposit. Prepare each check for deposit into your checking account.
2.4.2	Given a sample deposit slip, locate spaces where checks should be entered in space provided for bank number and for amount of check.	1. Locate the spaces on the front of the deposit slip where checks can be entered. 2. Locate the spaces on the back of the deposit slip where checks can be entered. 3. Locate spaces where bank number should be recorded.
2.4.3.1	Given sample checks, locate bank number on checks.	Review the sample checks below. Circle the bank number that should be recorded on the deposit slip.
2.4.3.2	Given sample checks, enter the checks on the deposit slip.	Record each of the sample checks on the deposit slip.
2.4.4	Given the back side of a deposit slip with the checks entered, total the amount to be deposited.	For the checks you have entered on the back side of your deposit slip, total them and record the total in the space provided.
2.4.5	Given a total of checks to be deposited from the back side of the deposit slip, record the total on the front side in the appropriate space.	Locate the sum of all checks marked on the back side of the deposit slip in Figure XX. Record this sum on the front side of the deposit slip in the space provided by the bank.
2.5	Given a deposit slip with the total amount of cash and checks entered on the front of the slip, determine the total amount of money to be deposited.	Sum the cash and checks recorded on the deposit slip in Figure XX, and enter the total amount of the deposit in the appropriate space on the slip.

TABLE *7.11* | (**Continued**)

Objectives		Test Items
2.6	When asked how to submit a completed deposit form, cash, and checks, tell how to submit the deposit.	Name two ways you can submit to the bank your deposit that includes cash and checks: 1. _____ 2. _____
2.7	Given a completed deposit slip and a bank receipt for the deposit, determine whether the amount of money on the receipt matches the deposit.	Examine the deposit slip and bank receipt in Figure XX. Is the bank crediting the customer with: a. The correct amount of money? b. Less money than appropriate? c. More money than appropriate?
2.8.1	Given a bank transaction register and a completed deposit form, record the date, transaction nature (deposit), and amount of deposit; then adjust the account balance.	Using the transaction register and completed deposit form in Figure XX, record the deposit transaction in the register. Complete all information to record the transaction accurately.
2.8.2	When asked how to ensure that you have been given credit for a deposit you have made, state that deposit receipts are stored for safety in a personal bank file.	Suppose when you receive your checking account statement that a deposit you made during the month is not recorded on your statement. How can you prove to the bank that you actually made the deposit?

V. Plan a design evaluation. If you were planning a design evaluation, you would create a chart with three columns: skills, objectives, and assessments.

1. In addition to the design evaluation chart you construct, what design document will help you determine the congruence of the information in column 1 of your chart?
2. What information will you need to judge the congruence and quality of the information in column 2 of your chart?
3. What information will you need to judge the congruence and quality of the information in column 3 of your chart?
4. How are these various design elements related during the evaluation?

FEEDBACK

I. 1. C
    2. C
    3. They must measure the behavior in the objective.
    4. They are derived from objectives.
    5. There may be no entry behaviors that require testing.
    6. C
    7. C
    8. C

II. Generally speaking, behavioral objectives for which test items should be included are:

    1. Entry behaviors: skills 1 through 4

2. Pretest: skills 5 through 14

3. Posttest: skills 5 through 14

III. Table 7.11 includes the performance objectives and sample test items for the objectives in the checking account goal (Table 7.10).

IV. Instructions to learners for the putting exam and Table 7.12.
The putting exam will consist of two parts: putting form and putting accuracy. You will be required to execute twenty-seven putts for the exam.

Your putting form will be judged throughout the test using the top part of the attached rating sheet. The aspects of your form that will be rated are listed in columns A and B. Your score depends on the number of OKs circled in the column labeled (1). You can receive a total score of ten on putting form if you do not consistently commit any of the mistakes named in the errors column. In the example, the student received a total score of seven. The errors consistently committed were all related to the swing: low backswing and follow-through and slow swing speed.

Your putting accuracy will also be judged on the twenty-seven putts. Nine of the putts will be uphill, nine will be downhill, and nine will be across

TABLE 7.12	Checklist and Tally for Evaluating Putting Form and Accuracy

Name _____ *Mary Jones* _____ Date _____ **3/26** _____

	A	B	(1)	Type of Errors		
1. Body		Comfort	(OK)	TNS		
		Aligned	(OK)	RT	LFT	
2. Grip		Pressure	(OK)	TNS		
		Height	(OK)	HI	LOW	
3. Backswing		Height	OK	HI	(LOW)	
		Direction	(OK)	RT	LFT	
4. Follow-through		Height	OK	HI	(LOW)	
		Direction	(OK)	RT	LFT	
5. Speed			OK	FST	(SLW)	JKY
6. Club face			(OK)	OPN	CLS	

Total **7**
(10)

Putting Accuracy Score

Area:	Uphill					Downhill					Across Hill					Totals
Points:	4	3	2	1	0	4	3	2	1	0	4	3	2	1	0	Totals
10'	//	/				/	/	/			/		/	/		*27*
15'		//	/				/	/	/		/		/		/	*18*
25'	/		/		/		/	/	/				/		//	*11*
Totals			*25*					*18*					*13*			*56*

Total

the hill to the cup. From each area, three putts will be from ten feet, three from fifteen feet, and three from twenty-five feet. Your accuracy score will depend on the proximity of each putt to the cup. Three rings are painted on the green at one-foot intervals from the cup to make a target area. The following points will be awarded for each area:

In cup = 4 points   Within 2 feet = 2 points   Outside 3 feet = 0

Within 1 foot = 3 points   Within 3 feet = 1 point

Balls that land on a ring will be assigned the higher point value. For example, if a ball lands on the one-foot ring, you will receive three points.

Each of your twenty-seven putts will be tallied on the form at the bottom of the sheet. The example is completed to show you how it will be done. Putting uphill from ten feet, the student putted two balls in the cup and another within the one-foot ring. Eleven points (four + four + three) were earned for putting uphill from ten feet. Look at the fifteen feet across hill section. One putt was within a foot, one was within three feet, and one was outside three feet for a total of four points (3 + 1 + 0). In summing the student's scores, all putts from each distance and from each area are added. For example, the student has a ten-feet score of 27 and an uphill score of 25. The student's overall score is 56.

The following score levels will be used to evaluate your overall putting performance on the test:

Acceptable = 27+ (27 × 1)   Excellent = 54 + (27 × 2)

Good = 41+ (27 × 1.5)   Perfect! = 108 (27 × 4)

Before reporting for your test, be sure to warm up by putting for at least fifteen minutes or thirty putts. Remain on the practice greens until you are called for the exam.

V. See Figure 7.1 and the discussion in the text.

REFERENCES AND RECOMMENDED READINGS

Baron, J. B. (1998). Using learner-centered assessment on a large scale. In Lambert, N. M., & McCombs, B. L. (Eds.) *How students learn.* Washington, DC: American Psychological Association. Provides a good definition of learner-centered assessment and its link to learning.

Bashaw, W. L. (1991). Assessing learner performance. In Briggs, L. J., Gustafson, K. L., & Tillman, M. H. (Eds.). *Instructional design: Principles and applications.* Englewood Cliffs, NJ: Educational Technology Publications.

Carey, L. M. (2001). *Measuring and evaluating school learning* (3rd ed.). Boston: Allyn and Bacon. Deriving and writing test items, product, performance, and attitude directions and rubrics, and portfolio assessment. Terminology is consistent with this text.

Dick, W. (1986). The function of the pretest in the instructional design process. *Performance and Instruction, 25* (4), 6–7. Discusses various issues related to the design and use of a pretest as part of the instructional design process.

Gagné, R. M., Briggs, L. J., & Wager, W. W. (1992). *Principles of instructional design* (4th ed.). New York: Holt, Rinehart and Winston. The chapter on assessing student performance includes not only the development of objective-referenced assignments, but also the concept of "mastery" and norm-referenced measures.

Haladyna, T. M., & Roid, G. H. (1983). Reviewing criterion-referenced test items. *Educational Technology, 23* (8), 35–39. The authors provide a data-based procedure for reviewing criterion-referenced test items.

Kubiszyn, T. & Borich, G. (2000). *Educational testing and measurement.* (6th ed.). New York: John Wiley & Sons, Inc. Good general textbook on criterion-referenced assessment. Contains information on item writing criteria, developing alternative assessments, and portfolio assessment.

Linn, R. L., & Gronlund, N. E. (2000). *Measurement and assessment in teaching* (8th ed.). Upper Saddle River, NJ: Prentice-Hall, Inc. The authors describe criteria for test item and assessment task formatting, portfolio assessment, and observational techniques.

FIGURE 7.1

Design Elements Gathered and Used in Conducting a Design Evaluation

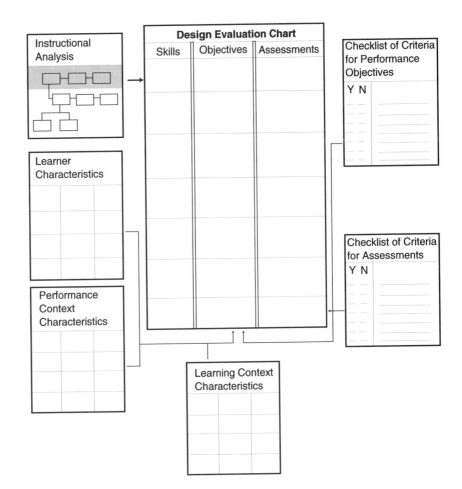

CHAPTER

8

DEVELOPING AN INSTRUCTIONAL STRATEGY

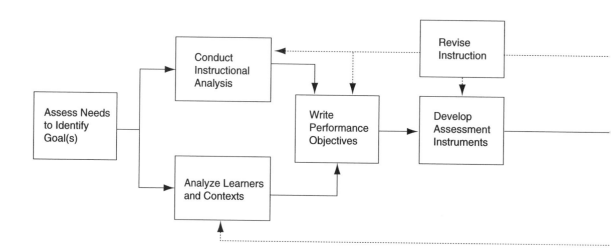

OBJECTIVES

- Describe considerations in selecting an instructional delivery system.
- Sequence content and arrange it in lesson-level clusters.
- Name the five learning components of an instructional strategy and list the primary considerations within each.
- Develop an instructional strategy, including preinstructional activities, content presentation, learner participation, assessment, and follow-through activities, for a set of objectives for a particular group of learners.
- Develop an instructional strategy congruent with learners' maturity and ability levels and the type of learning outcome.
- Select appropriate student groupings and media for the learning components of an instructional strategy.

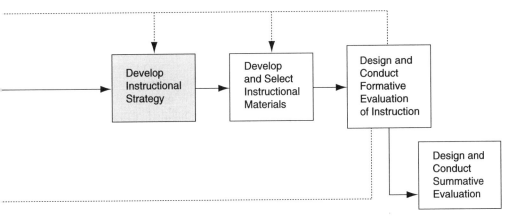

BACKGROUND

As the title indicates, this chapter addresses the ways in which a designer identifies how instruction will be presented to the learner. The term *instructional strategy* suggests a huge variety of teaching/learning activities, such as group discussions, independent reading, case studies, lectures, computer simulations, worksheets, cooperative group projects, and so on. These are essentially micro-strategies. Before the designer can make these kinds of decisions, it is necessary to develop a macro-strategy (i.e., a total strategy that begins with introducing learners to a topic and ends with learners' mastery of the objectives). To examine the difference between micro- and macro-strategies, consider the format of a typical textbook.

If you have another textbook nearby, pick it up and look it over. In what ways is the book structured to facilitate learning by the reader? The typical text, particularly for adults, has an introduction, a body of information, references, and an index. Sometimes review questions have been prepared and appear at the end of the chapters, or test items may be included in an instructor's manual. In essence, a textbook serves primarily as a source of information. The instructional strategy must be generated by the reader or an instructor. Usually, an instructor must do nearly everything to bring about learning: define the objectives, write the lesson plan and tests, motivate the learners, present the content, and administer and score the tests.

A well-designed set of instructional materials contains many of the strategies or procedures that a good teacher might normally use with a group of learners. When designing instruction, it is necessary to develop an instructional strategy that employs, to the degree possible, the knowledge we have about facilitating the learning process.

Educational psychologists have conducted much research over the past seventy-five years to determine how people learn. If you have read any of this research, then you may feel that it often seems esoteric and generally removed from real-life learning situations. Psychologists have been successful, however, in identifying several major components in the learning process that, when present, almost always facilitate learning. Three of these components are motivation, prerequisite and subordinate skills, and practice and feedback.

motivation
skills
practice/feedback

Many of the psychologists whose work influenced the original approaches to instructional design thirty to forty years ago were behaviorists. Some of the behaviorists' views were later modified by the cognitive approach to learning, with corresponding modifications and amplifications to the instructional design process. More recently, constructivists have made telling criticisms of instructional practices and suggested new approaches. Several of their ideas are reflected in the current instructional design process. The model used in this text is a generic process that will accommodate a variety of psychological points of view, especially with regard to the instructional strategy.

In this chapter, procedures will be described that can be used to design an instructional strategy for different types of instructional objectives. In the next chapter you will be shown how this instructional strategy applies directly to the selection or development of instructional materials and the development of classroom procedures.

CONCEPTS

The instructional design steps we have covered thus far have basically dealt with the question of what to teach. With that now determined, we turn to the question of how to teach it. The term *instructional strategy* is used generally to cover the various aspects of sequencing and organizing the content, specifying learning activities, and deciding how to deliver the content and activities.

In any kind of formal educational experience, there is usually a general methodology that is used for managing and delivering the teaching and learning activities that we call *instruction*. This general methodology is referred to as the *delivery system*. Delivery systems and instructional strategies are not synonymous. The delivery system is either an assumption that the designer takes into the development of an instructional strategy, or it is a decision that is made as a result of developing an instructional strategy. Choosing a delivery system is usually a course or curriculum management decision, while developing an instructional strategy is a lesson or unit planning process. The following sections explore selecting a delivery system and developing an instructional strategy.

SELECTION OF DELIVERY SYSTEM

The best way to define *delivery system* is through a list of examples. The following are a few examples of common delivery systems for conducting instruction:

- Traditional model—instructor with group of learners in classroom, training center, or lab
- Correspondence
- Large-group lecture
- Telecourse by broadcast or videotape
- Two-way, interactive videoconference
- Computer-based instruction
  - Can range from independent study to instructor facilitated
  - Can range from textual drill and practice to fully interactive multimedia
- Internet or intranet web-based instruction
  - Can range from independent study to instructor facilitated
  - Can range from textual drill and practice to fully interactive multimedia (within learners' access band-width limitations)
- Self-paced (sometimes open-entry, open-exit) programs that include a variety of combinations of instructor or tutor and print or mediated modules or learning packs
- Combinations and unique, custom systems

In an ideal instructional design process, one would work through the following considerations and decisions to arrive at the selection of the best delivery system:

1. Consider the goal, learner characteristics, the learning and performance contexts, objectives, and assessment requirements.
2. Review the instructional analysis and identify logical groupings of objectives that will be taught in appropriate sequences.
3. Plan the learning components that will be used in the instruction.
4. Choose the most effective student groupings for learning.
5. Specify effective media and materials that are within the range of cost, convenience, and practicality for the learning context.
6. Select or develop a delivery system that best accommodates the considerations in step 1 and the decisions made in steps 2–5.

This represents an ideal path for choosing a delivery system because the choice is based on careful consideration of needs and requirements before a solution is named. In this view, selecting a delivery system (step 6) is an output of the process of developing an instructional strategy (steps 2–5). Reversing the sequence and choosing a delivery system first would impose a solution (and its inherent constraints) before the requirements for delivering effective instruction are fully known.

There are three considerations to note about this ideal path to choosing a delivery system. First is that it almost never happens this way! One reason is that instructors and instructional designers often have preferred modes of course delivery, so in their minds the delivery system has been chosen before the instructional design process has even begun. A second reason is that the delivery system is often dictated by the learning context in which the organization delivers its instruction. The designer is typically required to work within this context, changing it only slightly for any given course or workshop. If the designer is working within a public school context, then the assumption may be that the teacher in a traditional classroom setting will be the delivery system. The same assumption can be made regarding training in business and industry that still is, for the most part, instructor-led platform instruction. A third reason is that there are situations in which new delivery systems such as video and computers have been purchased and installed, and the designer is told that these systems will be used for the delivery of instruction, often in an attempt to justify the purchase of the system. Now that Internet (and in some settings intranet) access is so ubiquitous and Web technology is advancing so rapidly, it is often chosen a priori as the delivery system when distribution of instruction to the home or desktop is desired across time and distance. When these situations prevail, as they usually do, the designer must be flexible and get everything out of the system that it is capable of delivering. If there is a mismatch between the skills to be taught and the system that is specified for delivering the instruction, then the designer must make the case and propose an alternative system.

A second consideration to note about the previously described ideal approach to selecting a delivery system is that the numbering 1 through 6 gives the appearance of a linear, step-wise sequence, when in fact steps 3, 4, and 5 are frequently considered at the same time. For example you may decide that a practice and feedback sequence is required for student mastery (step 3). While specifying that activity you would also be deciding that it would be most effective to do the practice and feedback in small groups of three to five learners (step 4) with three different scenarios prerecorded on videotape (step 5). Discussion will continue later in this chapter about putting together these pieces of an instructional strategy.

A final note is that the systems design model you are using is equally applicable whether the delivery system is chosen earlier or later in the process, and the generic instructional design steps that you are taking in this model are as relevant for a print-based correspondence delivery system as for a digital, interactive multimedia delivery system. We have included this discussion of selecting delivery systems at this point because it is where it usually happens in practice. The discussion will be reintroduced later in this chapter at the point where specifying media and selecting delivery systems would ideally occur. To reiterate for the purpose of clarity, the terms *delivery system* and *instructional strategy* are not synonymous. Figure 8.1 illustrates the process of developing an instructional strategy and the relationship between the instructional strategy and choosing a delivery system. The shaded area in Figure 8.1 includes the parts of developing an instructional strategy that we will describe in this chapter.

INSTRUCTIONAL STRATEGIES

An instructional strategy includes a sequence for teaching clusters of content, descriptions of learning components that will be included in the instruction, specifications of how students will be grouped during instruction, and selec-

Developing an Instructional Strategy and Selecting a Delivery System

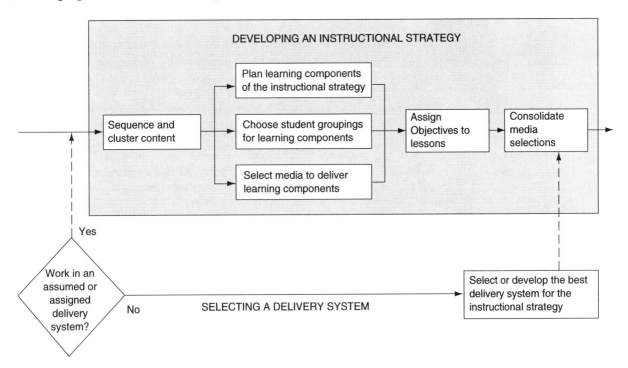

tions of media for delivering instruction. Each of these pieces of an instructional strategy is described next.

CONTENT SEQUENCE AND CLUSTERING

CONTENT SEQUENCE The first step in developing an instructional strategy is identifying a teaching sequence and manageable groupings of content. What sequence should you follow in presenting content to the learner? The most useful tool in determining the answer to this question is your instructional analysis. You would begin with the lower-level skills, that is, those just above the line that separates the entry behaviors from the skills to be taught, and then progress up through the hierarchy. At no point would you present information on a particular skill prior to having done so for all related subordinate skills.

The instructional sequence for a goal would, of course, logically be sequenced from the left, or the beginning point, and proceed to the right. If there are subordinate capabilities for any of the major steps, then they would be taught prior to going on to the next major component.

Because the goal analysis indicates each step that must be performed, and the subordinate skills analysis indicates the skills that must be acquired prior to learning the major steps in the goal, the instructional sequence tends to be a combination of bottom to top and left to right. That is, the subordinate skills for step 1 are taught first, then step 1. Next the subordinate skills for step 2 are taught, then step 2 itself. This sequence is continued until all the steps are taught. Finally, there is instruction on integrating and practicing all the steps in the instructional goal. See Figure 4.14 for an example of this approach. The boxes are numbered in the sequence in which they would be taught, beginning at the bottom, and working up to each major step.

There are two exceptions to this general approach to sequencing. The first occurs when two or more steps in a goal are the same and/or have the same subordinate skills. In this situation, it is not necessary to teach these skills again. The learner can simply be informed that a skill that has been previously learned will be used again at this point in the procedure.

A second exception to the general sequencing approach is when the instruction includes the use of several pieces of equipment, or the parts of a single piece of equipment. The instructional analysis may indicate that the learner will be required, for example, to be able to identify and locate various pieces of equipment at various points in the instruction. To avoid having to go back and forth to make identifications, it is usually both possible and desirable to present all of this instruction at the beginning of your unit. Similarly, it is sometimes desirable to present all the lower-level verbal information objectives, such as definitions, at one time at the beginning of the instruction. Use caution when doing this because you may be removing the context required to make the definitions meaningful. It may also make it more difficult for learners to store the information in memory and to retrieve it using contextual cues. Learners may also think that learning verbal information out of context is irrelevant and boring.

CLUSTERING INSTRUCTION   The next question in your instructional strategy deals with the size of the cluster of material you will provide in your instruction. At one extreme of the continuum is the linear programmed-instruction approach, which tends to break all the information down into very small units and requires constant responding by the learner. At the other extreme of the continuum is the conventional textbook in which a chapter is usually the unit of information. You may decide that you will present your information on an objective-by-objective basis with intervening activities, or you may wish to present the information on several objectives prior to any kind of learner activity.

You should take the following factors into consideration when determining the amount of information to be presented (or the size of "cluster"):

1. The age level of your learners
2. The complexity of the material
3. The type of learning taking place
4. Whether the activity can be varied, thereby focusing attention on the task
5. The amount of time required to include all the events in the instructional strategy for each cluster of content presented

For example, how much time will be required for informing learners of the prerequisites, presenting content, and providing practice? For younger children it is almost always advisable to keep the instruction, and the clusters within it, relatively small. More mature learners will be able to handle larger clusters of content. Regardless of the age of the learners, when content is varied with performance and feedback activities, the learners do not seem to tire of the activity as quickly.

The designer is often faced with clustering instruction into two- or three-day workshops or semester-long courses. How much goes into a half-day or a day? The nature of the delivery system will make a big difference. With self-instructional formats, such as print modules or computer-based instruction, the designer need not worry about exact time constraints. The nature of these systems allows time to vary among learners. Instructor-led and television approaches, however, require accurate time estimates, and there are no magic formulas for predicting time requirements. Develop a typical segment of instruction and try it out to estimate how long a total course or workshop might take. If timing is an important issue, then do not wait until all of the instruction is developed to estimate how much time is required to deliver it.

LEARNING COMPONENTS OF INSTRUCTIONAL STRATEGIES

An instructional strategy describes the general components of a set of instructional materials and the procedures that will be used with those materials to enable students' mastery of learning outcomes. You should note that an instructional strategy is more than a simple outline of the content that will be presented to the learner. For example, it would be insufficient to say that, in order to have students learn how to add two-digit numbers, you would first teach them single-digit numbers without carrying and then present the main concept of adding two-digit numbers. This is certainly a part of an instructional strategy and refers to content sequence and clustering, but this says nothing about what you will do before you present that content, what learners will do with that content, or how it will be tested or transferred to a performance context.

The origin of the concept of an instructional strategy is the events of instruction described in Gagné's *Conditions of Learning* (1970). In the cognitive psychologist's view, nine events represent external teaching activities that support internal mental processes of learning:

1. Gaining attention
2. Informing learner of the objective
3. Stimulating recall of prerequisite learning
4. Presenting the stimulus material
5. Providing learning guidance
6. Eliciting the performance
7. Providing feedback about performance correctness
8. Assessing the performance
9. Enhancing retention and transfer

Gagné's fifth event, providing learning guidance, has specific meaning within his system of instructional prescriptions for different domains of learning outcomes; but in a general sense, it is useful to think of all of the instructional events as forms of learning guidance. Learning is internal, occurring in the mind of the learner, and the purpose for developing an instructional strategy is planning how to guide learners' intellectual processing through the mental states and activities that psychologists have shown will foster learning.

To facilitate the instructional design process, we have organized Gagné's events of instruction into five major learning components that are part of an instructional strategy:

1. Preinstructional activities
2. Content presentation
3. Learner participation
4. Assessment
5. Follow-through activities

We will briefly describe each of these components and then provide detailed examples of how strategies could be developed for goals in each domain of learning.

PREINSTRUCTIONAL ACTIVITIES   Prior to beginning formal instruction, you should consider three factors. These factors include motivating the learners, informing them of what they will learn, and ensuring that they have the prerequisite knowledge to begin the instruction.

Motivating Learners   One of the typical criticisms of instruction is its lack of interest and appeal to the learner. One instructional designer who attempts to deal with this problem in a systematic way is John Keller (1987), who developed the ARCS model based on his review of the psychological literature on motivation. The four parts of his model are *A*ttention, *R*elevance, *C*onfidence, and *S*atisfaction. In order to produce instruction that motivates the learner, these four attributes of the instruction must be considered throughout the design of the instructional strategy.

The first aspect of motivation is to gain the attention of learners and subsequently sustain it throughout the instruction. Learners must attend to a task in order to learn to perform it. Their initial attention can be gained by using emotional or personal information, asking questions, creating mental challenges, and perhaps the best method of all, using human-interest examples.

According to Keller, the second aspect of motivation is relevance. Although you may be able to gain learners' attention for a short period of time, it will be difficult to sustain when they do not perceive the subsequent instruction as relevant to them. When instruction is thought irrelevant, learners ask, "Why do we have to study this?" and employees question the relationship between training and their job. When you use information from the learner and context analyses to help learners understand the relevance of the skills included in instruction, you will sustain their motivation; if not, you undoubtedly will lose them. In other words, instruction must be related to important goals in the learner's life.

The third major component of the ARCS model is confidence. For learners to be highly motivated, they must be confident that they can master the objectives for the instruction. If they lack confidence, then they will be less motivated. Learners who are overconfident are also problematic; they see no need to attend to the instruction because they already know it all. The challenge with under- and overconfident learners is to create the appropriate level of expectation for success. Learners who lack confidence must be convinced that they have the skills and knowledge to be successful, whereas the overconfident learners must be convinced that there are important details in the instruction that remain to be learned. On the other hand, if learners have, in fact, already mastered the instruction, they should be given more advanced instruction that more nearly meets the four aspects of the ARCS model.

The final component of Keller's model is satisfaction. High motivation depends on whether the learner derives satisfaction from the learning experience. Some would refer to this as reinforcement. Sometimes satisfaction is sustained through the use of rewards for successful performance such as free time, a high grade, a promotion in the workplace, or some other form of recognition. Of equal or greater importance is the intrinsic satisfaction a learner can gain by mastering a new skill and being able to use it successfully. Self-esteem can be greatly enhanced through meaningful learning experiences.

When taken alone, any of the four aspects of Keller's model may not be sufficient to keep a learner on task in a learning situation. When you can incorporate all four—attention, relevance, confidence, and satisfaction—into

F I G U R E 8.2

The Relationship Between
Each Major Component of
Instruction and ARCS

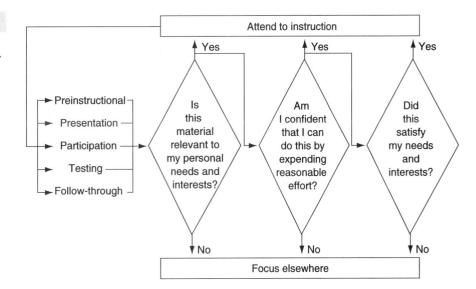

your strategy, the likelihood of maintaining the learners' interest is greatly increased.

There is a direct relationship between the five main learning components of the instructional strategy and the four aspects of motivation included in Keller's ARCS model. This relationship is illustrated in Figure 8.2. Following exposure to each component of the instruction, learners can ask themselves three questions. The first question relates to the relevance of the content presented or activity performed. If the materials are perceived as relevant to personal needs and interests, then attention is gained and maintained. The second relates to how confident they are that they can be successful. If they understand the material and are confident that they will be successful, then motivation is sustained. The third question relates to how satisfied they are that the content presented and activities provided meet their needs. If they are satisfied with each component, then motivation is maintained.

In designing the instructional strategy, we must devise ways to present each component to help ensure that learners continue to answer the three questions affirmatively. In order to do this, we can use the content from the learner analysis. We must understand their needs, interests, and performance levels well enough to infer how *they* will perceive the content and activities. In designing each learning component of the instructional strategy for the goal, designers should ask, "How does this relate to the learners' needs and interests and to their feelings of confidence and satisfaction?"

The most important aspect of maintaining learners' perceptions of relevance appears to be the congruence between the learners' expectations and the instruction they encounter. For example, the initial motivating material must be congruent with the learners' perceptions of their needs and interests. What material would best meet learners' initial expectations and hook them into the instruction? Should you judge that the congruence of the material in any component would not be immediately obvious to the learner, devise ways to illustrate the congruence so that they will perceive it as relevant. Problems will result when learners fail to see the relationships among their initial expectations, the content presented, the examples described, the practice activities provided, and the test questions administered.

As you develop the subsequent sections of your strategy, continued in the following paragraphs, you will want to continue to be aware of motivational concerns. For example, you will want to present the objectives so that the learners perceive them as achievable instead of overwhelming. A list of thirty or forty technically worded objectives would be likely to shatter the learners' confidence. A list of three or four global objectives written in the learners' language would tend to build confidence. Learners who are sure that they have previously mastered all prerequisites will be more confident than those who doubt their skill and knowledge.

Learners will have an immediate reaction to the volume of material presented initially; are learners more likely to feel comfortable and confident or overwhelmed with the amount of material you have chosen? Considering practice exercises, are learners likely to succeed on those you have provided and thus gain confidence in themselves? Has enough instruction preceded the practice for learners to be successful? You should also consider how learners will perceive pretests in deciding whether it is advisable to administer one. Will pretests demonstrate competence in the skills to be learned or create doubt and insecurity instead?

Learner satisfaction is the third general area of consideration. Will learners be rewarded for learning the skills? Will they consider the proposed rewards as adequate for the amount of effort required? Should you provide additional content to point out potential rewards? On your practice exercises, are they likely to succeed and thus gain intrinsic feelings of satisfaction and accomplishment? Are they likely to perceive the feedback you have designed as verification of their success or as criticism? After they complete your posttest, are they likely to be satisfied with their progress? Will they perceive the effort they had to expend as justified by the reward? Will they believe that the promises you made in the preinstructional materials were realized? Will they feel that they can do something better? If they believed that the rewards would be forthcoming, yet the rewards failed to materialize, then your task in motivating them for a subsequent unit undoubtedly will be more difficult.

Informing the Learner of the Objectives   The second component of the preinstructional activities is to inform the learners of the objectives for the instruction. Have you ever studied a text and wondered which key concepts you should be learning? If you had been informed of the objectives, then you would have known what to memorize, to solve, or to interpret.

By providing learners with the objectives, you help them focus their study strategies on these outcomes. They should not feel they are responsible for "knowing everything," but rather for being able to do certain specific things. Not only does this information help learners to use more efficient study strategies, but it also helps them determine the relevance of the instruction.

Informing the Learner of Prerequisite Skills   The third component of the preinstructional activities is informing learners of the prerequisite skills required to begin your instruction, if there are any significant ones. The first purpose for this component is a quick "reality check" to make sure that learners get an initial view of the relationship between the new content and what they already know. This can be done in either of two ways. One is to provide the learners with a brief test of the entry behaviors and inform them that they must demonstrate mastery of these skills to continue. Another is to provide them with a brief description of the required entry behaviors and tell them that the instruction will proceed with the assumption that they can perform these skills. Informing learners of prerequisites prepares them for the instruction that is to follow. If a test is used, it provides designers with information on the variability of students' entry behaviors, which helps them determine whether that variability is related to differences in the students' ability to learn from the instruction.

The second, and perhaps more important, purpose for this component is to promote learners' active recall of relevant mental contexts in which the new content can be integrated. In fact, all three preinstructional activities, taken together, can be viewed as the important first step in activating the mental processing that will enable learners to tie what they are learning with what they already know. This linking of new with old makes initial learning easier and eventual recall more successful.

CONTENT PRESENTATION AND EXAMPLES   The next step is to determine exactly what information, concepts, rules, and principles need to be presented to the learner. This is the basic explanation of what the unit is all about. The primary error in this step is to present too much information, especially when much of it is unrelated to the objective. It is important not only to define any new concepts, but also to explain their interrelationships with other concepts. You will also need to determine the types and number of examples you will provide with each of the concepts. Many research studies have investigated how we learn concepts and how we use examples and nonexamples to accomplish that task. A nonexample is a deliberate attempt by the designer to point out why a particular example is wrong. We know that learning is facilitated by the use of examples and nonexamples, so, generally, they should be included in your instructional strategy. In a later section we will consider, in more detail, what should be included in content presentation and learner participation for objectives in different domains of learning. Throughout this and following chapters, we will use the term *content presentation* to mean the totality of what is to be learned along with relevant examples and nonexamples in the form of illustrations, diagrams, demonstrations, model solutions, sample performances, and so on.

LEARNER PARTICIPATION   One of the most powerful components in the learning process is that of practice with feedback. You can enhance the learning process greatly by providing learners with activities that are directly relevant to the objectives. Learners should be provided an opportunity to practice what you want them to be able to do. Not only should they be able to practice, but they should also be provided feedback or information about their performance. Feedback is sometimes referred to as *knowledge of results*. That is, students are told whether their answer is right or wrong, or are shown a copy of the right answer or an example from which they must infer whether their answer is correct. Feedback may also be provided in the form of reinforcement. For adult learners, knowledge of correct completion of a task is often the best reinforcement and can be accompanied by positive statements such as, "Great, you are correct." Young children often respond favorably to forms of reinforcement such as an approving look from the teacher in classroom instruction, pop-up animations and audio flourishes in multi-media instruction, recognition in front of peers, special privileges, or the opportunity to do some other activity.

When the instructional strategy is formulated, it is typical to provide content, examples, practice, and feedback for each objective in the instructional analysis. Sometimes, it is more efficient and appropriate to combine several objectives into a cluster in order to provide more integrated content, examples, and practice with feedback. The decision to cluster the objectives is a subjective one, made by the designer based on knowledge of both the content and the learners. When it is an inappropriate decision, it will become apparent during the formative evaluations.

As indicated previously, there is a strategy for teaching each objective, including the terminal objective. It cannot be assumed that just because you have taught each of the objectives in your analysis, that learners will be able to integrate all of the skills and information in order to perform the terminal objective. The final element of your content and learner participation should be a summary of all of the instruction. It is structured like any other objective; namely there is a summary of the content that has been presented and an example of how to perform the terminal objective. Then the learner is given the opportunity to do a sample activity that includes the terminal objective, and to receive feedback on the activity. When that is done, then the learner will complete the assessment that is described in the next section.

ASSESSMENT   Three basic criterion-referenced tests were described in Chapter 7: entry behavior tests, pretests, and posttests. The general function of each was described, as well as how to develop them. At this point you must decide exactly what your strategy, as a designer, will be for assessing what learners have accomplished. This strategy may differ significantly from one that will eventually be used by an instructor who uses your completed instruction.

You must decide the following:

- Will I test entry behaviors? When will the assessment be administered?
- Will I have a pretest over the skills to be taught? When will it be administered? Exactly what skills will be assessed?
- When and how will I administer the posttest?

In addition to the formal testing that has been described, the designer may want to consider using embedded attitude questions. These questions indicate what learners thought of the instruction at the time that they encountered it. For example, the idea is not to wait until the end of the unit of instruction to ask general questions about the quality of the illustrations, but to ask questions during the instruction about the illustrations that have just been presented. These attitude or opinion questions can be physically located directly in self-paced instruction or included in unit guides.

What types of attitude items are most helpful? Items that are as specific as possible will provide the most information to the designer when the time comes to do the formative evaluation. The questions could refer to such aspects of the instruction as the clarity of a specific example or illustration, the sufficiency of a set of practice problems, or the general interest level of the content.

Sometimes there will be parts of the instruction in which the designer uses a special procedure or approach—either from a content or a pedagogical point of view. At these locations in the instruction, the designer can insert very specific questions about the learners' reactions to what has been done. This approach, as reported by Nathenson and Henderson (1980), does not seem to be disruptive to the learners. It seems instead to provide the kind of on-the-spot specific reaction to the instruction rather than the general reactions that are often received on a questionnaire that is administered at the end of an instructional unit. The end-of-unit questions can help the designer obtain an overall reaction to the instruction, but the embedded attitude questions will provide more precise, targeted information.

FOLLOW-THROUGH ACTIVITIES   The final learning component in the instructional strategy, follow-through, is a review of the entire strategy to determine whether learner memory and transfer needs have been addressed. These questions can be answered first by reviewing the performance context analysis, which should describe the conditions under which the learners will have to perform the instructional goal.

Memory Skills   Consider what learners will be doing when performing the instructional goal and consider what they will have to recall from memory. Is there anything that must absolutely be retrieved from memory? Must it be done rapidly and without prompts or reference materials? If so, then many of the techniques suggested later in this chapter for teaching verbal information are critical for inclusion in the instructional strategy.

Often the answer to the question of what learners need to remember is that memorization is not critical, just as long as they carry out the skill successfully. If this is the case with your goal, then you might want to consider the use of a job aid. A job aid is any device that is used by the performers to reduce their reliance on their memory to perform a task. For example, could the learner follow a checklist while performing the task? If so, this would greatly reduce the need to memorize a lot of information and could possibly reduce the length of the instruction. The interested reader should refer to Rossett and Gautier's (1991) book on the creation of job aids. Their approach is consistent with our instructional design process.

Transfer of Learning   The second question to ask about your instructional goal is, "What is the nature of the transfer of learning that will have to take place?" That is, "How different will the performance context be from the learning context?" Let's look at two somewhat extreme examples to make our case.

Suppose the instructional goal is to use a new computer application program, and it is taught in the training center on computers that are identical to those used in the workplace. During the training, learners work with actual forms used in their department while learning to use the application. It is expected that the learners will use the new application after they have completed their training.

From our description, it can be assumed that if the training is well designed, then there should be 100 percent transfer to the workplace. Transfer will occur because the systems and the application will be the same, and the forms will be similar to those used in training. The remaining components in the transfer context are the installation of the application on the learners' computers and the support environment established by their managers for learners' successful use of the new application.

Now consider a situation in which the instructional goal is to become effective participants in employee quality-improvement teams. The employees to be trained are from different divisions within the company; have various types of expertise, levels of education, commitment to the company, and attitudes about their supervisors; and face diverse problems in their respective divisions.

A situation like this requires careful consideration of the transfer of the skills learned during training. First of all, it is assumed that the designer has been able to determine the steps that are included in effective participation on a team. The content and examples should draw on a variety of situations from various parts of the company. The learners should receive ample opportunities to practice working on a team that seeks new solutions to troublesome problems. Unfortunately, the trainer will not be able to create practice situations that exactly match the job conditions, because people mixes on quality-improvement teams will vary, as will the nature of the problems. Will the learners be praised for using their new skills? Will anyone even notice them? Will they have the desired effect in terms of increasing the effectiveness of the teams?

Research indicates that, in general, learners transfer only some of what they learn to new contexts. Learning tends to be situation specific. The designer must therefore be aware of the tendency of learning not to transfer and to use every means possible to promote it. Broad and Newstrom (1992) have reviewed the literature on transfer and organized it in terms of what the trainer, the manager, and the learner can do to increase the probability that transfer will occur.

In addition to making the training and performance as similar as possible, it is also very helpful to require learners to develop a plan that indicates how they will use their new skills in the transfer context. The plan should include a list of possible problems the learner may have and suggestions for how these can be overcome. Commitment to the plan and periodic review of the plan will help to remind the learner of the skills that were learned and how they can be used.

Transfer of training from the classroom to the performance site is emerging as one of the most critical concerns of educators and trainers. No longer is end-of-instruction posttest performance considered the major criterion by which instructional effectiveness will be judged. Instruction is effective if learners can use it to further their study of more advanced topics or to perform skills on the job that make a difference in their organization's effectiveness. If these criteria are not met, then there are serious questions about the need for the instruction. Was it the wrong instruction, was it not taught effectively, were learners not motivated, or did it simply not transfer to the performance site? When we examine instruction that does not work, we can find potential problems at a variety of points in the instructional design process—from the needs assessment to the strategy for promoting transfer of learning.

DETAILED OUTLINE OF LEARNING COMPONENTS   The learning components of a complete instructional strategy are summarized below in their typical chronological sequence.

A. Preinstructional activities
   1. Motivate learners
   2. Describe objectives
   3. Describe or assess entry behaviors
B. Content presentation
   1. Instructional sequence
   2. Content
   3. Examples
C. Learner participation
   1. Practice
   2. Feedback
D. Assessment
   1. Entry behavior test
   2. Pretest
   3. Posttest

E. Follow-through activities
    1. Memory aids for retention
    2. Transfer considerations

Note that components B2, B3, C1, and C2 are repeated for each instructional objective or cluster of objectives. Components B and C are also repeated in summary form for the terminal objective.

LEARNING COMPONENTS FOR LEARNERS OF DIFFERENT MATURITY AND ABILITY LEVELS

Before beginning a discussion of instructional strategies for various learning outcomes we will take a moment to consider different learners' needs for instructional strategies. First, recall that the learning components of an instructional strategy are intended to guide learners' intellectual processing through the mental states and activities that foster learning. An ideal is that all learners could manage their own intellectual processing; that is, they would be independent learners or we could say that they had "learned how to learn." Indeed, this is an outcome of schooling that is now found in many mission statements for public, private, elementary, secondary, and post-secondary educational institutions.

This ideal exists, to a lesser or greater extent, in all of us. Generally speaking, younger students and less able students cannot manage their learning processes as well as older students and more able students. There is thus a greater need to provide the learning components in an instructional strategy for younger students and less able students; whereas older students and more able students can provide many of their own learning components. The learning components of an instructional strategy should be planned selectively rather than being provided slavishly for all learners in all instructional settings. Instruction for a first-grade student learning the concept of fractions should include all learning components. In contrast, a one-day in-service seminar for electronic engineers on the latest materials for circuit boards might include only content presentation with examples, practice, and feedback in the form of live question/answer discussion sessions. In this situation, a transfer activity might be conducted after the seminar in work-group problem discussions using group ware on the company intranet. The intent in planning instructional strategies should be to match learning components with the amount of guidance needed by the intended learners.

This same consideration is critical when designing instruction for distance students. Moore and Kearsley's (1996) theory of transactional distance is a "pedagogical" theory to be used as guidance for developing a distance course that will meet the needs of the intended student population. The implications of the theory are illustrated in Table 8.1; that is, more autonomous distance learners can manage greater transactional distance, thus requiring less course structure and course dialogue (meaning student interaction) for an effective course experience. The opposite is true for less autonomous learners. It can be seen that one would not provide a low-structure, low-dialogue course for students who are not self-directed. On the other hand, any combination of structure and dialogue can work quite well for independent learners. Structure makes intellectual content acquisition manageable and predictable while dialogue personalizes the student's experience and facilitates learner participation. Although not synonymous with our description of learning components, it is clear that course structure and dialogue are important vehicles for carrying the learning components of an instructional strategy. The value of course structure and learner interaction

TABLE *8.1* | **The Structure and Dialogue Dimensions of Moore and Kearsley's Theory of Transactional Distance**

Level of Course Structure	Level of Course Dialogue	Transactional Distance	Suitability for Learner Autonomy Level
Low: a flexible course in which student has control of course management	*Low:* little interactive communication with the instructor	*Greater*	Highly autonomous learner
↕	↕	↕	↕
High: a rigid course in which student conforms to a detailed course structure	*High:* lots of interactive communication and guidance from instructor (or through tutor, classmate, course materials, computer, etc.)	*Lesser*	Less autonomous learner who has not "learned how to learn" *or* Any range of learner autonomy up to and including the most independent learner

is supported in studies of distance learning students' perceptions of what works for them in distance courses (Moore and Kearsley).

LEARNING COMPONENTS FOR VARIOUS LEARNING OUTCOMES

The basic learning components of an instructional strategy are the same regardless of whether you are designing instruction for an intellectual skill, verbal information, a motor skill, or an attitude. They can thus be used as an organizing structure for your design. Within each component, however, there are distinctions you should consider for each type of learning outcome. These are noted in the sections that follow. Developing strategies to help ensure that material is motivational is omitted from this discussion because it was presented earlier.

INTELLECTUAL SKILLS The designer should be aware of both the way in which learners may have organized their entry knowledge in memory and the limits of their ability to remember new content. The strategy should provide ways in which the learner can link new content to existing prerequisite knowledge in memory. When the links may not be obvious to the learner, direct instruction about the links and the relationships between existing knowledge and new skills should be provided. The strategy should provide the learner with ways of organizing new skills so they can be stored along with relevant existing knowledge and thus be recalled more easily.

In presenting information about intellectual skills, it is important to recall the hierarchical nature of intellectual skills in determining the sequence for presentation. Subordinate skills should always come first. It is also important to point out the distinguishing characteristics of concepts that make up rules. These distinguishing characteristics may include physical characteristics or role and relationship characteristics. It is also important to focus learners' attention on irrelevant characteristics that may be present, as well as on common errors that learners make in distinguishing among concepts or in applying rules.

In selecting examples and nonexamples of a concept, the designer should select both clear examples and nonexamples. Direct information about why the examples fit or do not fit the definition may need to be provided. You should also ensure that the examples and illustrations selected are familiar to the learner. Teaching an unknown using an unfamiliar example unnecessarily increases the complexity of the skill for the learner; thus, you should select instances and examples likely to be contained in the learner's memory. To enhance transfer, you could progress from familiar examples to less familiar ones and to new instances.

There are several important things to consider when designing practice exercises for intellectual skills. One is the congruence of the practice to the conditions and behaviors prescribed in the objectives and covered in the instruction. This criterion helps separate relevant practice from busy work. Others are ensuring the link between prerequisite knowledge and new skills and progressing from less difficult to more complex problems. Yet another is providing a familiar context within which the skill can be rehearsed. Imagine having to practice analyzing an instructional goal in an unfamiliar skill area or having to write a paragraph on a topic you know nothing about. When you are skilled in performing the instructional goal, you are able to focus on the goal analysis process; when you are familiar with the paragraph topic, you are able to concentrate on the structure of the paragraph and the design of the message. As with designing the presentation of new content and examples, structuring practice exercises using unfamiliar contexts may unnecessarily increase the complexity of the skill for the learner.

The nature of feedback to learners is also important. It should be balanced in that it focuses on both the successes and failures in students' practice. Focusing only on errors may cause learners to perceive that nothing they did was meritorious, which is seldom the case. When errors are committed, learners should be provided with information about why their responses were inadequate. Learners tend to perceive corrective feedback as informative rather than criticism, especially when they can use the feedback to improve their performance.

We have indicated that content and examples should be presented in your instruction for all objectives or clusters of objectives, including the terminal objective! You will recall that in the Design Evaluation Chart you indicated the goal statement, a corresponding terminal objective, and an assessment of the terminal objective. Now, it is necessary to consider how to provide content, examples, practice, and feedback to prepare learners for taking the posttest.

Commonly designers say, "I taught all the subordinate skills, and I taught each of the steps in the goal. What is left to teach?" Yes, learners have been taught each of the steps, but they have not typically put them all together at one time. The content presentation for the terminal objective should therefore be at least a review of all of the steps that are required to perform the goal and an example of complete, correct performance of the goal. Then the learner should be given the opportunity to practice the terminal objective and to receive corrective feedback before the posttest.

If this suggestion is followed, learners perform the terminal objective a minimum of three times: first, as they learn each step in the process; second, as they practice on the terminal objective; and third, as they perform on the posttest. In many learning situations this is perfectly appropriate, acceptable to the learner, and results in effective instruction. If the terminal objective is a large and complex task, then this may seem to be too much.

What are the alternatives? You must always have a posttest, so that stays. You have to provide the step-by-step instruction about the process, so that stays. That leaves the practice on the terminal objective. If necessary, cut this short by only providing additional examples of the process and results, but do not require the learner to perform the skill again until the posttest.

The instructional strategy for assessment of learners' performance of intellectual skills involves determining when and how to test the skills. In order to make these decisions, the designer should consider how the test results will be used by both the designer and the learner. Premature testing, or tests administered prior to learners' readiness for them, can be more damaging than beneficial, because they tend to discourage learners and to provide incorrect information about the adequacy of presentations. In designing tests for complex intellectual skills, it is often desirable to test whether learners have mastered concepts and relationships and can describe the correct steps for performing a procedure prior to asking them to perform the terminal objective. For example, you might want to test whether students can describe the characteristics of a good paragraph and the criteria for judging paragraph quality prior to asking them to write paragraphs. Practicing incorrect constructions will not improve students' ability to write. Testing their writing skills prior to their mastery of subordinate skills will yield paragraphs that require a great amount of feedback from the instructor and frustration for the students.

Just as damaging as premature testing is applying inappropriate standards for judging the quality of intellectual skill products and performances. You should carefully consider levels of performance that reflect outstanding work, acceptable work, and unacceptable work for a given target group. Setting these standards is somewhat arbitrary, but they must be based on a realistic conception of what is possible for a particular age or ability group in a given situation.

It is critical to consider the requirements for retention and transfer of learning for hierarchically related skills especially when the skills from one instructional unit are subordinate to those in a subsequent one. You must consider whether corrective feedback following the posttest will suffice or whether additional instruction with practice and feedback will be required. You should also use data from the posttest to target additional instruction on specific subordinate skills where it is needed.

The review of the strategy for memory and transfer requirements is extremely important with intellectual skills. Where will the skill eventually be used, and has there been sufficient preparation for transfer to occur? Have learners been given authentic tasks to perform and a variety of tasks similar to those that will be encountered in the workplace? If the skill must be used from memory in the performance context, then have sufficient cues been provided in the instructional practice? Is it appropriate to create a job aid that enables, for example, animated pop-up explanations for each of the icons in the toolbar of a new computer interface, or could the steps for calibrating a quality-control instrument be listed on a card for use as needed? What about the environment in which the skills will be used? Has this been reproduced, both physically and interpersonally, in the instruction? And, finally, is the performance site prepared to support the learner? Are managers and supervisors aware of what is being taught and how the learners will expect to use the skills? Are teachers familiar with the performance context, and have they included instruction on how to integrate new skills into the work environment? Prompting the organization to encourage and reward the new skills of learners is a critical aspect of the overall instructional strategy. You can begin this part of the process, if it hasn't already been done, when you begin to try out the instruction.

VERBAL INFORMATION   Designing preinstructional activities is important for verbal information outcomes. When informing learners of the objectives, you should consider ways in which the objectives can be summarized using organizational structures. You could also consider informing learners about how they can use the information.

In presenting verbal information, the context for storing information and recalling it when needed is extremely important. Strategies that link new information to knowledge currently stored in memory will improve the effectiveness of the instruction. Ellen Gagné (1985) referred to this linking process as elaboration. The more detailed the elaboration or linking procedure, the greater likelihood that learners will store new information in a logical place and recall it later. She also suggests elaboration strategies such as providing analogies or asking learners to imagine something or to provide an example from their own experience for facilitating storage and recall of new information. These contextual links form the cues learners will use to recall the information.

Another strategy recommended for presenting verbal information is to present like information in subsets and to provide direct instruction on the relationship among items in the subset and among different subsets. This is referred to as organization. Procedures recommended by Gagné for aiding students in organizing new information include providing them with an outline or table that summarizes information by related subsets.

When information is entirely new and unrelated to prior learning, then the strategy should include a memory device, or *mnemonic,* to aid the learner in recalling the information. In developing mnemonics, however, those logically related to the material to be recalled are recommended. Cueing letters that form a familiar word and that are logically related to the information to be remembered can work well. Illogical mnemonics, however, can be as difficult to recall as the information they are designed to help retrieve.

What does it mean to "practice" verbal information? Rote repetition of unrelated facts is limited in its effectiveness to help learners recall information over time. Designing practice activities that strengthen elaborations and cues and that better establish an organizational structure are believed to be better. Practice in generating new examples, in forming images that cue recall, and in refining the organizational structure should also help. Focusing the exercise on meaningful contexts and relevant cues is another consideration for the strategy.

Just as with intellectual skills, feedback about the accuracy of verbal information recalled should be provided. Whenever possible the feedback should include the correct response and information about why a given response is incorrect.

In testing verbal information you will want to be sure to provide learners with cues that will be available in the performance context for recalling the information. You may also want to sequence verbal information items near related intellectual skills, motor skills, or attitudes to provide a relevant context for recalling the information. As noted previously, such a sequencing strategy for tests would suggest that all test items related to definitions and facts not be placed in a separate section at the beginning or end of the test.

Facilitation of the memorization of verbal information can be problematic. Although it will involve additional elaboration and organization strategies, it may also require a better motivational strategy. You may need to create something for learners to "do" with the information to hook them into learning it. Your strategy might include such activities as crossword puzzle contests for teams of learners that aid each other in recalling the information. A team approach to recall may provide them with practice in recalling for themselves and in coaching their teammates to recall. Although such an activity may seem like fun to learners, it can enrich elaborations and help ensure that the additional cues provided by teammates are based on their prior knowledge and are meaningful to them.

Since this is a verbal information goal, the assumption is that consideration has been given to why the learner must achieve it. With such goals, the learner does not use a job or memory aid. The motivation of the learner and the adequacy of practice are therefore critical. Also review the context in which the information will be used. Is the application context adequately represented in the learning context?

MOTOR SKILLS   The learning of a motor skill usually involves several phases. Initial learning concerns the development of an "executive routine," which consists of the "directions" that the learner is to follow. The mental statement of each step in the routine is followed by the performance of that step. With repeated practice and appropriate feedback, the steps in the routine begin to smooth out, there is less hesitation between each step, the mental rehearsal of the executive routine decreases, and the skill begins to assume its final form. Expert performance is often represented by the absence of dependency on the executive routine and an automatic execution of the skill.

What are the implications of this description of the learning of a typical motor skill for the presentation of content, examples, practice, and feedback? One very apparent implication is the requirement of some form of visual presentation of the skill. Obviously video or films can be used to capture movement, but often photos or drawings can be used, at least at the initial stages of learning a motor skill. The categories of content and examples in a strategy usually take the form of a verbal description of the skill followed by an illustration.

It is important to determine an effective way to group information on a motor skill. It is not unusual to cluster meaningful parts of the skill, which can later be integrated into the complete skill. In our earlier example of learning how to putt a golf ball, we showed that this skill can be broken down into lining up the ball with the cup, the backswing, hitting the ball, and follow-through.

Practice and feedback are the hallmarks of psychomotor skills. Research has shown that learners can benefit from mentally visualizing the performance of a skill before they physically engage in it. Actual practice of a skill should be repetitious. Immediate feedback on the correctness of the execution of the skill is very important, since incorrect rehearsal will not promote skill improvement.

A special problem that occurs when a motor skill involves the use of a piece of equipment is deciding at what points the learner should interact with the equipment. At one extreme all instruction is received before the learner practices on the actual equipment. Logistically this is the easiest approach, but it puts a great burden on the student to remember all the details of the instruction. The other extreme is to have the learner interact with the equipment at each step in the instruction. While there is less of a memory problem, this approach requires one piece of equipment per learner.

One solution to this instructional problem, which may later become a performance problem, is to provide the learner with a job aid. For example, if the learner must enter a coded number into a piece of equipment to make it operate in a particular way, then there may be no reason to require the learner to memorize all the possible codes. They could instead be listed on a plate on the equipment or on a card that the learner could easily review. Job aids can also include lists of steps to be executed or criteria to be used to evaluate a product or performance. If the designer chooses to incorporate a job aid into the training, then it is obvious that the learner must be taught how to use it.

The ultimate question in testing any motor skill is, "Can the learner execute the skill that has been taught?" The question of transfer of learning, which was raised with regard to intellectual skills and verbal information, must also be addressed with motor skills. What are the conditions under which this skill must be performed? Any requirements should be present as the skill is practiced in the instructional setting and should also be present for the posttest.

ATTITUDES   Researchers believe that our attitudes consist of three components: feelings, behaviors, and cognitive understandings. Feelings, in this case, can be described as pleasures or displeasures that are expressed through our tendency to approach or avoid a situation. This tendency is thought to depend on our success or failure in prior, similar situations or our observation of others in these situations. This is the key to a successful instructional strategy for an attitude. The content and example portion of the strategy should be delivered by someone or by an imaginary character who is respected and admired by the learners. This "human model" should display the behaviors involved in the attitude and indicate why this is an appropriate attitude. If possible, it should be obvious to the learner that the model is being rewarded for displaying this attitude.

The substance of the instruction for an attitude consists of teaching the behavior that is to be demonstrated by the learner, such as personal cleanliness, as well as the supporting information about why this is important. The behaviors should be demonstrated under the conditions described in the performance objectives.

You may also need to consider in your strategy whether you are developing an attitude or reshaping one. For existing negative behaviors (and attitudes) such as the learner becoming emotional or angry in a meeting when things do not go as anticipated, you may need to focus instruction on self-awareness and teach alternative ways of behaving in the circumstance. Creating simulations that evoke emotions that lead to damaging behaviors may be required. Guiding learners to more positive behaviors that they can associate with the same emotions can be difficult. You may wish to consider strategies such as videotaping them as they respond in context and then working with them as they analyze how they felt and reacted. You may want them to hear how others in the situation judged their reactions. You may want them to observe someone they admire react positively in a similar circumstance and, through remaining calm, direct the conclusion of the meeting to the anticipated outcome.

Undoubtedly the strategy you choose for instruction related to an attitude hinges on multiple factors. In addition to attempting to develop or reshape an attitude, several questions should be considered. Are the learners volunteers for the program because they perceive a need for it and wish to change? Are they satisfied with themselves but have been directed or "sentenced" to the program by a supervisor, school administrator, or judge? Are the attitude and behaviors ones the learners care little about, or do they represent strong convictions or sensitive feelings? How free can you be in delivering instruction, creating simulations, and providing feedback? Will group instruction suffice, or will individualized instruction be required? The answers to all such questions should have been obtained in the learner and context analyses and should be considered in designing an instructional strategy for attitudes.

How can the learner practice an attitude? Making inappropriate or ineffective choices that are followed by ineffective or even positive feedback will not help the learner make better choices. Practice, therefore, must incorporate opportunities to choose followed by consistent feedback (rewards/consequences) to help ensure that a given behavior becomes associated with a given response. The feedback should include information about what the learner did right and what the learner did wrong. Related to inappropriate responses, information about more appropriate responses should be provided.

Since attitudes can be learned vicariously, mental rehearsals may prove beneficial for practicing them. Such rehearsals might include dramatic scenes that present respected models who are faced with alternatives. Following the presentation of alternatives, the learners can observe the model reacting in positive ways and can observe the model receiving rewards considered positive and relevant by the learners. Additionally, other models could be observed reacting in negative ways and receiving negative consequences. These story simulations are especially useful because characters affected by the negative model's attitudes and behaviors can be observed by learners. When respected characters are injured, insulted, or angered by the "bad" model, the learner can associate or empathize with these reactions. This empathy will help the learner rehearse associating the attitude and behavior with the unpleasant consequences. These reactions of the respected characters constitute feedback to the learner. Reactors can be seen discussing the behavior of the negative model, and they can provide informative feedback by describing alternative ways the model should have behaved.

As discussed previously, an important consideration when designing tests for attitudes is whether learners will know they are being observed. Other considerations include tests of verbal information related to knowledge of the expected behaviors and the potential rewards and consequences for behaving in certain ways. The assessment strategy should also encompass any intellectual or motor skills required for exhibiting the required behaviors. For example, it would be difficult to demonstrate positive attitudes toward safe driving if one could not drive a car, could not state the rules of the road, and could not solve safety problems encountered while driving. Although this is an extreme example, it illustrates the point.

You may want to design questionnaires with situations and questions for the learners about how they would react to hypothetical circumstances. If this is your strategy, then you should be aware that research demonstrates there is little relationship between what we say about our attitudes in a written situation and what we do when confronted with a similar situation in real life. To the extent possible, the designer should try to create hypothetical situations that simulate those in which the attitude would influence the learners' choices and behaviors.

Perhaps the most important consideration in the instructional strategy for teaching an attitude is the adequacy of the components that will promote transfer. Rarely are we interested in a demonstration of an attitude in the presence of an instructor other than to show that the learner has mastered the skill associated with the attitude. We want the skill to be chosen by the learner as the desired behavior in situations when the instructor is not present. It is therefore critical to provide the learner with practice contexts that are similar to those in which we hope to see the attitude occur. The learner should also be provided with valid feedback to this attitude as part of the practice activity.

STUDENT GROUPINGS

When you are planning the learning components of an instructional strategy, you also need to plan the details of student groupings and media selections. Although all three are considered simultaneously, the learning components of the strategy remain the primary planning units, because they determine learning effectiveness. The emphasis should always be on planning student groupings and media selections *within* learning components. If a delivery system requiring distance learning or individualized instruction has been prescribed, then some limits on student groupings may exist; in most cases, however, this decision is in the hands of the instructional designer.

The primary question to ask when making decisions about student groupings is whether requirements for social interaction exist in the performance and learning contexts, in the statements of learning objectives, in the specific learning component being planned, or in one's foundational views of the teaching/learning process. The type of student grouping (individual, pairs, small group, large group) depends on specific social interaction requirements and is often mixed within and among the learning components in a lesson or unit. Remember that motivation is a key learning component and that social interaction and changes in student groupings provide variety and interest value even when not specifically required in the performance context or objectives. In other instances, pedagogical methods such as active learning and problem-based learning employ a variety of student groupings for managing different learning components of the instructional strategy.

SELECTION OF MEDIA AND DELIVERY SYSTEMS

As we begin this discussion of media selection, it is a good point for all of us to think back to our own experience as students in K through 12. Do you remember those few teachers who always seemed to have a video reserved for that last class on Friday afternoon? You remember the routine: class starts—lights off—video starts—video ends—bell rings—goodbye! Was that good instruction? Usually not, but why not? Think about the learning components of an instructional strategy described in this chapter. Would the Friday afternoon video be a complete strategy or just a part of an overall set of unit activities? The video probably could fit into a unit as part of preinstructional activities and content presentation, but what about the other learning components that are part of a complete strategy? They just did not happen on those Friday afternoons. This example illustrates the point of view in this chapter that media are useful to the extent that they effectively carry required learning components of an instructional strategy.

In the initial discussion in this chapter of the selection of a delivery system we noted that it most often occurs early in the instructional design process. When working under the constraint of an assigned or assumed delivery system, media selection becomes a choice among those formats that are available in that system. There are two reasons why this limit on available media is not of as much concern as one might think. The first reason is drawn from research on effects of media on students' learning. Such research began with military training films in the 1940s and has continued through radio, television, slide tape, multi-image, computer-based multi-media, and Web-based distance learning. The general conclusion of this research on effects of media is that the medium itself does not make a whole lot of difference in how much students learn. Clark's (1983) review of research established the basic argument that it is the design of instruction, rather than the medium used to deliver instruction, that determines student learning. In a summary of research ten years later, Russell (1993) focused more on distance learners' achievement with conclusions very similar to Clark's, and Russell's (1999) update of his review includes findings from research on Web-based instruction and reports the same general conclusions. The implication for the instructional designer (with some qualifications discussed in the following paragraphs) is that you can't go too far wrong with media selection because most media will work for most teaching/learning requirements.

A second reason why designing instruction under an imposed delivery system is not of as much concern as one might think, is that most media formats are available in most delivery systems. Consider a few common media formats ranging from text, graphics, audio, and motion video through real objects and authentic environments. These formats can be displayed or represented in a low-tech delivery system with an instructor and AV equipment in a classroom, or a high-tech delivery system using the Web. Regardless of whether instruction is low-tech or high-tech, the learning components of an instructional strategy are still the key predictors of learner success, and they must be provided by the instructor; by mediated materials; by classmates, workmates, colleagues, family, friends, and so on; or by the learners themselves.

Now we look at selection of media and a delivery system at the point where it would ideally occur in the instructional design process. Once decisions have been made about content sequencing and clustering, and the learning components have been planned, then appropriate decisions can be made regarding media selection and a delivery system. How are these choices made? Certainly there are practical considerations one immediately thinks of in terms of availability of resources and personnel. But there are prior decisions that should be made that relate to the selection of appropriate media for the various domains of learning and for certain task requirements found in objectives.

MEDIA SELECTION FOR DOMAINS OF LEARNING Reiser and Gagné (1983) have published a model showing how to select the best medium for instruction. The designer uses the model by *answering* questions about the skill to be taught, and then follows a flow diagram to the point that *several* media are suggested. The designer can then look at the practical aspects associated with the use of what are referred to as the *candidate media*. The Reiser and Gagné technique is based on a complete review of the research on the use of media in instruction, and interested readers may want to consult the source for details of the media selection logic and the decision flow charts. The critical decision points in the model really come down to two questions: (1) "Is intelligent, adaptive feedback required for learning?" and (2) "Is physical practice required for learning?" The answers to both of these questions are found in the domain of learning represented by the objectives being taught.

Consider, for example, the analysis of the type of media that might be used to teach intellectual skills. Research suggests that learners should be provided precise corrective feedback to responses made during the learning process. Often there is more than one "correct answer." In order to provide responsive feedback, one would choose interactive media such as a human instructor, a peer tutor, computer-based instruction, or programmed instruction. If broadcast TV were chosen, then supplemental student packages that require responses and provide feedback could be developed, or study groups could be organized.

If the instructional goal is in the domain of verbal information, there is still the requirement of eliciting responses from learners, but there is less need for intelligent, adaptive feedback. Students can easily compare their own responses to the correct answers, so there is less need for interactive media with verbal information goals.

The other two domains of goals that we have considered are motor skills and attitudes. If the learning of a motor skill begins with the learning of an executive routine (which is a description of what the learner will do and how it will be done under various circumstances), then this first phase can be treated as if it were an intellectual skill. As the learner masters the executive routine, however, it is necessary to practice in the real physical environment or with the equipment described in the instructional goal. Simulators or real objects should therefore be used for teaching psychomotor skills.

Research about how we learn attitudes suggests that one of the most powerful methods is to observe a person we highly regard doing something for which they are rewarded or have received approval. It is then likely that we will tend to make the same choice when we are in a similar situation. For teaching attitudes then, the visual media, such as television or digital video, are often suggested.

The purpose of this review has been to suggest that the differences in learning outcomes are reflected in the media used to deliver instruction; however, it cannot be assumed that the objectives are all in the same domain. For a short lesson, it is likely that all of the objectives might be intellectual skills or verbal information. On the other hand, as the size of instruction increases—for example, to a forty-hour course—there might be a mixture of domains represented in the objectives. It is necessary, therefore, to select a medium for a cluster of similar objectives, and attempt to mix compatible media for a variety of objectives.

MEDIA SELECTION FOR CERTAIN TASK REQUIREMENTS FOUND IN OBJECTIVES
In addition to matching media to learning domains, there are two instances when one must account for task requirements found in objectives. Both are fairly obvious but bear mention here to complete the considerations that go into media selection. First the designer should ask whether specific sensory discriminations (visual, auditory, tactile, etc.) are required to master the objective. If the answer is yes, then the medium or combination of media must be capable of managing the sensory requirements in content presentation, learner participation, and assessment. A second question the designer should ask is whether social interaction is required for mastery of the objective. If the answer is yes, then this requirement should probably be accommodated in learner participation and most certainly in assessment.

PRACTICAL CONSIDERATIONS IN CHOOSING MEDIA AND DELIVERY SYSTEMS An important factor in delivery system selection is the projected availability of various media in the environment in which the instructional package will be used. If the materials will be used in the learning resource center of a public school, community college, or university, then a whole array of media devices would probably be available to the learner and to the instructor. In contrast, if the package is designed for home study, use on the job, or use in a community center where equipment may be limited, then you must either develop a means of making that equipment available or limit media selection to reasonable expectations of availability. The ubiquity of computers and online access in recent years has changed how we think about "reasonable expectations of availability." If an Internet-capable computer is not available at home, then access can usually be obtained at work, at school, or in a public library, thus opening media selection to the Web and in some cases to CD, DVD, and proprietary software. A related concern is the ability of the instructor and the student to manage the media and software that you incorporate in the instructional package. If you select videotape, a PowerPoint presentation, an audiotape, and a workbook in combination, then the variety of media could create logistical problems. This is a practical consideration that might be solved by combining all components into a Web-based product. Another factor related to the learning environment is the skill levels that learners can bring to technological media. This is particularly critical in independent and distance learning delivery systems that require computer hardware and software capabilities.

Another factor in media selection is the ability of the designer or an available expert to produce materials in a particular medium. For example, you may find that computer-assisted instruction would be an ideal medium for a particular instructional objective, but because you do not already have the skills to develop instruction using computers or the time to learn them, or because there is no staff available to do it, another choice must be made. On the other hand, if such resources are available or you have these skills, then certainly they should be used.

The flexibility, durability, and convenience of the materials within a specified medium are other factors. If the materials are designed so that they require equipment found only in a learning center, is there a learning center available? Is it open during hours when students can participate in independent study? Are the materials in a form that students can handle alone without destroying either the materials or equipment required for the materials? Should the materials be portable and, if so, how portable can they be with the media you have chosen?

The final factor is the cost-effectiveness, over the long run, of one medium compared to others. Some materials may be initially cheaper to produce in one medium than another, but these costs may be equalized when one considers costs in other areas such as lecturers, evaluators, and feedback personnel. It might be cheaper to videotape a lecture for a large group of students to view again and again as needed, which frees the lecturer or specialist to work with small groups of students or to help individuals solve problems.

All the factors discussed here represent either theoretical or practical criteria that must be met. These criteria illustrate the importance of media selection in the instructional development process. In theory it would be ideal to delay the choice of a delivery system until media have been chosen for the components of the instructional strategy; however, in practice, nearly all projects begin with the delivery system already established. Regardless of the circumstance, most delivery systems offer a range of media alternatives. Matched with a thorough needs assessment and learning context analysis, the designer can maximize the effectiveness of the instruction with a variety of media formats in a course or workshop.

ALTERNATIVE VIEWS ABOUT DEVELOPING AN INSTRUCTIONAL STRATEGY

The approach in this chapter to developing and managing instruction is fairly prescriptive because we believe it to be the most effective and efficient in most professional and technical training and in many levels of school subjects. By prescriptive, we mean that the learning components of the instructional strategy are tied directly to a predetermined content structure and the teaching/learning process is tied directly to the learning components.

This prescriptive approach supports the emphasis on job skills in the training world; and whether one agrees with current trends, the prescriptive approach supports the standards and accountability movement in public education. Less prescriptive, learner-centered approaches to education based on Piaget's developmental theories and more recent constructivist theories can also have valuable roles in your design and management of instruction. After looking at a radical constructivist view that there is no objective reality, that knowledge is constructed internally and individually by learners, and is therefore unpredictable; an instructional designer might ask, "How can instructional designers determine what students need, prescribe instructional activities, and assess learning outcomes?" Carey (1998) and Ertmer and Newby (1993) provide balanced analyses of how aspects of a constructivist approach can be compatible with aspects of a prescriptive approach for specified types of learners and learning outcomes.

Constructivism shares roots in cognitive psychology from which the learning components of the instructional strategy presented in this chapter are derived. The literature on how constructivist instruction is done provides a set of guidelines that fit into the learning component categories. Table 8.2 summarizes guidelines within learning components to provide a model constructivist strategy. The constructivist strategy in Table 8.2 would be particularly applicable for learning ill-defined problem solving skills in the cognitive strategy area.

DEVELOPING AN INSTRUCTIONAL STRATEGY

Now that you have an idea of what is included in an instructional strategy, you can see that it would be inappropriate to go directly from a list of performance objectives to writing instructional materials without first planning and documenting your instructional strategy. The instructional strategy is a product that can be used as any of the following:

- Prescription to develop instructional materials
- Set of criteria to evaluate existing materials
- Set of criteria and a prescription to revise existing materials
- Framework from which class lecture notes, interactive group exercises, and homework assignments can be planned

Regardless of the availability of existing instructional materials, the instructor should develop an instructional strategy for a set of performance objectives before selecting, adapting, or developing instruction.

What is needed to develop an instructional strategy? The instructor should begin with an instructional design that includes: (1) an instructional

TABLE 8.2	**Constructivist Guidelines for Planning the Learning Components of an Instructional Strategy**

Learning Components of an Instructional Strategy	Guidelines for Designing Constructivist Learning Environments
1. Preinstructional Activities • Motivate learners • Describe objectives • Recall prerequisites	Foster motivation through "ownership" by giving students choices in the content they explore *and* control of the methods they use for exploration. Situate problem scenarios in meaningful (authentic) contexts that contain necessary elements for inquiry and are rich in the content of interest. Learning environments should require reflexive thought, looking back to incorporate foundational knowledge in construction of new knowledge.
2. Content Presentation with Examples	Learning environments should emphasize constructing process over finding answers; for example, the aim is for students to think like mathematicians rather than to compute a correct answer. Learning environments must be generative rather than prescriptive; that is, students construct their own, active investigation and knowledge acquisition rather than following steps in a prescribed process. Encourage group participation for negotiating new knowledge and process.

goal and goal analysis, (2) subskills identified through an instructional analysis, (3) a list of performance objectives, (4) associated test items (5) learner analysis, (6) learning context analysis, and (7) performance context analysis.

Having completed all these steps, you are ready to develop your instructional strategy. At this point you should realize that you have already completed some of the work needed to develop an instructional strategy. You have already (1) identified objectives, (2) identified prerequisite knowledge (through your analysis of the relationship among subskills in the instructional analysis), (3) identified the sequence for presenting instruction (when you completed your design evaluation table and your analysis diagram), (4) identified the content required (when you analyzed the knowledge and skills during the instructional analysis), and (5) identified appropriate test items for each objective. All this information, already included in your design evaluation table, can serve as input for the development of the instructional strategy.

Even though we recommend that learning components in an instructional strategy occur in the order presented in the previous section (preinstructional activities, presentation of content, student participation, assessment, and follow-through), we do not recommend that you try to develop your instructional strategy in this order. The developmental sequence differs from the suggested order in which students encounter learning components during a lesson.

The best sequence for developing your instructional strategy is as follows:

TABLE *8.2* | (Continued)

Learning Components of an Instructional Strategy	Guidelines for Designing Constructivist Learning Environments
3. Learner Participation • Practice	Use cooperative learning so that students can negotiate the meaning of what they are learning.
	Design learning environments of high complexity requiring use of multiple process strategies and knowledge and tool skills.
	Encourage multiple perspectives and interpretations of the same knowledge.
	Situate problem scenarios in authentic contexts.
• Feedback	Balance the potential frustration of aimless exploration with just enough facilitation to ensure progress (suggested facilitation techniques include modeling, scaffolding, coaching, and collaborating), but fade the facilitation as students become more skillful.
	Facilitate group interaction as needed to ensure peer review of knowledge and process.
4. Assessment	Suggest tools that students can use to monitor their own construction of knowledge and process; learning should be reflexive, encouraging review and critique of previous learning and newly constructed positions.
	Standards for evaluation cannot be absolute, but must be referenced to the students' unique goals, construction of knowledge, and past achievement.
	The ultimate measure of success is transfer of learning to new, previously unencountered, authentic environments.
5. Follow-through activities	Students should have opportunities to explore multiple, parallel problem scenarios where they will find application in a new scenario of information and processes that they have previously constructed.

1. Indicate the sequence of objectives and how you will cluster them for instruction. To do this, consider both the sequence and the size of clusters that are appropriate for the attention span of students and the time available for each session. In designing the sequence, remember to include review or synthesizing activities when needed. The decisions you make about sequence and clusters can be summarized using a form such as that shown in Table 8.5. Later, this prescription will help you assign objectives to lessons.

2. Indicate *what* you will do with regard to preinstructional activities, assessment, and follow-through. The relevant issues are listed in Table 8.3. These can be answered in narrative form with reference to each of the headings in the table. Note that decisions about student

groupings and media selection are made while these components of the strategy are planned. Note also that these components of the instructional strategy apply to all of your objectives; that is, they are normally planned once for your total unit or lesson. The next section will apply to individual objectives, or clusters of objectives.

3. Indicate the content to be presented and the student participation activities for each objective or cluster of objectives. To do this, you may wish to use a form similar to the one included in Table 8.4. The objective number from your list of performance objectives is identified at the top of the form. Your form should include two main sections: content to be presented and student participation. The presentation section should briefly describe the required content and a typical example. In selecting your example, remember to choose a congruent one that is most likely to be familiar and interesting to the learners. The participation section should illustrate a sample practice exercise and the type of feedback that will be provided in the instruction. Table 8.4 will be used as part of the information required for assigning objectives to lessons and for developing or selecting instructional materials. Don't forget to include a component that indicates your strategy for teaching the terminal objective at the end of your instruction, and remember to include notes about student groupings and media selection.

4. Review your sequence and clusters of objectives, preinstructional activities, assessment, content presentation, student participation strategies, and student groupings and media selections. Using this information—coupled with the amount of time available for each lesson and the predicted attention span of target learners—assign objectives to lessons. The first session will undoubtedly contain preinstructional activities, and the last will include the posttest or feedback from the posttest. Intervening lessons should include time for any needed review, presentation, and participation.

5. Review the entire strategy again to consolidate your media selections and either (1) confirm that they fit an imposed delivery system or (2) select a delivery system that is compatible with the learning and performance context.

Several things should be noted about developing an instructional strategy as outlined here. First of all, certain instructional components must be considered in terms of the entire sequence of instruction; that is, preinstructional, assessment, and follow-through activities apply to the whole lesson. On the other hand, the content presentation, practice, and feedback sections must be completed for each objective or cluster of objectives, including your terminal objective. It is not intended that you write the whole lesson in the strategy. If you do, then you have written too much. The purpose of the written strategy is to require you to think through the entire lesson before you start developing or selecting any instruction.

EVALUATING AN INSTRUCTIONAL STRATEGY

With the completion of the instructional strategy, you are at another important checkpoint in the instructional design process. Now is a good time to do some more checking with both SMEs and learners. Their reactions will save

TABLE *8.3*	**Format for Writing Instructional Strategy for Preinstructional, Assessment, and Follow-Through Activities**

Preinstructional Activities:

MOTIVATION: Explain how you will gain learners' attention and maintain it throughout instruction.

OBJECTIVES: Explain how you will inform the learners about what they will be able to do when they finish your lesson. Explain why doing this is important to the learners.

STUDENT GROUPINGS AND MEDIA SELECTIONS: Explain how you will group students (e.g., individualized, small subgroups, total group). Describe the media selection (e.g., live lecture, videotape, print, Web-based).

Assessment:

PRETEST: Explain whether you will test for entry behaviors and what you will do if a learner does not have them. Explain also whether you will test for skills you will teach.

PRACTICE TESTS: Explain how you will use practice tests and rehearsal activities and where they will be located in the instruction.

POSTTEST: Explain when and how the posttest will be administered.

STUDENT GROUPINGS AND MEDIA SELECTIONS: Explain how you will group students for assessments (e.g., individualized, small subgroups, total group). Describe the media selection (e.g., paper and pencil, product development, live performance (videotaped), computer-administered and scored).

Follow-Through Activities:

MEMORY AID: Describe any memory aids that will be developed to facilitate retention of information and skills.

TRANSFER: Describe any special factors to be employed to facilitate performance transfer.

STUDENT GROUPINGS AND MEDIA SELECTIONS: Explain how you will group students (e.g., individualized, small subgroups, total group). Describe the media selection (e.g., live lecture, videotape, print, Web-based).

TABLE *8.4*	**Format for Writing Instructional Strategy for Content Presentation and Student Participation**

Objective #

Content Presentation

CONTENT:

EXAMPLES:

STUDENT GROUPINGS AND MEDIA SELECTIONS:

Student Participation

PRACTICE ITEMS AND ACTIVITIES:

FEEDBACK:

STUDENT GROUPINGS AND MEDIA SELECTIONS:

needless writing and revision later on. The time required is small compared to the value of the feedback.

Subject-matter experts and individuals familiar with the needs, interests, and attention spans of learners can be asked to review all three of your strategy tables and to pinpoint potential problems. Spending a short time with selected reviewers now may save hours during later stages of the instructional development process. You may need to provide reviewers with additional information such as a description of your instructional goal, a list of your objectives, and a description of the characteristics of your intended learners. This information will help reviewers judge the quality of the information included in your strategy.

Now is also the time to try out your instructional strategy and assessments with one or two learners. The procedure is to explain to the learners that you are developing some instruction and would like to see whether you have an adequate outline of what you are going to teach. Go through the strategy just as you have written it, but in this case simply explain it to the learners. You might show them some of the examples and ask them to do the practice activities. Do they understand, and can they participate? Give them some or all of your test items and see how they do. This is a very informal process, but it can yield valuable information that you can use to revise the strategy before you begin to write the instructional materials or instructor guide, create a storyboard, or prepare a computer-based instructional lesson.

EXAMPLES

The five phases to planning the instructional strategy for a unit of instruction are as follows:

1. Sequence and cluster objectives.
2. Plan preinstructional, assessment, and follow-through activities for the unit.
3. Plan the content presentations and student participation sections for each objective or cluster of objectives.
4. Assign objectives to lessons and estimate the time required for each.
5. Review the strategy to consolidate media selections and confirm or select a delivery system.

We will consider each of these in turn, with an example drawn from the group leadership instructional analyses in Chapter 4. For an additional example, see Appendices E and F for instructional strategies related to the unit on writing skills.

SEQUENCE AND CLUSTER OBJECTIVES

The first step in planning the instructional strategy is to sequence and cluster performance objectives. The subskills and instructional goal from Figure 4.6, "Lead group discussions," are included in Table 8.5. Fourteen clusters of objectives are identified, and two hours of instruction are planned for each cluster. Although not broken out for this illustration, the objectives for main steps 1 through 4 are each assigned to their own cluster. The objectives for main step 5, "Manage thought line," are divided into four separate clusters. The objectives for main skill 6, "Manage cooperative group interaction," are broken out into clusters 9 through 12. The content and nature of the objectives

TABLE *8.5*

Performance Objectives for Main Step 6 from Table 6.2 Sequenced and Clustered

Clusters*	Instructional Goal Steps			
1	Main step 1: Prepare for discussion			
2	Main step 2: Set agenda			
3	Main step 3: Convene group			
4	Main step 4: Introduce task			
5–8	Main step 5: Manage thought-line			
	Cluster 5	Cluster 6	Cluster 7	Cluster 8
9–12	Main step 6: Manage cooperative group interaction			
	Cluster 9 Objectives:	Cluster 10 Objectives:	Cluster 11 Objectives:	Cluster 12 Objectives:
	6.1.1 6.3.1	6.6.1 6.7.1	6.11.1	6.1: Main step 6
	6.1.2 6.4.1	6.6.2 6.7.2	6.12.1	
	6.2.1 6.4.2	6.6.3 6.8.1	6.12.2	
	6.2.2 6.5.1	6.6.4 6.9.1	6.13.1	
		6.6.5 6.9.2	6.14.1	
		6.6.6 6.10.1	6.14.2	
		6.6.7	6.15.1	
13	Main step 7: Summarize/conclude discussion			
14	Terminal objective			

*All clusters are designed to require approximately two hours (allocated time in learning center).

in each cluster were analyzed to ensure that they represented a logical set of skills. Cluster 9 contains the objectives related to recognizing and engendering cooperative behavior, and cluster 10 includes objectives for recognizing and defusing blocking behaviors of group members. Cluster 11 deals with recognizing and alleviating group stress. Cluster 12 focuses on main step 6, "Manage cooperative group interaction." In this cluster, objectives for all subordinate skills will be addressed together. Cluster 13 contains all objectives subordinate to main step 7, "Summarize and conclude discussion." Cluster 14 contains the terminal objective of all seven main steps and their subordinate skills. This cluster reflects putting the entire leadership process together.

The clusters of subskills planned and the amount of time assigned may need to be revised as you continue to develop the strategy. This initial structure, however, will help you focus on lessons rather than on individual objectives.

PLAN PREINSTRUCTIONAL, ASSESSMENT, AND FOLLOW-THROUGH ACTIVITIES

These learning components of the instructional strategy relate to the overall lesson or lessons and do not refer to individual instructional objectives within a lesson. First, how will you design the preinstructional activities? Remember, this area contains three separate sections: motivation, objectives, and entry behaviors. Table 8.6 shows the instructional strategy plans for these components. Notice that the information that will be used in the lessons is not included in the table, the objectives are not written out, and the entry behaviors are not listed. Instead, what you will need to do when developing the instruction is briefly described, along with notes about student groupings and media selection.

Preinstructional Activities:

MOTIVATION: The County NCW Coordinator will welcome the new leaders, provide praise for the volunteers, and discuss the critical role of NCW leaders in improving and maintaining the quality of life in the community. A uniformed police officer will welcome participants, discuss the relationship between NCW associations and the police department, present statistics on current crime and trends in neighborhoods (nature and frequency) around the state, discuss the financial and emotional costs of such crimes to families, and present actual statistics on the effectiveness of local NCW programs in reducing neighborhood crime. Actual local instances of NCW *leader* effectiveness will be highlighted.

OBJECTIVES: The critical role of the discussion leader in NCW groups will be described. An overview of the tasks leaders perform before and during meetings will be presented. A video of an actual group discussion, highlighting the role of the leader at each step, will be shown.

ENTRY BEHAVIORS: Learners will all have completed the instruction on problem-solving group discussion methods. They will be heterogeneous in their group-discussion skill levels due to their varying ages, education levels, work experience, and group problem-solving experience. They will enter the leadership instruction regardless of their posttest performance levels in the group-membership instruction.

Let's focus now on the assessment and follow-through phases of the instructional strategy for the instructional goal. How would you plan these activities for NCW leaders? Table 8.7 includes plans for the pretests, posttests, and follow-through activities. A pretest focused directly on the objectives included in each session will be administered at the beginning of the session except for clusters 8, 12, and 14. No pretest will be administered in these sessions because pretest data for these objectives, main steps 5, 6, and the terminal objective, will have been collected in preceding sessions. Likewise, a cluster-focused posttest will be administered at the conclusion of each session. A terminal objective posttest will be administered during the final session. Given the characteristics of the leaders and their situation as volunteers in their neighborhoods, the tests will be administered informally and represented as practice activities rather than as tests. It will be made clear to learners that the assessments are included to help them focus and practice skills and to help the staff learn about the strengths and weaknesses in the instruction.

The bottom portion of Table 8.7 contains the designers' prescriptions for follow-through activities. Included are plans for memory aids and transfer support as leaders plan and conduct meetings in their neighborhoods. Student groupings and media selections are also noted in the table.

PLAN CONTENT PRESENTATION AND STUDENT PARTICIPATION

Content presentation and learner participation sections make up the interactive part of the lesson. They are considered the exchange or interface point. The presentation section has two parts—namely, the content and examples. The learner participation component has two areas: sample practice items and activities, and the planned feedback strategy.

Table 8.8 includes performance objectives for main step 6, "Manage cooperative interaction," as an illustration of how this format is used to sketch out

TABLE *8.7*

Testing and Follow-Through Activities for Unit on Leading Group Discussion

Assessment:

PRETESTS: Due to the heterogeneous nature of the NCW leaders and the varied group participation experiences they have had, a pretest will be administered at the beginning of each of the sessions. The pretest will be informal and administered as an instructional activity to be collected. For sessions 1 through 3, the pretest will be a print document. For sessions 4 through 14, it will consist of a staged NCW meeting (videotape) that leaders watch. During viewing, they will use an observation form to tally the number of times named leader behaviors occur in the meeting. After instructional materials are developed and formative evaluation activities are complete, trainers may choose to dispense with the pretest for evaluation purposes. They may choose, however, to maintain the pretest as a preinstructional learning tool to focus learner attention on the objectives.

POSTTESTS: A small learning-site posttest will be administered at the conclusion of each session. Clusters 8 and 12 will each consist of a performance posttest that requires leaders to manage the discussion thought-line and manage the cooperative group interaction.

A final posttest will be administered during the last evening of training. To maximize the authenticity of the assessment, the examination will be designed to accommodate learners who are volunteers in a community setting, and it will be completed in three sections: a product section, a process section, and an analysis/feedback section.

The product part of the final posttest will require learners to complete the first three main steps (1. Prepare for discussion; 2. Set agenda; and 3. Convene group) in preparation for the first actual NCW meeting they will lead in their own neighborhoods. Leaders will independently make these preparations between the thirteenth and fourteenth instructional sessions and bring copies of their plans and materials to the last session. They will submit one copy of their plans (product) for review.

For the process portion of the posttest, leaders will break into small groups of four persons. Within their small groups, each member will lead a fifteen-minute group discussion on the "problem" topic he or she has prepared for the first community meeting. Their leadership performances will be videotaped within each group.

For the last part of the posttest, learners will discuss the leadership performances of members within their groups. During these discussions, members will focus on each leader's strengths relative to introducing the task, managing the thought-line, engendering cooperative member behaviors, defusing blocking behaviors, and alleviating group stress. Through these discussions, members will receive feedback on the positive aspects of their performances. Leaders may also review the videotapes of their own meetings to "watch themselves in action."

The effectiveness of the overall instruction will be assessed through the plans learners submitted, the videotapes of their leadership, and the interactive discussion in which learners critiqued each other's performances.

Follow-Through Activities

MEMORY AID: Memory aids planned include checklists of member and leader behaviors that leaders can use to focus their attention as they read meeting transcripts or view videos of simulated meetings. Leaders will take copies of the checklists with them for reference as they plan for meetings in their neighborhoods.

TRANSFER: The NCW area coordinator schedules biannual meetings with NCW leaders. During these meetings successes, issues, and problems encountered in leading group discussions within the neighborhoods will be shared. In addition, the NCW coordinator will remain on call for leaders as they plan their meetings. Leaders will also be given names and telephone numbers of all NCW leaders attending the training sessions. Hopefully, these leaders will form a network of support for each other, sharing ideas and plans. Finally, a sample of leaders will be selected for a performance-site posttest. Information gathered during these sessions on any assistance needed by leaders will be shared with the local NCW coordinator and local police representatives.

TABLE *8.8*

Instructional Strategy for the Content Presentation and Student Participation Components for Cluster 9 Performance Objectives (Main Step 6, Manage Cooperative Group Interaction)

Performance Objectives Subordinate to Main Step 6

6.1.1 When requested in writing to name group member actions that facilitate cooperative interaction, name those actions. At least six facilitating actions should be named.

Content Presentation

CONTENT: Cooperative interaction within group discussions depends on spontaneous positive actions that group members demonstrate when introducing their own ideas and when reacting to ideas introduced by others. An annotated NCW meeting dialogue will be provided with characters in the meeting demonstrating positive actions that foster cooperative group interaction. The annotation will point out the particular actions used by group members. The dialogue format will be used for its interest value and context validity.

EXAMPLES:

Personal actions	Reactions to others in discussion
1. Prepares for discussion before meeting convened	1. Considers all members' ideas impartially
2. Readily volunteers ideas and information	2. Listens attentively to others' comments
3. Invites others to participate	3. Gives others credit for their ideas
4. Demonstrates good will	4. Demonstrates trust in others' motives
5. Demonstrates open-mindedness	5. Resists pressures to conform
	6. Respects others' loyalties and needs

Student Participation

PRACTICE ITEMS:

1. List positive personal **actions** that group members can take to facilitate cooperative interaction during problem-solving discussions.
2. List positive personal **reactions** to others that group members can take to facilitate cooperative interaction during problem-solving discussions.
3. Think back over interactive discussions you have had in the past. Name the actions and reactions of others that made you feel that those conversing with you were interested in you, in your comments, and in the problem being discussed.

FEEDBACK: Repeat list of positive personal actions and reactions group-discussion members can demonstrate.

6.1.2 When asked in writing to indicate what members should do when their ideas are questioned by the group, name positive reactions that help ensure cooperative group interaction. Learner should name at least three possible reactions.

Content Presentation

CONTENT: Problem-solving group discussions naturally require give and take and a good deal of interactive brainstorming that often includes proposals of half-baked ideas. During brainstorming sessions, a member's ideas may be questioned for a myriad reasons. The manner in which a member responds to these questions can demonstrate her or his goodwill and open-mindedness and can help ensure cooperative group interaction.

EXAMPLES:

1. Listens attentively to members' questions (without interrupting)
2. Explains ideas more fully to help others understand the ideas and direction
3. Resists abandoning ideas too quickly just because they are questioned
4. Participates in modifying initial ideas to make them more acceptable to the group
5. Readily admits errors in ideas or judgment

Student Participation

PRACTICE ITEMS:

1. List positive **reactions** a group member can make when her or his proposals or ideas are questioned by other group members.
2. Think back over interactive discussions you have had in the past. Name the **positive reactions** that you have seen others make when their ideas were questioned or not readily accepted by other members of the group.

FEEDBACK: Restate positive reactions to others' questions.

| TABLE *8.8* | (Continued) |

6.2.1 Given written descriptions of group members' facilitating actions during a meeting, indicate whether the actions are likely to facilitate cooperative group interaction. Learner should correctly classify at least 80 percent of the actions depicted.

Content Presentation

CONTENT: A written NCW meeting scenario will be presented with actual characters and dialogue. The dialogue will include both positive personal actions and positive personal reactions of meeting participants.
EXAMPLES: (See 6.1.1 above)

Student Participation

PRACTICE ITEMS:
Using a checklist of positive personal actions and reactions, identify characters in the written scenario who demonstrate each positive action or reaction.
FEEDBACK: Complete checklist with characters' names inserted for each action and reaction.

6.2.2 Given videos of staged NCW meetings depicting facilitating member actions, indicate whether the members' actions are likely to facilitate cooperative group interaction. Learner should classify correctly at least 80 percent of the actions demonstrated.

Content Presentation

CONTENT: A simulated NCW discussion group will be staged and videotaped with discussion members exhibiting positive personal actions and reactions during the meeting. Learners will watch the group members in action as they propose and discuss ideas.
EXAMPLES: (See 6.1.1 above)

Student Participation

PRACTICE ITEMS:
Using a checklist of positive personal actions and reactions, identify characters in the simulated meeting who demonstrate each positive action or reaction.
FEEDBACK: Complete checklist with characters' names inserted for those actions and reactions demonstrated.

6.3.1 When asked in writing to name leader actions that encourage and stifle discussion member cooperation, name these actions. Learner should name at least ten encouraging and corresponding stifling actions.

Content Presentation

CONTENT: As the discussion group leader, there are several actions you can take that encourage cooperative group interaction. For each of these cooperating actions, there are corresponding actions that tend to stifle group cooperation.
EXAMPLES:

Cooperation Encouraging Actions	Cooperation Stifling Actions
1. Suggests points of discussion as questions	1. Prescribes topics for the group to consider
2. Uses an investigative, inquiring tone	2. Uses an authoritative tone
3. Uses open terms such as *perhaps* and *might*	3. Uses prescriptive terms such as *must* or *should*
4. Hesitates and pauses between speakers	4. Fills quiet gaps with personal points of view or solutions
5. Willingly turns over the floor to group members who interrupt	5. Continues to talk over interrupting member, or interrupts member
6. Encompasses total group with eyes, and invites all to participate freely	6. Focuses gaze on a few members
7. Nonverbally (eyes, gestures) encourages speaker to address group	7. Holds speaker's attention
8. Uses comments that keep discussion centered in the group	8. Encourages discussion to flow through leader by evaluating member comments
9. Encourages volunteerism (e.g., "Who has experience with …")	9. Designates speakers and speaking order (e.g., "Beth, what do you think about …")

TABLE *8.8* | (Continued)

10. Refers to *us, we, our*	10. Refers to *I, me, mine,* or *your*
11. Acknowledges group accomplishments	11. Acknowledges own accomplishments or those of particular members
12. Praises group effort and accomplishment	12. Singles out particular people for praise

Student Participation

PRACTICE ITEMS:

1. List strategies you can use as group-discussion leader to encourage cooperative group interaction.

2. Think back over interactive discussions you have had in the past. Name the actions and reactions of the discussion leader that you believe engendered cooperative interaction among group members.

FEEDBACK: Repeat list of positive leader actions and reactions that engender cooperative interaction among group members.

6.4.1 Given written descriptions of a group leader's action during a meeting, indicate whether the leader exhibits actions that are likely to encourage or stifle cooperative group interaction. Learner should correctly classify at least 80 percent of the actions depicted.

Content Presentation

CONTENT: A written NCW meeting scenario will be presented with actual characters and dialogue. The dialogue will focus particularly on leader actions and reactions designed to encourage positive member interaction and participation.

EXAMPLES: (See 6.3.1 above)

Student Participation

PRACTICE ITEMS:

Using a checklist of actions the leader can take to encourage or stifle positive member interaction, identify the particular behaviors exhibited by the leader in the written scenario.

FEEDBACK: Complete checklist with described leader actions checked.

6.4.2 Given videos of staged NCW meetings depicting staged leader's actions, classify the leader's actions that are likely to encourage and stifle member cooperation. Learner should classify correctly at least 80 percent of the encouraging and stifling actions demonstrated.

Content Presentation

CONTENT: A simulated NCW discussion group will be staged and recorded with videotape. The group leader will exhibit actions designed to encourage and stifle member interaction during the meeting. Learners will watch the leader "in action" as he/she manages the group.

EXAMPLES: (See 6.3.1 above)

Student Participation

PRACTICE ITEMS:

Using a checklist of actions the leader can take to encourage and stifle positive member interaction, identify the particular behaviors exhibited by the leader in the video.

FEEDBACK: Complete checklist with exhibited leader actions checked.

6.5.1 In simulated NCW problem-solving meetings with learner acting as group leader, initiate actions to engender cooperative behavior among members. Group members cooperate with each other and with leader during discussion.

Content Presentation

CONTENT: Learners will break into small groups of four and each group will receive a written description and background information for a particular neighborhood safety problem as well as a meeting agenda for discussing the given problem. After reading the material, one member will serve as the discussion leader and the remaining three members will serve as group members. (Different problem scenarios will be provided for each of the four group members to enable each to rehearse group interaction leadership.)

Student Participation

PRACTICE: The leader will introduce the problem to the group, set the climate for cooperative interaction, and lead a simulated group discussion for ten minutes.

FEEDBACK: Following the discussion, group members will discuss positive aspects of the leader's performance. These discussions will be held within the small group only.

the instructional strategy. Each objective is stated, followed by a description of the content and examples to be presented. In cases where videotapes will be used to present content, a description of the action is described. Notice that no new content about the objective is included for objective 6.5.1 because the skill-related content was presented in the preceding objectives. Instead, media, materials, and general instructions for interactive meetings are described. In this instance the content presentation and student participation components are intertwined. This example illustrates how hierarchical skills build on each other and how the table format can be adapted for each objective.

At this point, we have completed examples of how to design the instructional strategy for the following: (1) sequencing and clustering objectives; (2) planning preinstructional, assessment, and follow-through activities; and (3) identifying content presentation and learner participation activities. Student groupings and media selections have also been noted as the instructional strategy was planned.

ALLOCATE ACTIVITIES TO SESSIONS

With this information complete, we should review it and allocate prescribed activities to lessons. Lesson prescriptions are included in Table 8.9. Compare the strategy for individual sessions in Table 8.9 with the initial sequence and cluster of objectives in Table 8.5. Notice that we predicted a total of fourteen two-hour clusters in Table 8.5, but added an additional two hours of instruction for fifteen sessions in Table 8.9. This was necessary to allow for preinstructional, motivational, and pretest activities in the first session. Within the remaining sessions, pretest and posttest activities are added. Again, you must consider the timelines tentative until you have developed the instruction and tested it with actual learners.

CONSOLIDATE MEDIA SELECTION AND CONFIRM OR SELECT DELIVERY SYSTEM

The last phase of planning is to review the instructional strategy to consolidate media selections and ensure compatibility with the delivery system. While you were planning the instructional strategy, you considered how you would mediate instruction by noting the domain of learning in each objective and examining the conditions, behavior, and content in the objective. You also considered which medium would best replicate conditions in the learning and performance contexts. You began by selecting the ideal media formats for the domains of learning and objective components, but you may have compromised and chosen the best medium given constraints such as budget, personnel, equipment, and delivery system and learning-site constraints. After choosing the best medium for each objective or cluster of objectives, it makes sense to examine the entire set of selections for patterns or common media prescriptions across the objectives.

Table 8.10 contains a summary of media prescriptions taken from the instructional strategy for the instructional goal "Lead group discussions, Step 6: Manage cooperative group interaction." The first column contains the class sessions and the second column contains the objectives in each session. Types of learning are listed in the third column, and the fourth column identifies the initial media selections based on the domain of learning, the objective, resources available for materials development, and facilities and equipment present in the county learning centers.

TABLE 8.9 | **Lesson Allocation Based on Instructional Strategy**

Session	Activities
1	Introductory and motivational materials: 1. NCW coordinator gives welcome, praise for leader volunteers, and overview of workshop (objectives). 2. Police officer gives welcome, presentation of statewide/countrywide neighborhood crime problems, and presentation of crime-reducing influence of active NCW groups. 3. Pretest with group discussion feedback pointing to main steps in leadership process.
2	Pretest; introduction; instruction and practice activities on objectives for main step 1, "Prepare for discussion"; and posttest.
3	Pretest; introduction; instruction and practice activities on objectives for main step 2, "Set agenda"; and posttest.
4	Pretest; introduction; instruction and practice activities on objectives for main step 3, "Convene group"; and posttest.
5	Pretest; introduction; instruction and practice activities on objectives for main step 4, "Introduce task"; and posttest.
6–9	Each of these sessions will contain a pretest; introduction; instruction and practice activities on objectives for main step 5, "Manage thought line"; and posttest.

Session 6	Session 7	Session 8	Session 9
2 hours	2 hours	2 hours	2 hours

Session	Activities
10–13	Sessions 10, 11, and 12 will contain a pretest; introduction; instruction and practice activities on objectives for main step 6, "Manage cooperative group interaction"; and posttest. Session 13 will contain an introduction and interactive groups in which leaders manage group interaction. No pretest or posttest will be administered. A debriefing and discussion session will follow group rehearsals.

Session 10 Objectives:		Session 11 Objectives:		Session 12 Objectives:	Session 13 Objectives:
6.1.1	6.3.1	6.6.1	6.7.1	6.11.1	6.1: Main step 6
6.1.2	6.4.1	6.6.2	6.7.2	6.12.1	
6.2.1	6.4.2	6.6.3	6.8.1	6.12.2	
6.2.2	6.5.1	6.6.4	6.9.1	6.13.1	
		6.6.5	6.9.2	6.14.1	
		6.6.6	6.10.1	6.14.2	
		6.6.7		6.15.1	

Session	Activities
14	Pretest; introduction; instruction and practice activities on objectives for main step 7, "Summarize/conclude discussion"; and posttest.
15	Give welcome, instructions for session, and three-part posttest for terminal objective, debriefing.

Considering the entire set of prescriptions in column 4 of Table 8.10, you can see that a pattern exists: live group simulations, videotapes, printed dialogue scripts, and printed dialogue with annotation are each repeated several times. In the performance site, newly trained leaders will work interactively within a group, so using live group simulations during instruction will closely resemble the context within which NCW leaders must work. They will also need to make inferences from group interactions, so observing televised groups as they interact will help support concept acquisition.

TABLE *8.10*

Consolidation of Media Selections and Choice of Delivery System for Main Step 6, Sessions 10–13 (from Table 8.9)

Session	Objectives	Type(s) of Learning	Media Selections and Student Groupings	Delivery System(s)
10	6.1.1–2 6.2.1–2 6.3.1 6.4.1–2 6.5.1	Verbal information and intellectual skills	Instructor-led, large-group lecture/discussion Videotaped simulations Printed dialogue with annotations	Web-based instruction with e-mail discussion group
11	6.6.1–7 6.7.1–2 6.8.1 6.9.1–2 6.10.1	Same as above	Same as above	Same as above
12	6.11.1 6.12.1–2 6.13.1 6.14.1–2 6.15.1	Same as above	Same as above	Same as above
13	6.1 (Main step 6)	Intellectual skills	Instructor-led, large group lecture/discussion Small group interactive role-play Small group discussion	Instructor-led, large group lecture/discussion Small group interactive role-play Small group discussion

Providing printed dialogue scripts of meetings rather than didactic descriptions of meetings is also prescribed for authenticity, because interpreting meeting dialogue and members' actions will be the focus during learners' actual work.

The first delivery system considered was classroom lecture/discussion, because the set of media prescriptions could be managed easily in a traditional county training center classroom with an instructor presenting content, distributing handouts, facilitating interaction, providing feedback, and managing assessment and mediated presentations. After reviewing the media selections a second time, reconsidering the learning and performance contexts, the decision was made to consolidate most media into a Web-based, distance learning delivery system. For authenticity and transfer, however, the live group simulations would have to be retained for advanced practice, feedback, and posttesting. These media consolidation and delivery system decisions are reflected in column 5 of Table 8.10.

The decision for independent, Web-based instruction was made for several reasons. The learners are mature, motivated adults who have volunteered for the NCW responsibility, and the novelty value and convenience of distance learning should engender some initial motivation. Most learners have computers with Internet access in their homes, and others have access at work or in a local branch library. Although the initial audience for the instruction is not large, the training program will be repeated and could be exported to other counties promoting development of NCW groups. There is some turnover in the job and new NCW volunteers could be trained with a combination of the Web instruction and peer tutoring from successful NCW leaders. From a practical perspective, the distance learning format will standardize instruction, ensure uniform results, save instructor time, and save a lot of student travel time and miles. Finally, there is sufficient money in the grant budget to pay for Web development, formative evaluation, and revision, and the county information systems division has agreed to provide server space and software maintenance.

After consolidating media selections and confirming or selecting a delivery system, it may be necessary to revisit the previous step, "Allocate activities to lessons," and touch up some of that planning. This is particularly true if selection of a delivery system was delayed until this point in the design process. In most instructional design contexts the delivery system would have been assumed or imposed at the outset of the process, and the designer merely confirms delivery system capability for the media selections. The reader is referred back to Figure 8.1 for a visual representation of the overall process of developing an instructional strategy and choosing a delivery system.

The instructional strategy for main step 6, "Manage cooperative group interaction," is now complete, and we have the prescriptions necessary to begin developing materials.

Recall that readers interested in a school-based example may refer to Appendix E.

SUMMARY

Materials you will need in order to develop your instructional strategy include the instructional goal, the learner and context analyses, the instructional analysis, the performance objectives, and the assessment items. You will need to reference these materials several times as you design your strategy.

The instructional strategy is a prescription that will be used for developing or selecting instructional materials. The first consideration is sequencing the content for teaching and making clusters of logical groupings of skills in the instructional analysis.

Four learning components in the instructional strategy are based on the work of educational psychologists, and these components guide learners' intellectual processing through the mental states and activities that foster learning. These four components include preinstructional activities, content presentation, student participation with feedback, and follow-through activities. The assessment component is included in the strategy to facilitate instructional management. Assessment enables us to tailor instruction to the needs of learners, to evaluate the quality of instructional materials, and to evaluate the progress of learners. Although the major function of assessment in the strategy is management, it also can support learning when corrective feedback about performance is provided to learners. As these components are being planned, the designer specifies student groupings and selects one or more media that can be used to deliver each component. The selection decision is based on theory and administrative (or logistical) considerations.

Instruction is presented to students in the sequence of the named components in the strategy; however, the strategy is not designed in this order. The first step in designing the strategy is to sequence and cluster objectives for presentation. The second is to prescribe the preinstructional, assessment, and follow-through strategies. The third is to prescribe the content presentation and student participation strategies. The fourth is to assign objectives to lessons. The final step is to review the instructional strategy to consolidate media selections and confirm or select a delivery system.

The type of instructional goal is an important consideration when designing your strategy. Whether intellectual skills, verbal information, motor skills, or attitudes, all five of the components of the strategy are important. Each type of goal, however, may require unique activities for each of the instructional strategy components.

In creating each component of your strategy, you should also consider the characteristics of your target students; their needs, interests, and experiences; and the information about how to gain and maintain their attention throughout the five learning components of instruction. Keller's ARCS model provides a handy structure for considering how to design materials that motivate students to learn.

With your strategy complete, you can begin to develop instruction based on the prescriptions in the strategy. Before proceeding, however, you should request an evaluation of your materials from content experts as well as from one or more of your target learners.

For readers who are doing an instructional design project as they work through this text, we suggest that you read Chapter 9 before developing your instructional strategy, paying particular attention to our recommendation that first-time designers plan self-paced instruction in illustrated text format.

PRACTICE

To provide practice in developing an instructional strategy for a unit of instructional materials, we have selected the checking account example. Recall that your target group consists of college-bound, high school seniors, all of whom have the required arithmetic entry behaviors for beginning your unit.

To complete this activity, work through the following steps.

1. Sequence and cluster objectives for lessons. Assume that each class period is fifty minutes long. Remember that at this point, you are simply predicting how many of the tasks can be accomplished during a fifty-minute period and clustering similar content together. (Refer to Figure 4.8 and concentrate only on the main steps in the goal, or 1.0 through 5.0.)

2. Develop a table that describes preinstructional and assessment activities for only the objectives included in step 2.0, "Deposit money into a checking account." The steps are illustrated in Figure 4.9, and the performance objectives and test items you will need for this exercise are included in Table 7.11. See Table 8.11 in the Feedback section for examples.

3. Develop presentation and practice components of an instructional strategy for the *depositing money* cluster of procedures, step 2 in Table

Sample Bank Deposit Slip,
Front and Back, and
Transaction Register

Front Side of Slip

	Dollars	Cents
Currency		
Coins		
C		
H___		
E		
C___		
K		
S		
Total from other side		
TOTAL		

Back Side of Slip

Bank Number	Dollars	Cents
TOTAL CHECKS		

Transaction Record

ITEM NUMBER	DATE	TRANSACTION DESCRIPTION	SUBTRACTIONS/ WITHDRAWALS	✓	ADDITIONS/ DEPOSITS	BALANCE

7.11. To aid you with this activity, a sample bank deposit slip and transaction register for a checking account are provided in Figure 8.3 as a reference for your work. See Table 8.12 in the Feedback section for examples.

FEEDBACK

1. Possible sequence and cluster of objectives for unit on opening and maintaining a checking account.

    LESSON 1: Introduction, pretest over all main steps in goal (1.0–5.0)

    LESSON 2: Step 1 and all related objectives

    LESSON 3: Step 2 and all related objectives

    LESSON 4: Step 3 and all related objectives

    LESSON 5: Step 4 and all related objectives

    LESSON 6: Step 5 and all related objectives

    LESSON 7: Posttest over all main steps in goal (1.0–5.0)

2. See Table 8.11 for preinstructional, assessment, and follow-through activities.

3. See Table 8.12 for content presentation and learner participation only for step 2, "Deposit money into a checking account."

TABLE *8.11*	**Preinstructional, Assessment, and Follow-Through Activities for Banking Instructional Goal**

Preinstructional Activities: (Entire unit)

MOTIVATION: Introductory material will be included regarding: (1) why students should have a checking account while in college, (2) the benefits of paying bills using checks, (3) who can legally have a checking account, and (4) legal penalties for purposefully misusing checking accounts. Several types of sample checks will be used as illustrations in the materials.

OBJECTIVES: A list of the overall objectives that includes only the five major steps in the checking account procedure will be provided.

PREREQUISITE SKILLS: It will be assumed that the entry behaviors of adding and subtracting decimal numbers will be present in college-bound high school seniors.

Assessment: (Entire unit)

PRETEST: There will be no entry behaviors tested. A pretest will be given since some students may already have their own checking accounts. The test will cover all major objectives in the unit.

POSTTEST: A posttest will be administered only at the conclusion of instruction. The test will be paper-and-pencil simulation and cover the following main objectives:

1. Given simulated signature cards and application to open a checking account, complete forms.
2. Given a specified amount of money and checks, complete a deposit form.
3. Given simulated checks and specified amounts of money, write checks to persons or organizations prescribed.
4. Given receipts for deposits and withdrawals, make specified entries in a simulated check register.
5. Given a simulated bank statement, sample checks, and a check register, balance the checking account.

Follow-Through Activities:

MEMORY AID: Banks provide preprinted forms customers use when making checking account transactions. These forms typically contain the titles and information customers need to conduct their work preprinted on the forms; thus, memorization of the procedures is unnecessary.

TRANSFER: Instructional materials mimicking actual bank forms in format and information will be created. With parents' permission, actual checking account forms from the family bank can be brought to class by students. Using authentic appearing forms will aid students in transferring the skills they learn in class to opening and managing their own checking accounts.

3. Information presentation and sample practice and feedback activities for only step 2, "Deposit money into a checking account."

TABLE *8.12*

Content Presentation and Learner Participation Activities for Banking Instructional Goal

Objective 2.1 Indicate where to obtain a deposit slip

Content Presentation

CONTENT:
Deposit slips are located in (1) back of checkbook, (2) from bank.

EXAMPLE:

1. Show preprinted form from back of checkbook with identifying information.

2. Show generic deposit slip from bank.

Student Participation

PRACTICE ITEMS:
1. List two places where you can obtain a deposit slip to deposit money into your checking account.
   a. _____
   b. _____

FEEDBACK:
1. Back of checkbook
2. From bank

Objective 2.2 Complete information to identify depositor and date

Content Presentation

CONTENT:
1. To identify the depositor, the user must add name, address, account number, and date on generic deposit slip.
2. User must add date to preprinted deposit slip.

EXAMPLE:
Sample preprinted and generic deposit slips will be illustrated with arrows pointing to where information should be placed.

Student Participation

PRACTICE ITEMS:
1. List information that should be provided on a generic deposit slip.
   a. _____
   b. _____
   c. _____
   d. _____
2. Complete the sample generic deposit slip to indicate the depositor and account.

TABLE 8.12	(Continued)

FEEDBACK:
1. a. Name
   b. Address
   c. Date
   d. Account number
2. Show generic deposit slip completed with information.

Objective 2.3.1 Determine where currency and coins are entered on deposit slip

Content Presentation

CONTENT:
1. The top line of this deposit slip is reserved for dollar bills. The word *currency* is used to indicate where to place the amount of money. Have students note the division for dollars and cents.
2. Show completed currency line:

Currency

Coin

Student Participation

PRACTICE ITEMS:
1. Given an illustration of a blank deposit slip, place an X beside the line where the amount of dollar bills to be deposited should be written.
2. Select the currency line that is correctly completed.

	Dollars	Cents
A. Currency	400	00
B. Currency		400
C. Currency	400	20

FEEDBACK:
1. Illustrate where amount of dollar bills should be inserted.
2. A is correct; B has the currency listed in the coin space; C has coins included in the currency line.

Objective 2.3.2 Count money and enter the totals in the appropriate spaces on the deposit slip

Content Presentation

CONTENT:
1. Count all dollar bills, total the amount, and enter the total on the currency line of the deposit slip.
2. Count all coins and record the total on the line marked "coins."

TABLE 8.12 | (Continued)

EXAMPLE:

1. *Dollars*

4	10 dollar bills =	$40.00
3	5 dollar bills =	$15.00
4	1 dollar bills =	$ 4.00
		$59.00

2. *Coins*

6	quarters	=	1.50
3	dimes	=	.30
4	nickels	=	.20
3	pennies	=	.03
			$2.03

	Dollars	Cents
Currency	59	00
Coin	2	03

Student Participation

PRACTICE ITEMS:

1. Total the money described below and enter the total amount in the appropriate lines in the deposit slip.

Dollars		*Coins*			Dollars	Cents
#	*Value*	#	*Value*			
1	50.00	4	.50	Currency		
3	20.00	3	.25	Coins		
6	10.00	7	.10	Checks		
2	5.00	2	.05			
7	1.00	3	.01	Total		

Feedback:
Dollars = $187.00
Coins =   3.58

	Dollars	Cents
Currency	187	00
Coins	3	58
Checks		
Total		

TABLE *8.12* | (Continued)

Objective 2.4.1 Sign checks and enter account number on each

Content Presentation

CONTENT:
Sign checks and record account number of depositor on each.

EXAMPLE:
Illustrate back of check with account number and signature included.

Student Participation:

PRACTICE ITEMS:
1. Sign your name as it appears on the signature card of your account and record your account number beneath it.

FEEDBACK:
Show illustration of back of check with signature and account number complete.

Objective 2.4.2 Identify where checks are entered on front and back of deposit slip

Content Presentation

CONTENT:
Checks are listed one at a time on the deposit slip. Record the bank number for each check, which is located in the upper right corner of the check, and total amount of the check in the money column. The bank number is recorded to the left.

EXAMPLES:

Back side of deposit slip

		Dollars	Cents
	C Bank Number		
	H _____		
Show sample check including bank number and value of check	E _____		
	C _____		
	K _____		
	S _____		

TABLE *8.12* | (Continued)

Student Participation

PRACTICE ITEMS:

1. Besides the amount of the check, what other identifying information about the check should you write on the deposit slip?
   _____

2. Circle the bank number on this sample check.

Sara Jones	400
402 Shadow Lane	<u>63-656</u>
	631

Date _____

Pay to the order of _____ $ _____

_____ Dollars

_____

4023010201

3. Where on the deposit slip should you write the bank number of checks being deposited?_____

FEEDBACK:

1. Bank number
2. Show check with bank number circled. Explain other numbers on check as check number and account number.
3. To the left of the amount of money on the same line.

Objective 2.4.3 Record each check, including the bank number and amount, on the deposit slip

Content Presentation

CONTENT:
Record each check deposited including the amount and the bank number on the deposit slip.

EXAMPLE: Provide students with several example checks of varying sizes and amounts from several different banks and a deposit slip. Point out on the deposit slip where to record the information for each check included.

TABLE *8.12* | (Continued)

		Dollars	Cents
C Bank number			
H			
E			
C			
K			
S			
	Total Checks		

Student Participation

PRACTICE ITEMS:
Provide students with a variety of checks and a deposit slip. Have students record relevant data from checks onto deposit slip.

FEEDBACK:
Provide a sample deposit slip correctly completed for sample checks used. Point out where each type of information is recorded on the deposit slip.

Objective 2.4.4 Sum the checks recorded on the back of the deposit slip

Content Presentation

CONTENT: Add together the total amount of checks listed on the back of the deposit slip and record the total at the bottom of the form.

EXAMPLE:

	Bank number	Dollars	Cents
C			
H	36-142	100	00
E	14-426	32	50
C	18-421	45	00
K	1-402	1000	00
S			
Total Checks		1177	50

TABLE *8.12* | (Continued)

Student Participation

PRACTICE ITEMS:

Sum the amount of checks listed and record the total at the bottom of the form in the space marked "Total Checks."

	Bank number	Dollars	Cents
C			
H	12-143	15	30
E	19-125	5	20
C	3-402	103	50
K	12-143	2000	75
S			

Total Checks

FEEDBACK: $2124.75

Objective 2.4.5 Record subtotal of checks onto front of deposit slip

Content Presentation

CONTENT:

The total amount of checks listed on the back side of the deposit slip should be transferred to the front and placed in the line marked "total from other side."

EXAMPLE: Deposit Slip Front Side

Currency		100	00
Coin		4	32
C	90-425	32	50
H	36-102	150	00
E	15-432	630	15
C			
K			
S			
Total from other side		2124	75

Deposit Slip Back Side

C	Bank number	Dollars	Cents
H	12-143	15	30
E	19-125	5	20
C	3-402	103	50
K	12-143	2000	75
S			
Total Checks		2124	75

TABLE *8.12* | (Continued)

Student Participation

PRACTICE ITEMS:
Locate the total amount of checks listed on the back of the deposit slip and transfer the total to the front of the deposit slip in the correct space.

Back side of slip

12-264	200	00
32-105	50	10
32-105	2	20
12-143	150	00
Total	402	30

Front side of slip

Currency		
Coin		
Total from other side		

FEEDBACK:
Front side of slip

Total from other side	402	30

Objective 2.5   Record total amount of deposit on slip

Content Presentation

CONTENT:
Record total amount of deposit (cash and checks) on slip.

EXAMPLE:
Provide illustration with correct total entered.

Student Participation

PRACTICE ITEM:
Sum the sample deposit slip and enter the total in the correct line.

FEEDBACK:
Provide illustration with correct total entered and highlighted.

TABLE *8.12* | (Continued)

Objective 2.6   Give deposit slip, checks, and/or money to teller

Content Presentation

CONTENT:
Give deposit slip, checks, and/or money to teller or deposit at automatic teller machine.

EXAMPLE:
Illustrate complete deposit slip, money, and checks, and give to a teller at the window.

Student Participation

PRACTICE ITEM:
To whom should you give the deposit slip and money?

FEEDBACK:
Teller

Objective 2.7   Verify total deposit on receipt

Content Presentation

CONTENT:
You will receive a receipt from the deposit.
1. Verify that the amount recorded as a deposit is correct.

EXAMPLE:
Show illustration of deposit receipt with amount of deposit highlighted.

Student Participation

PRACTICE ITEM:
When a deposit receipt is returned by the teller, what should you do?

FEEDBACK:
1. Verify amount.

Objective 2.8.1 Record transaction in check register

Content Presentation

CONTENT:
You should always record the amount of your deposit in your check register.
1. Record the date of the deposit
2. Under "Transaction Description," write *Deposit*.
3. In "Additions" column, write the total amount of the deposit.
4. Sum the deposit and the previous balance to obtain the new balance.
5. Record the new balance in the last column marked "Balance."

TABLE *8.12* | (Continued)

EXAMPLE:
Show illustration of check register with deposit information recorded and highlighted.

Student Participation

PRACTICE ITEM:
Examine the following deposit receipt and checking account transaction register form. Correctly enter the deposit in the transaction register.

FEEDBACK:
Repeat the transaction register form with the deposit information correctly entered.

Objective 2.8.2 Place deposit receipt in bank records

Content Presentation

CONTENT:
You should always store your deposit receipt in your banking records to prove that you have made a deposit should the bank make an error in crediting your account.

EXAMPLE:
Show illustration of file folder containing deposit receipts.

Student Participation

PRACTICE ITEM:
Suppose you discover when going over your bank statement that the bank has not given you credit for a deposit you recently made. What proof do you have that you actually made the deposit?

FEEDBACK:
The deposit receipt.

Beaudin, B. P. (1987). Enhancing the transfer of job-related learning from the learning environment to the workplace. *Performance and Instruction, 26* (9 & 10), 19–21. Tips on how to analyze the work site to plan instruction that results in the learning of skills that get used on the job.

Broad, M. L., & Newstrom, J. W. (1993). *Transfer of training.* Reading, MA: Addison-Wesley. Describes many factors regarding transfer that should be considered before, during, and after instruction.

Carey, J.O. (1998). Library skills, information skills, and information literacy: Implications for teaching and learning. *School Library Media Quarterly Online.* Vol. 1. Available: http://www.ala.org/aasl/SLMQ/skills.html.

Carey, L. M. (2001). *Measuring and evaluating school learning* (3rd ed.). Boston, MA: Allyn and Bacon. Includes several different approaches to analyze goals and identify content.

Clark, R. (1983). Reconsidering research on learning from media. *Review of Educational Research, 53* (4), 445.

Dills, C. R., & Romiszowski, A. J. (Eds.) (1997). *Instructional development paradigms.* Englewood Cliffs, NJ: Educational Technology Publications. A handbook that addresses many instructional strategy issues along with many other issues related to the field of instructional design.

Ertmer, P., & Newby, T. (1993). Behaviorism, cognitivism, constructivism: Comparing critical features from an instructional design perspective. *Performance Improvement Quarterly, 6* (40), 50–72. Excellent review of theories that affect instructional design practice. Indicates implications for the instructional designer.

Gagné, E. D. (1985). *The cognitive psychology of school learning.* Boston, MA: Little, Brown. Gagné describes different types of school learning and suggests strategies for teaching them.

Gagné, R. M. (1985). *Conditions of learning* (4th ed.). New York: Holt, Rinehart and Winston. Gagné describes in detail the factors that should be present to stimulate learning in each of the learning domains.

Gagné, R. M., Briggs, L. J., & Wager, W. W. (1992). *Principles of instructional design* (4th ed.). New York: Holt, Rinehart and Winston. The chapter on the events of instruction in this book will provide additional background on the major concepts that have been included.

Gagné, R. M., & Driscoll, M. P. (1988). *Essentials of learning for instruction.* Englewood Cliffs, NJ: Prentice-Hall. This book includes a description of the events of instruction as they are incorporated into an instructional strategy.

Gagné, R. M., & Medsker, K. L. (1996). *The conditions of learning: Training applications.* Fort Worth, TX: Harcourt Brace College Publishers. This book integrates much of Gagné's early work on conditions of learning with the current world of training in business and industry.

Hannafin, M. J., & Hooper, S. R. (1993). Learning principles. In Fleming, M., & Levie, W. H. (Eds.). *Instructional message design.* Englewood Cliffs, NJ: Educational Technology Publications. Description of fundamental principles for instructional presentations, practice, and feedback.

Journal of Educational Psychology includes a variety of research articles about the effectiveness of various instructional strategies that might be incorporated in instructional materials.

Keller, J. M. (1987). Strategies for stimulating the motivation to learn. *Performance and Instruction, 26* (8), 1–7.

Keller, J. M. (1987). The systematic process of motivational design. *Performance and Instruction, 26* (9), 1–8.

Keller, J., & Burkman, E. (1993). Motivation principles. In Fleming, M., & Levie, W. H. (Eds.). *Instructional message design.* Englewood Cliffs, NJ: Educational Technology Publications. Excellent review of both learner and text characteristics that are important to the designer.

Moore, M. G., & Kearsley G. (1996). *Distance education: A systems view.* New York: Wadsworth. 197–212. A good overview of distance education with summaries of research findings.

Okey, J., & Santiago, R. S. (1991). Integrating instructional and motivational design. *Performance Improvement Quarterly, 4* (2), 11–21. This article provides an example of the use of Keller's ARCS model.

Reiser, R. A., & Gagné, R. M. (1983). *Selecting media for instruction.* Englewood Cliffs, NJ: Educational Technology Publications. This book describes an easy-to-use media selection method that is based on Gagne's domains of learning.

Romiszowski, A. J. (1993). Psychomotor principles. In Fleming, M., & Levie, W. H. (Eds.). *Instructional message design.* Englewood Cliffs, NJ: Educational Technology Publications. One of the few sources that describes the principles of motor skills instruction for the designer. Excellent summary of the fundamentals.

Rossett, A., & Gautier-Downes, J. (1991). *A Handbook of Job Aids.* San Diego, CA: Pfeiffer and Co. Procedures for developing job aids, along with numerous examples.

Russell, T. L. (1993). The "no significant difference" phenomenon as reported in research reports, summaries, and papers. Raleigh: North Carolina State University Office of Instructional Telecommunications.

Russell, T. L. (1999). The "no significant difference" phenomenon: A comparative research annotated bibliography on technology for distance education. Raleigh: North Carolina State University Office of Instructional Telecommunications. Russell maintained a Web site on the NSD phenomenon with annual updates until 1999, when the site was scaled back in favor of a print version that can be ordered from NCSU.

Smith, P. L., & Ragan, T. J. (1999). *Instructional design* (2nd ed.). New York: John Wiley & Sons, Inc. In-depth descriptions of a variety of instructional strategies.

9 DEVELOPING INSTRUCTIONAL MATERIALS

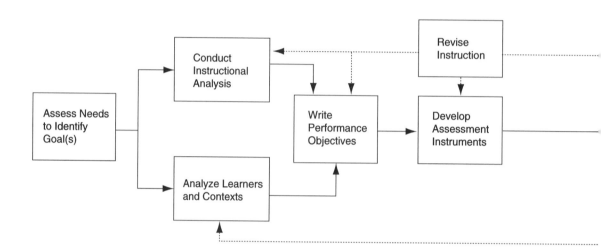

OBJECTIVES

- Describe factors that may cause revisions in media selections and delivery systems for given instruction.
- Name and describe the components of an instructional package.
- List four categories of criteria for judging the appropriateness of existing instructional materials.
- Describe the designer's role in materials development and instructional delivery.
- Name appropriate rough draft materials for various final media.
- Given an instructional strategy, describe the procedures for developing instructional materials.
- Develop instructional materials based on a given instructional strategy.

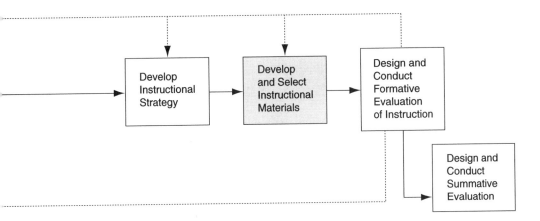

BACKGROUND

In a typical classroom setting, the instructor does many of the things we describe as being components of an instructional strategy. The instructor is often the motivator, the content presenter, the leader of practice activities, and the evaluator. The instructor makes decisions that affect the whole group as well as individual students. Instructors are usually required to use strategies whereby they must move the whole class forward through a sequence of instruction or retain the whole class at a particular point in the instruction until they feel that sufficient skill and knowledge have developed within a majority of the group.

The hallmark of individualized instruction is that many of the instructional events typically carried out by the instructor with a group of students are now presented to the individual student through instructional materials. As we have said elsewhere, this does not necessarily mean that the instructor is removed from the instructional setting. The instructor's role is different, and even more important than in lock-step instruction. The instructor is still the motivator, as well as a counselor, evaluator, and decision maker; and the instructor usually feels added responsibility for each student's mastery of the objectives.

We recommend that you produce self-instructional materials in your first attempt at instructional design; that is, the materials should permit the student to learn the new information and skills without any intervention from an instructor or fellow students. Once having performed this feat as a designer of print or mediated materials, you can move to instructor-led or various combinations of mediated materials with an instructor. As a first effort, however, learning components such as motivation, content, practice, and feedback should be built into the instructional materials. If you were to start your development with the instructor included in the instructional process, it would be very easy to use the instructor as a crutch in order to deliver the instruction. In your first effort as a designer, we recommend that you see how much can be done without having an instructor actively involved in the instructional process. Not only will this test your design skills and give you added insight into the learning components of an instructional strategy, but it will also give you a defined, replicable product to take into the formative evaluation process in Chapter 10.

CONCEPTS

THE DELIVERY SYSTEM AND MEDIA SELECTIONS

At this point in the instructional design process, a delivery system is specified and the instructional strategy has been developed, including clustering and sequencing, learning components, student groupings, and tentative media selections. If the designer will be working within an assumed or imposed delivery system, then the range of options will be limited and the media selections that have been made will probably be fairly stable. If one made open selections of media formats and an ideal delivery system, however, the likelihood is high that specifications will be revised during materials development. The point here is that our choices of theoretically best practice will run into a reality check as a natural part of the materials development process; some conflict is expected, and the resulting compromises usually help ensure a workable educational product that fits the learning environment. Three factors often cause compromise in media selections and the delivery system: (1) availability of existing instructional materials, (2) production and implementation constraints, and (3) the amount of facilitation that the instructor will provide during instruction.

AVAILABILITY OF EXISTING INSTRUCTIONAL MATERIALS Sometimes existing materials are an attractive alternative to going through the development and production process. Existing materials could be substituted for planned materials on a scale ranging from a single motivational sequence in one lesson, to an entire course or curriculum. Consider the example of our Neighborhood Crime Watch leadership training design. In Chapter 8 we specified a web-based delivery system, but suppose a review of existing materials turned up an appropriate, current instructional television series (ITV) on group leadership skills developed by a junior college consortium. If the duplication and distributions rights were not prohibitive, then distribution by the U.S. Post Office of student workbooks and VHS tapes might be a viable substitute for the time and cost of developing web-based instruction.

PRODUCTION AND IMPLEMENTATION CONSTRAINTS Media formats and delivery systems that look expensive *are* expensive. Cutting production corners to save money will usually not impact students' learning, but it will impact students' attention and perceptions of relevance and authority. Novice designers who have not worked with complex media often severely underestimate the costs of hiring commercial production, and equally underestimate the expertise, infrastructure, and time requirements for in-house production. Sometimes after development is completed, the costs of duplication, distribution, and maintenance can be just as prohibitive as unanticipated production costs. The key is to anticipate such constraints by due diligence during the learning context analysis, and to maintain an open, flexible viewpoint when entering the materials production phase. When faced with these dilemmas, the best strategy is to back down to simpler media formats and produce them well rather than sticking with complex media formats and producing them poorly. Using our Neighborhood Crime Watch example again, if it became apparent that quality, web-based streaming video was simply out of reach, it would be better to drop back to a good PowerPoint presentation developed for web delivery than to do amateurish video.

AMOUNT OF INSTRUCTOR FACILITATION The first steps in adoption of a new technology are usually attempts to replicate the features of the old technology; thus, as we began using ITV or computer-based instruction or web-based instruction, we tried to replicate features of the classroom experience for our students. Instructor facilitation is a particular feature of classroom instruction that has implications for how we develop instructional materials. Later in this chapter we will discuss how the facilitation factor affects development of face-to-face instruction, but here we will look at how it affects implementation of distance learning delivery systems. Instructor facilitation is a point at which distance learning philosophies sometimes diverge between academic programs, and professional and technical training programs. Table 9.1 contrasts academic and professional/technical training models of distance learning and includes the familiar *open university model* of distance learning as a reference point. Note that these models are not mutually exclusive and that the features of each are not as discrete as the tabular format might imply.

There are several implications in Table 9.1 for the development of materials in distance learning delivery systems. Recalling our discussion from Chapter 8 of Moore and Kearsley's concept of transactional distance, high levels of course dialogue in the academic model give learners perceptions of a more personal experience and feelings of group affiliation. Much of this dialogue is instructor participation in online discussion and practice with feedback, and it is generally reflected in more positive student evaluations of the course and the instructor. This is a feature of classroom instruction that the academic model attempts to replicate in distance learning. When discussion and feedback are provided by the instructor, initial materials development costs are lower; however, per-student costs are high and the course cannot be scaled up in size without hiring additional instructors.

The open university model uses differentiated staffing to limit the instructor costs, maintain a personalized course, and allow large student

TABLE *9.1* **Levels of Instructor Facilitation in Three Models of Distance Learning**

	Academic Model of Distance Learning	Open University Model of Distance Learning	Professional and Technical Training Model of Distance Learning
Delivery Systems	Web, two-way interactive television, videoconferencing	Web, broadcast television	Web, computer-based training
Purpose	Replicate classroom experience	Replicate large lecture hall experience	Replace classroom experience
Instructor Facilitation	•Instructor centered •Learning facilitated by instructor's active participation	•Instructor centered or materials centered •Learning facilitated by differentiated staff (e.g., proctor, learning center staff, graduate assistant, adjunct, tutor)	•Materials and software centered •Independent learning facilitated by software
Learners	Suitable for all learner independence levels	Suitable for fairly independent learners	Suitable for highly independent learners
Accountability	•Student learning outcomes •Student attitude about course •Student rating of faculty	•Student learning outcomes •Student attitude about course •Student rating of instructor and differentiated staff	•Student learning outcomes •Student attitude about course •Supervisor rating of student's job performance
Class Size Scalability and Per-Student Cost	•Limited scalability and high per-student cost •Add students by adding additional faculty	•More scalable, moderate to high per-student costs •Add students by adding additional staff	•Scalable, per-student costs dependent on sufficient audience size to amortize cost of development
Development and Implementation	•Low startup costs if technological infrastructure is in place •Can be developed and managed independently by a faculty member	•Low to high startup costs, depending on medium and sophistication of materials •Can require production team and will require network of facilitators	•High startup costs for intensive materials development and evaluation •Production team, but primary management task after implementation is accountability

audiences. The per-student costs, however, can still be high due to personnel and administrative expenses.

The professional and technical training model of distance learning opts for higher initial development expenses by assigning learning components to the instructional materials rather than to an instructor, and then it relies on large class sizes to bring down the per-student cost. Initial choices of ideal delivery system and media formats are often compromised when the instructional designer is faced with distance learning materials development and delivery cost options that are based on varying levels of instructor facilitation. The decision regarding the role of the instructor in instructional delivery needs to be considered and affirmed before selecting or developing materials.

COMPONENTS OF AN INSTRUCTIONAL PACKAGE

With your completed instructional strategy in hand, you are, at last, ready to start selecting existing instructional materials, developing materials yourself, or writing specifications for someone else who will be developing the materials. Before you begin you should be aware of the several components that usually make up an instructional package, and note that in the term *package* we include all forms of print and mediated materials.

INSTRUCTIONAL MATERIALS The instructional materials contain the content—either written, mediated, or facilitated by an instructor—that a student will use to achieve the objectives. This includes materials for the major objectives and the terminal objective, and any materials for enhancing memory and transfer. Instructional materials refer to any preexisting materials that are being incorporated, as well as to those materials that will be specifically developed for the objectives. The materials may also include information that the learners will use to guide their progress through the instruction. Templates for such student guidance are now available as part of commercial web-based distance course management systems such as WebCT, Blackboard Info, Learning Space, and eCourse. Student workbooks, activity guides, problem scenarios, computer simulations, case studies, resource lists, and other such materials would also be part of the instructional materials.

ASSESSMENTS All instructional materials should be accompanied by objective tests or by product or performance assessments. These may include both a pretest and a posttest. You may decide that you do not wish to have the tests as a separate component in the materials, but prefer to have them appear as part of the instructor's materials so they are not available to students. The package will be incomplete, however, unless you have included at least a posttest and the other assessments that are necessary for using the instructional package.

COURSE MANAGEMENT INFORMATION There often is a general description of the total package, typically called an instructor's manual, that provides the instructor with an overview of the materials and shows how they might be incorporated into an overall learning sequence for students. The manual might also include the tests and other information that you judge to be important for implementing the course. In addition to the student guidance templates provided in commercial, web-based instructional management systems, there is also course management support for the instructor. Instructor support often includes automated class listing, student tracking, online testing, project monitoring, grade book, and a variety of communication and messaging mechanisms. In some instances of self-paced, independent learning there really is no course instructor per se, so the instructor's guide is really a course management guide that can be customized for site-specific applications. Special attention should be paid to the ease with which course management information can be used by the instructor or course manager, and it should undergo the same type of formative evaluation as would tests and instruction.

SELECTING EXISTING INSTRUCTIONAL MATERIALS

The next step following the development of the instructional strategy is to determine whether there are existing materials that fit your objectives. In some content areas you will find an abundance of materials available, either superficial or greatly detailed, which are not really directed to the target population in which you are interested. On the other hand, occasionally it is possible to identify materials that will serve at least part of your needs. When you consider the cost of developing a video or a multi-media presentation, it is clearly worth the effort to spend several hours examining existing materials to determine whether they meet your needs.

To aid planning your materials evaluations, recall from Chapter 7 three of the categories of criteria for creating assessments, including goal-centered, learner-centered, and context-centered criteria. We will use all of these and add one more category—namely, learning-centered criteria.

GOAL-CENTERED CRITERIA FOR EVALUATING MATERIALS This category of criteria is focused on the content of the instruction, and your instructional analysis documents will provide a basis for determining the acceptability of the content in various instructional materials. Specific criteria in this area include (1) congruence among the content in the materials and your terminal and performance objectives, (2) adequacy of content coverage and completeness, (3) authority, (4) accuracy, (5) currency, and (6) objectivity.

LEARNER-CENTERED CRITERIA FOR EVALUATING MATERIALS The second area of consideration is the appropriateness of instructional materials for your target group. Your learner analysis documentation should provide the foundation for this evaluation. Specific criteria include the appropriateness of the materials for your learners' (1) vocabulary and language levels, (2) developmental, motivation, and interest levels, (3) backgrounds and experiences, and (4) special language or other needs. Other important learner-centered criteria include the materials' treatment of diversity and whether gender, cultural, age, racial, or other forms of bias appear to be present. Using these criteria to judge available materials can help you determine the appropriateness of the materials for your specific target group.

CONTEXT-CENTERED CRITERIA FOR EVALUATING MATERIALS The appropriateness of existing materials for your instructional and performance context should be evaluated. Your instructional and performance context analyses can provide the foundation for judging whether existing materials can be adopted as is or adapted for your settings. Criteria within the context category include the authenticity of the materials for your contexts and learners and the feasibility of the materials for your settings and budget. More specific within the feasibility category, you should examine the technical quality of existing materials, including packaging, graphic design and typography, durability, legibility, audio and video quality, and, when appropriate, interface design, navigation, and functionality.

Learning-Centered Criteria for Evaluating Materials Your instructional strategy can be used to determine whether existing materials are adequate as is, or whether they need to be adapted or enhanced prior to use. Materials can be evaluated to determine whether (1) the content sequencing is correct, (2) motivational concerns are addressed, (3) student participation and practice exercises exist, (4) adequate feedback is included, (5) appropriate assessments are available, (6) adequate follow-through directions are included for enhancing memory and transfer, (7) delivery system and media formats are appropriate for the objectives and the learning context, and (8) adequate learner guidance is provided to move students from one component or activity to the next. The instructional strategy should be used to evaluate each potential resource. It may be possible to combine several resources to create a complete set of materials. When materials lack one or more of the necessary learning components—such as motivation, prerequisite skills, and so on—it may be economically advantageous to make adaptations so that the missing components are made available for use by students. It may also make sense to "complete" existing materials by writing assessments and an instructor's guide.

If no appropriate materials are found that can be adopted or adapted for your instructional strategy, you are in the instructional materials development business. You must specify how you or a media production specialist will move from an instructional strategy to an instructional product that you can take into formative evaluation.

The Designer's Role in Materials Development and Instructional Delivery

When the Designer Is Also the Materials Developer and the Instructor In many instructional settings, the person who designs the instruction is also the person who develops materials and teaches students. For example, a human resources generalist in a small company may design, develop, and deliver all new employee orientation, benefits training, and "soft skills" training. Teachers and professors do their own lesson plans and syllabi, materials, and instruction; and professionals in all fields routinely design, develop, and present their own workshops and in-service training. These instructors may be involved at three different levels in the development and delivery of instruction. The differences between the three levels lie in the role the instructor plays in developing the instruction and in the actual delivery of instruction to target learners. Table 9.2 includes a description of the instructor's role in the materials development and delivery processes.

When instructors design and develop individualized materials, or materials that can be delivered independent of an instructor, their role in instructional delivery is passive, but their role as a facilitator is very active. In this case, their task during instruction is to monitor and guide the progress of students through the materials. Students can progress at their own speed through the instruction, with the instructor providing additional help for those who seem to need it. Except for the pretests and posttests, all learning components are included within the materials. In some materials, even these tests are included and submitted to the instructor only when learners complete them.

TABLE 9.2 | The Method of Delivering Instruction for Various Instructional Approaches

The Instructor's Role in Designing Materials	Instructional Strategy Components				
	Preinstructional Activities	Presenting Information	Student Participation	Follow-Through Activities	Pretest/Posttest and Unit Motivation
I Instructor designs individualized instructional materials	Materials	Materials	Materials	Materials	Instructor/ Materials
II Instructor selects and adapts existing materials to suit the instructional strategy	Materials and/ or Instructor	Materials and/ or Instructor	Materials and/ or Instructor	Materials and/ or Instructor	Instructor/ Materials
III Instructor uses no material but delivers instruction to suit the instructional strategy	Instructor	Instructor	Instructor	Instructor	Instructor/ Materials

In the second case, in which instructors select and adapt materials to suit their instructional strategy, it is probable that the instructor will have an increased role in delivering instruction. Some available materials may be instructor independent, but when they are not, the instructor must provide any instruction specified in the strategy, but not found in the materials. When an instructor uses a variety of instructional resources, he or she plays a greater role in materials management. By providing a learner guide for available materials, instructors may be able to increase the independence of the materials and free themselves to provide additional guidance and consultation for students who need it.

The third type of instruction illustrated in Table 9.2 is heavily dependent on the instructor. The instructor delivers all instruction according to the instructional strategy that has been developed. This commonly occurs in public schools or in other settings where there is a small budget for materials or where the content to be taught changes rapidly. The instructor uses the instructional strategy as a guide in producing outlines for lecture notes and directions for group exercises and activities. In professional and technical training, the designer often develops a formal instructor's guide that provides detailed lesson plan-like guidance for lectures, discussions, and participant activities.

This type of instruction has both advantages and disadvantages. A major advantage is that the instructor can constantly update and improve instruction as changes occur in the content. Instructors spend the majority of their time, however, lecturing and delivering information to a group, leaving little time to help individual learners with problems. Progress through a lesson is difficult because when the instructor stops to answer a question for one learner, the progress of the entire group is halted.

The intended delivery mode for instruction is a very important consideration in the development of materials based on the planned instructional strategy. If instruction is intended to be instructor-independent, then the materials will have to include all the learning components in the strategy. The instructor is not expected to play a role in delivering instruction.

If the instructor plans to combine available materials, then instructional delivery will combine materials and instructor presentation. The instructor may not be required to develop any new materials in this mode, but may be required to deliver some of the needed instruction. The amount of original materials developed for this type of instruction will depend on available time, budget, and staff support.

If instructors plan to deliver all the instruction with materials such as lecture notes, a data projector, and a chalkboard, then they may need to develop little besides lecture outlines, electronic presentations, practice worksheets or active learning exercises, and formal tests.

As the instructional designer you made decisions about the intended delivery system and media formats in planning your instructional strategy. Now, in the case when you are also the materials developer and the instructor, you may need to modify and adapt your original decisions to reflect existing materials you have found, the realities of development and production costs, and changes in your thinking about your role as instructor. These decisions will affect materials development activities as well as the required budget and staff.

When the designer is also the developer and the instructor, the whole process of materials development is rather informal; that is, much of what would be formal specification and communication between designer and materials developer remains as mental notes or informal planning notes. The thought also tends to reside in the back of the designer's mind that, as the instructor, "I will be able to manage the instruction, adapting and accommodating as needed on the fly." This thought results in less concern for the nitty-gritty details of developing and implementing instruction.

There is a commonly practiced division of responsibilities in which the designer is also the instructor, but is not solely responsible for materials production. This seldom happens in public schools, but in higher education, business, government, and military settings there is often technical assistance available for production of complex media such as video, web, and multimedia. The designer usually works collaboratively with an in-house media production specialist rather than turning over specifications, so the preceding discussion is generally applicable to this division of responsibilities.

WHEN THE DESIGNER IS NOT THE INSTRUCTOR In large companies with a significant training and development function, an instructional designer may work with a team responsible for design, development, and implementation of training. The same kind of team also exists in instructional design (ID) consulting firms, personnel training and development companies, and in some universities. The functions represented on such a team are usually manager, instructional designer, subject matter expert, materials developer (or coordinator), and evaluator.

In a smaller ID setting, one individual may be responsible for more than one function, while in a larger setting, multiple individuals may be assigned to each function. The team would also interact regularly with a representative of the internal or external client and sometimes with an instructor or instructional program manager. In ID teams it is common for the manager to be a senior-level instructional designer, and for the instructional designer also to be a materials developer or at least have working-level knowledge of a variety of media formats. The combination of instructional design and materials development skills is desirable, particularly in computer-based and web-based materials development, because of pressure to bring "just in time" training products to users as quickly as possible. Michael Greer's text (1992) is a good source for exploring team-based instructional design and ID project management.

Earlier in this chapter we mentioned that the process of specifying and developing materials is fairly informal when the designer is also the materials developer and the instructor. When the designer is neither the developer nor the instructor, however, a premium is placed on precision specifications and working in a team environment requiring communication and collaboration skills. There is no such thing as a standard operating procedure for the communication that occurs between a designer and a materials developer. It is always a unique collaboration that is determined by the mix of design and development skills possessed by each participant and the division of responsibilities in the team setting.

For example, a creative designer with good television production skills and the time to do so, might turn over a full production script with storyboarding to the materials developer. At the other extreme, a busy designer without production experience would probably meet with the developer, go over the learner and context analyses, review the instructional strategy, solicit production ideas from the developer, and then meet later to review a storyboard and script notes prepared by the developer. The best way for a designer to establish methods for communicating media specifications is to meet with and learn from the developer, because materials developers will already have planning and production tools that they use routinely in their media trade. The instructional designer should adopt the planning tools with which materials developers in a particular shop are comfortable.

Another reason why we have introduced the idea of an ID team is to point out a common problem in the instructional design process that stems from the relationship, or lack thereof, between the designer and the learners. When the designer is also the instructor of a given set of learners, the designer/instructor has a good understanding of the interests and motivations of the learners, of their preferences and expectations, and their general and specific knowledge of the content area. It is often the case, however, in team ID settings that the designer is not the instructor and is unfamiliar with the learners for whom the instruction is intended and may have little or no direct contact with them. When this situation exists the designer can depend on careful learner and context analyses, but in lieu of good information, may depend on his or her own stereotypes of what the learners are like. Such assumptions may result in more problems than if the designer had no knowledge of the learners at all.

If possible, designers should have conducted the on-site learner and context analyses themselves to observe a sample of the learners for whom the instruction is being designed. This step is equally important whether observing schoolchildren, military recruits, adult volunteer learners, middle-management trainees, or any others for whom instruction is to be designed. If the designer did not do the original learner and context analyses, then an opportunity for at least casual observation should be pursued. Based on these observations, the designer makes decisions as diverse as the size of content clusters, the features of a graphical user interface, or the types of role models that should be used to foster attitudes. Although it is impossible to indicate all the characteristics of a learner population that might be important to the design of new instruction, the instructional designer must become as knowledgeable as possible about the target population.

DEVELOPING INSTRUCTIONAL MATERIALS FOR FORMATIVE EVALUATION

ROUGH DRAFT MATERIALS We all know what the term *rough draft* means, because we have all written rough drafts of papers that have subsequently been revised into a final form. *Rough draft* means about the same thing when applied to instructional materials, but it carries the additional meaning that the product is developed in alternate, simpler, less expensive media formats.

The purpose for doing a rough draft of materials is to create a quick, low-cost version of your design, so that you will have something to guide final production and something to take into formative evaluation and try out with a subject-matter expert, several learners, or a group of learners. The thought is that the time to catch any problems with the instructional materials is when they can still be revised without going to great amounts of time and expense. The design model we have been following throughout this book has a feedback line that says "Revise instruction," and the concept of rough draft materials requires that revision process.

A troublesome thought at this point might be, "How can I determine whether my instructional planning and materials are effective from a rough draft version?" Research in learning from different media formats suggests that where actual mastery of knowledge and skills is concerned, there is very little difference between rough draft and finished product. For example, a student will learn just as much from watching a video as from looking at hand-drawn storyboard cards and listening to a person read the script. As one

| TABLE *9.3* | Examples of Suggested Rough Draft Formats |

If Final Medium Will Be:	Then Rough Draft Version Could Be:
• Illustrated text	Word processed, loose-leaf notebook with hand-drawn or clip-art illustration
• Laminated booklet	8½-by-11-inch card stock
• Overhead transparencies	Hand-lettered, word processed, or presentation graphic frames printed on 8½-by-11-inch paper
• Activity centers and learning centers	"Flimsy" versions of materials that, in final form, will need to be "heavy duty" to resist wear and tear
• Presentation graphics program (e.g., Astound, Free-lance, Harvard, Power-Point)	Hand-drawn storyboard with lecture notes; although if one has sufficient experience it is easiest to create rough-draft materials directly in the presentation program using drawing tools and a good clip-art collection, and then type lecture notes into the "notes view"
• Video	Hand-drawn storyboard cards with script notes or full script; although technological advances such as mini DV camcorders and user-friendly desktop video editing programs have made it possible to tape inexpensive draft footage and rough cut it into AVI or Quicktime format for formative tryouts
• Multi-media computer-based instruction (e.g., Authorware, Director, HyperStudio, IconAuthor, Toolbook II)	Hand-drawn screen designs with flowchart of decision points, media events, and hyperlinks; mockups with limited functionality are often developed for proof-of-concept and formative review; mockups are sometimes developed for testing in user-friendly, lower-tech programs (e.g., rough draft in Astound but final version in Authorware)
• Web-based and multi-media web-based instruction	Same as above (all programs mentioned can be ported for web access)

would expect, the attention and motivational effects of the experience will be different, but rough draft tryouts are used routinely in formative evaluation of complex, expensive media. Developers even use illustrator art or computer-generated art to determine whether children will like and identify with cartoon characters that will later be created for film or video. Table 9.3 lists examples of rough draft versions for a few final media formats. As you look at the suggested rough draft formats, recall that the purpose for the draft is a quick, cheap product to take into formative tryouts.

RAPID PROTOTYPING   Anyone who has experience with multimedia authoring knows the time and energy requirements for developing and testing complex computer-based instruction. The thought of "doing it several times" for the sake of formative evaluation is daunting; but that is exactly what happens in an instructional materials development process called *rapid prototyping.* In many learning contexts, technologies and training requirements change so quickly that instructional designers have rethought some of the traditional approaches to instructional design. The first strategy used in rapid prototyping is to go light on the early analysis steps of an instructional design model, then develop prototype instructional materials rapidly, and use quick interactive cycles of formative evaluation and revision to shape the final form of the materials. Rapid prototyping can be thought of as a series of informed, successive approximations. The emphasis must be on the word *informed* because this developmental approach relies absolutely on information gathered during tryouts to ensure the success of the final product.

The second strategy used in rapid prototyping is simultaneous design and development; that is, much of the front-end analysis work is conducted while the first rough draft materials are being developed. This might seem like getting the cart before the horse, but recall that rapid prototyping occurs primarily in high-tech, quickly changing learning contexts. The thinking here is that trainers designing cutting-edge technological products will not know answers to critical design questions unless they are also involved in product development with those technologies. In team instructional design settings there is a premium on accurate, continuous communication between those working in design and those working in materials development if the benefits of simultaneous activity are to be realized.

The concept of using rough-draft materials for tryouts still holds in rapid prototyping, with the focus of early approximations being on the functionality of the user interface, the flow of program events, learner navigation through the instruction, and learners' performance. In later iterations as the instruction nears its final form, the fancy artwork and graphics are added to the product.

The rapid prototyping process is quite complex in large instructional development projects involving interactive, computer-based and web-based multi-media. In such efforts, many stages of instructional design, materials development, and formative evaluation occur simultaneously. For example, in production of computer-based instruction, one feature could be in the design phase while another was undergoing development and yet another was in prototype testing. It is easy to fall into a pattern of thinking that instructional design is a strictly linear process, but this is misleading because tracking design and development activities would reveal a sequence of overlapping, circular patterns that duplicates the iterative product design and development process.

MATERIALS DEVELOPMENT TOOLS AND RESOURCES   Production of mediated materials requires a whole set of skills, both artistic and technical, that can range from simple word processing to writing lines of computer code. To develop familiarity and skills with typical materials planning and production tools, readers are referred to the list of references and recommended readings at the end of this chapter. The texts by Heinich, Molenda, Russell, and Smaldino (1999) and Kemp and Smellie (1994) both provide overviews of current instructional media formats, along with guidelines and tips for materials planning, design, and development. There are few references at the end of this chapter on digital audio and video, and on computer-based and web-based multi-media. The reason is that the technologies change so quickly that any listing in this book would soon be outdated. However, there are two good sources for this type of specialized information. The first source is the paperback literature available in computer stores, bookstores, and through web-based vendors. These are the "how to" manuals that quickly follow new releases of computer applications, programming, and authoring tools. The other source is the web itself. To find the most current information on a computer application or authoring tool that you are using, just type the brand name into a web index or search engine, and you will likely find web sites maintained by the publisher and other users as well as references for USENET newsgroups and user mailing lists.

BEGINNING THE DEVELOPMENT PROCESS

Earlier in this chapter we discussed the advantages for a first-time instructional designer of developing self-paced materials rather than instruction that is presented by an instructor. Another piece of advice for the novice designer is that the first materials development be done in illustrated text format. This is a very natural starting point because it avoids the problem of being required to have complex media development skills. Anyone with decent word processing skills can quickly create rough drafts of text and either draw by hand or electronically insert pictorial and graphic illustration. Another reason for beginning with illustrated text is that there is an abundance of good examples of text designs and formats that you can emulate for a wide range of content and learner ages. Even low-end, user-friendly desktop publishing applications such as PrintShop Pro and Publisher include style guides and templates that make good-looking illustrated text easy to produce. Sticking with illustrated text also keeps one's focus on the whole point of this book—that is, the design, development, and validation of effective instruction—rather than production of mediated materials. The purpose for the materials development step in this chapter is to produce only a draft product that will communicate well enough to allow a formative tryout with intended learners. With illustrated text you can take a manageable product into formative evaluation where the focus can be on learning outcomes rather than media production variables.

For the designer who chooses to prepare instruction for media other than illustrated text, the processes described in this and succeeding chapters still apply. In other words, the instructional strategy must be developed before preparing the first draft of the instruction, regardless of the medium; and once that first draft of the instruction is prepared, then the formative evaluation process should begin.

We will show in our examples how the instructional strategy is used as a guide for developing the first draft of your instruction. The strategy should keep you on track as you write your materials to motivate and inform the learners, present each objective, provide practice and feedback, and implement your assessment and memory and transfer strategies. The next section discusses the general steps you will follow from the development of the instructional strategy to the completion of the first draft of the instruction and support materials.

STEPS IN THE DEVELOPMENT OF INSTRUCTION

1. Review the instructional strategy for each objective in each lesson.
2. Survey the literature and ask subject-matter experts to determine what instructional materials are already available.
3. Consider how you might adopt or adapt available materials.
4. Determine whether new materials need to be designed. If so, proceed to step 5. If not, begin organizing and adapting available materials, using the instructional strategy as a guide.
5. Review your analysis of learners and for each lesson, consider the instructor's role in facilitating instruction and determine the degree to which you want the instruction to be self-paced or group-paced.

6. Review your analysis of the learning context and your assumptions about resources available for developing materials. Reconsider the delivery system and the media chosen to present the materials, to monitor practice and feedback, to evaluate, and to enhance learner memory and transfer.

7. Plan and write the instructional materials based on the instructional strategy in rough draft form. You will be amazed at how stick figures and rough illustrations can bring your ideas to life for a first trial. Printed, visual, or auditory materials in this rough form will allow you to check your sequence, flow of ideas, accuracy of illustration of ideas, completeness, pace, and so on. Make a rough set of materials as complete as is reasonably possible for each instructional activity.

8. Review each completed lesson or class session for clarity and flow of ideas.

9. Using one complete instructional unit, write the accompanying instructions to guide the students through the activities if they are required.

10. Using the materials developed in this first inexpensive, rough draft, begin evaluation activities. Chapter 10 introduces and discusses procedures and activities for evaluating and revising instructional materials.

11. You may either develop materials for the instructor's manual as you go along or you can take notes as you develop and revise the instructional presentations and activities. Using the notes, you can later write the instructor's guide.

EXAMPLES

Selected parts of the instructional strategy for the group leadership unit will be used to illustrate materials development. While there are many performance objectives that could be illustrated, we have chosen to illustrate only two as an example. These include objective 6.3.1, "Naming strategies that encourage and stifle member cooperation," and objective 6.4.1, "Classifying strategies that encourage and stifle member cooperation." See Table 8.9 for a complete list of the objectives included in Session 10.

All materials illustrated are scripts for web-based, distance instruction. Learners will study independently at home, coming to the learning center only for interactive meeting participation and interactive group leadership. These in-center meetings are only for objective 6.5.1, "In simulated NCW problem-solving meetings with learner acting as group leader, initiate actions to engender cooperative behavior among group members."

The assumption underlying these examples of rough-draft materials development is that the instructional designer is sharing development responsibilities with a production specialist. The designer specified web-based instruction in the instructional strategy and has now written the scripting for what will appear on the web pages. For the specific objectives being illustrated in the example, the production specialist will take the scripting and create a web page design and insert cartoon characters and callouts to simulate a comic book style. In the example that follows, a comment on mediation is included as each component of the instructional strategy is described. Readers should note that the materials specified for web-based delivery in

Learning Component	Instruction
Introduction/ motivation	Throughout America, we as citizens have good intentions of working together to make our neighborhoods safe for our families and us. We bond together in times of crisis, forming search parties for a missing neighbor or chaperoning schoolchildren to and from a bus stop. We always work relentlessly until the crisis is resolved. When there is no immediate crisis, however, we often have difficulty forming cohesive groups that persist in systematic efforts to improve and sustain neighborhood safety. We have seen illustrations of the positive differences that effective NCW associations can make in our neighborhoods, and we have examined the activities and impact of several NCW associations around the state. The key factor in forming and maintaining an effective NCW group is **leadership.** In your neighborhood, *you* are the key ingredient to an effective NCW association and improved safety for all citizens.
Linking to previous skills	During previous sessions we practiced group leadership skills related to planning and preparation skills for NCW meetings. You also rehearsed techniques for managing the thought line for the group, and you experienced the difference you can make using thought-line management techniques during a problem-solving meeting. To this point in discussion groups, your actions have been rather directive: preparing materials, inviting participants, and keeping the group on the topic with thought-line management techniques. Your direction in these areas is critical for helping your neighbors examine different facets of safety issues and plan safety programs.
Session objectives	There is another important ingredient in effective group leadership: **managing cooperative group interaction during meetings.** Regardless of the topic of the meeting, the level of members' preparation, or the resulting plan of action, participants are most likely to view the NCW association and your meetings as worth their time and effort when their interaction in the group is comfortable and cooperative. Leader actions for managing cooperative interaction are more democratic than those we have covered to this point; their purpose is to draw out participants. These actions are interwoven in a discussion with actions you use to manage the thought line. In this session, however, we will set aside thought-line actions and focus specifically on actions for encouraging cooperative group interaction. You can use three main strategies as the NCW leader to manage cooperative group interaction during meetings: 1. Engender cooperative member behaviors. 2. Recognize and defuse members' blocking behaviors if they occur. 3. Recognize and alleviate group stress if it appears. You will spend the next four sessions practicing and refining your leadership skills in these three main areas. During this session, our focus will be on skills related to engendering cooperative member behaviors, and we will work on the following three main skills: 1. Recognizing cooperative member behaviors 2. Recognizing leader actions that encourage and stifle member cooperation during meetings 3. Using leader actions ourselves to encourage member cooperation during meetings Many of you have participated in problem-solving discussion groups in the past, and a few of you have served as leaders for discussion groups. As a beginning, watch a NCW leader lead a group-discussion meeting and see how many of these leader behaviors you already recognize.

this example lesson could have been specified with equivalent learning effectiveness for broadcast television with a workbook, for illustrated text with videocassette, for traditional classroom instruction, or for many other delivery systems. One caveat is that any delivery system chosen for the entire unit on group leadership skills would have to preserve students' opportunities to observe and participate in small group interaction.

PREINSTRUCTIONAL ACTIVITIES

MEDIATION OF PREINSTRUCTIONAL ACTIVITIES   The web-based instructional materials prescriptions for this session are scripts for the web presentations. In addition to the scripts, the web-based instruction will include the graphic and color enhancements that are readily available and inexpensive in web-based instruction. These enhancements are intended to stimulate motivation and interest value.

MOTIVATION MATERIALS AND SESSION OBJECTIVES   Table 9.4 contains the motivational materials and session objectives. (Recall that the instructional strategy for these materials appears in Table 8.6.) The left column identifies particular learning components from the instructional strategy and the right column contains the instruction. This is done to highlight links between instruction and the instructional strategy, making the relationships easier for you to follow. (The session information and left-hand column would not appear in the actual instruction.)

Figure 9.1 includes an illustration of how graphics and comic book style characters can be used in the conversion of these preinstructional activities scripts to web-based instructional materials. This sample of how the web presentation would be developed is provided to spark your imagination and to illustrate how the scripts can be given personality and interest value. Imagine the conversion of the remainder of the materials to web-based instruction as you study the examples. In studying these scripts, you should focus on the nature of the content and its relationship to the components of the instructional strategy.

F I G U R E *9.1*

Graphic Example of How Preinstructional Text Material Can Be Converted as Graphics for Web-Based Delivery

TABLE 9.5

Sample Pretest for Group Leadership Instructional Goal (Session 10, Objective 6.4.2 in Table 8.9 and Instructional Strategy in Table 8.8)

Learning Component	Pretest Directions
Pretest	**Detecting leader behaviors that encourage or stifle group cooperation during meetings**
	Directions: Print web form #6.1, then watch web video #6.1: *Leader Behaviors that Encourage and Stifle Cooperative Learning.* In the video, a NCW meeting is underway, and members are discussing neighborhood problems with vandalism. They are examining possible actions they can take to eliminate opportunities for vandals and community actions that can lessen vandalism in the future.
	The form that you printed contains twelve specific **leader actions** that either encourage or stifle group members' cooperation during a meeting. Study the list carefully. Can you pick out these actions used by the group leader in the meeting? As you watch the video presentations:
	1. Check all the *purposeful actions* that Eloise McLaughlin, the NCW leader, directly makes during the meeting to *encourage her neighbors' participation and cooperation.* She may exhibit some of the behaviors more than once and others not at all. Each time she exhibits an encouraging behavior, place a checkmark (✔) in the "Do" column next to the behavior.
	2. Check in the "Don't" column each time that Eloise takes one of the actions that stifles cooperation. For example, if Eloise uses questions as a way to suggest points of discussion five times, you should place a checkmark (✔) in the "Do" column of your checklist each time she demonstrates this skill. On the other hand, if she directly tells the group what she wants them to discuss two times, you should place a checkmark in the "Don't" column each time she directly tells the group what to discuss. Notice how her actions are recorded on the response form in the following example:

Example:

Do Tally	Eloise's Cooperation-Encouraging Actions	Eloise's Cooperation-Stifling Actions	Don't Tally
✔✔✔ ✔✔	Suggests points of discussion as questions	Prescribes topics for the group to consider	✔✔

The NCW meeting segment you will watch runs for eight minutes. Watch the video meeting straight through; then watch it a second time. As you watch the meeting progress, use the form to record your judgments about the group management skills Eloise exhibits during the meeting. When you finish marking your checklist, go to web pretest #6.1. Use the form you have been working on to fill in the pretest and click the "send pretest" button when you are done.

PRETEST   The pretest for Session 10 will cover only objective 6.4.2, "Given videos of staged NCW meetings, classify leaders' actions that are likely to encourage or stifle member cooperation." Objectives 6.3.1 and 6.4.1 are both subordinate to 6.4.2 and are embedded in the pretest exercise for 6.4.2. Objective 6.5.1, the highest-level skill in this cluster, is not included in the pretest because it requires the learner to lead an actual interactive group meeting. Requiring a public demonstration of skill prior to instruction on the skills does not seem appropriate for this adult group of volunteers.

TABLE 9.5 | (Continued)

Instructional Strategy Component: Learners' Response Form

Do Tally	Eloise's Cooperation-Encouraging Actions	Eloise's Cooperation-Stifling Actions	Don't Tally
	1. Suggests points of discussion as questions.	1. Prescribes topics for the group to consider	
	2. Uses an investigative, inquiring tone	2. Uses an authoritative tone	
	3. Uses open terms such as *perhaps* and *might*	3. Uses prescriptive terms such as *must* or *should*	
	4. Hesitates and pauses between speakers	4. Fills quiet gaps with personal points of view or solutions	
	5. Willingly turns over the floor to group members who interrupt	5. Continues to talk over interrupting members or interrupts member	
	6. Encompasses total group with eyes, inviting all to participate freely	6. Focuses gaze on a few members	
	7. Nonverbally (eyes, gestures) encourages speaker to address group	7. Holds speaker's attention	
	8. Uses comments that keep discussion centered in the group	8. Encourages discussion to flow through leader by evaluating member comments	
	9. Encourages volunteerism (e.g., "Who has experience with...")	9. Designates speakers and speaking order (e.g., "Beth, what do you think about...")	
	10. Refers to *us, we, our*	10. Refers to *I, me, mine* or *your*	
	11. Acknowledges group accomplishments	11. Acknowledges own accomplishments or those of particular members	
	12. Praises group effort and accomplishment	12. Singles out particular people for praise	

MEDIATION OF PRETEST   As prescribed in the objective and the instructional strategy, the pretest will consist of directions for learners, a learner-response form, and a streaming video of a simulated NCW meeting. Learners will print from the web site a "working copy" of the response form that they can use as they view the video. For the pretest, they can view the video only twice, marking their responses on the response form as they watch. Following the second viewing, they access the interactive pretest form on the web site, and respond to questions about the number and type of leader and member actions they observed in the meeting. Table 9.5 contains the directions and the learners' response sheet.

FIGURE 9.2

Rough Example of Content
Presentation Script in
Table 9.4 Converted for
Web-Based Instruction

CONTENT PRESENTATION

MEDIATION OF INSTRUCTION   Due to the length of instruction for the objectives in Session 10, we will present only a segment in this chapter. Assume that instruction for objectives 6.1.1 through 6.2.2 is already complete, and that we are developing instruction only for objectives 6.3.1 and 6.4.1. The instruction will be web-based and made available to participants in their homes. Participants who do not have the equipment at home can access the materials in the learning center's computer laboratory or in another site more convenient to their homes. The web-based instruction for these two objectives will be created using a comic book style instructor with a conversational format such as that illustrated in Figure 9.2 for objective 6.4.1. The figure is a rough illustration of how the NCW committee members will appear in the web-based instruction. Jackson, the NCW leader in this example, is offering introductory comments to the group. Encouraging behaviors are highlighted for learners using callout boxes and arrows.

INSTRUCTION   Table 9.6 contains the content and examples for session 10 for only objectives 6.3.1 and 6.4.1, naming and recognizing leader actions that encourage and stifle cooperative interaction among members. Notice that for objective 6.4.1, an actual script of a NCW meeting is provided. The numbers beside each person's comments during the meeting are a key to link the comments to the leader actions presented in objective 6.3.1. This presentation exercise begins to link the verbal information actions to interactive human actions during a meeting.

LEARNER PARTICIPATION

MEDIATION OF LEARNER PARTICIPATION AND FEEDBACK   The learner participation component will also be formatted for web-based instruction enabling learners to study independently and at home throughout the county. Learners can print the pages containing the script, locating and marking all instances of behavior directly on the pages they print. After completing the exercise, they can scroll down the screen to the feedback

TABLE 9.6	Content Presentation for Group Leadership Instructional Goal

Session 10, Engendering Cooperative Member Behaviors: Content and Examples for Objective 6.3.1, When asked in writing to name leader actions that encourage and stifle member discussion and cooperation, name these actions.

As the discussion leader, there are many actions you can take to encourage cooperation among group members. All of these actions are designed to draw out members' ideas and suggestions and to demonstrate the importance of their participation. Your actions during a discussion should place participating members in the foreground, while placing yourself in the background. Your personal ideas, solutions, and conclusions are put on hold during the meeting; your job is to get all members actively involved in examining the problem, volunteering ideas and suggestions, weighing the strengths and problems with ideas suggested, and settling on "best solutions" that will alleviate or minimize given problems in the community. Remember that good solutions identified in meetings are most likely to be carried out *if* group members participate in forming the solutions and have a personal commitment to them.

Although you can use many actions to encourage or stifle cooperative behavior during a discussion, let's focus our attention on twelve key actions. These twelve actions each have a cooperation and a stifling complement (e.g., do this [encouraging] rather than that [stifling]) that forms opposite action pairs. The twelve action pairs (encouraging and stifling) can be divided into four main categories, with three action pairs in each one. The following list illustrates the four main categories and behaviors within each.

Leader actions that facilitate and stifle cooperative interaction
(Notice that each encouraging and stifling action pair is bridged with the terms *rather than*.)

I. Appearing open-minded and facilitating to group members *rather than* directive when introducing or changing the topic or suggesting paths the group might take. You can take specific actions during a meeting to achieve this impression:
    1. Suggesting points of discussion as questions rather than prescribing topics for the group to consider
    2. Using an investigative inquiring tone rather than an authoritative one
    3. Using open terms such as *perhaps* and *might* rather than prescriptive terms such as *must* or *should*
II. Demonstrating a genuine desire for others to contribute rather than providing you with an audience. Certain actions effectively leave this impression with your group members:
    4. Hesitating and pausing between speakers rather than filling quiet gaps by offering personal points of view or solutions
    5. Willingly turning over the floor to group members who interrupt you rather than continuing to talk over the interrupting member
    6. Encompassing total group with eyes, inviting all to participate freely, rather than focusing your gaze on a few members you know are ready contributors
III. Helping group members focus on themselves, their needs, and their ideas rather than on you as the leader. You can achieve this objective through these actions:
    7. Nonverbally (eyes, gestures) encouraging speakers to address the group rather than you
    8. Using comments that keep discussion centered in the group rather than encouraging discussion to flow through you (e.g., "Are there any more thoughts on that idea?" rather than "I like that, Karen, tell me more about it")
    9. Encouraging volunteerism rather than designating speakers and speaking order

TABLE 9.6 | (Continued)

(e.g., "Who has experience with . . ." rather than "Beth, what do you think about . . .")

IV. Moving ownership of ideas from individual contributors to the whole group. Owner-ship transfer can be accomplished in the following ways:

10. Referring to *us, we, our*, rather than *I, me, mine*, or *your*

11. Acknowledging group accomplishments rather than your own or those of particular members

12. Praising group efforts and accomplishments rather than singling out particular peo-ple for praise

When you consistently exhibit these twelve encouraging behaviors in leading group discussions, your group members will be more productive and reach better decisions than they will if you use the alternative stifling ones

Session 10, Engendering Cooperative Member Behaviors: Content and Examples for Objective 6.4.1, Given written descriptions of a group leader's actions during a meeting, in-dicate whether the actions are likely to encourage or stifle cooperative group interaction.

It may be helpful to examine a NCW leader using each of these twelve cooperation-en-couraging actions as he leads a group discussion. In the following NCW meeting script, Jackson, the leader, demonstrates each of the behaviors. The meeting script appears in the right column and the left column is used to highlight particular actions. The actions are linked to the previous list by number (1–12).

Leader Actions	Neighborhood Watch Meeting Script
6. Eyes group inclusively	**Jackson:** (*Smiling, eyes encompassing whole group*) I'm pleased that so many of *us* can be here
10. Use of terms *us, our, we*	tonight. During *our* last meeting, *we* discussed the problems we are having with graffiti and planned ways to try to reduce the amount of graffiti we
11. Praises group for accomplishment	see. *Our* three point program *appears to be having an incredible impact*; the old graffiti is gone, and we have fewer instances of new graffiti.
12. Does not praise individuals	
	Sam: (*Addressing Jackson*) I think the new paint on buildings and fences looks good. It dresses up the community.
4. Hesitates, waiting for others to join	(*Jackson does not verbally respond; he awaits other mem-bers' comments.*)
	Dorothy: I think we should send letters of apprecia-tion to the businesses who contributed the paint and to the student–parent groups that volun-teered their time through the school to paint out the graffiti that had been building for so . . .
	Frank: (*Interrupting Dorothy*) The letters have been sent.
6. Eye contact with all	**Dorothy:** Good.
11. *We* agreed	**Jackson:** (*Looking around group*) Last meeting *we agreed* to invite Officer Talbot to talk with us about ways we can help protect ourselves
1. Pose topic as question	from home burglaries. Is this still the area we wish to address this evening?

TABLE *9.6* | (Continued)

9. Not designating speaker	*(Jackson again looks around the group and hesitates without calling on a particular member.)*
	Gwen: *(Addressing Jackson)* I want to talk about ways to protect ourselves from burglars. As I told you, our house was robbed last month while we were visiting John's mother in Pittsburgh.
7. Nonverbal gesture for speaker to address group	*(Jackson gestures with eyes and hands for Gwen to address her comments to the group.)*
	Gwen: *(Continuing to group)* I thought we had done everything we needed to do by stopping the mail and newspaper, but obviously that wasn't enough.
4. Hesitates	*(Jackson hesitates, awaiting other members' responses to Gwen.)*
	Sam: *(Looking at Jackson)* I would like some information on the nature of burglaries in our neighborhood.
8. No comment, evaluation	*(Jackson does not comment; instead, he looks inquiringly at Officer Talbot, the resource officer.)*
	Officer Talbot: During the past year, there were 125 burglaries in our community, and over 90 percent of them occurred between 10 a.m. and 3 p.m. when you were at work and the children were at school. Most burglaries have been crimes of opportunities . . . we have made entering our homes relatively easy. The intruders entered homes through unlocked doors and windows, especially through garage doors, bathroom windows, and back doors and windows where they were less likely to . . .
	Gwen: *(Interrupting Talbot)* Our doors and windows *were* locked. Still they entered. They broke the kitchen window on the back porch and crawled in over the sink!
	Officer Talbot: It does happen, Gwen. I'm sure your intruders felt more safe entering your house from the back side. They are typically looking for cash or items they can readily sell for cash such as jewelry, electronic equipment, silver, guns, or other valuables easy to carry away. Typical burglars in this neighborhood are local, male teenagers. Only 15 percent of our burglaries have been committed by individuals who are pros.

TABLE *9.6* | (Continued)

<table>
<tr><td></td><td>**Sam:** Thank you.</td></tr>
<tr><td>2. Uses inquiring tone
3. Uses terms *perhaps, might*</td><td>**Jackson:** *(Using inquiring tone)* It seems that the majority of our crimes are opportunities. Perhaps we might consider ways of removing . . .</td></tr>
<tr><td></td><td>**Sam:** *(Interrupting Jackson)* Exactly. How can we remove the opportunities?</td></tr>
<tr><td>5. Willingly turns over floor</td><td>*(Jackson turns interestedly to Sam.)*</td></tr>
<tr><td></td><td>**Frank:** I found a home security survey that helps homeowners locate areas where they might be lax.
Officer Talbot: I have seen those. What areas does your survey cover?
Frank: Let's see. It covers examining windows, doors, garages, landscaping, exterior lights, and interior lights. It's in a checklist format and would be easy for us to use and to share with all members of the neighborhood.</td></tr>
<tr><td>12. Doesn't praise individual
2. Inquiring tone and response</td><td>**Jackson:** *(Does not praise Frank, although he believes that bringing the survey to the meeting was a good idea since it will provide a catalyst for further group discussion)* May we make a copy of the survey to share around the group? Is it copyrighted?</td></tr>
<tr><td></td><td>**Officer Talbot:** These surveys are typically provided by public service groups, and citizens are encouraged to copy and use them.
Frank: Yes. We can copy and distribute it. It is produced and distributed from the county sheriff's office. In fact, it gives a number here for obtaining more copies. I thought it was a good idea for our meeting this evening, so I brought enough copies for everyone. *(He passes copies of the survey to members around the table.)*
Officer Talbot: I'll contact the office and get the extra copies. How many copies will we need?</td></tr>
<tr><td>3. Using term *probably*
12. Not praising individual
10. Moving ownership of survey from Frank to group with "our survey"</td><td>**Jackson:** We will probably want enough copies for all homes in our four-block area. *(Turning to the group, without addressing or praising Frank)* Well, what does our survey say?</td></tr>
</table>

TABLE 9.6 | (Continued)

Notice that during Jackson's meeting, he exhibited each of the twelve positive behaviors at least once. Each of these group-encouraging behaviors is so subtle that it often is unnoticed by group members. The behaviors taken together, however, communicate clearly to group members that Jackson believes their input is valuable, he wants them to contribute, and he is not going to broker who gets to speak or when. Jackson's actions demonstrate clearly that he does not perceive his neighbors to be an audience or backdrop for him and one or two of his friends in the community.

section where the meeting script is repeated with the behaviors, *enhancing* and *stifling,* marked. Learners can then compare their classification of the behaviors with the classifications made by the designer. Learners will be instructed to mark any discrepancies between their classifications and those of the designer. These discrepancies can then be discussed in person at the learning center when NCW leaders come for the next interactive session.

LEARNER PARTICIPATION SCRIPT The learner participation script for the web-based materials is illustrated in Table 9.7. Only a part of the script is illustrated; the actual script would continue until all twelve cooperation encouraging and corresponding stifling behaviors are illustrated. We stop here because the nature of the student participation is established.

FEEDBACK To illustrate feedback, only a segment of the participation exercise follows. Table 9.8 contains the feedback, and learners would locate this material after completing the exercises in Table 9.7. In Table 9.8, the pluses and minuses shown in the left column indicate the designer's classification and whether the action was seen as enhancing (+) or stifling (−). Learners are to compare their classifications with those of the instructor. The right-hand column contains a repeat of the script in Table 9.7 so that learners are not required to scroll up and down the screen to match the participation and feedback materials. Learners will continue with the feedback material until they have compared all their responses and marked their inconsistent ratings for group discussion.

Following the learner feedback for objective 6.4.1, participants will begin instruction for objective 6.4.2, "Classifying leaders' actions during interactive meetings." A video will be used, and learners will observe segments of three NCW meetings in progress. The information presentation and example segments will demonstrate each of the encouraging and discouraging behaviors as well as demonstrate how the leader could have molded each of the stifling actions into complementary, encouraging actions.

As a learner participation activity, they will again classify all the encouraging actions the leader takes during the meeting session. In addition, for

Session 10, Engendering Cooperative Member Behaviors: Learner Participation for Objective 6.4.1

Directions: Can you locate each time one of these twelve key interaction leadership actions occurs in the following NCW meeting? Darcy, the new NCW leader, is a law student and new to her community, which is located in a high crime area near the university. She has had several leadership roles in college, but this is her first community-based leadership activity. Young and inexperienced, she may commit errors or stifling actions as she manages her group's interaction. Having completed communications courses and participated in problem-solving discussions in college, however, she will undoubtedly demonstrate several of the encouraging actions. Each time you see Darcy demonstrate one of the encouraging actions, write the number of the action with a plus sign (+) in the left column of the same line. If she uses the action incorrectly (stifling), write down the action number with a minus sign (–). For example, if Darcy suggests a point of discussion as a question, you would place a + 1 in the left column of that line. On the other hand, if she tells the group what to discuss, you will place a –1 in the left column preceding the line. Use a list of numbered leader actions identical to the one used in the pretest to aid your responses.

Mark Leader Actions in This Column	Neighborhood Watch Meeting Script
	Darcy: Thank you all for coming this morning. I am so pleased to see this many of you returning and also to see several new faces. Why don't we begin by introducing ourselves? Some of you may want to share your reasons for joining us. Shall we start here on my left?
	(*The fourteen neighbors in attendance begin to introduce themselves.*)
	Darcy: At the conclusion of the last meeting, several of you suggested that we discuss ways to be more safe as we move about the neighborhood and campus. On this topic, I have invited Sharon Wright, who will share some of the strategies they use with students who come to the Victims' Advocacy Center on campus.
	Darcy: (*Turning to Sharon*) Thank you for coming this morning, Sharon. Some of you may know Sharon. We are certainly lucky to have her with us. She has her Ph.D. in criminology with a master's in counseling and victim advocacy.
	Sharon: Thank you, Darcy. I am very pleased to have been invited.
	Darcy: (*Looking around total group, smiling*) I have also made a list of topics suggested in Mann and Blakeman's book *Safe Homes, Safe Neighborhoods* on personal safety in the neighborhood.
	Darcy: (*Continuing*) Our basic plan this morning is to generate information for a personal safety-tips brochure that we will stuff in all community mailboxes and that Sharon will distribute through the Victims' Advocacy Center on campus. I think we should begin with the issue of safety in the home since we are having such problems with robberies.
	Ben: I think that street safety is more problematic here, so . . .
	Darcy: (*Interrupting Ben*) That's a very good idea, Ben, and we should get to street safety as well. (*Darcy remains quiet, looking around room for other suggestions from group.*)
	Sharon: We should perhaps discuss safety in public parking lots on campus and at the mall. There are several strategies we can use there to improve our chances of being safe.

TABLE *9.7* | (Continued)

> **Darcy:** That's a good idea, Sharon. Well, that's three good topics. Home safety, street safety, and parking lot safety. Let's begin with these and see where they take us. Bob, you haven't said anything yet. Where would you like to start?
>
> **Bob:** Like Ben, I understand there are a lot of problems in our neighborhood with street crimes such as muggings, purse snatchings, and so forth. Let's consider this area since most of us walk from campus down Third Street and across Garfield. Those are some of the most dangerous sidewalks in this city!
>
> . . .

The student participation script continues until all twelve cooperation and corresponding stifling behaviors are illustrated. We stop here because the nature of the student participation is established.

TABLE *9.8* | **Feedback for the Group Leadership Instructional Goal**

Session 10, Engendering Cooperative Member Behaviors: Feedback for Objective 6.4.1 (To illustrate feedback, only a segment of the exercise follows.)

Directions: Once you have finished analyzing Darcy's cooperation enhancing and stifling actions, you should compare your marked script with the following one. Each time your behaviors column differs from the following one, circle the behavior on your script that is different than the one(s) marked on this script. Reread the script at the point of difference to see whether you wish to change your mind about the category. If not, we will discuss differences before moving on.

Mark Leader Actions in this Column	Neighborhood Watch Meeting
	Darcy: Thank you all for coming this morning. I am so pleased to see this many of you returning and also to see several new faces. ***Why don't we begin by introducing ourselves?*** Some of you
+1	
+3,+10	*may* want to share your reasons for joining *us*.
+1	Shall *we* start here on my left?
	(The 14 neighbors in attendance begin to introduce themselves.)
	Darcy: At the conclusion of the last meeting, *several members suggested* that *we discuss* ways
+11,+10	to be more safe as *we* move about the neighborhood and campus. On this topic, *I* have

TABLE *9.8* | **(Continued)**

Mark Leader Actions in this Column	Neighborhood Watch Meeting
-10	invited Sharon Wright, who will share some of the strategies they use with students who come to the Victims' Advocacy Center on campus.
-11, -12	**Darcy:** *(Turning to Sharon)* Thank you for coming this morning, Sharon. Some of you may know Sharon. *We are certainly lucky to have her with us. She has her Ph.D. in criminology with a master's in counseling and victim advocacy.* **Sharon:** Thank you Darcy. I am very pleased to have been invited.
+6 -10 -1, +10 -10, +10 -3 +10	**Darcy:** *(Looking around total group, smiling) I have* also made a list of topics suggested in Mann and Blakeman's book *Safe Homes, Safe Neighborhoods* on personal safety in the neighborhood. *Our basic plan* this morning is to generate information for a personal safety-tips brochure that *we* will stuff in all community mailboxes and that Sharon will distribute through the Victims' Advocacy Center on campus. *I think* **we** *should* begin with the issue of safety in the home since *we* are having such problems with robberies.
	Ben: I think that street safety is more problematic here, so . . .
-5,-8 +10, -3 +4	**Darcy:** *(Interrupting Ben) That's a very good idea,* Ben, and *we should* get to street safety as well. *(Darcy remains quiet, looking around room for other suggestions from group.)*
	Sharon: We should perhaps discuss safety in parking lots on campus and at the mall. There are several strategies we can use there to improve our chances of being safe.
-8 -1	**Darcy:** *That's a good idea* Sharon. Well that's three good topics. Home safety, street safety, and parking lot safety. *Let's begin with these . . .*

each stifling action encountered, they will prescribe the action the leader should have taken instead. The feedback for this objective will also be delivered using the video, with guided trips through the same meeting to revisit particular leader behaviors. During the feedback trip, as each stifling action is revisited, the leader changes actions before the learner's eyes and uses the complementary encouraging one instead. Following instruction on objective 6.4.2, the learners will finish session 10 on objective 6.5.1 by leading a small group discussion of their own.

Readers interested in examples of material development for the school subject unit on story writing should review Appendices G, H, and I.

SUMMARY

You have the following resource materials for developing your instruction:
- Instructional goal
- Instructional analysis
- Behavioral objectives
- Sample test items
- Characteristics of the target learners
- Characteristics of the learning and performance contexts
- Instructional strategy that includes prescriptions for the following:
  - Cluster and sequence of objectives
  - Preinstructional activities
  - Assessments to be used
  - Content presentation and examples
  - Learner participation (practice and feedback)
  - Strategies for memory and transfer skills
  - Activities assigned to individual lessons
  - Student groupings and media selections
  - Delivery system

It is a good idea to keep two of your resources close at hand while writing the materials. The first is the design evaluation chart (see Tables 7.2 and 7.3 and Figure 7.1). The performance objectives in the design evaluation chart will help ensure congruence between the instruction created and the objective. Other critical resources include the learner analysis, the context analysis, and the instructional strategy documents. Constant reference to these documents while you work will keep your efforts targeted and help avoid introducing interesting—but extraneous—information. Focus carefully on the conditions specified in the objectives as well as the characteristics and special needs of the learners.

When you complete this phase of the instructional design, you should have a draft set of instructional materials, draft assessments, and draft instructor's manual.

We should caution you on one important point: Do not feel that any of the materials you develop on the first attempt will stand for all time. It is extremely important that you consider the materials you develop as draft copies. They will be reviewed and revised based on feedback from learners, instructors, and subject-matter experts. You should not begin engaging in elaborate and expensive production procedures. You should be considering the use of hand-printed 8½-by-11 sheets of paper instead of professionally prepared overhead transparencies; the use of crude pictures instead of finished artwork; the use of storyboards and "homemade" videos instead of studio-produced tapes. Delay the development of any mediated materials, particularly ones that will be expensive, until you have completed at least one revision of your materials.

You can be assured that no matter how humble your materials may be at this point, there will be costs associated with them. Try to minimize the costs now in order to gather the data that you will need to make the correct decisions about the final version. We will have more to say about this in succeeding chapters.

PRACTICE

I. Developmental Considerations
1. List below the three major components of an instructional package.
   a. _____
   b. _____
   c. _____
2. What types of learning components would you be most likely to include in the instructional materials?
   a. _____
   b. _____
   c. _____
   d. _____
   e. _____
3. What would you be likely to include in the instructor's guide portion of course management information?
   a. _____
   b. _____
   c. _____
   d. _____
4. Number from 1 to 3 the following materials to show the order in which you believe you would develop them: ( ) instructional materials, ( ) assessments, and ( ) instructor's guide. (There is no set answer to this question, but with your developmental project in mind, it is time to give the developmental procedure some thought. This will enable you to collect pertinent information at the proper time.)

II. Developing Instructional Materials
For this exercise, you should practice developing materials based on the instructional strategy you developed for depositing money into a checking account. The entire instructional strategy appears in the Feedback section of the previous chapter. Because this task is complex, select only the following components to develop:
1. A pretest for objectives 2.1 through 2.4.5.
2. Actual content presentation materials for objectives 2.1 through 2.4.5 (3 in Feedback section of Chapter 8).
You may like the instructional strategy that you developed for depositing money better than the example we provided in the last chapter. If this is the case, use your original strategy rather than ours found in Table 8.12 to develop materials.

It may help you to use the script format we used earlier to develop your material. Simply divide a sheet of paper into three sections and label each component and objective as you work.

Component	Subskills	Text

This format will help keep you on track. Of course you would not use this format when field-testing your own instruction. The first two columns would be omitted. Compare your content presentation materials with the sample materials in Table 9.10 in the Feedback section that follows.

3. Learner participation activities (practice tests) with feedback for objectives 2.3.1, 2.3.2, 2.4.1, 2.4.2, 2.4.3.1, 2.4.3.2, 2.4.4, 2.4.5, and 2.5. For feedback, see sample student participation activities in Table 9.11 in the Feedback section.

FEEDBACK

I. Developmental Considerations
1. The three major components of an instructional package are
   - Instructional materials
   - Assessments
   - Course management information
2. Types of information you are likely to include in the instructional materials are
   - Preinstructional activities, including objectives and review materials as well as motivational materials and activities.
   - Content that must be presented to students to enable them to achieve your objectives, including examples and nonexamples of information, concepts, or skills that need to be learned.
   - Participation activities that enable students to practice or to try out the concept or skills for themselves, and feedback on students' performance that enables them to reconsider their ideas or adjust their techniques.
   - Assessments of learners' mastery of new information and skills.
   - Activities that enhance memory and transfer.
3. Types of materials you may want to include in an instructor's guide are
   - Information about the target population for the materials
   - Suggestions on how to adapt materials for older, younger, higher achieving, or lower achieving students
   - Overview of the content
   - Intended learning outcomes of the instruction
   - Suggestions for using the materials in a certain context or sequence
   - Suggestions for materials management for individualized learning, small-group learning, learning-center activities, or classroom activities
   - Retention and transfer activities
   - Tests that can be used to evaluate students' performance on terminal objectives
   - Evidence of the effectiveness of the materials when used as suggested with the intended target populations
   - Suggestions for evaluating students' work and reporting progress
   - Estimation of time required to use the materials properly
   - Equipment or additional facilities needed for the materials

4. A rigid pattern of development for the three components of the instruction—the instructional materials, assessments, and course management information—does not exist. The following order of events may serve as an example of how you might proceed. Constraints on your time, materials, and resources may cause you to deviate. The suggested order of development remains the same whether developing an instructional strategy, a unit of instruction, or a whole course:
   - Assessments that were probably completed in a previous design step and may just need final formatting
   - Instructional materials
   - Course management information including the instructor's guide and other information for implementing distance learning and self-paced instructional programs

II. 1. See pretest in Table 9.9.
   2. See content presentation in Table 9.10.
   3. See learner participation with feedback in Table 9.11.

TABLE 9.9 | **Pretest for Checking Account Instructional Goals (Objectives 2.1–2.5)**

Component	Subskill	Text
Pretest		Score_____ Name_____ Date_____Period_____ *Depositing Money in a Checking Account*
	2.1	1. List the places where you can obtain a deposit slip to deposit money into a checking account. a. _____ b. _____
	2.2	2. If the deposit slip you use is not printed specifically for your checking account, what information should you add to it so that banks can identify it as yours? a. _____ b. _____ c. _____
Pretest	2.3.1 2.3.2 2.4.2 2.4.3.1 2.4.3.2 2.4.4 2.4.5 2.5	3. Use the descriptions of money and checks in Table 1 to complete the sample deposit slip provided in Table 2. Both sides of the deposit form are illustrated. Place the correct information in the appropriate space on the deposit slip.

TABLE 1

COINS		BILLS		CHECKS	
Number	Coin	Number	Bill	Bank #	Amount
5	50¢	14	$100.	63-656	$145.20
8	25¢	12	50.	12-402	235.00
9	10¢	8	20.	13-320	500.00
3	5¢	4	10.	63-656	25.00
6	1¢	3	0.	17-402	650.00
				19-200	892.00
				16-420	200.00
Your account number is 4023161020.				13-920	100.00

TABLE 2
Front Side of Deposit Slip

	CURRENCY			
	COIN			
Name	C_____			
	H_____			
	E_____			
	C_____			
Address	K_____			
	S			
Date _____	Total from other side			
	TOTAL			
	Less Cash Received			
Sign here only if cash received from deposit	Total Deposit			

TABLE *9.9* | (Continued)

Component	Subskill	Text
Pretest		*Back Side of Deposit Slip*

Please list each check separately by financial institution		
Number	Dollars	Cents
Checks by Financial Institution		
TOTAL		

TABLE *9.10* | **Content Presentation for Checking Account Instructional Goal**

Component	Subskill	Text
Content Presentation	2.1	After you have opened a checking account, you will want to continue to deposit money in it. Banks have specially printed forms you should use to deposit your money. One type of deposit form is provided along with your checks. It has your name, your address, and your account number printed on it. It is wise to use these printed slips because it helps ensure that your money is credited to the appropriate account.
Content Presentation	2.2	Sometimes you may need to deposit money into your account when you do not have your personalized deposit forms with you. For this purpose, banks have general deposit slips that can be used by any of their customers. These forms may be obtained in the bank lobby or in the automatic teller machine. Before using these deposit slips, you should always print your name as it appears on your account in the appropriate space. You should also print the number of your checking account in the boxes provided for the account number. Failure to provide this identifying information on general deposit slips will result in delays and possibly errors because the bank will not know where to put the money you have deposited.
Example	2.1 2.2	The following form is a personalized checking account deposit slip. Notice the name of the customer is printed in the upper left corner (A), and the checking account number is located in the bottom center of the form (B). There is also a line provided where you can write the date when the money is deposited (C). It is a good idea to always put the date on your deposit tickets to help identify them.

TABLE *9.10* | (Continued)

Component	Subskill	Text

| | | (A) Sara Jones   63-656
302 Shadow Lane   631
Tampa, Florida 33617 |

(C) Date_____

CURRENCY		
COIN		
C_____		
H_____		
E_____		
C_____		
K_____		
S		
Total from other side		
TOTAL		
Less cash received		
Total Deposit		

Sign here only if cash
received from deposit

(B) 6401121010

Component	Subskill	Text
Content	2.3.1	After obtaining a deposit slip and ensuring that your name, your account number, and the date are recorded, you are ready to enter the amount of money you wish to deposit into your account. Three different forms of money can be deposited into your account: dollar bills, coins, and checks. There is a separate space on the deposit slip for each. It is a good idea to separate the kinds of money you wish to deposit. Make one pile of bills, one pile of coins, and another pile of checks.
Example	2.3.1	Locate on the deposit slip where you are to record each type of money. Dollar bills are recorded on the line marked "currency," and coins are entered on the line marked "coins."

TABLE 9.10 | (Continued)

Component	Subskill	Text

Currency		
Coins		
C		
H		
E		
C		
K		
S		
Total from other side		
TOTAL		

Content — 2.3.2

Add together all the bills you wish to deposit, and record the total amount on the "currency" line. For example, if you have two fifty-dollar bills and three ten-dollar bills, what would you enter? Since these bills total $130, you would write this amount on the currency line.

The second step is to record the total amount of coins you wish to deposit. Sum the coins you have, locate the line marked "coins" and enter the total on that line. If you have two half dollars, two quarters, and five nickels, what would you write on the coin line?

Example

$$2 \times .50 = 1.00$$
$$2 \times .25 = .50$$
$$5 \times .05 = .25$$
$$\overline{\$1.75}$$

	Currency	130	00
→	Coins	1	75

Content — 2.4.1

You should prepare the checks you wish to deposit into your account. Each check to be deposited should be signed on the back using the *name* and signature you have registered on your signature card. After signing your name, you should record your *account number* beneath your name. This will help if your checks become separated from your deposit slip during bookkeeping.

Example

Back Side of the Check

For deposit only
Sara Jones
4023161020

TABLE *9.10* | (Continued)

Component	Subskill	Text
	2.4.2	You are now ready to enter the checks on the deposit slip. Each check should be listed separately in spaces provided for checks, and the amount of the check as well as the bank number should be written on the deposit slip. The bank number should be recorded on the left side of the line, and the amount of the check should be written on the right side.
Content	2.4.3.1	The first step is to locate the bank number on the check. It is usually located on the upper right corner of the check, above the date. The bank number is the top one in a set of two numbers. The sample check illustrates the bank number and its location.
Example	2.4.3.1	
Content	2.4.3.2	Notice the number $\frac{63\text{-}656}{631}$ on the sample check. The top number of this set identifies the bank. The amount of the check and the identifying bank number would be recorded on the deposit slip. Each check you wish to deposit should have the identifying number of the issuing bank and the total amount of the check recorded.
Example	2.4.3.2	
Content	2.4.4	If you have more checks to deposit than will fit on the front side, then turn over the deposit slip. There is room on the reverse side of the slip to list additional checks you wish to deposit. To complete this side of the deposit form, simply list the identifying number of the issuing bank and the amount of each check.

TABLE *9.10* | (Continued)

Component	Subskill	Text
Example	2.4.4	Checks included on the back side of a deposit slip are totaled and the sum is written on the "total" line provided at the bottom of the list. This total is then entered on the front side of the slip. The sample reverse-side of a deposit ticket illustrates how it should be completed.

Please list each check separately by financial institution

Financial Institution	Dollars	Cents
42-301	100	00
24-206	5	00
13-925	43	00
63-402	50	00
Total (enter on front side)	198	00

Component	Subskill	Text
Content	2.4.5 2.5	With all the cash and the checks you wish to deposit entered on the deposit ticket, you are ready to total the deposit. Remember to write the total amount of the checks listed on the back side of the deposit slip on the front in the space labeled "Total from other side." Add together the amount of money listed on the front of the form, and record the sum on the line marked "TOTAL." The following illustration shows a deposit slip completed to this point.
Example	2.5	

Sara Jones
402 Shadow Lane

Date _____

_____

	Dollars	Cents
Currency	130	00
Coins	1	75
C H 63-656	40	00
E C 42-301	300	25
K S 12-924	402	16
Total from other side	198	00
TOTAL	1072	16
Less Cash Received		
Total Deposit	1072	16

6401121010

TABLE *9.11*

Learner Participation with Feedback for Checking Account Instructional Goal

Component	Subskill	Text
Learner Participation	2.3.1 2.3.2 2.4.1 2.4.2 2.4.3.1 2.4.3.2 2.4.4 2.4.5 2.5	Using the following dollars, coins, and checks in column A, fill out the sample deposit slip in column B. Use both sides of the deposit slip.

A

Bills:
  3 x $100.00 =
  2 x $ 20.00 =
  1 x $ 5.00 = _____

Coins:
  4 x $.25 =
  3 x $.10 =
  2 x $.05 =
  7 x $.01 = _____

Checks:
  24-102 $32.00
  16-904 12.00
  52-129   5.00
  32-926 15.00
  40-524 26.00
  13-240 80.00
  52-160 95.00

B

Front Side of Slip

	Dollars	Cents
Currency		
Coins		
C		
H		
E		
C		
K		
S		
Total from other side		
TOTAL		

Back Side of Slip

Bank Number	Dollars	Cents
TOTAL CHECKS		

TABLE *9.11* | (Continued)

Component	Subskill	Text
Feedback	2.3.1–2.5	

Front Side of Slip

	Dollars	Cents
Currency	*345*	*00*
Coins	*1*	*47*
C H *24-102*	*32*	*00*
E C *16-904*	*12*	*00*
K S *52-129*	*5*	*00*
Total from other side	*216*	*00*
TOTAL	*611*	*47*
4023161020		

Back Side of Slip

Bank Number	Dollars	Cents
32-926	*15*	*00*
40-524	*26*	*00*
13-240	*80*	*00*
52-160	*95*	*00*
TOTAL	*216*	*00*

REFERENCES AND RECOMMENDED READINGS

Barron, A., & Orwig, G. (1995) *Multimedia technologies for training: An introduction.* Englewood, CO: Libraries Unlimited. A survey of tools and techniques for training with multimedia technologies.

Chute, A. G., Thompson, M. M., & Hancock, B. (1998). *The McGraw-Hill handbook of distance learning: A "how to get started guide" for trainers and human resources professionals.* New York: McGraw-Hill. Includes sections on designing effective distance learning and supporting materials for video conferencing, audio conferencing, the Internet.

Fleming, M., & Levie, W. H. (Eds.) (1993). *Instructional message design.* Englewood Cliffs, NJ: Educational Technology Publications. Excellent chapters on concept learning, problem solving, psychomotor skills, attitude change, and motivation.

Gagné, R. M., & Driscoll, M. P. (1988). *Essentials of learning for instruction.* (2nd ed.) Hinsdale, IL: Dryden Press, 71–96. The conditions of learning are related to the types of learning outcomes desired.

Gagné, R. M., Wager, W., & Rojas, A. (1981). Planning and authoring computer-assisted instruction lessons. *Educational Technology, 21* (9), 17–26. In this article the authors provide specific examples of procedures that could be employed with CAI to present the events of instruction for various types of learning outcomes.

Gibbons, A. S., & Fairweather, P. G. (1999). *Computer-based instruction: Design and development.* Englewood Cliffs, NJ: Educational Technology. Authoring tools, interface design, and message design for delivering instruction by computer or web.

Greer, M. (1992): *ID project management: Tools and techniques for instructional designers and developers.* Englewood Cliffs, NJ: Educational Technology Publications. Good guide to ID team organization and management with chapters on creating and testing rough draft materials.

Hannafin, M. J., & Peck, K. L. (1988). *The design, development, and evaluation of instructional software.* New York: Macmillan. Excellent source for process of developing computer-based materials from instructional strategy prescriptions.

Harrison, N. (1994). *How to design self-directed and distance learning: A guide for creators of Web-based training, computer-based training, and self-study materials.* New York: McGraw-Hill. Follows a systems design model with commentary on special considerations for developing self-directed and distance learning.

Heinich, R., Molenda, M., Russell, J. D., & Smaldeano, S. (1999). *Instructional media and technologies for learning* (6th ed.) Upper Saddle River, NJ: Merrill. A classic text on the design and utilization of media in instruction.

Jonassen, D. H. (Ed.). (1982). *The technology of text: Vol. I.* Englewood Cliffs, NJ: Educational Technology Publications.

Jonassen, D. H. (Ed.). (1985). *The technology of text: Vol. II.* Englewood Cliffs, NJ: Educational Technology Publications.

Jonassen, D. H., Peck, K. L., & Wilson, B. G. (1999.) *Learning with technology: A constructivist perspective.* Upper Saddle River, NJ: Merrill. Focuses on the use of technology for engaging students in meaningful learning rather than the use of technology to deliver instructional content to learners.

Kemp, J. E., & Smellie, D. C. (1994). *Planning, producing, and using instructional technologies* (7th ed.) New York: HarperCollins College Publishers. Similar to Heinich text in scope and emphasis on wide range of media formats.

Kyker, K., & Curchy, C. (1993). *Television production: A classroom approach.* Englewood, CO: Libraries Unlimited.

Mann, S., & Blakeman, M. C. (1993). *Safe homes, safe neighborhoods: Stopping crime where you live.* Berkeley, CA: Nolo Press.

Merrill, P. F., Hammons, K., Vincent, B. R., Reynolds, P. L., Christensen, L., & Tolman, M. N. (1996). *Computers in education.* Boston: Allyn and Bacon. General focus is on public education, but contains views on roles that computers can play in education and information on software evaluation, multimedia systems, and curriculum integration.

Reynolds, A., & Iwinski, T. (1996). *Multimedia training: Developing technology-based systems.* New York: McGraw-Hill.

Slatkin, E. (1991). *How to write a manual.* Berkeley, CA: Ten Speed Press. Good suggestions for writing and formatting information.

Vaughan, T. (1998). *Multimedia: Making it work* (4th ed.) Berkeley, CA: Osborne/McGraw-Hill. Comprehensive overview of multimedia technologies including hardware, software, and authoring systems.

Williams, M. L., Paprock, K., & Covington, B. (1999). *Distance learning: The essential guide.* Thousand Oaks, CA: Sage Publications. Useful tips for development and management of distance learning programs.

Zettle, H. (1996). *Television production handbook* (6th ed.). Belmont, CA: Wadsworth.

DESIGNING AND CONDUCTING FORMATIVE EVALUATIONS

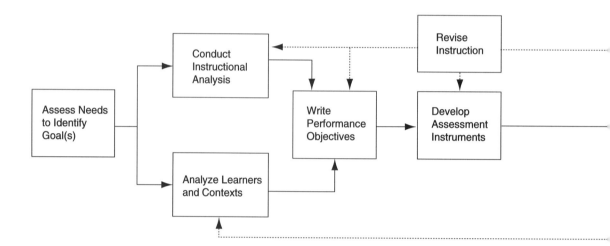

OBJECTIVES

- Describe the purposes for and various stages of formative evaluation of instructor-developed materials, instructor-selected materials, and instructor-presented instruction.
- Describe the instruments used in a formative evaluation.
- Develop an appropriate formative evaluation plan and construct instruments for a set of instructional materials or an instructor presentation.
- Collect data according to a formative evaluation plan for a given set of instructional materials or instructor presentation.

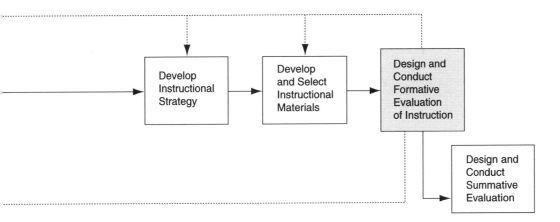

BACKGROUND

If you had been developing instructional materials thirty years ago, then it is likely that your initial draft, or perhaps a revised draft, of those materials would have been put into final production and distributed to the target population. As a consequence, it was almost certain that many problems would occur in their use due to the limited effectiveness of first draft instructional materials. Too often instructors have been blamed for poor teaching and learners for poor learning when, in fact, the materials were not sufficient to support the instructional effort.

The problem of untested materials was magnified in the 1960s with the advent of large curriculum development projects. At that time the concept of *evaluation* tended to be defined as a comparison of the effectiveness of an innovation with other existing products. When such studies were carried out, researchers often found a relatively low level of student achievement with the new curriculum materials. In reviewing this situation, Cronbach and Scriven concluded that we must expand our concept of evaluation. They proposed that developers conduct what has come to be called *formative eval-*

uation—the collection of data and information during the development of instruction that can be used to improve the effectiveness of the instruction.

Studies have shown that thousands of the instructional products sold in the United States each year have not been evaluated with learners and revised prior to distribution. Other studies have demonstrated that simply trying out materials with a single-learner and revising the materials on the basis of that data can make a significant difference in the effectiveness of materials. This component of the instructional design model therefore emphasizes the necessity of gathering data from members of the target population about the use and effectiveness of materials and using that information to make the materials even more effective.

You should note that all of the design and development steps in the instructional design process are based on theory, research, and some common sense. At this point, you are about to become an evaluator as you collect data about the effectiveness of your own instructional materials. By following the instructional design model, you hope you have generated instructional materials that will produce significant achievement for learners who initially cannot perform your terminal objective. You are now at the point of testing that assumption.

Formative evaluation was originally used as a process to improve instruction after the first draft of instruction was developed. Experienced designers, however, found that it was better to try out earlier components of the design process, thereby avoiding a lot of problems that would otherwise not be discovered until after the draft of the instruction was complete.

Recall we suggested that during the context analysis you use your instructional analysis to explain what you will be teaching to some learners from the target population. We also suggested a similar approach when you completed your instructional strategy—that you use it to "teach" some learners in an attempt to find the problems in the strategy prior to its use as a guide for developing the instruction. Both of these procedures can be referred to as formative evaluations in that you are gathering information from learners in order to revise the materials before proceeding with the design process. Now you will be doing the same thing, in a more systematic manner, with the instruction that you have developed.

A rather arbitrary division of content has been made between this chapter and the next. We typically think about formative evaluation and revision of instructional materials as one major step. For the sake of clarity and to emphasize the importance of re-examining the whole instructional design process when instructional materials are to be revised, we have separated the design and conduct of the formative evaluation study from the process of revising the instructional materials.

In this chapter we will discuss how to apply formative evaluation techniques to newly developed materials, to selected and adapted materials, to instructor-delivered instruction, and to combinations of these three presentation modes. We will also show how to apply these techniques to instructional procedures as well as to instructional materials to ensure that instruction, regardless of the presentation mode, is properly implemented and managed.

CONCEPTS

The major concept underlying this chapter is *formative evaluation*. Formative evaluation is the process designers use to obtain data that can be used to revise their instruction to make it more efficient and effective. The emphasis in formative evaluation is on the collection and analysis of data and the revision of the instruction. When a final version of the instruction is produced, other evaluators may collect data to determine its effectiveness. This latter type of evaluation is often referred to as *summative evaluation*. It is summative in that the instruction is now in its final form, and it is appropriate to compare it with other similar forms of instruction.

There are three basic phases of formative evaluation. The first is one-to-one, or clinical evaluation. In this initial phase the designer works with individual learners to obtain data to revise the materials. The second stage of formative evaluation is a small-group evaluation. A group of eight to twenty learners who are representative of the target population study the materials on their own and are tested to collect the required data. The third stage of formative evaluation is usually a field trial. The number of learners is not of particular consequence; often thirty are sufficient. The emphasis in the field trial is on the testing of the procedures required for the installation of the instruction in a situation as close to the "real world" as possible.

The three phases of formative evaluation are typically preceded by the review of instruction by interested specialists who are not directly involved in the instructional development project, but have relevant expertise. The role of these reviewers is described, followed by descriptions of the three learner-oriented phases of formative evaluation.

ROLE OF SUBJECT-MATTER, LEARNING, AND LEARNER SPECIALISTS IN FORMATIVE EVALUATION

Although the focus of the formative evaluation process is on the acquisition of data from learners, it is also important to have the instruction reviewed by specialists. It is assumed that the designer is knowledgeable about the content area or is working with a content specialist, and is also knowledgeable about the target population. Still, there are several good reasons to have the instruction reviewed by outside specialists.

When the first draft of the instruction has been written, designers appear to experience a "forest and trees" problem. They have seen so much that they cannot see anything; it is invaluable to the designer to get others to review what has been developed. One type of reviewer is usually a person outside the project who has special expertise in the content area of the instruction. This subject-matter expert (SME) should comment on the accuracy and currency of the instruction. Although many suggestions for improvement may be received, the designer should give considerable thought before making any changes that are counter to the instructional strategy already developed. Another type of reviewer is a specialist in the type of learning outcome involved. A colleague who is familiar with the suggestions for instruction related to the type of learning might be able to critique your instructional strategy related to what is known about enhancing that particular type of learning.

It is also helpful to share the first draft of the instruction with a person who is familiar with the target population—a person who can look at the instruction through the target population's eyes and react. This specialist may be able to provide insights into the appropriateness of the material for the eventual performance context.

The designer is not obligated to use the suggestions of these specialists. There may be some recommendations that the designer may want to consider after data from learners have been collected and summarized. At least the designer is sensitized to potential problems before learners become involved in the formative evaluation process.

ONE-TO-ONE EVALUATION WITH LEARNERS

In this discussion of the three phases of formative evaluation of instruction, we will assume that the designer has developed original instruction. In subsequent sections we will discuss the differences in procedures when existing materials are used, or when instructor-led instruction has been created.

The purpose of the first stage of formative evaluation, the one-to-one stage, is to identify and remove the most obvious errors in the instruction, and to obtain initial performance indications and reactions to the content by learners. This is accomplished through direct interaction between the designer and individual learners. During this stage, the designer works individually with three or more learners who are representative of the target population.

CRITERIA   During the development of the instructional strategy and the instruction itself, designers and developers make a myriad of translations and decisions that link the content, learners, instructional format, and instructional setting. The one-to-one trials provide designers with their first glimpse of the viability of these links and translations from the learners' perspective. The three main criteria and the decisions designers will make during the evaluation are as follows:

1. **Clarity:** Is the message, or what is being presented, clear to individual target learners?

2. **Impact:** What is the impact of the instruction on individual learner's attitudes and achievement of the objectives and goals?

3. **Feasibility:** How feasible is the instruction given the available resources (time/context)?

The one-to-one trials help verify whether the designers' and developers' hunches were correct or were reflections of their misconceptions of the target group.

SELECTING LEARNERS   One of the most critical decisions that is made by the designer in the formative evaluation is the selection of learners to participate in the study. This is not an experiment; there is no need for random selection of large numbers of learners. Actually, the designer wants to select a few learners who are representative of the target population. They should represent the range of ability in the group because prior learning or ability is usually one of the major determiners of ability to learn new skills and information. The designer therefore selects at least one learner from the target population who is above average in ability (but certainly not the top student), one who is average, and at least one learner who is below average. The designer then works on an individual basis with each learner. After the initial evaluations with the three learners, the designer may wish to select more learners from the target population to work in a one-to-one mode, although three is usually sufficient.

The designer should be aware of learner characteristics other than ability that may be highly related to the learners' achievement, and therefore should be systematically represented in the formative evaluation. As noted in Chapter 5, attitudes and previous experience can be very important, and such variables should be a consideration during formative evaluation. For the

TABLE 10.1 | **Formative Evaluation Criteria for One-to-One Trials and the Types of Information for Each Criterion**

Criteria

	Message	Links	Procedures
Clarity of instruction	•Vocabulary level •Sentence complexity •Message complexity •Introductions •Elaborations •Conclusions •Transitions	•Contexts •Examples •Analogies •Illustrations •Demonstrations •Reviews •Summaries	•Sequence •Segment size •Transition •Pace •Variation

	Attitudes	Achievement
Impact on learner	•Utility of the information and skills (relevance) •How easy/difficult the information and skills are to learn (confidence) •Satisfaction with skills learned	•Clarity of directions and items for posttests •Scores on posttests

	Learner	Resources
Feasibility	•Maturity •Independence •Motivation	•Time •Equipment •Environment

one-to-one phase of the formative evaluation, the designer may wish to select one learner with a very positive attitude toward that which is being taught, one who is neutral, and one who is negative. Likewise, if experience on the job is an important factor, select someone who has been on the job ten or more years, one who has been there two to five years, and someone who has been there for less than a year. The point is that ability might not be the only critical factor in selecting learners for a formative evaluation. The designer will have to make this decision for each particular instructional design situation.

DATA COLLECTION The three main criteria and the decisions to be made during one-to-one trials help evaluators focus on the kinds of information that would be useful. Table 10.1 contains the types of information that can be obtained for comparisons with clarity, impact, and feasibility criteria. The lists in each criterion category are intended to be illustrative rather than exhaustive because the degree of relevance of each kind of information may differ by learner maturity, instructional content, and delivery method.

For clarity of instruction, there are three main categories of illuminating information—message, links, and procedures. The first category, *message*, relates to how clear the basic message is to the learner. Concerns related to the basic message include the following: vocabulary, sentence complexity, and message structures. Regardless of whether the learner reads, hears, or sees the message, he or she must be able to follow it. The second category, *links*, refers to how the basic message is tailored for the learner. These links include the contexts, examples, analogies, illustrations, demonstrations, and so forth.

When these links are also unfamiliar to the learner, the basic message will undoubtedly be more complex. The third area, *procedures*, refers to characteristics of the instruction such as the sequence, the size of segment presented, the transition between segments, the pace, and the variation built into the presentation. The clarity of instruction may change for the learner when any one of these elements is inappropriate for her or him. The instruction can be so slow and iterative that the learner loses interest, or it can proceed so quickly that comprehension becomes difficult.

Descriptive information rather than quantitative data will probably yield the best information about clarity for revising the instruction. If the instruction is delivered through print, whether on paper or on a computer screen, then the learner can be directed to underline or highlight in some way all unfamiliar words; unclear examples, illustrations, and paragraphs; and to mark directions within any figures or tables that are confusing. The learner can be directed to jot down unclear terms and note confusing material when using a videotape or slide tape, or directed to stop the equipment at any point in order to interact with the evaluator about confusing passages or terms. Regardless of the delivery format during a one-to-one trial, the learner can be asked about the procedural characteristics of the instruction such as segment size and pace. Information about the procedural characteristics can also be collected by observation as the learner listens to the instructor, reads the material, or watches a screen. Such observations can help the evaluator determine whether anxiousness, boredom, fatigue, or all three conditions become apparent at different points in the instruction.

The second criterion in Table 10.1, *impact on learner*, relates to the learner's attitudes about the instruction and her or his achievement on specific objectives. Related to attitudes, the evaluator needs to determine whether the learner perceives the instruction as being (1) personally relevant to her or him, (2) accomplishable with reasonable effort, and (3) interesting and satisfying to experience. Related to achievement, posttests will help determine whether the individual can recall the information and perform the tasks. The format of these achievement measures will differ depending on the instructional delivery medium. Questions or directions for performance can be presented orally by the instructor. Learners can be asked to respond (1) using paper and pencil or keyboard, (2) orally in response to the instructor's questions, or (3) by developing or performing something requested.

The third criterion in Table 10.1, *feasibility*, relates to management-oriented considerations that can be examined during the one-to-one trial. Feasibility considerations include the capability of the learner, the instructional medium, and the instructional environment. Examples of questions of interest include the following: (1) How will the maturity, independence, and motivation of the learner influence the general amount of time required to complete the instruction? (2) Can learners such as this one operate or easily learn to operate any specialized equipment required? (3) Is the learner comfortable in this environment? and (4) Is the cost of delivering this instruction reasonable given the time requirements?

PROCEDURES   The typical procedure in a one-to-one evaluation is to explain to the learner that a new set of instructional materials has been designed and that you would like his or her reaction to them. You should say that any mistakes that learners might make are probably due to deficiencies in the material and not theirs. Encourage the learners to be relaxed and to talk about the materials. You should have the learners not only go through the instructional materials, but also have them take the test(s) provided with the materials. You might also note the amount of time it takes a learner to complete the material.

Instructional designers have found this process invaluable in the preparation of materials. When learners use the materials in this manner, they find typographical errors, omissions of content, missing pages, graphs that are improperly labeled, inappropriate links in their web pages, and other kinds of mechanical difficulties that inevitably occur. Learners often are able to describe difficulties that they have with the learning sequence and the concepts being taught. They can critique the tests in terms of whether they think they measure your objectives. You can use all of this information to revise your materials and tests and correct relatively gross problems as well as small errors.

In contrast to the earlier stages of instructional design, which emphasize the analytical skills of the designer, the first critical hallmark of the one-to-one formative evaluation is that it is almost totally dependent on the ability of the designer to establish rapport with the learner and then to interact effectively. The learner has typically never been asked to critique instruction; the assumption has been made that if learning does not occur, then it is the student's fault. Learners must be convinced that it is legitimate to be critical of what is presented to them. This is sometimes particularly difficult for the young person who is being asked to criticize an authority figure. The designer should establish an atmosphere of acceptance and support for any negative comments from the learner.

The second critical hallmark of the one-to-one approach is that it is an *interactive process*. The power of the process is greatly diminished when the designer hands the instruction to the learner and says, "Here, read this and let me know whether you have any problems." Sitting diagonally beside the learner, the designer should read (silently) with the learner and, at predetermined points, discuss with the learner what has been presented in the materials. The dialogue may focus on the answers to practice questions or may be a consideration of special points made in the content presentation. Before each one-to-one session, the designer should formulate a strategy about how the interaction will take place, and how the learner will know when it is appropriate to talk with the evaluator.

It is clear that a one-to-one session can take place with only one learner at a time. It is simply not feasible to do the process with two or more learners. As the designer proceeds with the evaluation, it is necessary to note the comments and suggestions made by the learner as well as any alternative explanations made by the designer that seem effective. These can be noted on one copy of the instruction, or a tape recorder can be used during the session, which students seem to adapt to quite readily.

ASSESSMENTS AND QUESTIONNAIRES   After the students in the one-to-one trials have completed the instruction, they should review the posttest and attitude questionnaire in the same fashion. After each item or step in the assessment, ask the learners why they made the particular responses that they did. This will help you spot not only mistakes, but also the reasons for the mistakes. This information can be quite helpful during the revision process. You will also find that some test items that appear to be perfectly clear to you will be totally misinterpreted by the learner. If these faulty items remain in the assessment for the small-group evaluation, then there will be major problems in determining whether only those items or the instruction is defective. Exert as much care in evaluating your assessment instruments as you do the instruction itself.

Test directions and instruments to evaluate performances, products, and attitudes should also be formatively evaluated before they are actually used to evaluate examinees' work. Just as with paper-and-pencil tests, you must ensure that the directions are clear to the learner and that learners can follow the instructions to produce the anticipated performance or product.

You must also evaluate the utility of the evaluation instrument. Particular criteria to use in evaluating the elements included in the instrument are the following: (1) the observability of each of the elements to be judged, (2) the clarity of the manner in which they are paraphrased, and (3) the efficiency of the sequencing order. Related to the evaluator's responding format, you should check whether the response categories and criteria are reasonable in terms of the number and type of judgments you need to make and the time available for you to observe, judge, and mark the judgment. If you are unable to keep up with the performer, then the accuracy of your judgments will be affected.

The reliability of your judgments should be evaluated. This can be done by rating the same performance or product two or more times with an intervening time interval. You can also check reliability by having two or more evaluators use the instrument to judge the same performance or product. When the multiple ratings obtained from a single evaluator on a single product differ or the ratings of multiple evaluators differ for a single product, the instrument should be revised. Instrument areas to reconsider are the number of elements to be judged, the number of levels of judgments to be made, and the clarity of the criteria for each level. The number of elements to be observed and the number of judgment categories should be reduced to a point where consistency is obtained. This implies that several iterations of instrument evaluation are necessary to verify the utility of the instrument and the consistency of judgments made using it.

Finally, you should evaluate your scoring strategy. Using the data you gather during the formative evaluation of the instrument, combine or summarize element-level scores as planned. Review these combined scores in terms of objective-level and overall performance. Are the scores logical and interpretable? Can they be used to evaluate particular parts of the instruction and performance? If not, then modify the rating and/or scoring procedure until usable data are obtained.

LEARNING TIME   One of the interests of the designer during the one-to-one evaluation is to determine the amount of time required for learners to complete their instruction. Only a very rough estimate can be obtained from the one-to-one evaluation because of the inclusion of the interaction between the learner and the designer. You can attempt to subtract a certain percentage of the time from the total time, but experience has indicated that such estimates can be quite inaccurate.

One final comment about the one-to-one evaluation process is in order. Rarely are learners placed in such a vulnerable position and required to expose their ignorance. There will be occasions even with adults who must admit that they do not know the meaning of a fairly common word—they always meant to look it up in the dictionary, but forgot. In the one-to-one stage, the designer is in control and thus has the responsibility for providing a comfortable working situation. Learners may deplore what they reveal about their current state of knowledge. Every possible effort should be made to be both objective about the instruction and supportive of the learner. Without the learner, there is no formative evaluation.

DATA INTERPRETATION The information on the clarity of instruction, impact on learner, and feasibility of the instruction needs to be summarized and focused. Particular aspects of the instruction that are found to be weak can then be reconsidered in order to plan revisions that are likely to improve the instruction for similar learners. One caution about data interpretation from one-to-one trials is critical. Take care not to overgeneralize the data gathered from only one individual. Although ensuring that the participating target learner is representative of the intended group will help ensure that his or her reactions are typical of other members of the target group, there is no guarantee that a second target learner will respond in a similar manner. Differing abilities, expectations, and personalities among members of the target group result in different data from each. Information gathered from the one-to-one trial should be viewed as a "first glimpse" that may or may not generalize. Gross errors in the instruction will likely become apparent during the trial and will lead to immediate, accurate revisions. Other areas of the instruction that are questionable may not be revised until after the instruction is retried with other individuals or with a small group.

OUTCOMES The outcomes of one-to-one trials are instruction that (1) contains appropriate vocabulary, language complexity, examples, and illustrations for the participating learner; (2) either yields reasonable learner attitudes and achievement, or is revised with the objective of improving learner attitudes or performance during subsequent trials; and (3) appears feasible for use with the available learners, resources, and setting. The instruction can be refined further using small group trials.

In the next chapter, we will discuss how to summarize the information from the one-to-one trials and how to decide what revisions should be made. In this chapter, we will continue with our discussion of the next phase of formative evaluation, which takes place after the revisions from the one-to-one evaluation have been completed.

SMALL-GROUP EVALUATION

There are two primary purposes for the small-group evaluation. The first is to determine the effectiveness of changes made following the one-to-one evaluation and to identify any remaining learning problems that learners may have. The second purpose is to determine whether learners can use the instruction without interacting with the instructor. (At this point in our discussion, we are continuing to assume that the designer is designing some form of self-instructional materials.)

CRITERIA AND DATA Typical measures used to evaluate instructional effectiveness include learner performance scores on pretests and posttests. Pretests typically encompass entry behaviors as well as instructional objectives, and posttests measure learners' performance on the subordinate and terminal objectives for the instruction. Besides learner performance levels, their attitudes about the instruction are obtained through an attitude questionnaire and sometimes a follow-up interview. Information gathered about the feasibility of the instruction usually includes the following: (1) the time required for learners to complete both the instruction and the required performance measures, (2) the costs and viability of delivering the instruction in the intended format and environment, and (3) the attitudes of those implementing or managing the instruction.

SELECTING LEARNERS   For the small-group evaluation, you should select a group of approximately eight to twenty learners. If the number of learners is fewer than eight, the data will probably not be very representative of the target population. On the other hand, if you obtain data on many more than twenty learners, then you may find that you have more information than you need, and that the data from additional learners does not provide you with a great deal of additional information.

The selection of learners to participate in your small-group trial is important. The learners who evaluate the materials should be as representative of your target population as possible. In an ideal research setting, you would select the learners randomly, which would enable you to apply your findings generally to the entire target population. In typical school, industrial, and adult education settings, however, true randomization is often impossible, and perhaps not even desirable.

When you cannot select your learners at random, or when the group you have available to draw from is relatively small, you want to ensure that you include in your sample at least one representative of each type of subgroup that exists in your population. Examples of such subgroups might include the following:

- Low-, average-, and high-achieving students
- Learners with various native languages
- Learners who are familiar with a particular procedure (e.g., web-based instruction), and learners who are not
- Younger or inexperienced learners as well as more mature learners

When your target group is homogeneous, these subgroups are not a problem. When the target population is made up of persons with varied skills and backgrounds, the designer should consider including representatives of each group in the small-group sample. For example, it is almost impossible to predict how a low-achieving learner will perform on your materials based on the efforts of a high-achieving learner. By selecting a representative sample, you will be able to be more insightful about changes you may need to make in your instruction.

Small-group participants are sometimes a biased sample because they consist of people who participate more willingly than the group at large. The designer must be aware of this problem and obtain the most representative group possible, considering all the constraints usually present in obtaining participants for small-group trials.

It is also important to note that while this stage is referred to as *small-group evaluation,* the term refers to the number of learners and not the setting in which the learners actually use the materials. For example, if your materials require the use of highly specialized equipment, and you have access to only one piece of equipment, then you would attempt to obtain eight to twenty learners who would use your materials in an individualized setting. It is not necessary to get all the learners together in one room at one time to conduct a small-group evaluation.

PROCEDURES   The basic procedures used in a small-group evaluation differ sharply from those used in a one-to-one evaluation. The evaluator (or the instructor) begins by explaining that the materials are in the formative stage of development and that it is necessary to obtain feedback on how they may be improved. Having said this, the instructor then administers the materials in the manner in which they are intended to be used when they are in final form. If a pretest is to be used, then it should be given first. The instructor should intervene as little as possible in the process. Only in those cases when equipment fails, or when a learner becomes bogged down in the learning process and cannot continue, should the instructor intervene. Each learner's difficulty and the solution should certainly be noted as part of the revision data.

ASSESSMENTS AND QUESTIONNAIRES   Additional steps in small-group evaluation are the administration of an attitude questionnaire and, if possible, in-depth debriefings with some of the learners in the group. The primary purpose for obtaining learner reactions to the instruction is to identify, from their perceptions, weaknesses and strengths in the implementation of the instructional strategy. The questions should therefore reflect various components of the strategy. The following questions would usually be appropriate:

- Was the instruction interesting?
- Did you understand what you were supposed to learn?
- Were the materials directly related to the objectives?
- Were sufficient practice exercises included?
- Were the practice exercises relevant?
- Did the tests really measure your knowledge of the objectives?
- Did you receive sufficient feedback on your practice exercises?
- Did you feel confident when answering questions on the tests?

These questions might be included in an attitude questionnaire, and then pursued at some depth in a discussion with learners. By using questions directed at components of the instructional strategy, such as those just described, it is possible to relate the learners' responses directly to particular components of the instructional materials or procedures. In the discussion with the learners after the materials have been completed, the instructor can ask questions about such features as the pacing, interest, and difficulty of the materials.

DATA SUMMARY AND ANALYSIS   Both the quantitative and descriptive information gathered during the trial should be summarized and analyzed. Quantitative data consist of test scores as well as time requirements and cost projections. Descriptive information consists of comments collected from attitude questionnaires, interviews, or evaluator's notes written during the trial.

OUTCOMES   The goal of the small-group trial and instructional revisions is refined instruction that should be effective with most target learners in the intended setting. Refinements required in instruction may be simple, such as changing examples and vocabulary in test items or increasing the amount of time allocated for study. Modifications might also require major changes in the instructional strategy (e.g., motivational strategies, sequence of objectives, instructional delivery format), or in the nature of information presented to learners. Once instruction is adequately refined, the field trial can be initiated.

In the next chapter, we will illustrate how to summarize this data and determine the implications they have for the revision process. In this chapter, we have focused our concern on the formative evaluation study and the collection of data.

FIELD TRIAL

In the final stage of formative evaluation the instructor attempts to use a learning context that closely resembles that intended for the ultimate use of the instructional materials. One purpose of this final stage of formative evaluation is to determine whether the changes in the instruction made after the small-group stage were effective. Another purpose is to see whether the instruction can be used in the context for which it was intended—that is, is it administratively possible to use the instruction in its intended setting?

In order to answer these questions, all materials, including the tests and the instructor's manual, should be revised and ready to go. If an instructor is involved in implementing the instruction, then the designer should not play this role.

LOCATION OF EVALUATION   In picking the site for a field evaluation, you are likely to encounter one of two situations. First, if the material is tried out in a class that is currently using large-group, lockstep pacing, then using self-instructional materials may be a very new and different experience for the learners. It will be important to lay the groundwork for the new procedure by explaining to the learners how the materials are to be used and how they differ from their usual instruction. In all likelihood you will obtain an increase in interest, if not in performance, simply because of the break in the typical classroom instructional pattern. Second, if the materials are tried out in an individualized class, then it may be quite difficult to find a large enough group of learners who are ready for your instructional materials because learners will be "spread out" in the materials they are studying.

CRITERIA AND DATA The field trial is much like the final dress rehearsal in theater since the instruction is polished and delivered in a manner that is as close as possible to the final format. Also, similar to dress rehearsals, the main purpose of the field trial is to locate and eliminate any remaining problems in the instruction. There are many similarities between the small group trial and the field trial. The decisions to be made during both types of trials are whether learner performance is adequate and delivery of instruction is feasible. Another similarity to the small group trial is that information is gathered on learner achievement and attitudes; instructor procedures and attitudes; and resources such as time, cost, space, and equipment. The main differences between the two trials are in the actual sophistication of the materials, learners, procedures, instructors, and setting.

SELECTING LEARNERS   You should identify a group of about thirty individuals to participate in your field trial. Again, the group should be selected to ensure that it is representative of the target population for which the materials are intended. Because a "typical" group is sometimes hard to locate, designers often select several different groups to participate in the field trial. This ensures that data will be collected under all intended conditions such as an open classroom, traditional instruction, and/or distance learning centers.

The use of multiple tryout sites may be necessary if such sites will vary a great deal. The designer may not be able to be present while the instruction is used; therefore, it is important that the designer inform the instructor about the procedures to be followed and the data to be collected.

PROCEDURE FOR CONDUCTING FIELD TRIAL The procedure for conducting the field trial is similar to that for the small group, with only a few exceptions. The primary change is in the role of the designer, who should do no more than observe the process. The instruction should be administered or delivered by a typical instructor. This being the case, the designer may have to design and deliver special training to the instructor so that he or she will know exactly how to use the instruction.

The only other change might be a reduction in testing. Based on experience in the small group, the pretest and posttest might be modified or reduced to only assess the most important entry behaviors and skills to be taught. The reasoning is that by this point in the development process the main concern in the formative evaluation is feasibility in the learning context.

The questionnaire may be modified to focus on the environmental factors that the designer thinks will be critical to the success of the instruction. Essentially, the questions should focus on anything that might interfere with the success of the instruction. Observation of the instruction in use and interviews with learners and the instructor will be very valuable.

DATA SUMMARY AND INTERPRETATION Data summary and analysis procedures are the same for the small group and field trials. Achievement data should be organized by instructional objective, and attitudinal information from both learners and instructors should also be anchored to specific objectives whenever possible. Summarizing the data in these formats will aid locating particular areas where the instruction was and was not effective. This information from the field trial is used to plan and make final revisions in the instruction.

OUTCOMES The goal of the field trial and final revisions is effective instruction that yields desired levels of learner achievement and attitudes and that functions as intended in the learning setting. Using data about problem areas gathered during the field trial, appropriate revisions are made in the instruction. With the revisions complete, we can begin the formative evaluation in the performance context.

FORMATIVE EVALUATION IN THE PERFORMANCE CONTEXT

We have discussed three phases of formative evaluation that focus on gathering information and data about learner performance and attitudes toward the instruction. The context of the instruction changes in each phase from an informal setting in the one-to-one trials to the actual learning context in the field trial. But the question remains about whether the learner can use the new skills in what we have called the *performance context*—the site where the skills are ultimately required.

Almost no newly learned skills are intended for use only during the learning process; the goal is their use at some other time, in some other location. The designer cannot ignore this, but rather should, when appropriate and feasible, include it in the formative evaluation plan. The designer should determine whether the skills that have been taught are retained and used in the performance context, and whether the use of the skills has the desired effect on the organization. If negative results are obtained, then the designer must determine what the implications are for the revision of the training. The process we will describe next for doing formative evaluation in the performance context could be used after any of the three phases of learning-context formative evaluation.

	Questions, Data Sources, and Data Gathering Methods for Performance Context Formative Evaluation		

TABLE 10.2 — **Questions, Data Sources, and Data Gathering Methods for Performance Context Formative Evaluation**

Questions	Data Sources	Methods
1. Did the skills transfer?	•Learners	•Interviews
2. How are the skills used (frequency, context)?	•Colleagues/ peers of learners	•Questionnaires
3. What physical, social, managerial factors enhanced transfer and use of the skills?	•Subordinates of learners •Supervisors •Customers •Company records	•Observations •Records analysis
4. What physical, social, managerial factors inhibited transfer and use of the skills?		
5. Does using the skills help resolve the original need? How? What is the evidence?		
6. How might training be refined or improved?		

The purpose of the in-context formative evaluation is to determine fundamentally three things. First, do the learners find that it is appropriate to use their new skills in the workplace, and have they been doing so? Second, if they have been used, what has been the impact on the organization? Third, what suggestions do the learners and others that they work with have for improving the instruction? Instruction that works fine, in terms of learner performance on a posttest, may not result in learners being able to be successful on the job.

CRITERIA AND DATA   Criteria and data in the performance site will vary greatly from one context to another, and appropriate methods for the evaluation must be tailored to the site. In selecting the most appropriate procedures for collecting evidence of training impact, you should consider performance data from both direct observation and company records. Also include perceptual information such as views and attitudes from learners, from those who work with them, and, perhaps, from customers. Basic questions, possible data sources, and data gathering methods are compiled in Table 10.2. In framing your own questions, be more specific about *which* skills are of interest in your evaluation.

You may assume that performance-context formative evaluation only applies to workshops and skills training. This is not necessarily the case, although it is easier to conceptualize in those situations. The greatest barrier to the use of this procedure may be timing. For some instruction, learners will begin using the skills immediately because the skills are part of a hierarchical flow (such as the use of sentence writing skills to write essays), and the designer can do a follow-up within weeks. But what about the public school student who might not be using the skills for years, or a training manager who rarely gets to use newly learned skills? For some instruction, this delay can be tolerated because of the length of the overall project and the importance of the information.

SELECTING RESPONDENTS Who should participate in this phase of the formative evaluation? Certainly all of the one-to-one learners should participate if the evaluation is done following that phase. Perhaps only a sample of the learners from the small group and field trial would be included. They could be specifically selected based on their performance on the posttest and attitude questionnaire. It would be appropriate to select several high achievers and several low achievers, along with any other learners who presented special circumstances of interest to the designer. These same evaluation questions should be presented to the manager or supervisor of the learner. Their reactions might be identical to the learners or quite different. Peers and subordinates may also offer insights into the effectiveness of the instruction. Did they notice the learners using the skills? Were the learners effective? How could they have performed better?

PROCEDURE At the completion of the formative evaluation, regardless of the phase, the learners should be told that they will be contacted sometime in the future to discuss the instruction they have just completed and its usefulness. Then, when sufficient time has passed to permit the skills to be used—and this will vary according to the nature of the goal—the learners should be contacted. Ideally, the designer would go to the location where the skills are being used, but the contact could be done via telephone.

OUTCOMES Data gathered during the performance-site formative evaluation are used to document the strengths and weaknesses in the instruction, the transfer of skills to the performance site, the use of skills, and the degree to which the original need was reduced or eliminated through the instruction. These data should be summarized and shared with learners, their supervisors, and those requesting the instruction as a way to reduce or eliminate the original need. In addition, problems detected in the workplace that block transfer and implementation of the new skills should be described and shared with the organization. The result of the performance-site formative evaluation is documentation of (1) the strengths and weaknesses in the instruction, (2) areas where transfer and use of skills can better be supported, and (3) suggestions for revising instruction to remove any instructional barriers to implementing the new skills in the work setting. In the next chapter we will indicate how this documentation will be used to refine instruction by eliminating observed weaknesses.

COLLECTING DATA ON REACTIONS TO INSTRUCTION

What frame of reference can you use to design the formative evaluation? Keeping in mind that the purpose for the formative evaluation is to pinpoint specific errors in the materials in order to correct them, the evaluation design—including instruments, procedures, and personnel—needs to yield information about the location of and the reasons for any problems. Focusing the design only on the goals and objectives of the instruction would be too limited. Data on learners' achievement of the goals and objectives would be insufficient, though important, because these data will only provide information about where errors occur, not why they occur. Similarly, a shotgun approach to the collection of data would also be inappropriate. Although collecting data on everything you can imagine will produce a variety of information, it may yield some data that are irrelevant and incomplete.

*Inst. strategy is key** [handwritten note in margin]

Perhaps the best anchor or framework for the design of the formative evaluation is the instructional strategy. Since the strategy was the foundation for creating the materials, it is likely to hold the key to the nature of errors you made in producing them. Using the instructional strategy as the frame of reference for developing evaluation instruments and procedures should help you avoid designing a formative evaluation that is either too narrowly focused or too broad.

How? matrix [handwritten note in margin]

How can the instructional strategy be used to aid the design of the formative evaluation? One way is to create a matrix that lists the components of the instructional strategy along one side and the major areas of questions about the instruction along the other. In the intersecting boxes of the component-by-question matrix, you can generate questions that should be answered in the evaluation related to each area and component. Using these questions, you can then plan the appropriate instruments and procedures to use and the appropriate audiences to provide the information.

The different components of the strategy should be quite familiar to you by now. What general areas of questions should be asked about each component of the materials? Although undoubtedly there are questions that would be unique for a given set of materials, the five following areas of questions would be appropriate for all materials. These areas are directly related to the decisions you made while developing the materials.

5 ?'s appropriate to all material [handwritten note in margin]

1. Are the materials appropriate for the type of learning outcome? Specific prescriptions for the development of materials were made based on whether the objectives were intellectual or motor skills, attitudes, or verbal information. You should be concerned about whether the materials you produced are indeed congruent with suggestions for learning each type of capability. The best evaluator of this aspect of the materials would undoubtedly be an expert in the type of learning involved.

2. Do the materials include adequate instruction on the subordinate skills, and are these skills sequenced and clustered logically? The best evaluator for this area of questions would be an expert in the content area.

3. Are the materials clear and readily understood by representative members of the target group? Obviously, only members of the target group can answer these questions. Instructors familiar with target learners may provide you with preliminary information, but only learners can ultimately judge the clarity of the materials.

4. What is the motivational value of the materials? Do learners find the materials relevant to their needs and interests? Are they confident as they work through the materials? Are they satisfied with what they have learned? Again, the most appropriate judges of these aspects of the materials are representative members of the target group.

5. Can the materials be managed efficiently in the manner they are mediated? Both target learners and instructors would be appropriate to answer these questions.

Table 10.3 contains an example of the suggested framework for designing the formative evaluation. Using such a framework will help ensure that you include relevant questions about different components of the materials and that appropriate groups and individuals are included.

TABLE *10.3* | **Example Framework for Designing a Formative Evaluation**

	Main Areas of Questions about Materials				
Main Components of Materials	Type of Learning	Content	Clarity	Motivation	Management
Preinstructional Initial motivation Objectives Entry behaviors					
Presentation Sequence Size of unit Content Examples					
Participation Practice Feedback					
Assessment Pretests Posttests Performance context					
Who Judges?	Learning Specialists	Content Expert	Target Learners	Target Learners	Target Learners/ Instructors
How Is Data Gathered?	Checklist Interview	Checklist Interview	Observations Interviews Tests Materials	Observations Interviews Tests	Observations Interviews

Notice the two rows at the bottom of the matrix. The first indicates those individuals or groups most appropriate for evaluating each aspect of the materials. The second provides a reminder that you must consider how to gather each type of information needed from the evaluators. You may want to create a checklist or list of questions to accompany the materials for soliciting information from the specialists you choose. You may also want to interview them to determine why they believe particular parts of the material are inadequate and to obtain their suggestions about how the materials might be improved.

In designing instrumentation for gathering information from learners, you must consider the phase (i.e., one-to-one, small-group, and field trial), the setting (learning or performance context), and the nature of the information you are gathering. In the one-to-one evaluations, the materials themselves make up one instrument. You will want learners to circle words or sentences and to write comments directly in the materials. The questions included in the intersecting blocks of the matrix should help you develop other instruments such as checklists to guide your observations and questions to include in your interviews and questionnaires. It is important to note that although different areas of questions about the materials are described separately here, it does not mean to imply that they must be on separate instruments. The instruments you produce should be efficient in gathering information from participants.

At a minimum, the types of data you will probably want to collect include the following:

- Test data collected on entry behaviors tests, pretests, posttests, and performance context.
- Comments or notations made by learners to you or marked on the instructional materials about difficulties encountered at particular points in the materials.
- Data collected on attitude questionnaires and/or debriefing comments in which learners reveal their overall reactions to the instruction and their perceptions of where difficulties lie with the materials and the instructional procedures in general.
- The time required for learners to complete various components of the instruction.
- Reactions of the subject-matter specialist. It is the responsibility of this person to verify that the content of the module is accurate and current.
- Reactions of a manager or supervisor who has observed the learner using the skills in the performance context.

FORMATIVE EVALUATION OF SELECTED MATERIALS

The three phases of formative evaluation previously described are not totally applicable when the instructor has selected existing materials to try with a group of learners. The kinds of editorial and content changes that are made as a result of one-to-one and small-group evaluations are typically not used when one uses existing materials. These procedures are avoided not because they would be unproductive in improving the instruction, but because in reality the instructor who selects existing materials seldom has the time or resources to conduct these phases. In this circumstance the instructor should proceed directly to a field trial with a group of learners. One primary purpose of formative evaluation with existing materials is to determine whether they are effective with a particular population and in a specific setting. Another is to identify ways in which additions to and/or deletions from the materials or changes in instructional procedures might be made to improve the effectiveness of the materials. For these reasons, the formative evaluation procedures for selected materials most nearly resemble those in a field trial.

Preparations for the field trial of existing materials should be made as they would be for a field trial of original materials. An analysis should be made of existing documentation on the development of the materials, the effectiveness of the materials with defined groups, and particularly any description of procedures used during field evaluations. Descriptions of how materials are to be used should be studied, any test instruments that accompany the materials should be examined for their relationship to the performance objectives, and the need for any additional evaluations or attitude questionnaires should be determined.

In the field trial study, the regular instructor should administer the pretest unless he or she knows the learners already have the entry behaviors and lack knowledge of what is to be taught. A posttest and an attitude questionnaire should certainly be available to evaluate learners' performance and their opinions of the materials.

The instructor who conducts a field trial is able to observe the progress and attitudes of learners using a set of adopted or adapted materials. It is even possible to examine the performance of different groups of learners using modified or unmodified materials to determine whether the changes increased the effectiveness of the materials. The instructor should certainly take the time following the field evaluation to thoroughly debrief the learners on their reactions to the instruction because additional insights about the materials or procedures can be gained during such debriefing sessions. After completing a field trial of selected materials, the instructor should have collected approximately the same types of data that would have been collected if original materials were being formatively evaluated.

FORMATIVE EVALUATION OF INSTRUCTOR-LED INSTRUCTION

If the instructor plans to deliver the instruction to a group of students using an instructor's guide, then the purposes of formative evaluations are much the same as they are for the formative evaluation of independent instructional materials: to determine whether the instruction is effective and decide how to improve it. Once again, the formative evaluation of an instructional plan most nearly approximates that of the field trial phase for instructional materials. In all likelihood, there will be little time for a one-to-one or even a small-group evaluation.

In preparing for a field trial of instructor-led instruction, the instructor should be concerned with the entry behaviors and prior knowledge, the posttest knowledge, and the attitudes of learners. In addition, the instructor is in a unique position to provide interactive practice and feedback. Interactive practice and feedback should be included in the instructional strategy, because it will provide learners with the opportunity to demonstrate specific skills they have acquired. These sessions also serve to identify those skills not yet acquired. This form of in-progress practice and assessment may be administered in one of two formats. The instructor may deliver it orally to a variety of learners and keep notes on their performance, or the instructor may periodically distribute various printed practice and feedback exercises during the lesson. This latter approach provides concrete evidence of the learners' progress.

The instructor can also use the field trial as an opportunity to evaluate the instructional procedures. Observation of the instructional process should indicate the suitability of grouping patterns, time allocations, and learner interest in various class activities.

Many instructors already use these types of formative evaluation in their instruction. Our point is to stress the thorough and systematic use of these techniques to collect and analyze data in order to revise the lesson plan. To identify weak points in the lesson plan, and to provide clues to their correction, in-progress data can be compared to results obtained with the posttest, attitude questionnaire, and students' comments during debriefing sessions.

Very often, the field testing of selected materials and the field testing of instructor-led instruction are interwoven. Frequently the use of selected materials will require an interactive role for the instructor and, likewise, the use of an instructor's guide may well involve the use of some prepared instructional materials. Under either of these circumstances, approximately the same types of field evaluation procedures should be employed and similar types of revisions carried out.

Data Collection for Selected Materials and Instructor-Led Instruction

Much of the information dealing with the collection of data in a field trial of original instructional materials applies equally well to the data collection procedures used in the evaluation of selected materials and instructional procedures. For example, it is critically important that any equipment to be used during instruction is in good running order, and that the environment in which the field trial is conducted be conducive to learning.

When an instructor evaluates self-instructional materials, selected materials, or an instructor guide, existing rapport with learners can be a great advantage. It is important during the evaluation of materials and guides that students understand the critical nature of their participation in, and contributions to, the study. The instructor, in working with familiar learners, also has knowledge of the learners' entry behaviors and, quite possibly, is able to predict accurately the pretest performance of students. The instructor should, however, avoid relying entirely on such predictions. If there is any doubt at all concerning the learners' performances, then they should be tested to verify the need for instruction in specified skills.

When the instructor selects materials to implement an instructional strategy, a number of unique concerns arise. Information can be gathered about these concerns by observation and the use of questionnaires. The major question will be, "Did the instruction have unity?" To answer this question, the instructor should determine the adequacy of the learner guide in directing students to various resources. Redundancy and gaps in the instructional materials should be noted. Was sufficient repetition and review built into the strategy? If the instructor is presenting the instruction, then events that reflect the same types of problems should be noted as the presentation progresses. The types of questions raised by learners will provide a key to the strategy's inadequacies.

Concerns Influencing Formative Evaluation

The formative evaluation component distinguishes the instructional design process from a philosophical or theoretical approach. Rather than speculating about the instructional effectiveness of your materials, you will be testing them with learners. You will therefore want to do the best possible job of collecting data that truly reflect the effectiveness of your materials. There are several concerns about the formative evaluation context and the learners who participate in the evaluation that the designer should keep in mind when planning and implementing data collection procedures.

CONTEXT CONCERNS One concern in any evaluation of your materials is to ensure that any technical equipment is operating effectively. More than one instructor has been discouraged because a new set of instructional materials was tried with a particular piece of equipment and the equipment failed to operate correctly. Consequences are that the data from learners were invalid, and the instructor learned little more than that the equipment must operate effectively to try out materials.

It is also important in the early stages of formative evaluation, especially in the one-to-one trials, that you work with learners in a quiet setting—one in which you can command their full attention. At this point you are concerned about how the materials will work under the best possible conditions. As you move to the small-group sessions and field trial you are increasingly concerned with how the materials will work in more typical contexts. If the typical setting is an individualized classroom that has a relatively high noise level, then you will want to know whether the materials work in that situation. But you should not begin the formative evaluation under these conditions.

CONCERNS ABOUT LEARNERS   In the selection of learners for participation in any phase of formative evaluation, avoid depending entirely on the instructor to assess entry knowledge of the learners. Whenever possible, administer entry-behavior tests to learners to verify that they are actually members of the target population for whom the materials are intended. Experience has shown that instructors, for whatever reason, sometimes make poor estimates of the readiness of learners who are recommended for participation in formative evaluation studies. Do what you can to verify the entry knowledge of the learners.

When you get the information on entry knowledge and skills of learners, you sometimes encounter the problem of what to do with those learners who have already mastered some or all of the skills to be taught, or learners who do not have the required entry behaviors. Do you drop them from the formative evaluation?

It is preferable to include some of these learners who do not exactly match the skill profile of the real target population. Those who already know some of the content can serve as "subject matter sophisticates" who can infer how other students, who do not know the content, will respond. You can also determine whether your instruction can bring these learners up to approximately 100 percent performance. If it does not work for these learners, then it is unlikely that it will be effective with learners who have less entering knowledge.

Learners who do not have the entry behaviors should also be included in a formative evaluation. The entry behaviors have been theoretically derived and therefore are in need of validation. If the learners who cannot demonstrate the entry behaviors do, in fact, struggle through the instruction with little success, while those with the entry behaviors are successful, then it suggests that you have identified skills that learners must have to begin the instruction. If, on the other hand, learners without the entry behaviors are successful with the instruction, then you must seriously reconsider the validity of the entry behaviors you have identified.

We have suggested that in the one-to-one formative evaluation, the designer should use at least three learners—one high, one average, and one low in ability. This is a vague recommendation that can be made more specific by identifying a high-ability learner as one who already knows some of the content to be taught. The average learner can be identified as one who has the entry behaviors, but no knowledge of the skills to be taught, and the low-ability learner as one who does not have some or all of the entry behaviors. By using these definitions the designer can be much more sure of getting the desired range of abilities. Research indicates that these three types of learners will provide different but useful information to the designer, and thus all three should be included in the formative evaluation.

CONCERNS ABOUT FORMATIVE EVALUATION OUTCOMES A final word of caution: Be prepared to obtain information that indicates that your materials are not as effective as you thought they would be after going through such an extensive instructional design process. It is common to become tremendously involved when putting a great deal of time and effort into any kind of project. It is just as common to be sharply disappointed when you find that your efforts have not been entirely satisfactory.

You should note, however, that in the formative evaluation process, positive feedback from students provides you with little information about how you might proceed to change anything. Positive feedback only indicates that what you have is effective with the students who used the materials. You can then only make the limited inference that the materials would be effective with learners who are of similar ability and motivation.

As you move through the formative evaluation process, it might be helpful to pretend that another instructor has developed the materials and that you are merely carrying out the formative evaluation for that person. We do not suggest that you mislead the learners about it, but rather that you adopt this noninvolved psychological set in order to listen to what learners, instructors, and subject-matter experts might say. These kinds of feedback must be integrated into an objective assessment of the extent to which your materials are meeting the objectives you have set for them, and how they can be improved.

CONCERNS WITH IMPLEMENTING FORMATIVE EVALUATION While the ideal instructional design process is to conduct three phases of formative evaluation prior to distributing instruction for general use, it is sometimes simply not possible to follow this procedure. In many cases, there is not enough time to conduct the formative evaluation or no funds have been budgeted to do so. What responsibility does the designer have in this situation?

The first consideration should be to determine whether any kind of formative evaluation can be conducted before the formal usage of the instruction. Are there ways to combine some of the one-to-one techniques with the field trial? Can we get someone to read through the materials and see whether they make sense? Can we walk through a role play to make sure it works? Most designers would acknowledge that to use newly designed instruction without some type of tryout is extremely risky, but sometimes it is unavoidable.

If instruction is being used with the target population without the benefit of any formative evaluation, then it is still possible to use that opportunity to gather information that can be used to do revisions of the instruction. In these situations, the procedures typically applied are those of the field trial. Questionnaire data and assessment information can be combined with observations of learners and direct discussions of the instruction to determine what kinds of changes should be made.

The general principle for the designer is that formative evaluations are always conducted; it is just a question of when, where, and how. Sometimes there is enough time and resources to conduct the three phases of formative evaluation that have been described in this chapter. When it is not possible to do so, it is the designer's responsibility to improvise ways in which to gather as much information as possible about the instruction so that it can be appropriately revised.

PROBLEM SOLVING DURING INSTRUCTIONAL DESIGN

In the instructional design process the designer is often faced with questions that can best be answered with data from learners. It is interesting to find how often it is possible to settle a design argument by saying, "Let's have the learners tell us the answer to that." The whole formative evaluation process is one of gathering data from learners to answer questions you may (or may not) have had about your instruction.

Assume that following a series of one-to-one evaluations, it becomes clear that there is a question about the use of illustrations in your instruction. Several students liked and used them, while several others said they were of no use. Since it may be expensive to use illustrations in instruction, a significant question must be answered, "Should illustrations be used in your instruction?"

In order to answer this question, the designer might develop two versions of the instruction for use in the small-group evaluation. Ten randomly selected learners might receive the instruction with illustrations, while ten receive it with no illustrations. Then the performance and attitudes of both groups could be compared. How did they do on the posttest? How did they do on those items directly related to the illustrations? What did they say on the attitude questions about their use of (or the absence of) the illustrations? How did the learning times of the two groups compare?

Is this research? Not really. The purpose is to make a decision about what to do with a particular unit of instruction, not to determine the benefits of using illustrations in instruction. The designer could collect enough data in the formative evaluation about the illustrations to make at least a tentative decision about their continued use in the instruction. This same methodology can be used by the designer to answer a wide array of questions that will inevitably arise during the design process.

EXAMPLES

The following list includes information that you can use for planning a one-to-one, a small-group, and a field-trial evaluation. While looking through these suggested procedures, assume that you know your intended target population, but are unsure whether they possess the required entry behaviors. The examples that follow are not offered as the only activities you should pursue in formative evaluation, but as a list of suggestions you can use to begin thinking about your own project. You may be able to identify other activities for your project.

FORMATIVE EVALUATION ACTIVITIES

ONE-TO-ONE EVALUATION
    I.   Participation by learners from the target population
        A. Identify learners who are typical of those you believe will be found in the target population. (Include each major type of learner that can be found in the target population.)
        B. Arrange for the learner(s) to participate.
        C. Discuss the process of a one-to-one evaluation of the materials with each learner separately.

D. Evaluate the pretest you have constructed to measure entry behaviors.
   1. Can the learner read the directions?
   2. Does the learner understand the problems?
   3. Does the learner have the required prerequisite skills?
E. Sit with the learner while he or she studies the materials.
   1. Instruct the learner to write on the materials to indicate where difficulty is encountered or to discuss ideas and problems.
   2. If the learner fails to understand an example, then try another verbal example. Does this clarify the issue? Note in writing the changes and suggestions you make as you go through the materials.
   3. If the learner fails to understand an explanation, then elaborate by adding information or changing the order of presentation. Does this clarify the issue? Note the changes you make in writing.
   4. If the learner appears to be bored or confused while going through the materials, then you may want to change the presentation to include larger or smaller bits of information before practice and feedback. Record your ideas concerning the regrouping of materials as you go along.
   5. Keep notes on examples, illustrations, information you add, and changes in sequence during the formative evaluation process. Otherwise, you may forget an important decision or idea. Note taking should be quick and in rough form so the learner is not distracted from the materials.
F. You may choose to test another learner from the target population before you make any changes or revisions in your materials in order to verify that the changes are necessary. If errors pointed out by your first learner "consultant" are obvious, then you may want to make revisions before testing the next learner. This will save testing time and enable the next learner to concentrate on other problems that may exist in the materials.

II. Participation by subject-matter experts
A. You should provide the expert with the following:
   1. Instructional analysis
   2. Behavioral objectives
   3. Instruction
   4. Tests and other assessment instruments
   These materials should be in rough form because major revisions could well be the outcome of this one-to-one testing. You may want to present your materials in the order described above.
B. You should be looking for verification of the following:
   1. Objective statements
   2. Instructional analysis
   3. Accuracy and currency of the content
   4. Appropriateness of the instructional materials in vocabulary, interest value, sequence, chunk size, and learner-participation activities
   5. Clarity and appropriateness of test items and assessment situations
   6. Placement of this piece of instruction relative to prior and

subsequent instruction

    C. The number of subject-matter experts you should approach for assistance will vary with the complexity of the information and skills covered in your materials. For some instruction one expert will be sufficient, while for others four may still seem inadequate. The nature of the learning task will dictate the number and type of expert consultants you will need.

III. Outcomes of one-to-one formative evaluation

    A. Consider again the types of information you are looking for in the one-to-one testing:

        1. Faulty instructional analysis

        2. Errors in judgment about entry behaviors of learners in the target population

        3. Unclear or inappropriate objectives and expected outcomes

        4. Inadequate information presentation and examples

            a. Examples, graphs, or illustrations that are too abstract

            b. Too much or too little information at one time

            c. Wrong sequence of information presented

            d. Unclear examples

        5. Unclear test questions, test situations, or test directions

        6. Faulty wording or unclear passages

IV. Performance-context formative evaluation

    A. Determine whether it is appropriate and feasible to contact learners after they complete the one-to-one.

    B. By phone or in person, determine when and how learners use skills taught in the training.

    C. Determine the organizational level of support from managers for using the skills.

    D. Observe learners as they use skills, interview peers and subordinates, or both.

    E. Determine whether using skills resolved the problems identified through the needs assessment.

    F. Ask for suggestions for revision of the instruction.

SMALL-GROUP EVALUATION

I. Participation by learners from the target population

    A. Identify a group of learners that typifies your target population.

    B. Arrange for a group to participate.

        1. Adequate time should be arranged for required testing as well as instructional activities.

        2. Learners should be motivated to participate.

        3. Learners should be selected to represent the types of people expected in the target population. You may want to include several learners from each expected major category in your target population.

    C. During the pretest, instruction, and posttest, you may want to make notes about suggestions for instructors who will use the materials. You may also note changes you want to make in the instruction or procedures as a result of your observation of learners interacting with the materials.

    D. Administer the pretest of required entry behaviors if one is appropriate.

        1. Check the directions, response patterns, and questions to

ensure that the wording is clear.

    2. Instruct learners to circle words they do not understand and place a check beside questions or directions that are unclear.

    3. Do not stop and discuss unclear items with learners during the test unless they become bogged down or stop.

    4. Record the time required for learners to complete the entry test.

E. Administer the pretest of skills to be taught during instruction. This test and the test of required entry behaviors could be combined into one pretest if desirable.

    1. Have learners circle any vocabulary that is unclear to them.

    2. Have learners place a check beside any directions, questions, or response requirements that are unclear to them.

    3. Have learners write additional comments in the test if they desire.

    4. Do not discuss problems with learners during the test.

F. Administer the instructional materials. Have the instructional setting close to reality with all required equipment and materials present. Any instructional assistance required should also be available during the trial.

    1. Instruct learners that you will need their help in evaluating the materials.

    2. Have learners sign their work so you can compare their performance on the lesson with their performance based on their entry behaviors.

    3. Instruct learners to circle any unclear words and place a check beside any illustrations, examples, or explanations that are unclear in the instruction. Learners should keep working through the materials to the end without stopping for discussion.

    4. Record the time required for learners to complete the instructional materials. Time required may be more than anticipated if learners need instruction on unfamiliar equipment or procedures.

G. Administer the posttest.

    1. Have learners sign their posttest to enable comparisons with the pretest and questionnaires.

    2. Have learners circle any unclear vocabulary and place a check beside any unclear directions, questions, or response requirements.

    3. Have learners respond to as many items as they can, regardless of whether they are sure of the answer or just guessing. Often incorrect guesses can provide clues to inadequate instruction. You may want them to indicate which answers reflect guessing.

    4. Record the time required for learners to complete the posttest.

H. Administer an attitude questionnaire to learners.

    1. You may want to ask questions such as these:

       • Did the instruction hold your attention?

       • Was the instruction too long or too short?

       • Was the instruction too difficult or too easy?

       • Did you have problems with any parts of the instruction?

- Were the cartoons or illustrations appropriate or distracting?
- Was the use of color appealing or distracting?
- What did you like most?
- What did you like least?
- How would you change the instruction if you could?
- Did the tests measure the material that was presented?
- Would you prefer another instructional medium?

I. Arrange for learners to discuss the pretest, instruction, and/or posttest with you or their instructor after they have completed all the work.
1. You may want to structure the discussion with planned questions.
2. You may want to ask questions such as, "Would you change the exercises in section X?" or "Did you like the example in section X?"

J. See Section IV under one-to-one evaluation for ideas on the performance context formative evaluation. You may want to continue to evaluate only a sample of the learners in the small-group evaluation.

FIELD TRIAL

I. Select an appropriate sample from the target population.
A. Arrange for the selected group to try the materials.
1. Ensure that there is an adequate number of learners in the group. Thirty is an often-suggested number of learners to participate in a field trial.
2. Ensure that selected learners reflect the range of abilities and skills of learners in the target population.
3. Ensure that there are adequate personnel, facilities, and equipment available for the trial.
B. Distribute the instructional materials as well as the instructor's guide, if it is available, to the instructor conducting the field test.
C. Discuss any instructions or special considerations that may be needed if the instruction is out of context.
D. Personally play a minimal role in the field trials.
E. Conduct performance context formative evaluation as previously described.
F. Summarize the data you have collected. Summarized data may include a report of the following:
1. Scores on the entry-behavior part of the pretest
2. Pretest and posttest scores on skills taught
3. The time required for students to complete each test used
4. The time required for students to complete the instruction
5. The attitudes of learners as well as participating instructors

FORMATIVE EVALUATION OF SELECTED MATERIALS AND INSTRUCTOR-LED INSTRUCTION

I. Selected materials
In addition to the formative suggestions for self-instructional materials, you should determine whether the following are true:
A. All parts of the instructional strategy are accounted for in the selected materials or provided by the instructor.

B. The transitions between sources are smooth.

C. The flow of content in the various instructional resources is consistent and logical.

D. The learners' manual or instructor adequately presents objectives.

E. Directions for locating instruction within each source are adequate.

F. Sections of the instructional strategy that must be supplied by the instructor are adequate.

G. The vocabulary used in all the sources is appropriate.

H. The illustrations and examples used are appropriate for the target group.

II. Instructor-Led Instruction

A major factor in evaluating instruction that is delivered by instructors is that they are an interactive part of the instruction. In addition to all the considerations we have mentioned previously, several important evaluation considerations are unique to this type of instruction.

A. Is the instructor convincing, enthusiastic, helpful, and knowledgeable?

B. Is the instructor able to avoid digressions to keep instruction and discussions on relevant topics and on schedule?

C. Does the instructor make presentations in an interesting, clear manner?

D. Does the instructor use the chalkboard and other visual aids to help with examples and illustrations?

E. Does the instructor provide good feedback to learners' questions?

F. Does the instructor provide adequate practice exercises with appropriate feedback?

You should record events that occur during instruction so that you can study them for what they imply about the effectiveness of the instruction.

INSTRUMENTS FOR ASSESSING LEARNERS' ATTITUDES ABOUT INSTRUCTION

Instruments for assessing learners' achievement of group leadership skills were illustrated and discussed in the preceding chapter. No attitude questionnaires, however, were presented, and good formative evaluation includes assessing both achievement and attitudes.

Table 10.4 contains an attitude questionnaire for the instructional goal, "Lead group discussion aimed at solving problems." The questionnaire is designed to be administered following session 10: Engender cooperative member behaviors during group meetings (objectives 6.1.1 through 6.5.1). It contains six sections. Four of the sections relate to facets of Keller's ARCS model including attention, relevance, confidence, and satisfaction. Another section enables learners to rate the clarity of instruction. The last section asks learners to provide their comments on the strengths and weaknesses of instruction from their perspective. To aid their work, different aspects of instruction are named in the far-left column. The last two rows, marked other, are included to invite learners to comment on aspects of the instruction that were not specifically named on the form.

In addition to evaluating the instruction, instruments used to gather information are also assessed for their clarity and utility during the formative evaluation. For example, if several learners ask questions about instructions

TABLE *10.4*

Attitude Questionnaire for Main Step 6: Manage Cooperative Group Interaction, Session 10, Objectives 6.1.1 Through 6.5.1

Session 10: Engendering Cooperative Member Behaviors   Date_____

INSTRUCTIONS: Use the following questionnaire to judge the effectiveness of today's session on engendering cooperative member behaviors. Please rate the quality of the instruction in each of the five main categories included on the form. For each of the instructional areas listed on the left, circle the response on the right that best reflects your perception of the quality level. At the bottom of the form, please comment on aspects of tonight's session that you consider to be particular strengths or problems. Thank you.

I. Attention: To what degree did the following instructional activities hold your interest or attention?

Instructional Areas	Attention Level (circle one level for each area)
A. Reading, analyzing annotated dialogues of NCW meetings illustrating:	
1. Member actions that aid cooperative interaction	Little 1 2 3 4 5 Very attentive
2. Strategies leaders use to encourage group cooperation	Little 1 2 3 4 5 Very attentive
B. Watching, analyzing videotapes of NCW meetings depicting:	
3. Positive member actions that aid cooperative interaction	Little 1 2 3 4 5 Very attentive
4. NCW leaders engendering cooperative member behaviors	Little 1 2 3 4 5 Very attentive
C. Performing myself as group leader to:	
5. Engender cooperative member behaviors in my group	Little 1 2 3 4 5 Very attentive

II. Relevance: To what degree do you believe the following skills are *relevant* for helping you provide effective leadership in NCW problem-solving meetings?

	Relevance Level
6. Recognizing cooperative member behaviors during meetings	Little 1 2 3 4 5 Very relevant
7. Engendering cooperative member behaviors during meetings	Little 1 2 3 4 5 Very relevant

or particular items on the attitude questionnaire or tend to leave items or sections blank, then the related areas should be examined for clarity and modified. In addition, if any section of the instrument does not yield data useful for pinpointing strengths and weaknesses and for revising instruction, then it should also be revised or eliminated.

Readers interested in a school-based example may refer to Appendix J.

TABLE *10.4* | **(Continued)**

III. Confidence: What level *of confidence* do you have that you can effectively use these group interaction management skills in NCW problem-solving discussion?

Confidence Level

8. Recognizing cooperative member behaviors during meetings

Little 1 2 3 4 5 Very confident

9. Engendering cooperative member behaviors during meetings

Little 1 2 3 4 5 Very confident

IV. Clarity: What level of *clarity* do you believe the following instructional materials and activities have?

Clarity Level

10. Session introduction

Little 1 2 3 4 5 Very clear

11. Objectives for session

Little 1 2 3 4 5 Very clear

12. Annotated written dialogues of NCW meetings

Little 1 2 3 4 5 Very clear

13. Videotapes of NCW meetings

Little 1 2 3 4 5 Very clear

14. Performing ourselves as group leaders

Little 1 2 3 4 5 Very clear

15. Instructions for our group leadership activity

Little 1 2 3 4 5 Very clear

16. Checklists we used to find positive leader actions

Little 1 2 3 4 5 Very clear

17. Feedback on exercises for positive member and leader actions

Little 1 2 3 4 5 Very clear

V. Satisfaction: Overall, how satisfied were you with:

Satisfaction Level

18. The facilities

Little 1 2 3 4 5 Very satisfied

19. The instructor(s)

Little 1 2 3 4 5 Very satisfied

20. The pace

Little 1 2 3 4 5 Very satisfied

21. The instruction

Little 1 2 3 4 5 Very satisfied

22. Yourself, relative to the new skills you have developed/refined

Little 1 2 3 4 5 Very satisfied

SUMMARY

Formative evaluation of instructional materials is conducted to determine the effectiveness of the materials and to revise them in areas where they are ineffective. Formative evaluations should be conducted on newly developed

| TABLE 10.4 | (Continued) |

VI. **Please comment on aspects of this session that were strengths or problems for you personally.**

	Strengths	Problems
Introduction:		
Objectives:		
Annotated dialogues:		
Videotapes:		
Interactive leadership session:		
Assessments:		
Other:		
Other:		

materials as well as existing materials that are selected based on the instructional strategy. Evaluations are necessary for both mediated and instructor presented materials. The evaluations should be designed to produce data to pinpoint specific areas where the instruction is faulty, and to suggest how it should be revised.

An iterative process of formative evaluation containing at least three cycles of data collection, analysis, and revision is recommended. Each cycle focuses on different aspects of quality. The first cycle, one-to-one evaluation, is conducted to pinpoint gross errors in the materials. These errors typically relate to both the clarity of vocabulary, concepts, and examples used, and the motivational value of all five components of the instructional materials. Evaluations can also be conducted with content experts and individuals familiar with the characteristics of target learners. One-to-one evaluations must be conducted with individuals who are representative of the target population. An interactive, interview process is used so the evaluator can learn not only what was wrong with the materials but also why it was wrong.

The second cycle, the small-group evaluation, follows the correction of major errors identified in the instruction. The group typically consists of from eight to twenty representative members of the target population. The purpose of the small-group evaluation is to locate additional errors in the instructional materials and management procedures. The elements of the instructional strategy are again the anchor for the evaluation instruments and procedures. During this cycle the evaluator plays a less interactive role, performance and attitude data are collected, and in-depth debriefings are conducted to obtain both quantitative and qualitative data.

The final cycle, a field trial, is conducted following refinement of the materials based on the small-group evaluation. The purpose of this evaluation is to pinpoint errors in the materials when they are used as prescribed in the intended setting. Similar to the first two cycles, evaluation instrumentation and procedures should be anchored in the five components of the instructional strategy. Instruments to gather data on learner performance and attitudes are important. The gathering of management data such as the time required to use the materials and the feasibility of the management plan is also important. During the trial, the evaluator does not interfere as data are gathered from the learners and perhaps the instructor, although observation while materials are used can provide insights for the interpretation of data gathered.

Following any phase of formative evaluation, the designer should determine the feasibility of collecting additional data from the learners as they return to the context in which they will use the skills that they learned in the instruction. The intent is to find out whether the skills are being used and with what effect. The result is more information to use in the revision of the instruction.

This chapter has focused on the design of the formative evaluation and the data-gathering procedures. The next chapter describes data analysis and materials revision based on the data.

PRACTICE

The following exercises are based on the instructional analysis and strategy of main step 6, "Manage cooperative group interaction" presented in Chapter 8. Again, the target population is Neighborhood Crime Watch leaders of varying levels of knowledge and skills. For each type of formative evaluation (one-to-one, small-group, and field trial), you are to consider the questions and identify decisions you would make based on the purposes of the evaluation, the nature of the instruction, and the target population.

I. One-to-One Evaluation
 1. Describe how many NCW leaders you would select for a one-to-one evaluation of the cooperative group interaction instruction and explain why you would include each learner in your sample.
 2. Describe the kinds of information you would be seeking during the one-to-one evaluation.
 3. Describe the appearance (typed, rough copy, polished copy, etc.) of your materials for the one-to-one evaluation.

II. Small-Group Evaluation
 1. Describe the number and achievement level of learners that you would include in your small-group trial.

2. Describe how you would determine whether one small-group evaluation session was sufficient.
3. Describe the materials (level of completeness, rough copy, polished copy, etc.) you would use for a small-group evaluation session.
4. Describe the information you would record to help evaluate the instruction on managing cooperative group interaction for leaders with varying backgrounds and levels of achievement.

III. Field Trial
1. Why would you be interested in a field trial of the materials?
2. What information would you collect during the field trial that you would not have collected during the small-group evaluation session?
3. Describe an appropriate sample group and instructional setting that could be used to evaluate the materials on managing cooperative group interaction.
4. What materials would you include in the field trial?

IV. Performance Context Formative Evaluation
1. Would you do a performance context formative evaluation for any of the phases? If so, which one(s), and why?
2. What procedure would you use?

V. Formative Evaluation of Selected Materials and Instructor-Led Instruction
1. How would your procedures differ if you were conducting a field trial of adapted or adopted materials, rather than a set of "original" materials?
2. Describe the major procedural differences between the field trial of selected materials and the field trial of instructor-led instruction.

VI. Develop an attitude questionnaire to use with learners when conducting the small-group evaluations and field trials for the lesson on depositing money into a checking account.

FEEDBACK

I. One-to-One Evaluation
1. The exact number of learners selected for one-to-one evaluation is arbitrary. The sample should include learners with different levels of education and group leadership experience. There should be at least one learner from each of the levels you identify. Should you discover that the instruction is inappropriate for those with no experience in leadership, you will need to adapt the instruction to include these learners. Learners with high school diplomas only should be included to check vocabulary; reading difficulty level; pacing; entry skills; and the clarity of examples, exercises, and feedback. You should also include advanced-degree leaders with leadership experience to determine the following:
   a. Can some sections be skipped?
   b. Are examples clear and are exercises challenging but clear?
   c. Are exercises and feedback appropriate?
2. Types of information you should obtain during the one-to-one evaluation are the following:

a. Does the initial motivation material interest the learner?

b. Are the objectives clear and interesting as well as relevant to the learner?

c. What skills from the instruction do the learners already possess?

d. Are the instructional materials adequate in the following categories?
   - Vocabulary
   - Pacing
   - Chunk size
   - Clarity of descriptions
   - Clarity of examples
   - Adequacy of sequence of content and activities
   - Interest level of exercises
   - Student performance on practice exercises
   - Clarity of feedback information
   - Motivation

e. Are the test instructions, vocabulary, questions, and response expectations clear to the learners?

3. The appearance of materials is again arbitrary and rests on the judgment of the instructor. A set of materials to teach the objectives may consist of loose pages of instruction with directions typed and illustrations hand drawn. Each new idea and any required student responses should be placed on one page, with feedback on a separate page. This way sequences can be changed easily. Another benefit of grouping instruction and learner performances for one concept together is that it will help pinpoint concepts that have been inadequately explained or examples, illustrations, and feedback that confuse rather than clarify an idea. Illustrations, graphs, and figures should be "roughed in" because learners will "see" the idea whether you have stick figures or artistically-drawn characters. Learners should be encouraged to write on the materials, to circle unclear words, and to place a check by unclear parts. You will need as many copies of materials as learners you intend to sample, plus extra copies on which to tally your results and make revisions.

II. Small-Group Evaluation

1. You should include at least three or four learners from each expected education and leadership experience level. This will help you avoid the error of assuming that all learners at a particular level will respond in the same manner. It will give you a basis for comparing the responses of learners who are at various education and experience levels. As a guideline you should have at least eight learners.

2. One session of small-group evaluation may not be enough. A good way to judge is to consider the amount and types of revisions made in the materials as a result of the previous evaluation. If only a few slight revisions are made and you believe that similar learners would react the same way to the instruction, then continued small-group evaluation is unnecessary. If, however, you make several revisions as a result of the previous evaluation, then you may need another small-group session to

evaluate your new version of the materials. Some of your decisions may result in improvements; others may not.

3. Your materials should be developed to the appropriate level of sophistication. Problems resulting from the medium itself cannot be detected unless the instruction appears in that medium. Tests used prior to and after instruction should also be complete and administered in their intended format. If possible, the instructor's guide should be complete and tested at this time and necessary revisions should be made before the field evaluation. Information from the field evaluation session will probably be included in the information section of the instructor's guide, but it will be necessary to evaluate the clarity of instructions and suggestions for using the materials.

4. After the small-group evaluation, you may want to summarize the various types of information for the following groups:

   a. Divide the sample into no, some, and formal leadership training or experience.

   b. Record their responses on the pretest.
      - Record performance on each subskill required to reach the terminal objective.
      - Tally any vocabulary words circled as unclear.
      - Tally any questions checked as unclear.
      - Tally directions marked as unclear.

   c. Record their responses in the instructional package.
      - Tally any explanations, examples, illustrations, vocabulary, and feedback that have been marked as being unclear.

   d. Record their responses on the posttest.
      - Tally correct and incorrect objective-by-objective responses.
      - Tally any questions marked unclear.
      - Tally any directions marked unclear.
      - Tally any response requirements marked unclear.
      - Tally any vocabulary circled or marked unclear.

   e. Record time required for pretest, instruction, and posttest activities.

III. Field Trial

   1. Materials are field tested to determine their effectiveness with the target population when used under specified conditions. Field trials answer the question, "Do these materials work for given learners when used in the planned learning context, and are there any improvements that can be made?" It helps to determine the instructional effectiveness of the materials in the absence of coaching by an instructor. It also aids in determining whether the materials are actually ready for use. The materials, tests, and instructions for both learners and instructors should be examined during the field trial. Have the materials had enough revision, or is more revision required? Revision at this point can be either in the materials themselves or in suggestions for using the materials.

   2. You would probably want to collect the same types of information that were obtained during the small-group evaluation. Other information might include learners' attitudes about the following:

      a. Was instruction interesting?

      b. Was instruction too easy, too difficult, or just right?

      c. Was instruction too fast, too slow, or just right?

      d. Were the materials easy to use or were they complicated?

You might also want to include instructors' attitudinal information about whether the materials are easy to use, complicated, or just right, and why the instructors hold these opinions.

3. An appropriate population to field test the instruction on leading cooperative group interaction would be current NCW leaders or block captains with high school through advanced graduate degrees and with various levels of leadership experience—perhaps twenty current leaders in a county area. This would provide information about performance levels, attitudes, and instructional time requirements when materials are used under normal learning center conditions.

4. All materials developed should be included and evaluated in the field trial. This should include all print materials, Web-based materials, equipment, assessments, and the instructor's guide.

IV. Performance-Context Formative Evaluation

1. You could chose to do a performance-context formative evaluation after any of the three phases of formative evaluation. Perhaps the one-to-one would be the wisest place to start because if any major changes were to be made as a result of the evaluation, then there would be several more phases in which those changes could be evaluated. The argument for waiting until later phases of formative evaluation to do the performance-context evaluation is that more learners will be involved who may be returning to a variety of contexts. This clearly provides more information to the designer; however, less time is left to do anything about it!

2. The context for use of the skills in this lesson is actual neighborhood meetings convened by leaders. The designer could interview learners several weeks or a month after the instruction to determine whether they are using the group leadership skills, what effect they are having, and any problems they are encountering. The designer could also use the posttest observation form to evaluate the actions of leaders in managing their actual meetings. In this case the designer could report back to the task force or funding agency that identified the need for the instruction. They could review the instructional products to determine, from their perspective, whether the instruction meets the need as they had identified it. Finally you could assess the impact of NCW activity in neighborhoods where leaders received the training. Variables you might consider include the following: (1) the number of NCW meetings leaders held during the last six to twelve months, (2) the number and nature of crime prevention programs initiated during the period, (3) the number and nature of police contacts made by area citizens during the time period, (4) the trends (increases, decreases by

type) of actual crimes committed within these areas, (5) the number of active members in the NCW groups, (6) trends in the amount of graffiti visible in the neighborhood, and so forth.

V. Formative Evaluation of Selected Materials and Instructor-Led Instruction

1. The major difference between field evaluation of selected materials and original materials is that the instructor is present during the evaluation of selected existing materials. This provides the instructor with the opportunity to observe the use of the materials and to determine the adequacy of the various components of the instructional strategy.

2. With instructor-led instruction, the instructor interacts with the learners while delivering the instruction. The instructor controls the practice and feedback components of the instruction. The instructor is more passive when evaluating selected materials.

VI. Attitude Questionnaire

The attitude questionnaire (Table 10.5) can be given to learners to complete during the small-group and field trials. During the one-to-one trials, however, you should use the questionnaire as an interview form. You can write responses learners make on the form. The one-to-one trials will help you formatively evaluate the attitudinal questionnaire to determine whether the questions you have asked are clear. If you get several "I don't know" responses, then rephrase the questions until the learner understands the question and expresses an opinion. Note on the questionnaire changes you need to make to clarify what you are asking.

The attitudinal questionnaire can be used as an interview guide during the debriefing session as well. It will help you focus the evaluation on important components in the materials.

TABLE *10.5*

Attitude Questionnaire for Instruction on Depositing Money into a Checking Account

**Instructional Quality for Lesson on
Depositing Money into a Checking Account**

Class _____ Date _____

DIRECTIONS: We need your help in evaluating the quality of this lesson. The left column names particular parts of the lesson. For each part named, rate its overall quality on a scale from 1 = Poor to 5 = Good (circle the level you believe best describes each lesson part). In the right column, note ways you think we can improve each lesson part to make it more clear, more interesting, and more relevant for your needs in managing your own checking account. Thank you; your comments are very important to us!

Lesson Part	Quality Rating (Circle Value)	Suggest Improvements for Clarity, Interest Value, and Relevance to you
1. Introduction	Poor 1 2 3 4 5 Good	Clarity:
		Interest:
		Relevance:
2. Objectives	Poor 1 2 3 4 5 Good	Clarity:
		Interest:
		Relevance:
3. Information presentation (including examples)	Poor 1 2 3 4 5 Good	Clarity:
		Interest:
		Relevance:
4. Practice Activities	Poor 1 2 3 4 5 Good	Clarity:
		Interest:
		Relevance:
5. Feedback	Poor 1 2 3 4 5 Good	Clarity:
		Interest:
		Relevance:
6. Assessments	Poor 1 2 3 4 5 Good	Clarity:
		Interest:
		Relevance:
7. Other:	Poor 1 2 3 4 5 Good	
8. Other:	Poor 1 2 3 4 5 Good	

REFERENCES AND RECOMMENDED READINGS

Cronbach, L. J. (1975). Course improvement through evaluation. Reprinted in Payne, D. A., & McMorris, R. F. (Eds.), *Education and Psychological Measurement.* Morristown, NJ: General Learning Press, 243–256. This is one of the original articles on the need for formative evaluation of instructional materials.

Dick, W., & Carey, L. M. (1991). Formative evaluation. In Briggs, L.J., Gustafson, K. L., & Tillman, M. H. (Eds.), *Instructional Design: Principles and Applications.* Englewood Cliffs, NJ: Educational Technology Publications.

Dick, W., & King, D. (1994). Formative evaluation in the performance context. *Performance and Instruction.* 33(9), 3–10. Discussion of follow-up evaluation in the workplace.

Flagg, B. N. (1990). *Formative evaluation for educational technologies.* Hillsdale, NJ: Lawrence Erlbaum Associates. Examples of use of formative evaluation strategies when developing sophisticated instructional systems.

Nathenson, M. B., & Henderson, E.S. (1980). *Using student feedback to improve learning materials.* London: Croom Helm. A detailed description of the use of the formative evaluation process with Open University courses in England.

Newby, T. J., Stepich, D. A., Lehman, J. D., & Russell, J. D. (1996). *Instructional technology for teaching and learning.* Englewood Cliffs, NJ: Prentice-Hall, Inc. An excellent resource for instructional design in the school setting as well as the integration of computers into the instructional process.

Performance and Instruction Journal, 22 (5), 1983. Special issue on formative evaluation. This issue carries a number of articles of interest to the designer. See especially: Wager, "One-to-One and Small Group Formative Evaluation"; Komoski, "Formative Evaluation"; Lowe, "Clinical Approach to Formative Evaluation"; and Golas, "Formative Evaluation Effectiveness and Cost."

Russell, J. D., & Blake, B. L. (1988). Formative and summative evaluation of instructional products and learners. *Educational Technology, 28* (9), 22–28. This article distinguishes between the formative evaluation of instruction and the formative evaluation of learners.

Scott, R. O., & Yelon, S. R. (1969). The student as a co-author—The first step in formative evaluation. *Educational Technology,* October, 76–78. This is one of the few articles that describes procedures to be used in one-to-one formative evaluation with students.

Scriven, M., Tyler, R., & Gagné, R. (1967). Perspectives of curriculum evaluation. AERA Monograph Series on Curriculum Evaluation. Chicago: Rand McNally. In this monograph the authors made the first functional distinction between formative and summative evaluation.

Shambaugh, R. N., & Magliaro, S. G. (1997). *Mastering the possibilities.* Needham Heights, MA: Allyn & Bacon.

Tessmer, M. (1993). *Planning and conducting formative evaluations.* London: Kogan Page Limited. A complete description of the major phases of formative evaluation.

Tessmer, M. (1994). Formative evaluation alternatives. *Performance Improvement Quarterly,* 7(1), 3–18.

Thiagarajan, S. (1991). Formative evaluation. In Performance Technology. *Performance Improvement Quarterly, 4* (2), 22–34. Discusses follow-up evaluation six months after implementation. Excellent references.

CHAPTER

11 REVISING INSTRUCTIONAL MATERIALS

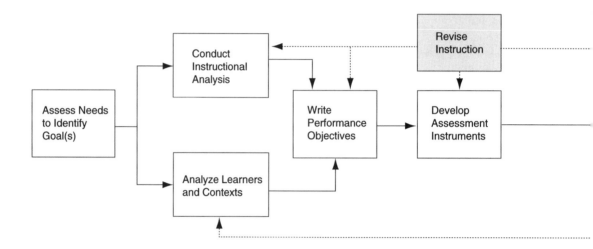

OBJECTIVES

- Describe various methods for summarizing data obtained from formative evaluation studies.
- Summarize data obtained from formative evaluation studies.
- Given summarized formative evaluation data, identify weaknesses in instructional materials and instructor-led instruction.
- Given formative evaluation data for a set of instructional materials, identify problems in the materials, and suggest revisions for the materials.

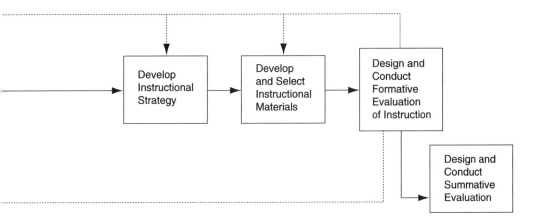

Design and Conduct Formative Evaluation of Instruction

Develop Instructional Strategy

Develop and Select Instructional Materials

Design and Conduct Formative Evaluation of Instruction

Design and Conduct Summative Evaluation

BACKGROUND

If you examine almost any instructional design model, you will find major emphasis on the concept of formative evaluation, that is, on collecting data to identify problems and to revise instructional materials. Models often indicate that after data have been collected and summarized, you should revise the materials "appropriately." Although a number of studies have indicated the benefit of revising instructional materials, few have proposed any theories around which to gather the data. In our approach to formative evaluation, we interpret the data in light of our instructional strategy and then make changes that seem to be indicated by the data and our understanding of the learning process.

There are two basic types of revisions you will consider with your materials. The first is changes that are made to the content or substance of the materials to make them more accurate or more effective as a learning tool. The second type of change is related to the procedures employed in using your materials.

In this chapter, we will point out how data from various formative evaluation sources can be summarized and used to identify portions of your

change content or procedures

323

materials that should be revised. You will note that you will not be concerned about the use of complex statistics in this step of the instructional design process because simple descriptive summaries of the data are sufficient. Elaborate statistical tests are almost never employed in the formative evaluation and revision process.

CONCEPTS

There are many different ways in which the data collected in a formative evaluation may be summarized to point to areas of learner difficulties and possible revisions. The methods we describe here are merely suggestions. As you begin to work with your own data, you may find other techniques that will help you derive more insight from them. We will first look at what you can do with the data and information from a one-to-one formative evaluation, and then consider the small-group and field-trial phases.

ANALYZING DATA FROM ONE-TO-ONE TRIALS

Following the one-to-one formative evaluation the designer has very little data because information typically is available for only three to five learners. Since these learners were selected based on their diversity, the information they provide will, in all likelihood, be very distinct, rather than blending into some type of group average. In other words, the designer must look at the similarities and differences among the responses of the learners, and determine the best changes to make in the instruction.

The designer has five kinds of basic information available: learner characteristics and entry behaviors, direct responses to the instruction, learning time, posttest performance, and responses to an attitude questionnaire, if used.

The first step is to describe the learners who participated in the one-to-one evaluation and to indicate their performance on any entry-behavior measures. Next, the designer should bring together all the comments and suggestions about the instruction that resulted from going through it with each learner. This can be done by integrating everything on a master copy of the instruction using a color code to link each learner to his or her particular problems. It is also possible to include comments from a subject-matter expert, and any alternative instructional approaches that were used with learners during the one-to-one sessions.

The next set of data to be summarized is that associated with the posttest. Begin by obtaining individual item performance and then combine item scores for each objective and for a total score. It is often of interest to develop a table that indicates each student's pretest score, posttest score, and total learning time. In addition, student performance on the posttest should be summarized, along with any comments, for each objective. The same type of summary can be used for examining the data on the attitude questionnaire, if one is used at this point in the instruction.

With all this information in hand, the designer is ready to revise the instruction. Of course, certain obvious revisions may have been made before completing the one-to-one sessions. Now the more difficult revisions must be made. Certainly the place to begin is within those sections that resulted in the poorest performance by learners and in those that resulted in the most comments.

First, try to determine, based on learner performance, whether your rubric or test items are faulty. If flawed, then changes should be made to make them consistent with the objectives and the intent of the instruction. If the items are satisfactory, and the learners performed poorly, then the instruction must be changed. You have three sources of suggestions for change: learner suggestions, learner performance, and your own reactions to the instruction. Learners often can suggest sensible changes. In addition, the designer should carefully examine the *mistakes* made by learners in order to identify the kinds of misinterpretations they are making and, therefore, the kinds of changes that might be made. You should not ignore your own insights about what changes will make the instruction more effective. You have used systematic design procedures, so you have made careful descriptions of what is to be learned and have provided examples; you have offered students the opportunity to practice each skill and they have received feedback. The basic components are there! The usual revisions at this stage are ones of clarification of ideas and the addition or deletion of practice activities. Hopefully, the three sources of data will suggest the most appropriate steps to take.

There will be times when it is not obvious what to do to improve your instruction. It is sometimes wise simply to leave that part of the instruction as is and see how it works in the small-group formative evaluation. Alternatively, the designer can develop several approaches to solving the problem and try these out during the small-group evaluation.

ANALYZING DATA FROM SMALL-GROUP AND FIELD TRIALS

The small-group formative evaluation provides the designer with a somewhat different data summary situation. The data from eight to twenty learners are of greater collective interest than individual interest; that is, these data can show what problems and reactions this representative group of learners had. The available data typically include the following: item performance on the pretest, posttest, and responses to an attitude questionnaire; learning and testing time; and comments made directly in the materials.

The fundamental unit of analysis for all the assessments is the individual assessment item. Performance on each item must be scored as correct or incorrect. If an item has multiple parts, then each part should be scored and reported separately so that the information is not lost. This individual item information is required for three reasons:

1. Item information can be useful in deciding whether there are particular problems with the item or whether it is effectively measuring the performance described in its corresponding objective. The method for doing this will be described in a later section.

2. Individual item information can be used to identify the nature of the difficulties learners are having with the instruction. Not only is it important to know that, for example, half the learners missed a particular item, but it is just as important to know that most of those who missed it picked the same distractor in a multiple-choice item or made the same type of reasoning error on a problem-solving item.

3. Individual item data can be combined to indicate learner performance on an objective, and eventually, on the entire test. Sometimes, the criterion level for an objective is expressed in terms of getting a certain percentage of items correct on a set of items. The individual item data can be combined not only to show percentage of items correct for an objective, but the number and percent of learners who achieved mastery.

TABLE *11.1* | Item-by-Objective Analysis Table

Objectives		1		2		3			4			Items		Objectives	
Items		1	2	3	4	5	6	7	8	9	10	#	%	#	%
Students	1	X	X	X	X	X	X	X	X	X	X	8	100	4	100
	2	X	X	X	X	X	X	X	X	X	X	8	100	4	100
	3		X	X	X	X	X	X	X	X	X	7	88	3	75
	4	X			X		X	X		X		X	4	50	0	0
	//														
	20	X	X				X	X	X	X			4	50	2	50
# Students Correct		18	19	15	17	17	6	18	18	10	9				
% Students Correct		90	95	75	85	85	30	90	90	50	45				
% Mastering Objectives		90		75		85			45						

*Summaries represent totals after items 6 and 8 were removed from the analysis.

Note: Although there were twenty students in the analysis group, data for only 5 students are illustrated.

After the item data have been collected and organized into a basic item-by-objective table, it is then possible to construct more comprehensive data tables.

GROUP'S ITEM-BY-OBJECTIVE PERFORMANCE   The first data summary table that should be constructed is an item-by-objective table. An example is illustrated in Table 11.1. Assume that we have a ten-item test that measures four objectives. Twenty learners were in the small-group formative evaluation.

The objectives are listed across the top of the table, and items are inserted in the second row within the objectives they measure. Learners' data are recorded in the rows beneath the items and objectives. An X in the column beneath an item indicates a correct response, and a blank indicates an incorrect response for each learner.

With the raw data displayed in this manner, we can use the table to create two summaries for analysis: item quality and learner performance. You should analyze item quality first, because faulty items should not be considered when analyzing learner performance. The bottom rows contain the data summaries needed for the item analysis. The first row contains the number of the twenty students who answered each item correctly. The next row contains the percentage of learners who answered each item correctly. These figures are obtained by dividing the total number of students in the evaluation into the number of students who answered correctly—that is, for item 1, 18/20 =.90 or 90 percent. The last row contains the percentage of the group that mastered each objective. This value is calculated by dividing the number of students who mastered each objective by the total number of students in the analysis. In this example, learners must correctly answer all the questions for an objective in order to master the objective.

The purpose for the item-by-objective analysis is threefold: to determine the difficulty of each item for the group, to determine the difficulty of each objective for the group, and to determine the consistency with which the set of items within an objective measures learners' performance on the objective.

Item difficulty values above 80 percent reflect relatively easy items for the group, whereas lower values reflect more difficult ones. Similarly, consistently high or low values for items within an objective reflect the difficulty of the objective for the group. For example, the difficulty values for items 1 and 2 in Table 11.1 (90 and 95) indicate that nearly all the learners mastered the items associated with objective 1. If these data were from a posttest, then we could infer that the instruction related to objective 1 is effective. Conversely, if they are low, then they point to instruction that should be considered for revision.

The consistency of item difficulty indices within an objective typically reflects the quality of the items. If items are measuring the same skill, and if there is no inadvertent complexity or clues in the items, then learners' performance on the set of items should be relatively consistent. With small groups, differences of 10 or 20 percent are not considered large, but differences of 40 percent or more should cause concern. Notice in Table 11.1 that item data are consistent within objectives 1 and 2. In contrast, the data are inconsistent within objectives 3 and 4. For objective 3, two items are quite consistent (85 and 90), while one item, 6, yielded a much lower difficulty index (30). Such a pattern reflects either inadvertent complexity in the item or a different skill being measured. The pattern in objective 4 illustrates two consistent items (50 and 45) and one outlier (90). This type of pattern reflects either a clue in item 8 or a different skill being measured. When inconsistent difficulty indices are observed within an objective, it indicates that the items within the set should be reviewed and revised prior to reusing them to measure learner performance. If the item is judged sound, then it reflects an aspect of instruction that should be reconsidered.

LEARNERS' ITEM-BY-OBJECTIVE PERFORMANCE The second type of analysis that can be conducted using the item-by-objective table is individual learner performance. Before conducting this analysis, you should eliminate any items judged faulty during the item analysis. The last four columns in the table contain the individual performance data. The first two of these columns contain the number and percent of items answered correctly by each learner. The last two columns contain the number and percent of objectives mastered by each learner. Answering all items within an objective was set as the criterion for mastery.

The hypothetical data for learners in Table 11.1 illustrate that individuals in the group performed quite differently on the test. Two individuals mastered all four objectives, and the scores for the other three learners range from no objectives mastered to 75 percent. If these data represented performance on entry behaviors or skills to be included in the instruction, then they would suggest who was ready for instruction and whether instruction was actually needed by some members of the sample. In contrast, if they reflected posttest performance, then the designer could make inferences about the necessity of revising the instruction. Data about learners' performance on items and objectives provide different information, and for the formative evaluator, data on objectives mastered are more informative than raw scores.

LEARNERS' PERFORMANCE ACROSS TESTS The item-by-objective table provides the data for creating tables to summarize learners' performance across tests. Table 11.2 illustrates how learner-by-objective mastery can be illustrated across tests administered. The data are presented for only five of the twenty students in the analysis, and a summary for the twenty students is presented

TABLE **11.2**

Student Performance on the Pretest and Posttest by Objective

Objectives	1		2		3		4	
Test	PR	PS	PR	PS	PR	PS	PR	PS
Students 1		X		X	X	X	X	X
2		X		X		X		X
3	X	X		X	X	X		
4		X		X		X		X
//								
20		X		X	X	X		X
%								
Mastering	20	100	10	100	50	100	40	60
Diff.		80		90		50		20

PR = pretest; PS = posttest; X = mastered

Note: Table includes data for only 5 of 20 students in the evaluation but summary percentages reflect data for entire group.

TABLE **11.3**

Entry-Behavior, Pretests, and Posttest Data Summarized by the Percent of Total Possible Objectives

Student Number	3 Entry Behavior Objectives	9 Pretest Instructional Objectives	9 Posttest Objectives
1	100	11	89
2	100	22	89
3	100	22	89
4	100	11	100
//			
20	67	0	67
Mean	92	14	88

Note: The mean scores are based on the performance of all twenty students even though the data for only five are illustrated.

at the bottom of the table. The first row identifies the objectives, the second row identifies the tests, and subsequent rows are used to record students' mastery of objectives on each test. The two summary rows at the bottom of the table contain the percentage of the twenty learners who mastered each objective on each test and the increase or decrease in percentages from pretest to posttest for each objective. Ideally, the percentages of learners who mastered each objective should increase from pretests to posttests. Such a pattern is illustrated for all four objectives in Table 11.2.

You may also want to summarize learners' performance across tests using the percentage of objectives mastered on each test. Such a summary is illustrated in Table 11.3. The top row identifies the test and the number of objectives measured by each one. Subsequent rows contain the percentage of objectives mastered by each student on each test. The bottom row contains the average percentage of objectives mastered by the group on each test.

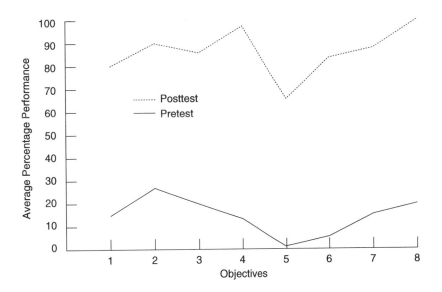

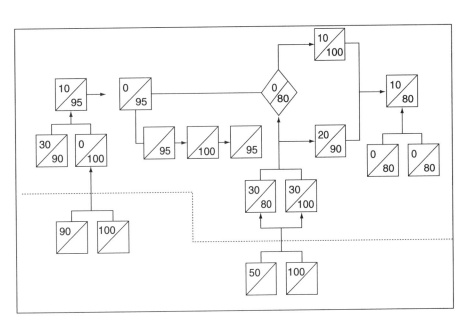

From these data the designer could infer that: (1) the group selected was appropriate for the evaluation, (2) the instruction covered skills not previously mastered by the group, and (3) the instruction was effective in improving learners' skills.

GRAPHING LEARNERS' PERFORMANCES Another way to display data is through various graphing techniques. A graph may show the pretest and posttest performance for each objective in the formative evaluation study. You may also want to graph the amount of time required to complete the instructional materials as well as the amount of time required for the pretest and posttest. An example of a pretest/posttest performance graph appears in Figure 11.1.

Another graphic technique for summarizing formative evaluation data involves the instructional analysis chart. This procedure requires the determination of the average pretest and posttest performance of learners participating in the formative evaluation on each of the skills indicated on the instructional analysis chart. The designer uses a copy of the instructional analysis chart, without the statement of skills. See Figure 11.2 for an example of this technique. The pretest and posttest scores for each objective are entered in the appropriate boxes. This provides an interesting display of the interrelationships of the scores on the various skills in the instructional materials. It will become apparent if learners' performance declines as they approach the top of the hierarchy. You may also find a skill mastered by only a few learners that seems to have little effect on the subsequent mastery of superordinate skills.

OTHER TYPES OF DATA   There are other kinds of data to summarize and analyze in addition to learners' performance on objectives. It has been found that a good way to summarize data from an attitude questionnaire is to indicate on a blank copy of the questionnaire the percent of learners who chose each alternative to the various questions. If you also request open-ended, general responses from the learners, then you can summarize them for each question.

Another important type of data is the comments obtained from learners, from other instructors involved in the formative evaluation, and from subject-matter experts who react to the materials. Data and information that are collected in performance context formative evaluations may have to be summarized in descriptive fashion. Since it is almost impossible to summarize these comments in tabular or graphic form, it is better to try to relate each of these comments to the instructional materials themselves, or to the objective in the materials to which they refer. These comments can be written directly on a copy of the materials.

The final type of data summary you may wish to prepare is related to any alternative approaches you may have used during either the small-group or field-trial evaluations. These data may be performance on specific test items, responses on an attitude questionnaire, or even an indication of total learning time.

SEQUENCE FOR EXAMINING DATA   As you prepare summaries of your data, you will quickly begin to get an overall picture of the general effectiveness of your instructional materials and the extent of revisions you may be required to make. After generally examining the data, we suggest that you use the data in the following sequence.

ENTRY BEHAVIORS   First, after removing data for any defective items, you should examine the remaining data with regard to the entry behaviors of learners. Did the learners in the formative evaluation have the entry behaviors you anticipated? If so, did they succeed with the instructional materials? If they did succeed, but did not have the required entry behaviors, then you must question whether you have identified critical entry behaviors.

PRETESTS AND POSTTESTS   The second step is to review the pretest and posttest data as displayed on the instructional analysis chart. If you sequenced the materials appropriately and if you identified skills that are hierarchically dependent on each other, then learner performance should decrease as you move upward through the hierarchy—that is, there should be poorer learner performance on the terminal objective than on the earlier skills. When the instruction is working well, there will, of course, be no decline in learner performance as learners complete the skills at the top of the analysis. These data will help you identify exactly where problems exist and perhaps even suggest a change in the instructional sequence for certain skills.

Third, you might examine the pretest scores to determine the extent to which individual learners, and the group as a whole, had already acquired the skills that you were teaching. If they already possess most of the skills, then you will receive relatively little information about the effectiveness of the instruction or how it might be improved. If they lack these skills, then you will have more confidence in the analyses that follow.

By comparing pretest with posttest scores objective by objective, which is usually what is done when you examine the instructional analysis chart, you can assess learners' performance on each particular objective and begin to focus on specific objectives and the related instruction that appear to need revision.

As you identify objectives on which the learners performed poorly, examine the exact wording of the objective and the associated test items, and the exact student answers to the items. Before revising the instructional materials, refer to your item analysis table to see whether poor test items, rather than the materials, indicated poor learner performance. All that may be needed is revised test items rather than a major revision of the instructional materials.

INSTRUCTIONAL STRATEGY   The next step is to examine the instructional strategy associated with the various objectives with which learners had difficulty. Was the planned strategy actually used in the instructional materials? Are there alternative strategies that might be employed? The final step is to examine the materials themselves to evaluate the comments about problem areas made by learners, instructors, and subject-matter experts.

LEARNING TIME   An important concern in any formative evaluation is the amount of time required by students to complete the instructional materials. It may be necessary for you to revise the materials to make them fit within a particular time period. This is an extremely difficult task, and it must be done with great care. With individualized materials it is not unusual for the slowest learner to take two or three times longer than the fastest learner. Knowing what to remove from the materials or change without interfering with learning is very difficult to determine. Often the decision can be made only after a trial/revise/trial/revise process with target learners.

INSTRUCTIONAL PROCEDURES   Data that relate to the implementation of the instructional materials must also be examined. We suggested earlier that you might gather misleading data because of the faulty operations of media equipment. There may also have been disruptions in the classroom, an extended lunch break, or any one of a variety of other kinds of activities that are common to various instructional settings. Since these disruptions cannot be controlled, they simply must be noted and explained.

On the other hand, there are procedural concerns that can be controlled. Were learners hindered by the logistics required to use the materials? Were there questions about how to proceed from one step to the next? Were there long delays in getting test scores? These are the kinds of implementation procedural problems that often are identified in questionnaires and debriefing discussions. Solutions to such problems must be found and incorporated into either the instruction or the instructors' manual to make the instructional activity run more smoothly.

REVISION PROCESS

We suggest that as you begin the revision process, you summarize your data as suggested in this chapter. We recognize that the needs of instructional designers will differ according to the type of materials with which they are working; however, the strategy suggested here should apply to almost any instructional design effort. For example, if you have taught a psychomotor skill, then your posttest performance would be recorded on a rubric of some sort, and summarized on your instructional analysis chart. There might also be a paper-and-pencil test of subordinate skills and knowledge. These scores should be examined in connection with their associated motor skills. The use of attitude responses and learning time would be the same for any type of instruction.

Given all the data from a small-group or field-trial evaluation, the designer must make decisions about how to make the revisions. It is almost always apparent where the problems are, but it is not always apparent what changes should be made. If a comparison of several approaches has been embedded in the formative evaluation, then the results should indicate the type of changes to be made. Otherwise, the strategies suggested for revising instruction following the one-to-one evaluations also apply at this point—namely, use the data, your experience, and sound learning principles as the bases for your revisions.

One caution: Avoid responding too quickly to any single piece of data, whether it is the learners' performance on a particular objective, a comment from an individual learner, or an observation by a subject-matter expert. They are all valuable pieces of information, but you should attempt to corroborate these data with other data. Look for performance as well as observational data that will help you focus on particular deficiencies in the instructional materials.

An additional suggestion: When summarizing data from the field evaluation, you should be careful to summarize it in an accurate and clear fashion. You will find that these data will be of interest not only to you as the instructional designer, but will also serve as an effective vehicle to show others how learners performed with your instruction. The table and graphs can provide both a general and a detailed description of the overall performance of the learners.

REVISING SELECTED MATERIALS AND INSTRUCTOR-LED INSTRUCTION

The data summary and revision procedures described previously are equally appropriate whether the instructor develops original instructional materials, uses a variety of selected materials, or works from an instructor's guide. The types of data that are collected, the ways in which they are summarized, and the ways in which they are used to direct the revision process are all similar. When working with selected materials, however, there is little opportunity to revise the materials directly, especially if they are commercially produced and copyrighted. With copyrighted materials, the instructor can consider the following adaptations for future trials: (1) omit portions of the instruction, (2) include other available materials, or (3) simply develop supplementary instruction. Procedures for the use of materials should also be reconsidered in light of formative evaluation data.

Instructors working from an instructor's guide have the same flexibility as the developer for changing instruction. A pretest and a posttest, together with an attitude questionnaire, should provide data for a thorough analysis of the instruction. Summary tables that indicate performance on each objective should be prepared. Examine learner performance on test items and objectives and then relate learner performance by objective to the instructional analysis diagram.

The instructor's notes from the guide should reflect questions raised by learners and responses to those questions. Learners' questions should be examined to determine whether basic misunderstandings have developed. Were the responses to the questions sufficient to provide adequate performance by learners on the related test items?

An instructor who used an instructor's guide is also likely to obtain a greater "spread" in the scores on tests and reactions on attitude questionnaires. Research data indicate that, by the very nature of group-paced, interactive instruction, some students are unlikely to understand the concepts as rapidly as others do during a given class period. Since there are typically no embedded remedial strategies in group instruction, such learners learn progressively less during a series of lessons, and receive progressively poorer scores; their attitudes will likely reflect this situation. In this interactive, group-paced mode, learners' performance is likely to resemble a bell curve distribution (i.e., a few high scores, a few low scores, and mostly average scores).

Identifying learners who are performing poorly and inserting appropriate activities are important components of the revision process for the instructor who is using an interactive instructional approach. Unlike using written instructional materials, the instructor can revise the presentation during its implementation and note the reasons for the change.

One final observation needs to be made. We have stressed that you are working with a systems approach to build an instructional system, and when you change one component of the system, you are changing the whole system. You need to be aware, therefore, that when you make changes through the revision process, you cannot assume that the remaining unchanged instruction will necessarily maintain its initial effectiveness. You may hope your changes are for the better, but you cannot assume that they always are.

one change can affect other stuff

EXAMPLES

Data from the instructional goal on leading group discussions will be used to illustrate techniques for summarizing and analyzing data collected during formative evaluation activities. Examples provided in this section are designed to illustrate procedures you might use for either a small-group or field-trial evaluation of materials and procedures. Of course the types of tables, graphs, and summary procedures you actually use should be tailored to your instructional materials, tests, instructional context, and learners. These examples simply show some ways the information gathered could be summarized for the group leadership unit.

Recall that, based on interviews with learners in the performance context (current NCW leaders and police support personnel), some decisions were made about how these adult learners would be tested. Due to learner sensitivity, they would not be pretested on verbal information or leadership performance objectives; pretests would simply assess their ability to recognize leadership skills demonstrated by others during staged NCW meetings. The decision was also made not to have individual learners identify themselves on their pretest or practice exercise papers. Learners were identifiable on the posttests because these consisted of actual group leadership. Not having identified the learners, individual member performance cannot be traced across tests; however, total group performance can be monitored, which will provide evidence of instructional effectiveness.

In this example, formative evaluation data for twenty learners were collected during a field trial of the instruction. Assessment data are presented for the twelve leader actions that encourage and stifle group cooperation contained within objectives 6.4.2 and 6.5.1. Recall that the same twelve actions are embedded within these two objectives. During the pretest, learners viewed a simulated NCW meeting on videotape and marked their observation form each time the leader exhibited one of the twelve enhancing or stifling actions (objective 6.4.2). Assessment data for objective 6.4.2 were also collected during learner participation activities within the instruction. Posttest data were collected only for the learners' group leadership actions exhibited during simulated NCW meetings (objective 6.5.1). Attitudinal data were collected using a questionnaire and debriefing at the end of session 10.

Summarizing Item-by-Objective Data Across Tests

Table 11.4 contains a summary of learners' responses on the pretest for objective 6.4.2. There are twelve behaviors within the objective, and they can be summarized similar to test items within an objective on an objective-style test. Each of the twelve encouraging and stifling actions is listed across the top of the table, and the twenty learners are listed in the far-left column. The first step in summarizing performance data from any test is to determine how to score learners' responses. When you administer an objective-style test, obtaining a score is relatively easy for each learner by counting the number of test items answered correctly. Scoring live performance assessments, however, requires some planning. (See pretest in Table 9.5.)

In scoring the pretest, we made the following decisions. Each of the enhancing and stifling actions was exhibited by the leader three times during the simulated meeting. Learners were given credit if their tally was within one point of the exhibited actions; thus, a tally of 2, 3, or 4 occurrences earned credit, and an X was placed in the student-by-behavior cell in the summary chart in Table 11.4. Further, enhancing and stifling behaviors for each of the twelve actions were combined to create a total test score from 0 to 12. To receive credit for any one of the twelve actions, learners had to classify correctly both the enhancing and stifling behaviors within a skill. For example, if they correctly classified the enhancing behaviors for action 3 but not the stifling behaviors for action 3, then they did not receive credit for action 3. Notice the shaded pairs of cells for each learner in the table. These pairs of cells reflect the skills for which learners received credit.

The row totals (each learner's score in the far-right column) were obtained by summing the shaded action pairs within each learner's row. The first row of column totals at the bottom of the table reflects the percentage of learners classifying each enhancing and each stifling action correctly. The last row on the bottom of the chart contains the percentage of the group that classified each of the twelve pairs of actions correctly.

With the pretest data summarized in this manner, you can begin the analysis and interpretation. First, examine individual learner performance (far-right column). Is the group heterogeneous in their group leadership skills as anticipated? You would undoubtedly conclude that their performance on the pretest was heterogeneous or very different. The highest possible score on

TABLE 11.4 | **Pretest Data Summarized by Learners Across Behaviors (Horizontal) and Behaviors Across Learners (Vertical)**

	Encouraging (+) and Stifling (−) Behaviors Exhibited by Leaders																								TOTAL
LRNS	1+	1−	2+	2−	3+	3−	4+	4−	5+	5−	6+	6−	7+	7−	8+	8−	9+	9−	10+	10−	11+	11−	12+	12−	
1	X	X	X	X	X	X	X	X	X	X	X	X	X	X	X	X	X	X	X	X	X	X	X		11
2	X	X	X	X	X		X	X	X	X	X		X	X	X				X	X	X	X	X		7
3	X	X	X	X	X	X	X		X	X	X	X	X	X			X		X	X	X			X	8
4	X	X	X	X	X	X	X	X						X	X	X	X		X		X	X		X	6
5	X	X	X		X					X	X	X	X	X	X				X	X	X	X	X		5
6	X	X	X	X	X	X	X		X	X			X				X	X			X	X	X		5
7	X	X			X						X	X	X	X	X	X			X	X	X	X	X		6
8	X		X	X	X	X	X	X			X	X			X						X	X			4
9	X				X								X	X						X	X	X			2
10		X	X	X	X	X	X	X	X		X	X	X		X	X	X	X	X	X	X	X	X	X	9
11										X		X							X		X				0
12	X	X	X	X	X								X							X					2
13			X	X	X	X			X		X	X	X	X	X	X	X	X	X	X	X	X	X	X	9
14	X	X	X								X	X							X		X	X			2
15													X	X	X	X	X		X		X				2
16	X		X	X	X	X					X	X		X							X		X		3
17	X		X	X	X	X	X						X						X	X		X	X		3
18					X					X		X	X				X				X				0
19	X			X	X	X				X							X		X						1
20		X			X	X					X	X	X	X	X		X		X	X	X	X	X		5
*	70	50	70	60	85	55	40	30	30	50	50	55	80	60	50	35	45	25	70	50	80	60	55	15	
**	45		55		55		25		25		40		50		25		25		40		55		10		

* Percentage of learners receiving credit for correctly classifying each enhancing (+) and stifling (−) behavior

**Percentage of learners receiving credit for correctly classifying both the enhancing and the stifling actions within a skill.

the test was twelve points, and their scores ranged from 11 to 0. Three of the learners earned scores of 9 (75 percent) or above, four earned scores between 6 and 8, four earned scores of 4 and 5, and nine, or almost half the group, earned scores of 3 (25 percent) or less.

The next step is to examine the total group's performance on each of the behaviors (bottom row). A reasonable question to answer from pretest data is, "Do the learners need this instruction, or do they already possess the skills?" Between 10 and 55 percent of the group correctly classified each pair of skills. From these data you can conclude that, with the possible exception of learner 1, instruction in enhancing cooperative group interaction is warranted. In addition, you can contrast their performance in classifying the enhancing and stifling actions (next to last row). The learners are better at recognizing the enhancing behaviors demonstrated than the stifling ones. In fact, they were better at classifying stifling behaviors for only one skill, 5, willingly turns over the floor to group members who interrupt rather than talking over interrupting members.

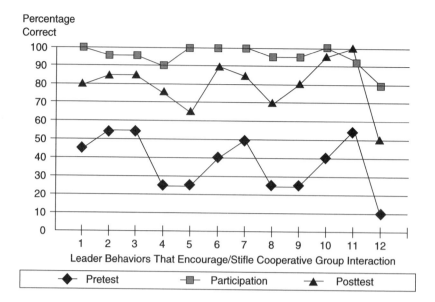

FIGURE 11.3

Percentage of Group Recognizing 12 Leader Actions that Encourage and Discourage Cooperative Group Interaction on the Pretest and Posttest (Objective 6.4.2) and Demonstrating Encouraging Behaviors as They Lead Group Discussions (Objective 6.5.1 Posttest Only)

In this instruction, objective 6.4.2 was not included on the posttest since the posttest consisted of demonstrating the twelve encouraging actions and avoiding the stifling ones while leading a discussion group. We contrasted the learners' pretest performance for objective 6.4.2 with their performance on the participation exercise embedded within instruction. Although this is not typical, we have no other data following instruction that can be used to compare with their pretest performance. This contrast will allow us to loosely examine the effects of instruction for objectives 6.1.1 through 6.4.2. Learner participation data should always be considered tentative; however, it might provide some evidence of growth or change from the pretest. The observation sheet learners used in the learner participation exercise was scored in the same manner as the pretest, which made comparisons possible.

SUMMARIZING AND ANALYZING DATA ACROSS TESTS

Figure 11.3 contains a graph of learners' achievement for objectives 6.4.2 and 6.5.1. The left side of the graph contains percentage levels used to identify the percentage of the twenty students who mastered each of the twelve behaviors. The twelve actions are listed along the bottom of the graph. With the data arranged as in Figure 11.3, you will be able to make observations about instruction related to the encouraging actions and the learners' achievement.

The lower line in the figure represents learners' pretest performance on objective 6.4.2, and these data were transferred directly from the bottom row of Table 11.4. The top row of data illustrates their classification skills on the learner participation activity that was included within the instruction. This activity followed instruction on objectives 6.1.1 through 6.4.2. Notice that at this point in the instruction, 80 percent or more of the group correctly classified all twelve of the leader behaviors. This high level of performance across the twelve skills and the learners' growth between the pretest and the practice activity indicate that instruction was effective in helping learners recognize these encouraging and stifling actions when they are exhibited by others.

The center row of data illustrates learners' demonstration of the twelve behaviors during the posttest administered at the end of session 10. Setting the criterion for effective instruction at 80 percent of the group successfully demonstrating each skill, you can see that instruction was adequate for eight of the twelve behaviors. It was ineffective, however, for helping learners consistently demonstrate the following encouraging actions:

#4 Hesitates and pauses between speakers rather than filling quiet gaps with personal points of view (75 percent)

#5 Willingly turns over floor when interrupted rather than continuing to talk or interrupting group members (65 percent)

#8 Uses comments to keep the discussion centered on the group rather than encouraging the discussion to flow through the leader (e.g., evaluating speaker's comments) (70 percent)

#12 Praises group effort and accomplishment rather than singling out particular people for praise (50 percent)

Notice in this data that learners are better at recognizing the twelve encouraging or stifling behaviors in other leaders than they are at consistently exhibiting the actions themselves during a meeting. This differentiation is consistent with the hierarchical order of these two skills in the instructional goal analysis.

SUMMARIZING ATTITUDINAL DATA

At the end of session 10, learners were asked to complete the attitudinal questionnaire contained in Table 10.4. The questionnaire was scored by summing the ratings of all learners (twenty) for each question and then dividing the sum by twenty to obtain the group's mean rating for each question. These values were then rounded to the nearest whole number. The range of responses (highest and lowest rating given for each question) was also identified.

These data are recorded on a blank copy of the questionnaire that is included in Table 11.5. The mean rating for each item is circled on the questionnaire, and the range is indicated using a vertical line over the lowest and highest rating for each item. At this point, items indicating potential problems can be flagged. In this instance, we defined a potentially problematic question as one having a mean or average score ($\bar{x}$) of 3 or lower and placed an asterisk to the right of items with means in this area.

Related to learners' perceptions of their attention levels during instruction, they were attentive during all activities, and they believed all objectives

| TABLE *11.5* | **Summary of Field Test Group's Responses on the Attitude Questionnaire for Main Step 6: Manage Cooperative Group Interaction, Session 10, Objectives 6.1.1 Through 6.5.1** |

Session 10: Engendering Cooperative Member Behaviors   Date: _____

Instructions: Use the following questionnaire to judge the effectiveness of today's session on engendering cooperative member behaviors. Please rate the quality of the instruction for you in each of the five main categories included on the form. For each of the instructional areas listed on the left, circle the response on the right that best reflects your perception of the quality level. At the bottom of the form, please comment on aspects of tonight's session that you consider to be particular strengths and/or problems.
Thank you.

TABLE *11.5* | (Continued)

I. Attention: To what degree did the following instructional activities hold your interest or attention?

Instructional Areas	Attention Levels (Circle one level for each area)
A. Reading and analyzing annotated diaglogues of NCW meetings illustrating the following:	
1. Member actions that aid cooperative interaction	Little 1 2 3 (4) 5 Very Attentive
2. Strategies leaders use to encourage group cooperation	Little 1 2 3 (4) 5 Very Attentive
B. Watching and analyzing videotapes of NCW meetings depicting the following:	
3. Positive member actions that aid cooperative interaction	Little 1 2 3 4 (5) Very Attentive
4. NCW leaders engendering cooperative member behaviors	Little 1 2 3 4(5) Very Attentive
C. Acting as group leader to:	
5. Engender cooperative member behaviors in my group	Little 1 2 3 4 (5)Very Attentive

II. Relevance: To what degree do you believe the following skills are *relevant* for helping you provide effective leadership in NCW problem-solving meetings?

	Relevance Levels
6. Recognizing cooperative member behaviors during meetings	Little 1 2 3 4 (5)Very Relevant
7. Engendering cooperative member behaviors during meetings	Little 1 2 3 4 (5)Very Relevant

III. Confidence: What level of *confidence* do you have that you can effectively use these group interaction management skills in NCW problem-solving discussions?

	Confidence Levels
8. Recognizing cooperative member behaviors during meetings	Little 1 2 3 (4) 5 Very Confident
9. Engendering cooperative member behaviors during meetings	Little 1 2 (3) 4 5 Very Confident ✳

IV. Clarity: What level of *clarity* do you believe the following instructional materials and activities have?

	Clarity Level
10. Session introduction	Little 1 2 3 (4) 5 Very Clear
11. Objectives for session	Little 1 2 3 4 (5)Very Clear
12. Annotated written dialogues of NCW meetings	Little 1 2 3 (4) 5 Very Clear
13. Videotapes of NCW meetings	Little 1 (2) 3 4 5 Very Clear ✳
14. Performing ourselves as group leaders	Little 1 2 3 4 (5)Very Clear
15. Instructions for our group leadership activity	Little 1 2 3 (4) 5 Very Clear

TABLE *11.5* | (Continued)

16. Checklists we used to find positive leader actions	Little 1　2　3 ④ 5　Very Clear
17. Feedback on exercises for positive member and leader actions	Little 1　2　3 ④ 5　Very Clear
V. Satisfaction: Overall, how satisfied were you with the following:	**Satisfaction Level**
18. The facilities	Little 1　2　3　4 ⑤ Very Satisfied
19. The instructor(s)	Little 1　2　3 ④ 5　Very Satisfied
20. The pace	Little 1　2 ③ 4　5　Very Satisfied　✳
21. The instruction	Little 1　2　3 ④ 5　Very Satisfied
22. Yourself, relative to the new skills you have developed/refined	Little 1　2 ③ 4　5　Very Satisfied　✳

VI. Please comment on aspects of this session that were strengths and problems for you personally.

Strengths	**Problems**
Introduction: *Good, interesting*	*Need food*
Objectives: *Good; Clear; Liked outline format; Easy to follow*	
Annotated dialogues: *Easy to follow; Easy to find actions; Relevant topics*	
Videotapes: *Relevant topics; Interesting new groups*	*Moved too fast; Would like to stop video while marking observation form; Help!*
Interactive leadership session: *Liked problem areas; Relevant topics for our own meetings*	*Too hurried—not enough time to get into leadership role; Some people not serious*
Assessments: *Like checklists; Like testing format— Seemed like part of instruction*	*Videos were too fast, missed stuff; Frustrating*
Other: *Will be able to use skills on job for quality team*	*Some stifling actions conflict with good manners (e.g. should comment on speaker's ideas to demonstrate attentiveness and understanding)*

covered were relevant to their new positions as NCW leaders ($\bar{x} > 4$). Moving to the confidence questions, you can see that the range of responses, or distance between the lowest and highest rating, increased, and the mean score for their confidence in actually using these actions dropped to 3. Within the clarity category, all instruction was rated satisfactorily except for the videos of NCW meetings. For overall satisfaction, problems were identified for pace of instruction and self-satisfaction.

At this point we examined the four questions with means at or below the criterion for unsatisfactory ratings. Instructional parts with potential problems are the following:

#9   Confidence in engendering cooperative group behavior

#13 Videos of meetings

#20 Pace of instruction

#22 Self-satisfaction with new skill levels

It is possible that these four questions are related. For example, questions 9 and 22, confidence and self-satisfaction, may be linked; they may also be related to the reported pacing and video problems.

Learners' open comments provided more information on these topics. Each learner's comments were content analyzed, similar comments were clustered across learners, and a summary of the issues they discussed is included on the questionnaire form. Related to the video problem, they thought the televised meetings went too fast for careful observation, and they were unable to watch the meeting progress and mark their observation forms at the same time. They also reported not having enough time to practice their leadership skills in the interactive meetings. Finally, several noted that they had trouble with some of the cooperation-stifling actions and believed the actions are in direct conflict with conventions of polite conversation. In follow-up interviews, we discovered that learners believe it is polite to comment when someone suggests a new idea because the comment illustrates to the speaker that others are listening and understand the comment. The difference between conventions of polite conversation and leader behaviors that stifle cooperative interaction may account for learners' poor posttest performance in actions 4, 5, 8, and 12. It is typically not considered polite to leave a large, obvious gap in a conversation (#4), allow others to interrupt (#5), not comment on others' ideas (#8), and not praise individuals for particularly good ideas and contributions (#12). The difference between cooperation-engendering behaviors in a group and conventions of polite conversation should be directly addressed in the instruction.

DETERMINING HOW TO REVISE INSTRUCTION

It is premature to make final decisions about all the changes that may need to be made in the materials for one segment of a total unit of instruction. Before actually making some changes, other lessons should be field-tested and analyzed. The changes should be made based on the overall effectiveness of the unit; however, we can use data gathered in session 10 to create an instructional revision analysis table such as the one in Table 11.6. The table has four parts. The component being evaluated is listed in the left column. Problems identified and potential changes are described in the next two columns. The last column contains the evidence used to justify the change and its source. The resources used to complete the table are (1) test data and observations of

TABLE *11.6* | **Instructional Revision Analysis Form**

Instructional Strategy Component	Problem	Proposed Change in Instruction	Evidence and Source
Motivational, introductory material	None	None	Learners reported good attention levels, clarity of purpose, and relevance of instruction (attitude questionnaire and debriefing session).
Pretest	Video meeting was too quick; learners had difficulty watching meeting and marking their observation form at the same time.	Add instructions to pause video while marking the observation form.	Comments came from attitude questionnaires, instructor comments, and debriefing session.
Information presentation	Performance levels on skills 4, 5, 8, and 12 were inadequate.	Add more information and examples of these behaviors in the presentations.	Information came from the following sources: •Posttest scores for these skills •Attitude questionnaire •Debriefing session
	Conflict was reported between stifling behaviors and conventions of polite conversation.	Directly address the differences between leadership actions that engender cooperative group behavior and conventions of polite conversation. State differences and explain the purpose for the differences.	•Observation during interactive meetings
Learner participation	(6.4.2) Video meeting was too quick; learners had difficulty watching meeting and marking their observation form at the same time.	Add instructions to pause video while marking the observation form.	Attitude questionnaire
Posttest	There was inadequate time available for each learner to perform.	Move learners into groups as they finish individualized activities. Watch, however; this may tend to place all the strong performers together and the novices together.	Attitude questionnaire
Attitude questionnaire	None	None	Questionnaire did detect areas of weakness and obtain explanations for them. Information obtained was corroborated with posttest data, debriefing, and instructor's comments.

students using the materials, (2) notes and remarks students make in the materials, and (3) information taken from the attitude questionnaire. By reviewing the materials revision prescriptions, you can see the value of the verbal descriptions of each item analysis table made previously.

It is important to remember that changes you make in your materials may have consequences other than the ones you anticipate. If extensive changes are made, such as inserting instruction for skills considered previously to be prerequisites for below-average learners and excusing above-average students from selected lessons, then you should conduct another field trial with these changes in place to see whether the desired impact was realized.

Readers interested in a school-based example may refer to Appendix K.

SUMMARY

The data you collect during the formative evaluation should be synthesized and analyzed in order to locate potential problems in the instructional materials. Your data summaries should include learners' remarks in the materials, their performance on the pretest and posttest, their responses on the attitude questionnaire, their comments during debriefing sessions, and information gained from the performance context. Once you get the data summarized you should perform the following analyses:

1. Examine the summarized data relative to entry behaviors and draw implications about the entry behaviors of students in your target group.

2. Review summarized pretest and posttest data both for total performance and objective-by-objective performance. Superimpose the averages on your instructional analysis chart. Draw inferences about your group's performance on each test item and each objective. You may want to compare data obtained from the entry-behavior items with pretest and posttest data as well.

3. Examine the objectives, test items, and instructional strategy for those objectives for which student performance failed to meet your established criteria. Check the objectives, test items, vocabulary, sequence, and instructional strategy for those objectives prior to making direct changes in the instructional materials.

4. Check procedures and implementation directions as well as equipment required for instruction for possible guides to revision.

5. Develop a materials revision analysis table that describes problems, changes, evidence that changes are needed, and sources of evidence cited for each component in the materials.

6. Revise instruction based on your prescriptions in the materials revision analysis table. Delay any revisions that may depend upon information from the field testing of other lessons.

These data synthesis and analysis activities are undertaken following each of the one-to-one, small-group, and field-trial formative evaluations. If you make major revisions in your materials following the field trial, then another trial is advisable to check the effectiveness of your revisions.

The final revision of your materials should be effective in bringing about the intended learning with members of your target audience. Then you are ready to reproduce or publish an effective set of instructional materials.

TABLE 11.7 | Item-by-Objective Analysis Table

Objective	1			2			3			4			Raw Score	Percent Correct	Objectives Passed	Percentage of Objectives Passed
Item	1	2	3	4	5	6	7	8	9	10	11	12				
Student 1	X	X	X		X	X				X	X					
2	X	X	X	X	X	X	X	X	X	X	X					
3				X	X	X				X	X					
4	X			X	X	X	X	X	X	X	X					
5	X	X	X	X	X	X	X	X	X	X	X					
Total correct																
Percent correct																
Percent passing objective																

X = Correct answer
Incorrect answer is left blank
To pass an objective, all items within the objective must be correct since each item was constructed to test a different facet of the objective.

PRACTICE

1. What data would you use to determine whether learners in your target group actually possessed the entry behaviors identified in your instructional analysis and whether those you identified were relevant to your instruction?

2. When should you develop instruction for prerequisite skills?

3. What type of data table should you create to provide the information necessary to determine the exact nature of problems that learners have with the instruction?

4. Why should you construct a narrative explanation from data tables of problems that are identified with each test?

5. Why should you summarize performance by objective across pretest and posttest?

6. What materials should you evaluate using an attitude questionnaire?

7. What information should you include in an instructional revision analysis table?

8. Table 11.7 contains an incomplete item-by-objective table for five learners. Use the raw data to calculate the following:

   a. Raw score for each learner
   b. Percent of items correct for each learner
   c. Number of objectives passed by each learner
   d. Number of learners answering each item correctly
   e. Percent of learners answering each item correctly
   f. Percent of learners passing each objective

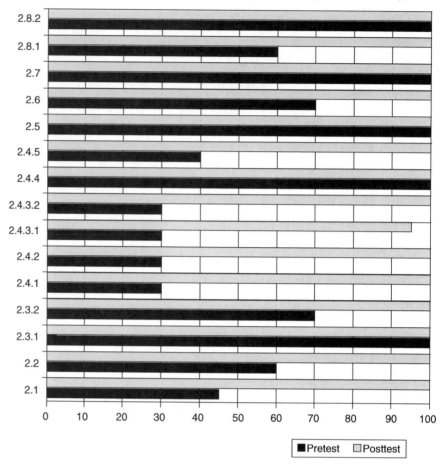

FIGURE 11.4

Percentage of Students Answering Objective-Based Items Correctly on Checking Account Pretest and Posttest

9. Figure 11.4 contains the percentage of students answering objective-based test items correctly for the checking account pretest and posttest. Answer the following questions based on the data in the chart.

a. Did students appear to need instruction on all of the skills?

b. Which of the skills had students mastered prior to entering the instruction?

c. Based on pretest and posttest data, for which skills did students appear to benefit from the instruction?

d. Apart from those skills students had mastered prior to instruction, for which skills was instruction *not* effective?

FEEDBACK

1. You would use item and objective analysis data from the items on the pretest and posttest. Data from the entry behaviors' pretest would tell you whether students possessed the entry behaviors. Data from tests

used with the instructional materials would tell you whether you had actually identified relevant entry behaviors. If students perform poorly on the entry behaviors items, yet are successful on subsequent tests, then you need to reexamine the entry behaviors you have identified.

2. You should *not* develop instruction for prerequisite skills prior to at least the one-to-one evaluation of your materials. As you could see in the Examples section, data from the field test will tell you whether such materials are needed and for what specific objectives they are needed.

3. You should construct an item/objective analysis table. It should be constructed in a manner to enable you to analyze correct answers as well as incorrect answers. Correct-answer analysis tells you whether your instruction was effective; incorrect-answer analysis tells you what went wrong and helps you focus on revisions that might help.

4. You should construct a narrative analysis from the data for each test while the information is fresh in your mind, because this information becomes one basis for the instructional revisions analysis table. If you do not do it and have many raw data tables from several tests before you, then it is very difficult to focus and pinpoint problems that have occurred.

5. The summary tables highlight trends in performance. If learners failed to master an objective on the pretest, was it mastered on the posttest?

6. All components of the materials should be evaluated on the attitude questionnaire. It is recommended that an attitude questionnaire be administered at the same time that materials are used by learners. We recommend embedding attitude questions within the lessons so students comment while the material is fresh in their minds. If this approach is used, then care must be taken not to disrupt the flow of learning.

7. An instructional revision analysis table should contain five types of information: (a) the name of the component, (b) problems identified with the component, (c) changes to be made in the instruction, (d) evidence from either test or questionnaire data, remarks in materials and observations of how procedures worked, and (e) the source of evidence cited as the reason(s) for changes.

8. See Table 11.8.

9. Based on the pretest/posttest data in the chart:

   a. Students do *not* appear to need instruction on all of the skills.

   b. Prior to entering the instruction, students had already mastered the following skills: 2.3.1, 2.4.4, 2.5, 2.7, and 2.8.2.

   c. Based on pretest and posttest data, students appeared to benefit from instruction for the following skills: 2.1, 2.2, 2.3.2, 2.4.1, 2.4.2, 2.4.3.1, 2.4.3.2, 2.4.5. 2.6, 2.8.1.

   d. Apart from those skills mastered prior to instruction, students appeared to benefit from instruction for all other skills.

TABLE *11.8* | Item-by-Objective Analysis Table

	Objective 1			Objective 2			Objective 3			Objective 4						Percent
Item	1	2	3	4	5	6	7	8	9	10	11	12	Raw Score	Percent Correct	Objectives Passed	Objectives Passed
Student 1	X	X	X		X	X				X	X		7	58	1	25
2	X	X	X	X	X	X	X	X	X	X	X		11	92	3	75
3				X	X	X				X	X		5	42	1	25
4	X			X	X	X	X	X	X	X	X		9	75	2	50
5	X	X	X	X	X	X	X	X	X	X	X		11	92	3	75
Total students correct	4	3	3	4	5	5	3	3	3	5	5	0				
Percent students correct	80	60	60	80	100	100	60	60	60	100	100	0				
Percent students passing objective		60			80			60			0					

X = Correct answer
Incorrect answer is left blank
To pass an objective, all items within the objective must be correct since each item was constructed to test a different facet of the objective.

REFERENCES AND RECOMMENDED READINGS

Carey, L. M. (2001). *Measuring and evaluating school learning* (3rd ed.). Boston: Allyn and Bacon. Carey illustrates ways to display criterion-referenced data within items and objectives to identify learner mastery and judge instructional effectiveness. Terminology is consistent with this text.

Kemp, J. E., Morrison, G. R., & Ross, S. M. (1998). *Designing effective instruction* (2nd ed.). New York: Merrill Publishing. This edition covers both formative and summative evaluation, including designs, data displays, and interpretations. *Performance and Instruction, 22* (5), 1983. This is a special issue on formative evaluation.

Smith, P. L., & Ragan, T. J. (1998). *Instructional design* (2nd ed.). New York: Macmillan. Chapters on formative and summative evaluation with data displays and interpretations for revision of instruction.

Wager, W. (1976). The formative evaluation outcomes matrix. *Educational Technology, 16* (10), 36–38. Wager describes a procedure for determining what revisions should be made in the instruction, based on the pattern of performance of the learners.

Wolf, R. M. (1974). Data analysis and reporting considerations in evaluation. In Popham, W. J. (Ed.). *Evaluation in education, Current applications.* Berkeley, CA: McCutchan Publishing Corp., 205–242. This chapter suggests various ways of setting up evaluation studies, how to analyze data, and how to display data.

*Most of the references listed at the end of Chapter 10 are also applicable to this chapter.

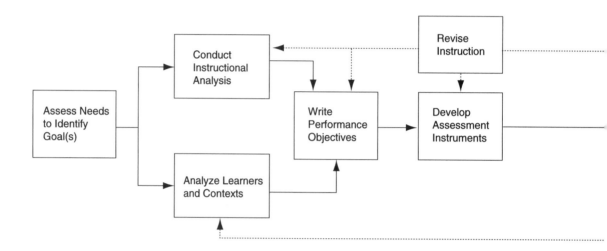

12 DESIGNING AND CONDUCTING SUMMATIVE EVALUATIONS

- Describe the purpose for summative evaluation.
- Describe the two phases of summative evaluation and the decisions resulting from each phase.
- Design a summative evaluation for comparing alternative sets of candidate instructional materials.
- Contrast formative and summative evaluation by purpose and design.

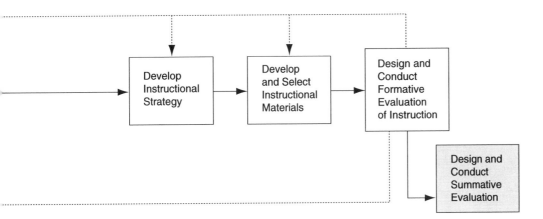

You have learned that formative evaluation is the process of collecting data and information in order to improve the effectiveness of instruction. In sharp contrast is summative evaluation. It is the process of collecting data and information in order to make decisions about the acquisition or continued use of some instruction.

The distinction between formative and summative evaluation became important several decades ago when advocates for each new public school curriculum and each new media delivery system claimed that it was better than its competitors. Studies were conducted as soon as possible to determine the "winner." Often the innovation did not do as well as traditional instruction. This came as no surprise to experienced evaluators, who knew that the innovation was really in draft form while the traditional instruction had been used, and revised, for many years.

Persuasive arguments were made to postpone such comparisons until an innovation had been formatively evaluated and revised to the point that all the major problems were removed, and it was suitable for routine use. *Then* it would be appropriate to compare the innovation to other forms of instruction or to document exactly what the new innovation could do in terms of learner performance, attitudes, instructor reactions, costs, durability, and compatibility with other instruction in a curriculum or organization. It is not necessary to have a comparison between or among instructional products to have a summative evaluation. A summative study can be done to document the effects of a single innovation.

For the designer, the fundamental importance of formative evaluation for the effective use of the systematic design process cannot be overstated. Every designer should be able to conduct formative evaluations with confidence. Such is not as much the case with summative evaluation as it was originally conceived. When it came to an impartial study of the effects of an innovative delivery system or an innovative curriculum, or both, most decision makers did not want the study to be conducted by a developer or advocate for one of the competing formats of instruction. So external or third-party evaluators were often hired to conduct summative evaluations.

In recent years the tenor of summative evaluations has changed. The question is no longer, "Which is better?" Instead it is, "Did the intervention, including the instruction, solve the problem that led to the need for the instruction in the first place?" In other words, instruction is being considered as a solution to a problem, and the ultimate summative evaluation question is, "Did it solve the problem?"

But, is this not the question we were also asking in performance-context formative evaluation? Yes, it is, but with a very different purpose. In the formative evaluation phase we wanted to use the information to revise the instruction so it would promote use of skills and the effectiveness of the skills in the performance context. Now, in the summative evaluation, we are asking whether, after the formative evaluation (or whatever design strategy has been used by the developer) is complete, the instruction is effective in solving our performance problem.

Interest has shifted from comparisons of innovations and statements of posttest performance to demonstrations of learner performance in the context in which the skills were intended for use. Are they used, and do they work? In order to answer these questions, there are two phases of summative evaluation. The first focuses on the relationship between the instruction of interest and the needs of the organization. This analysis is done through the use of available documentation. The second phase is a field trial of the instruction that is similar to the third phase of formative evaluation, except it is now conducted for a different purpose—namely, to determine whether it produces the desired results for the decision maker.

In the sections that follow, we will refer at different times to *instruction* and *instructional materials*. We use these terms synonymously. Our intent is to refer to the summative evaluation of any form that instruction might take, whether that is video, instructor guided, self-instructional materials, or computer-based instruction. So, when we use the terms *instruction* or *instructional materials*, you should consider them to mean any form of instruction.

CONCEPTS

Summative evaluation is defined as the design of evaluation studies and the collection of data to verify the effectiveness of instructional materials with target learners. Its main purpose is to make go–no-go decisions about maintaining currently used instructional materials or about adopting materials that have the potential for meeting an organization's defined instructional

SUMMATIVE EVALUATION

Expert Judgment Phase	Field Trial Phase
Overall Decisions	
Do the materials have the potential for meeting this organization's needs?	Are the materials effective with target learners in the prescribed setting?
Specific Decisions	
Congruence Analysis: Are the needs and goals of the organization congruent with those in the instruction?	**Outcomes Analysis:**
	Impact on Learners: Are the achievement and motivation levels of learners satisfactory following instruction?
Content Analysis: Are the materials complete, accurate, and current?	
Design Analysis: Are the principles of learning, instruction, and motivation clearly evident in the materials?	**Impact on Job:** Are learners able to transfer the information, skills, and attitudes from the instructional setting to the job setting or to subsequent units of related instruction?
Feasibility Analysis: Are the materials convenient, durable, cost-effective, and satisfactory for current users?	**Impact on Organization:** Are learners' changed behaviors (performance, attitudes) making positive differences in the achievement of the organization's mission and goals (e.g., reduced dropouts, resignations; improved attendance, achievement; increased productivity, grades)?
	Management Analysis:
	1. Are instructor and manager attitudes satisfactory?
	2. Are recommended implementation procedures feasible?
	3. Are costs related to time, personnel, equipment, and resources reasonable?

needs. The materials evaluated may or may not have undergone formative evaluation and revision. Materials evaluated may come from commercial publishers, a consulting firm, or an individual. The scope of the materials varies as well. They may be intended for a one-day workshop, a short course of some type, or for a semester or year of instruction. The scope of the materials does not change the basic design of the study. Rather, it influences the amount of time required to complete it.

A summative evaluation has two main phases: expert judgment and field trial. The purpose of the expert judgment phase is to determine whether currently used instruction or other candidate instruction has the potential for meeting an organization's defined instructional needs. The purpose of the field-trial phase is to document the effectiveness of promising instruction with target group members in the intended setting. The analyses and decisions to be made during each phase and the evaluation activities supporting each one are listed in Figure 12.1.

The activities undertaken in the expert judgment phase to decide whether candidate instruction is promising include (1) evaluating the congruence between the organization's instructional needs and candidate instruction, (2) evaluating the completeness and accuracy of candidate instruction, (3) evaluating the instructional strategy contained in the candidate instruction, (4) evaluating the utility of the instruction, and (5) determining current users' satisfaction with the instruction. When instruction has been tailored to the defined needs of the organization, systematically designed and developed, and formatively evaluated prior to the summative evaluation, then the expert judgment phase has been accomplished. The expert judgment phase is imperative when the organization is unfamiliar with the instruction and its developmental history.

The field trial phase has two components. The first is *outcomes analysis,* which involves determining the effect of instruction on learners' skills, on the job (transfer), and on the organization (need resolution). The second component, called *management analysis,* includes assessing instructor and supervisor attitudes related to learner performance, implementation feasibility, and costs.

The field trial for the summative evaluation includes documenting learner performance and attitudes, documenting instructor/implementor attitudes, and documenting procedures and resources required to implement the instruction. The main purpose of the field trial is to locate both the strengths and weaknesses of the instruction, to determine their causes, and to document the strengths and problems.

Both the expert judgment and the field trial can be focused on one set of instructional materials or on competing sets of materials. Typically the expert judgment phase is used to choose among available instruction in order to select one or two sets of materials that appear most promising for a field trial. Both phases are described in more detail in the following sections. In reading the material on the expert judgment phase, assume that the instruction to be evaluated is unfamiliar to you and that you are faced with the decision of whether to recommend expending additional effort and cost for a field trial.

EXPERT JUDGMENT PHASE OF SUMMATIVE EVALUATION

CONGRUENCE ANALYSIS

ORGANIZATION'S NEEDS Regardless of whether the summative evaluation involves materials comparisons or is focused on one set of instructional materials, the evaluator must determine the congruence between the organization's needs, the characteristics of their target learners, and the needs and characteristics the candidate materials were designed to address. To perform the congruence analysis, you should first obtain a clear description of the organization's needs, which includes an accurate description of the entry behaviors and characteristics of the target learners. After obtaining this information, you should locate instructional materials that have potential for meeting the organization's needs. For each set of candidate materials identified, you should obtain a clear description of the goals and objectives of the instruction and the target audience for which it is intended. This information can sometimes be found in a foreword or preface in the materials themselves or in the instructor's manual. If these descriptions are too general, then you may wish to contact the publisher of the materials for more detailed information.

RESOURCES   You should also analyze the congruence between the resources the organization has available for purchasing and implementing instructional materials and the costs of obtaining and installing candidate materials. Materials that are too costly, however effective, often cannot be considered by an organization. The facilities and equipment available in the organization and those required to implement the instruction should also be contrasted.

Once adequate descriptions are obtained, you should compare (1) the organization's needs versus needs addressed in the materials, (2) the organization's target groups versus target groups for the materials, and (3) the organization's resources versus requirements for obtaining and implementing the instruction. The information from your congruence analysis should be shared with appropriate decision makers. Although you may be asked to make recommendations, the persons who make the final decisions about which of the candidate materials to include in a summative evaluation, or whether to even continue the evaluation, will vary greatly from one organization to another.

Several groups of questions related to the design of quality materials should be addressed for any instruction selected for a summative evaluation. These questions should be answered prior to engaging in any field trials of the materials with learners.

1. Are the materials and any accompanying assessments accurate and complete?

2. Is the instructional strategy adequate for the anticipated types of learning outcomes?

3. Can the materials be used effectively?

4. Are current users of the materials satisfied?

If some or all of the candidate materials are judged to be unsound in these important aspects, then continuing the summative evaluation would be fruitless. Supervisors should be informed of your judgments following this phase of the summative evaluation, and again they should be asked whether they wish to continue the summative evaluation.

The manner in which we design and conduct this phase of the summative evaluation is similar to some of the strategies used in the one-to-one formative evaluation, but it has some distinctive features as well. Let's consider each cluster of questions in turn.

CONTENT ANALYSIS

Since you may not be a content expert in the materials you evaluate, it may be necessary to engage a content expert as a consultant. What you must consider is how best to use this expert. One strategy would be to provide the experts with copies of all candidate materials and ask them to judge the accuracy and completeness of the materials for the organization's stated goals. A better, more cost-effective strategy would be to work with the expert(s) to produce an instructional analysis of the stated goal. The document the expert(s) produces should include both the goal analysis and the subordinate skills analysis. A framework that identifies and sequences the main steps and subordinate skills in the goal would be a valuable standard against which you can evaluate the accuracy and completeness of any candidate materials.

How can the framework be used? The skills included in the framework can be converted to a checklist or rating scale the evaluator uses to review and judge the quality of the candidate materials and any accompanying tests.

DESIGN ANALYSIS

Similar to the one-to-one formative evaluation, you need to evaluate the adequacy of the components of the instructional strategy included in the candidate materials. As an external evaluator, you may not know whether particular components of the strategy are present, and if present, whether they have the potential for gaining and maintaining learners' attention. Again, checklists that can be used for reviewing and comparing candidate materials would be the most thorough and time-saving approach.

In developing the checklists, you should list the components of the instructional strategy in the far-left column and use the remaining columns for recording related information about candidate materials. Although the basic components of the strategy do not change, you may want to adopt criteria related to each component based on the type of learning outcome(s) addressed in the materials. The evaluator's response format can also be expected to vary based on the nature of the instruction.

UTILITY AND FEASIBILITY ANALYSIS

The third area of questions about the instructional materials relates to the utility of the candidate materials. For each set, you should consider such factors as the availability of a learner guide or syllabus and an instructor's manual. Factors related to the durability of the materials are another consideration. Another is any special resources, such as instructor capabilities, equipment, or environments (e.g., learning centers) that are required. A utility concern is whether the materials require group or individual pacing. You may also wish to revisit the issue of the relative costs of obtaining and implementing the materials. In fact, any factors that might enhance or restrict the utility of the materials for the organization should be considered.

To design this part of the summative evaluation, you may need to interview the persons in the organization who requested the evaluation. Through discussions with them you can ensure that you have determined their needs, resources, and constraints. They may help to identify utility questions that you may not have considered.

Using the utility questions you select, you can design a summary form to focus your attention on each question as you reevaluate all the candidate materials. As in the previous examples, the important questions can be listed in the left column of your checklist and a separate response column provided for each set of materials. One possible difference between this checklist and the preceding ones is that you may need to include descriptive information related to each set of materials rather than simply judging the presence or absence of selected criteria. Briefly summarizing the descriptive information in tabular form will assist you in making the appropriate comparisons across materials and in formulating your recommendations.

CURRENT USER ANALYSIS

There is one other analysis that you may wish to include in your design. It is to seek additional information about the candidate materials from organizations that are experienced in using them. The names of current users can often be obtained from the publishers of the materials.

What types of information should you seek from the users? One type of information involves data about the target learners in the other settings. For example, what are their entry behaviors and motivations for studying the materials? What are their pretest and posttest performance levels using the instruction? Finally, what are their attitudes about the materials?

Another type of information relates to the instructor's perceptions of the materials. For example, are the materials easy to use? What problems have they experienced in implementing the materials? What resources are required to use them? Do they plan to continue using the materials, and if not, why?

Depending on the logistics involved, you may wish to travel to the other organization, or you may decide to gather the information through questionnaires and telephone interviews. Either way you should plan carefully before obtaining the information.

At this point you have concluded the expert judgment phase of the summative evaluation. Based on the data you have gathered, you should be able to determine whether a field-trial phase of the summative evaluation is warranted and to recommend the most promising set or sets of materials for the field-trial phase. The evaluation design and procedures used to conduct this part of the evaluation should be documented in your evaluation report, together with your recommendations and rationale. Figure 12.2 illustrates the

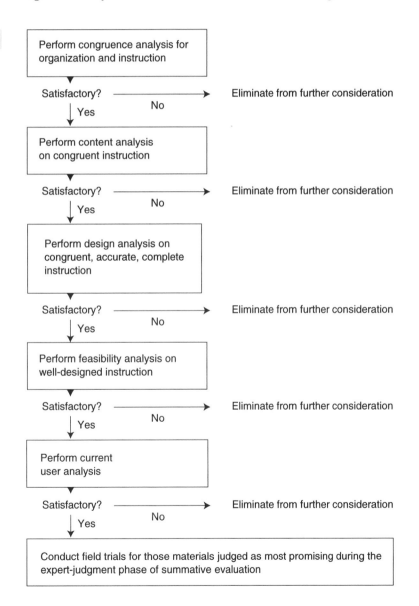

FIGURE 12.2

Sequence of Stages of Analysis During the Expert-Judgment Phase of Summative Evaluation

sequence of tasks involved in the expert-judgment phase and the decisions summative evaluators make as they progress toward a field trial of given instruction.

FIELD-TRIAL PHASE OF SUMMATIVE EVALUATION

OUTCOMES ANALYSIS

The second phase of the summative evaluation is the field trial. During the trial the instruction is implemented as intended, within the organization, and with selected target learners. The field trial typically includes the following parts: planning for the evaluation, preparing for the implementation, implementing instruction and collecting data, summarizing and analyzing data, and reporting results.

Table 12.1 contains a matrix that summarizes the activities related to each part of the evaluation. Each column is headed by one of the main parts, and activities related to each are listed beneath. All activities in the first column, "Planning," should be completed from top to bottom before beginning the activities in the second column, "Preparing." Similarly, activities in the second column should be sequenced from top to bottom, and they should be completed prior to moving to the third column, "Implementing/Collecting Data." At the point of instruction implementation and data collection, however, this top-to-bottom sequencing pattern within each part ceases. Data related to each area (across rows) should be collected using the most time- and cost-efficient schedule. This is true for the sequence of data summary and report sections, as well. The activities in the last three columns are presented in this sequence simply to illustrate their relationship to the activities named in the first two columns. The following paragraphs describe each of these summative field-trial activities in more detail.

PLANNING   The first planning activity is the design of your field trial. The exact nature of the design depends on several factors, including the needs assessment, the nature of materials, and whether competing materials are included. You may need to evaluate only one set of materials using one group, one set of materials using several groups with different characteristics or in different settings, or competing sets of materials using comparable groups and settings.

Another design activity is to describe clearly the questions to be answered during the study. Basically, your questions should yield information for both outcomes analysis (impact on learner, job, and organization) and management analysis. Questions will undoubtedly relate to learners' entry-behavior levels, their pretest and posttest performance on the objectives, and their attitudes. They may also relate to any resources, equipment, or facilities needed. They could relate to the skills and attitudes of those responsible for implementing the instruction. Others might relate to the implementation procedures and schedules. The precise areas of questions you include will depend on the nature of and resources for the study.

In addition to the questions related to performance in the learning context, there is the whole set of questions about performance in the transfer context. Plans must be made to do follow-through activities with some or all of the participants in the instruction. Interviews, questionnaires, and observations can be used with both learners and managers, peers, and subordinates in order to determine the impact in the performance context. The same kinds

TABLE 12.1   Overview of Activities for a Summative Evaluation Trial

Planning	Preparing	Implementing/Collecting Data	Summarizing and Analyzing Data	Reporting Results
Design evaluation	Obtain instruments Set schedule for instruction and testing Create/Modify syllabus			Describe limitations of design
Outcomes analysis Describe resources, facilities, equipment needed	Obtain resources, facilities, equipment	Adequate? (Observation, Interview, Questionnaire)	Describe problems by resources, facilities, and equipment	Recommendations and rationale
Describe ideal entry behaviors/characteristics of target group	Select sample Verify entry behaviors (data) Schedule learners	Learner performance? (Pre-Posttests) Learner attitudes? (Observation, Interview, Questionnaire) Learner performance in job context (Use, Effect?)	Item–by–objective analysis for group and individual Cross-test summary by group and individual by objective Attitude summary	Explanation, recommendations, rationale for learner, job, and organization impact
Describe number of groups and individuals needed				
Management analysis Describe skills/capabilities of instructors or managers Describe number of instructors needed	Select instructors Verify skills Schedule instructors	Validity of implementation? Modifications? (Observation, Interview)	Describe problems by instructor by objective	Recommendations and rationale
Plan and develop any training needed for instructors/managers	Provide training for instructors	Training effective? (Observation, Interview)	Describe implementation problems by objective and activity	Recommendations and rationale

of questions that were included in the field trial in the formative evaluation would also be asked here and should be planned for well in advance of the study.

With the instructional materials and a skeleton of the evaluation design in hand, you can describe the resources, facilities, and equipment appropriate for the study. This activity is included prior to planning for the sample, because any limitations you encounter in this area will undoubtedly influence the nature of the group you can use. Plan initially for the ideal requirements and then negotiate to determine the feasibility of these requests.

With the available resources issue settled, you can turn your attention to describing the ideal target learners. Your prescription should include their entry behaviors and any other characteristics that are relevant for the materials (e.g., prior experiences, present position, and personal goals). You also need to determine the number of learners you will need (or can afford) and how many groups you will need. In making this determination you should estimate conservatively, because quality and not quantity of data is the criterion. Often twenty to thirty carefully selected individuals who are truly representative of the target group will suffice. The term *group* is not intended to infer group-paced instruction; it refers to the number of individuals from whom data will be collected.

Once you know how many learners will be included in the study, you can decide how many instructors or managers you will need. Besides the ideal number to include, you should describe any skills they will need to implement the instruction. The availability of appropriate instructors may cause you to modify the number of learners in the design. If limiting learners is not feasible, then you may need to plan to train several instructors.

The final planning activity is to develop orientation and perhaps training for the instructors. A good summative evaluation will require the cooperation of those who are implementing the instruction. They must feel that they are an important part of the study, that they are informed, and that their opinions count. Developing initial rapport with this group and maintaining a cooperative relationship throughout the study will enhance the quality of the field trial and the data you are able to obtain. One final caution: the instructors must believe that you are not evaluating either them or the learners. From the outset the focus must be on evaluating the instruction. Building trust and being sensitive to learners' needs will help ensure your access to the setting and to the data. In fact, it may be a good idea to refer to them as implementor/evaluators throughout the study.

PREPARING   The activities in the preparation stage flow from the decisions made during the planning stage. They involve obtaining all the materials, instruments, resources, and people prescribed. When a trade-off must be made between what is prescribed and what is available, you may need to note these changes in the limitations section of your report.

IMPLEMENTING/COLLECTING DATA   During the implementation of instruction you will need to collect all the types of data prescribed. You might include performance measures, observations, interviews, and questionnaires. The density of your data collection will depend both on your questions and on your resources. At a minimum you will want pretest–posttest data and information about learners' perceptions of the materials and procedures. This information usually can be obtained inexpensively and unobtrusively by the instructors. After an appropriate amount of time has passed, conduct the follow-up evaluation in the performance context.

SUMMARIZING AND ANALYZING DATA   The data summary techniques described for the formative evaluation field trial are appropriate for the summative field trial. At a minimum you will want to produce objective-by-item tables and to summarize learners' performance by group and individual. You will also want to create tables to compare individual and group progress from pretests to posttests and to describe their use in the performance context.

In analyzing the data, you will want to document areas of the instruction that were ineffective and the potential reasons for the weaknesses. You will also want to document areas of the instruction that were effective. During a summative evaluation field trial, it is important to provide a balanced analysis of both the strengths and weaknesses of the materials. Focusing only on weaknesses will result in a biased report of the worth of the materials.

REPORTING RESULTS   The nature of your summative evaluation report depends on your design. If you included both the expert judgment and the field-trial phases, then both should be documented in the report. For each one you should describe the general purpose, the specific questions, the design and procedures, the results, and your recommendations and rationale. The rationale for your recommendations should be anchored in the data you present in the results section.

You should always consider the reader as you design and produce your report. After analyzing several program evaluation reports, Worthen, Sanders, and Fitzpatrick (1997) concluded that, although the reports were informative, they were also arsenic in print! You may want to follow their formatting suggestion for remedying this problem. They suggest beginning the report with an executive summary or abstract that highlights your final recommendations and rationale. Readers can then selectively read the remainder of the technical documentation to verify the quality of your procedures or the validity of your conclusions. (You can formatively evaluate technical reports just as you would formatively evaluate instruction.)

COMPARISON OF FORMATIVE AND SUMMATIVE EVALUATION

Formative and summative evaluation differ in several aspects. These differences are summarized in Table 12.2. The first difference is related to the purpose for conducting each type of evaluation. Formative evaluations are undertaken to locate weaknesses and problems in the instruction in order to revise it. Summative evaluations are undertaken to locate both strengths and weaknesses in instruction and to document the findings for decision makers who must decide whether to maintain or adopt the materials.

The second difference involves the stages of the evaluations. The formative evaluation includes three stages—the one-to-one, small group, and field trial—all conducted directly with target learners. During each stage, a great deal of time is spent observing and interviewing learners in order to understand the nature of problems they encounter with the instruction. The summative evaluation, conversely, contains only two stages: expert judgment and field trial. The expert judgment stage resembles evaluative decisions made by the designer and context expert during the design and development of materials. Target learners are not involved in this stage of summative evaluation. The field-trial stage is conducted with target learners, but little if any time is spent interviewing learners to determine why they did or did not

	Formative Evaluation	Summative Evaluation
Purpose	Locate weaknesses in instruction in order to revise it	Document strengths and weaknesses in instruction in order to decide whether to maintain or adopt it
Phases or stages	One-to-one Small group Field trial	Expert judgment Field trial
Instructional development history	Systematically designed in-house and tailored to the needs of the organization	Produced in-house or elsewhere not necessarily following a systems approach
Materials	One set of materials	One set of materials or several competing sets
Position of evaluator	Member of design and development team	Typically an external evaluator
Outcomes	A prescription for revising instruction	A report documenting the design, procedures, results, recommendations, and rationale

TABLE 12.2 | **A Comparison of Formative and Summative Evaluation**

succeed with particular objectives in the instruction. Data are typically obtained through unobtrusive observations, questionnaires, and criterion-referenced tests, both at the end of instruction and in the performance context.

The materials subjected to formative and summative evaluations typically have different developmental histories. Instruction subjected to formative evaluations usually has been systematically designed and developed, and thus holds promise for being effective with target learners. Conversely, materials included in a summative evaluation may or may not have been developed following systematic design procedures. Those for which field trials are conducted, however, should have many of the characteristics of systematically designed instruction and thus should also hold promise for being effective with target learners.

Yet another difference between formative and summative evaluations is the number of sets of instruction that are evaluated. Formative evaluations are conducted on only one set of materials. Summative evaluations may focus on either one set of materials or on competing sets of promising materials. Summative evaluations may involve one set of materials and groups with different characteristics or several sets of materials and groups with similar characteristics.

Another contrast between formative and summative evaluations is the relationship of the evaluator to the materials. Typically, formative evaluators have a personal investment in the materials and thus seek valid judgments about the materials in order to produce the best materials possible. Evaluators with personal investments in the outcome of the evaluation are called internal evaluators. It is wise for summative evaluators not to have a personal investment in the materials being evaluated because such detachment helps them maintain objectivity in designing the evaluation and in describing both the strengths and weaknesses in the materials. Detached evaluators are commonly referred to as external evaluators.

A final difference between formative and summative evaluations is the outcome. The results of a formative evaluation include prescriptions for revising the instruction and the actual materials revisions between the three stages of the evaluation. The outcome of the summative evaluation is not a prescription for revisions. Instead it is a report for decision makers, which documents the strengths and weaknesses of the instruction that has been evaluated.

EXAMPLES

This section contains examples of the evaluation instruments for the expert judgment phase of the summative evaluation. Instrumentation and data analysis procedures required for the field-trial phase were described in detail in the chapter on formative evaluation and will not be repeated here. Basically, the instruments required for the expert judgment stage consist of information summary charts and product evaluation checklists or rating scales to be completed by the evaluator.

DATA SUMMARY FORM FOR THE CONGRUENCE ANALYSIS

Table 12.3 contains an example information summary form for completing the congruence analysis. The left-hand column is used to describe the instructional needs of the organization, the entry behaviors and characteristics of the target group in the organization, and the organization's resources for obtaining and implementing the instruction. Additional columns can be included to record related information about sets of potentially promising materials. Summarizing the information in this manner will enable both you and the decision makers to make judgments about the appropriateness of candidate materials.

CHECKLIST FOR CONTENT ANALYSIS: EVALUATING THE COMPLETENESS AND ACCURACY OF MATERIALS

A hypothetical goal framework and materials checklist are illustrated in Figure 12.3. The goal analysis appears in the top portion of the table, and the checklist appears in the lower portion. Using such a checklist, the completeness of the materials and tests as well as the sequence of information in the materials can be evaluated. You could develop any number of response formats to record your judgments. In the example, three response columns are used for each set of materials. The first is for indicating the presence and sequence of subordinate skills in the instruction. The second and third columns are for indicating whether related test items are included in the pretest and posttest.

After evaluating each set of materials for its accuracy and completeness, you can tally the number of positive marks for each one in the bottom row of the table, and then compare the relative value of the candidate materials. In the hypothetical example, candidate instruction 2 appears to be the most promising because it includes instruction on all twenty-two steps and subordinate skills identified by content experts. The accompanying tests also appear to be the most thorough in measuring the prescribed skills.

TABLE *12.3* | Congruence Analysis Information Summary Form

Statements of Organization's Characteristics	Candidate Materials (Set 1)	Candidate Materials (Set 2)	Candidate Materials (Set 3)
Organization's instructional needs (goals and main objectives)	Stated goals and objectives in materials	Etc.	Etc.
Entry behaviors of organization's target group	Stated entry behaviors for learners	Etc.	Etc.
Characteristics of organization's target group Characteristics of performance contexts	Stated characteristics of learners and contexts	Etc.	Etc.
Organization's resources available for obtaining and implementing instruction	Costs of purchasing and implementing materials	Etc.	Etc.
Organization's facilities and equipment available for implementing instruction	Facilities required to implement materials (learning centers, equipment)	Etc.	Etc.

Comprehensiveness, however, is only the second criterion for summatively evaluating instructional materials.

Following your data analysis, you may wish to use the data to answer questions about the instruction from a systematic instructional design perspective. Sample questions might include the following:

1. How clear are the goal(s) and the main objectives of this instruction?
2. How accurate and current is the information included in the instruction?
3. How logical is the sequence of information in the instruction?
4. How appropriate is the instruction for the entry behaviors and characteristics of target learners (skills; contexts; understandings; gender, racial, cultural bias)?
5. Are measures of performance (paper-and-pencil tests and rubrics) congruent with the goals and objectives in the instruction and the target learners' characteristics?

CHECKLISTS FOR DESIGN ANALYSIS: EVALUATING THE LEARNING AND INSTRUCTIONAL STRATEGIES IN MATERIALS

Instructional designers who are conducting a summative evaluation of their own materials are keenly aware of the principles of learning and instruction

F I G U R E *12.3*

A Framework for
Evaluating the Accuracy
and Completeness of
Candidate Instructional
Materials and the Content
Validity of Accompanying
Tests

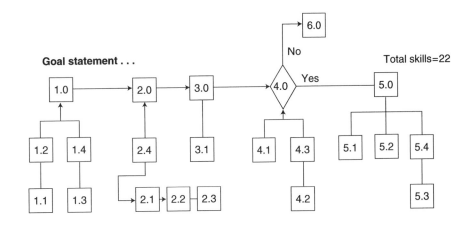

Subordinate Skill Statements	Candidate 1 MAT PRE POST			Candidate 2 MAT PRE POST			Candidate 3 MAT PRE POST		
1.0	X	X	X	X	X	X			
1.1	X			X		X			
1.2	X		X	X	X	X			
1.3	X			X		X			
1.4	X		X	X	X	X			
2.0	X	X	X	X	X	X	X	X	X
2.1	X			X		X			
2.2	X			X		X			
2.3	X			X		X			
2.4	X		X	X	X	X	X	X	X
3.0	X	X	X	X	X	X	X	X	X
3.1				X	X	X			
4.0				X	X	X			
4.1				X		X			
4.2				X		X			
4.3				X		X			
5.0	X	X	X	X	X	X	X	X	X
Etc.									
Totals	16	5	11	22	16	22	4	4	4

Note: MAT = Instructional materials content; PRE & POST = test item contents; X = skill
addressed in materials or tests

foundations for their materials. Independent evaluators who were not
involved in the production of the materials should determine whether these
principles were employed in the creation of the instruction.

Effective instruction, regardless of whether it is for learning verbal information, intellectual skills, attitudes, or motor skills, has certain characteristics
that are based on the research of cognitive and constructive psychologists and
learning specialists. Quality instruction should gain the attention of the learner. It should also help the learner focus on the relevant aspects of what is
learned, store the information logically in memory, and efficiently recall the

| TABLE 12.4 | Summative Evaluation Questions from Principles of Motivation (Attention, Relevance, Confidence, Satisfaction) |

ARCS Motivation Model	Question Areas for Summative Evaluation	Instruction 1		Instruction 2		Etc.	
Attention:	1. Are strategies used to gain and maintain the learners' attention (e.g., emotional or personal appeals, questions, thinking challenges, human interest examples, etc.)?	Yes ___	No ___	Yes ___	No ___	Yes ___	No ___
Relevance:	2. Is the instruction relevant for given target groups and how are learners informed and convinced of the relevance (e.g., information about new requirements for graduation, certification, employment, advancement, self-actualization, etc.)?	___	___	___	___	___	___
Confidence:	3. Are learners likely to be confident at the outset and throughout instruction so that they can succeed (e.g., learners informed of purposes and likely to possess prerequisites; instruction progresses from familiar to unfamiliar, concrete to abstract; vocabulary, contexts, and scope appropriate; challenges present but realistic; etc.)?	___	___	___	___	___	___
Satisfaction:	4. Are learners likely to be satisfied from the learning experience (e.g., relevant external rewards such as free time, employment, promotion, recognition; actual intrinsic rewards such as feelings of success, accomplishment, satisfaction of curiosity, intellectual entertainment, etc.)?	___	___	___	___	___	___

information and skill at a later time. The summative evaluator should be aware of the current principles for designing effective instruction and transfer these design principles to criteria and standards for the evaluation of the materials. Areas of instructional principles that should be used in designing summative evaluations should at least include those from motivation, types of learning (i.e., intellectual skills, verbal information, attitudes, and motor skills), and the instructional strategy.

MOTIVATION You should particularly focus on the potential of the instruction for motivating learners and learners' perceptions of how interested they were in learning the information and skills presented. The ARCS model (Keller, 1987) provides a helpful summary of the motivational principles that can be used by designers in producing instructional materials and by evaluators in determining the quality of existing instruction. ARCS represents the principles for (1) gaining and then maintaining learner *attention* through instruction that is (2) perceived by the learners to be *relevant*

TABLE 12.5	Checklist for Examining Characteristics of Instruction Based on Principles of Instruction for Intellectual Skills, Verbal Information, Attitudes, and Motor Skills

I. Intellectual Skills	Instruction 1		Instruction 2		Etc.	
	Yes	No	Yes	No	Yes	No
1. Are learners reminded of prerequisite knowledge they have stored in memory?	____	____	____	____	____	____
2. Are links provided in the instruction between prerequisite skills stored in memory and new skills?	____	____	____	____	____	____
3. Are ways of organizing new skills presented so they can be recalled more readily?	____	____	____	____	____	____
4. Are the physical, role, and relationship characteristics of concepts clearly described and illustrated?	____	____	____	____	____	____
5. Are application procedures clearly described and illustrated for rules and principles?	____	____	____	____	____	____
6. Are quality criteria (characteristics) directly addressed and illustrated for judging adequate versus inadequate results such as answers, products, or performances?	____	____	____	____	____	____
7. Are obvious but irrelevant physical, relational, and quality characteristics and common errors made by beginners directly addressed and illustrated?	____	____	____	____	____	____
8. Do the examples and nonexamples represent clear specimens of the concept or procedure described?	____	____	____	____	____	____
9. Are examples and contexts used to introduce and illustrate a concept or procedure familiar to the learners?	____	____	____	____	____	____
10. Do examples, contexts, and applications progress from simple to complex, familiar to unfamiliar, and/or concrete to abstract?	____	____	____	____	____	____
11. Do practice and rehearsal activities reflect application of the intellectual skills or merely recall of information about the performance of the skill?	____	____	____	____	____	____
12. Does feedback to learners provide corrective information and examples, or does it merely present a correct answer?	____	____	____	____	____	____
13. When appropriate, are follow-through activities such as advancement, remediation, and enrichment present and logical (e.g., address prerequisites, focus on improved motivation, provide additional examples and contexts)?	____	____	____	____	____	____

for their personal needs and goals, (3) at the appropriate level of difficulty so that learners are *confident* they can succeed if they try, and (4) perceived by learners as *satisfying* in terms of rewards for their investments. The concepts in this principle of motivation can be converted to complementary summative evaluation questions such as the ones presented in Table 12.4.

TYPES OF LEARNING The principles of instruction for different types of learning can be used as anchors for focusing the expert judgment phase of a summative evaluation. Table 12.5 contains a checklist based on principles of

TABLE *12.5* | (Continued)

II. Verbal Information	Instruction 1		Instruction 2		Etc.	
	Yes	No	Yes	No	Yes	No
1. Is new information presented in a relevant context?	___	___	___	___	___	___
2. Are strategies provided for linking new information to related information currently stored in memory (e.g., presentation of familiar analogies, requests for learners to imagine something, or to provide examples from their own experiences)?	___	___	___	___	___	___
3. Is information organized into subsets, and are the relationships of elements within and among subsets explained?	___	___	___	___	___	___
4. Are lists, outlines, tables, or other structures provided for organizing and summarizing information?	___	___	___	___	___	___
5. Are logical mnemonics provided when new information cannot be linked to anything stored in memory?	___	___	___	___	___	___
6. Does rehearsal (practice) include activities that strengthen elaborations and cues (e.g., generating new examples, forming images that will cue recall, refining organizational structure)?	___	___	___	___	___	___
7. Does feedback contain information about the correctness of a response as well as information about why a given response is considered incorrect?	___	___	___	___	___	___
8. Does remediation include additional motivational strategies as well as more rehearsal for recall cues?	___	___	___	___	___	___
III. Attitudes						
1. Are the desired feelings clearly described or inferred?	___	___	___	___	___	___
2. Are the desired behaviors clearly described or inferred?	___	___	___	___	___	___
3. Is the link (causality) between the desired feelings and behaviors, and the link between them and the subsequent positive consequences clearly established?	___	___	___	___	___	___
4. Is the link between the undesirable feelings and behaviors, and the link between them and the subsequent negative consequences clearly established?	___	___	___	___	___	___
5. Are the positive and negative consequences that are presented true and believable from the learners' perspective?	___	___	___	___	___	___
6. Are the positive and negative consequences that are presented ones that are likely to be considered important by target learners?	___	___	___	___	___	___
7. If vicarious learning is involved, are the target learners likely to generate emotions such as admiration, scorn, empathy, or pity for characters and situations presented to tap these emotions?	___	___	___	___	___	___
8. If vicarious learning is involved, are the contexts and situations presented familiar and relevant to target learners?	___	___	___	___	___	___
9. In the feedback, are the positive and negative consequences promised for specific actions experienced either directly or vicariously by learners?	___	___	___	___	___	___

TABLE *12.5* | (Continued)

IV. Motor Skills	Instruction 1		Instruction 2		Etc.	
	Yes	No	Yes	No	Yes	No
1. Does the instruction address similar skills the learner can already perform?	___	___	___	___	___	___
2. Does the instruction include a visual presentation of the motor skill that illustrates its sequence and timing?	___	___	___	___	___	___
3. Are complex skills broken down into logical parts for learners' analysis, experimentation, and rehearsal?	___	___	___	___	___	___
4. Is there provision for integrating the logical parts into performance of the complete skill?	___	___	___	___	___	___
5. Are common errors and strategies for avoiding them directly addressed?	___	___	___	___	___	___
6. Is repetitive practice provided to enable learners to smooth out the routine and automate the skill?	___	___	___	___	___	___
7. Is immediate feedback provided to help learners avoid rehearsing inaccurate executions?	___	___	___	___	___	___

instruction for intellectual skills, verbal information, attitudes, and motor skills. The questions contained in the checklist are not intended to exhaust the list of learning principle-based questions that could be posed. Instead, they are intended to illustrate the role of these principles in the design of a summative evaluation. Readers who want more information on these principles or their derivation and use in instruction should consult texts on the principles of instruction.

INSTRUCTIONAL STRATEGIES   Table 12.6 contains a checklist for evaluating the instructional strategies contained in the candidate materials. The left-hand column contains the parts of the instructional strategy, excluding pretests and posttests. Space is provided for two response columns for each set of materials. The first can be used to judge the presence or absence of each strategy component, and the second, marked "Attention," can be used to judge the perceived motivational value of each component for the intended learners. Remember that the motivational value depends on the relevance of the material for the learners' interests and needs, their confidence that they can succeed, and the satisfaction they will gain from learning the skills and knowledge. You may choose to check each criterion separately instead of holistically, as formatted in the example. You might also prefer to use a rating scale instead of a yes–no checklist.

A summary row is included at the bottom of the checklist to tally the number of positive responses given for each set of materials. Comparing the candidate materials in this way (Tables 12.3 through 12.6), you can begin to make recommendations about which set of materials appears to be most promising for the organization.

Strategy Component	Candidate 1		Candidate 2		Candidate 3	
	Present	Attention	Present	Attention	Present	Attention
I. Preinstructional						
A. Initial motivation	X	X	X	X		
B. Objectives	X	X	X	X		
C. Entry behaviors						
1. Described	X	X	X	X		
2. Sample items	X	X	X	X		
II. Information presentation						
A. Organizational structures						
1. Headings	X	X	X	X	X	X
2. Tables and illustrations	X	X	X	X	X	X
B. Elaborations						
1. Analogies/synonyms	X	X	X	X		
2. Prompts to imagine/consider	X	X	X	X		
3. Examples and nonexamples	X	X	X	X	X	
4. Relevant characteristics of examples	X	X	X	X		
5. Summaries/reviews	X	X	X	X	X	
III. Learner participation						
A. Relevant practice	X	X	X	X	X	X
B. Feedback						
1. Answers	X	X	X	X	X	X
2. Example solutions	X	X	X	X		
3. Common errors and mistakes	X	X	X	X		
IV. Follow-through activities						
A. Memory aids	X	X	X	X		
B. Transfer strategy	X	X	X	X		
TOTALS	17	17	17	17	6	4

FORM FOR UTILITY AND FEASIBILITY ANALYSIS: EXPERT JUDGMENT

Table 12.7 contains a form for summarizing and comparing expert judges' perceptions of the utility of the candidate materials. The elements to be judged for each set of materials are listed in the left-hand column, and space for noting the characteristics of each set of materials is included in subsequent columns. The particular elements you choose to compare across sets of materials will depend on the organization's stated needs and resources. The information you record about each set of materials will tend to be descriptive rather than a check indicating the presence or absence of an element or a rating of the quality of the element.

FORM FOR CURRENT USERS' ANALYSIS

Information collected about competing materials from current users is similar to that collected during a field trial. The difference is that most of these data are attitudinal rather than performance based. Table 12.8 contains a summary of the types of information you may wish to gather from users.

TABLE 12.7 | **Form for Documenting and Comparing the Utility of Competing Materials**

	Candidate 1 Materials		Candidate 1 Users' Satisf.		Candidate 2 Materials		Candidate 2 Users' Satisf.		Etc.
Feasibility Questions	Yes	No	Yes	No	Yes	No	Yes	No	
1. Characteristics of materials									
A. Do materials contain:									
1. Learner guides/syllabi?	___	___	___	___	___	___	___	___	
2. Instructor's manual?	___	___	___	___	___	___	___	___	
3. Test items or item bank?	___	___	___	___	___	___	___	___	
B. Can the materials be:									
4. Individually paced?	___	___	___	___	___	___	___	___	
5. Group paced?	___	___	___	___	___	___	___	___	
6. Used in a traditional classroom?	___	___	___	___	___	___	___	___	
7. Used in a learning center?	___	___	___	___	___	___	___	___	
8. Used at home or in library?	___	___	___	___	___	___	___	___	
C. Do the materials require:									
9. Special instructor capabilities?	___	___	___	___	___	___	___	___	
10. Special equipment?	___	___	___	___	___	___	___	___	
11. Special environments?	___	___	___	___	___	___	___	___	
D. How long does it typically take to:									
12. Complete one study session?	___	___	___	___	___	___	___	___	
13. Complete one unit?	___	___	___	___	___	___	___	___	
14. Complete the instruction?	___	___	___	___	___	___	___	___	
15. Complete the test?	___	___	___	___	___	___	___	___	
E. (Current users opinions) Do the materials lead to:									
16. Expected achievement level?	___	___	___	___	___	___	___	___	
17. Expected attitude and motivation?	___	___	___	___	___	___	___	___	
18. Adequate transfer to job or next unit?	___	___	___	___	___	___	___	___	
19. Accomplished goals and mission?	___	___	___	___	___	___	___	___	
F. Costs	$_____		$_____		$_____		_____		

The factors to consider are again listed in the left-hand column. The evaluator response format you use will differ from the previous ones for this data-gathering activity. You will need space to record the opinions of multiple users for each set of materials. Space for the responses for two users of each set of materials is included on the form in Table 12.8.

SUMMARY

Summative evaluations are conducted to make decisions about whether to maintain or adopt instruction. The primary evaluator in a summative evaluation is rarely the designer or developer of the instruction; the evaluator is frequently unfamiliar with the materials, the organization requesting the evaluation, or the setting in which the materials are evaluated. Such evalua-

TABLE 12.8   **Information Gathered from Current Users of the Materials**

	Candidate 1		Candidate 2		Candidate 3	
	User 1	User 2	User 1	User 2	User 1	User 2
1. Instructional needs for which materials are used?						
2. Entry behaviors of target learners?						
3. Characteristics of target learners?						
4. Achievement level of learners on pretests?						
5. Achievement level of learners on posttests?						
6. Achievement of learners in the performance context?						
7. Attitudes of learners about materials?						
8. Setting in which materials are used?						
9. Current satisfaction with materials?						
10. Plans for continuing use of materials?						

tors are referred to as external evaluators; these evaluators are preferred for summative evaluations because they have no personal investment in the instruction and are likely to be more objective about the strengths and weaknesses of the instruction.

Instructional designers make excellent summative evaluators because of their understanding of the instructional design process, the characteristics of well-designed instruction, and the criteria for evaluating instruction. These skills provide them with the expertise for designing and conducting the expert judgment as well as the field-trial phases of the summative evaluation.

The design of the expert judgment phase of summative evaluation is anchored in the model for systematically designing instruction. Similar to initially designing instruction, the materials evaluator begins by judging the congruence between the instructional needs of an organization and the goals for candidate instructional materials. Inappropriate materials are rejected, and promising materials are further evaluated. Next, the completeness and accuracy of the content presented in the materials are evaluated. The standard for this evaluation is an instructional goal analysis with required subordinate skills. Content experts are involved in either producing or verifying the quality of the skills diagram. Again, inappropriate materials are rejected, and promising materials are further evaluated. These materials are then evaluated for the quality of their instructional strategies, their utility, and their influence on current users. Materials that appear sound following these evaluation activities are then subjected to a field trial.

During the field-trial phase, the instruction is evaluated for its effectiveness with the target group in the intended setting. Following the evaluation, both the strengths and the weaknesses of the instruction are documented in the areas of learner performance and attitudes, instructor attitudes, and implementation requirements.

The evaluation report should include the expert judgment analysis (if one was conducted), as well as the field-trial phase of the evaluation. It should be designed and written with the readers' needs in mind.

PRACTICE

1. What is the main purpose of a summative evaluation?

2. What are the two main phases of a summative evaluation?

3. Why is the first phase of a summative evaluation often necessary?

4. Name five different types of analyses conducted during the first phase of a summative evaluation and the types of instruments used to collect the information.

5. What is the main decision made following the second phase of a summative evaluation?

6. Name two different types of analyses conducted during the second phase of a summative evaluation and the procedures used to collect information for each type.

7. Contrast the purposes for formative and summative evaluation.

8. Contrast the position of the evaluator in a formative and summative evaluation.

9. Contrast the final products of formative and summative evaluation.

FEEDBACK

1. Purpose: to document the strengths and weaknesses of instruction

2. Phases: expert judgment and field trial

3. Expert judgment: to determine the potential of candidate instruction for meeting the needs of the organization

4. Types of analyses conducted during expert judgment phase:
    a. Congruence analysis—information summary form
    b. Content analysis—product checklist or rating scale
    c. Design analysis—product checklist or rating scale
    d. Utility and feasibility analysis—information summary form, product checklist, or rating scale
    e. Current users' analysis—information summary form, product checklist or rating scale

5. Field trial: to document the effectiveness of instruction with target learners in the intended setting

6. Types of analyses conducted during the field trial:
    a. Outcomes analysis (instructional impact on learner, job, organization)—criterion-referenced tests, attitude questionnaires, interviews, observations, company records
    b. Management analysis (attitudes satisfactory, implementation feasible, costs reasonable?)—questionnaire, interview, observation, company records

		Formative Evaluation	*Summative Evaluation*
7.	Purpose:	To collect data in order to revise instruction	To collect data in order to document the strengths and weaknesses of the instruction
8.	Evaluator Position:	Evaluators are typically designers with a personal investment in the improvement of the instruction	Evaluators are external personnel who can objectively evaluate the quality of instruction produced by others
9.	Final Products:	Prescriptions for the revision of materials and revised materials	An evaluation report for decision makers that documents the purpose, procedures, results, and recommendations from the study

REFERENCES AND RECOMMENDED READINGS

Brinkerhoff, R. O. (1987). *Achieving results from training.* San Francisco, CA: Jossey-Bass. A six-stage evaluation model is presented, which includes assessments in the workplace and impact of training on the organization.

Carey, L. M., & Dick, W. (1991). Summative evaluation. In Briggs, L. J., Gustafson, K. L., & Tillman, M. H. (Eds.). *Instructional design: Principles and applications.* Englewood Cliffs, NJ: Educational Technology Publications.

Cronbach, L., & Associates. (1980). *Toward reform of program evaluation.* San Francisco: Jossey-Bass. This book takes the position that the evaluator serves in a supportive role in the instructional design process.

Draper, S. W. (1997). The prospects for summative evaluation of CAL in HE. *Association of learning technology journal.* vol. 5, no. 1 pp. 33–39. Draper describes the utility of summative evaluation and some strategies for evaluating instructional software for computer assisted learning. His article can be accessed at the following web address. http://www.psy.gla.ac.uk/~steve/summ.html

Gagné, R. M., & Briggs, L. J. (1979) Principals of instructional design. New York: Holt, Rinehart, & Winston, 236–238. This test includes a brief description of the summative evaluation process from the instructional designer's point of view.

Smith, M. E., & Brandenburg, D. (1991). Summative evaluation. *Performance Improvement Quarterly, 4* (2), 35–58. Summary of summative evaluation issues, includes extensive list of references.

Stufflebeam, D. (1973). Educational evaluation and decision making. In B. Worthen and J. Sanders (Eds.), *Educational evaluation: Theory and practice.* Belmont, CA: Wadsworth Publishing, 128–150. Stufflebeam's CIPP model is the one now predominantly used in educational evaluation.

Worthen, B. R., Sanders, J. R., & Fitzpatrick, J. L. (1997). *Program evaluation* (2nd ed.). White Plains, NY: Longman. The second edition provides new chapters on qualitative education; conducting multiple-site evaluation studies; evaluation approaches for business and industrial settings; and recent developments in the field. The focus of the text is program rather than instructional materials evaluation.

Note: The references at the end of Chapters 10 and 11 are appropriate for this chapter on summative evaluation. Readers can also access a myriad of summative evaluation projects, papers, course descriptions, and applications in a variety of settings on the Internet.

GLOSSARY OF TERMS

ARCS Acronym for Keller's theory of motivation (attention, relevance, confidence, and satisfaction).

Attitude An internal state that influences an individual's choices or decisions to act under certain circumstances. Attitudes represent a tendency to respond in a particular way.

Behavior An action that is an overt, observable, measurable performance.

Behavioral objective See Objective.

Candidate media Those media that can present the desired information, without regard to which may be the most effective. The distinction is from *noncandidate media*. A book, for example, cannot present sound, and thus would be an inappropriate choice for delivering instruction for certain objectives.

Chunk of instruction All the instruction required to teach one objective or a combination of two or more objectives.

Cluster analysis A technique used with goals in the verbal information domain to identify the specific information needed to achieve the goal and the ways that information can best be organized or grouped.

Complex goal A goal that involves more than one domain of learning.

Concept A set of objects, events, symbols, situations, etc., that can be grouped together on the basis of one or more shared characteristics, and given a common identifying label or symbol. Concept learning refers to the capacity to identify members of the concept category.

Congruence analysis Analyzing the congruence between (1) an organization's stated needs and goals and those addressed in candidate instruction; an organization's target learners' entry behaviors and characteristics and those for which candidate materials are intended; and an organization's resources and those required for obtaining and implementing candidate instruction. Conducted during the expert judgment phase of summative evaluation.

Content stability The degree to which information to be learned is likely to remain current.

Criterion A standard against which a performance or product is measured.

Criterion-referenced test items Items designed to measure performance on an explicit set of objectives; also known as objective-referenced test items.

Delivery system Term used to describe the means by which instruction will be provided to learners. Includes instructor-led instruction, distance education, computer-based instruction, and self-instructional materials.

Design evaluation chart A method for organizing design information to facilitate its evaluation. The chart relates skills, objectives, and associated test items, allowing easy comparison among the components of the instructional design.

Discrimination Distinguishing one stimulus from another and responding differently to the various stimuli.

Domain of learning A major type of learning outcome that can be distinguished from other domains by the type of learned performance required, the type of mental processing required, and the relevant conditions of learning.

Embedded attitude question Question asked of learners about the instruction at the time they first encounter it.

Entry behavior test item Criterion-referenced test items designed to measure skills identified as necessary prerequisites to beginning a specific course of instruction. Items are typically included in a pretest.

Entry behaviors Specific competencies or skills a learner must have mastered before entering a given instructional activity.

Evaluation An investigation conducted to obtain specific answers to specific questions at specific times and in specific places.

Expert judgment evaluation Judgments of the quality of instructional materials made by content experts, learner specialists, or design specialists. The first phase of summative evaluation.

Feedback Information provided to learners about the correctness of their responses to practice questions in the instruction.

Field trial The third stage in formative evaluation, referring to the evaluation of the program or product in the setting in which it is intended to be used. Also, the second phase of summative evaluation.

Formative evaluation Evaluation designed to collect data and information that is used to improve a program or product; conducted while the program is still being developed.

General learner characteristics The general, relatively stable (not influenced by instruction) traits describing the learners in a given target population.

Goal A broad, general statement of an instructional intent, expressed in terms of what learners will be able to do.

Goal analysis The technique used to analyze a goal to identify the sequence of operations and decisions required to achieve it.

Group-based instruction The use of learning activities and materials designed to be used in a collective fashion with a group of learners; interactive, group-paced instruction.

Hierarchical analysis A technique used with goals in the intellectual skills domain to identify the critical subordinate skills needed to achieve the goal, and their interrelationships. For each subordinate skill in the analysis, this involves asking, "What must the student know how to do in order to learn the specific subskills being considered?"

Individualized instruction The use, by students, of systematically designed learning activities and materials specifically chosen to suit their individual interests, abilities, and experience. Such instruction is usually self-paced.

Instruction A set of events or activities presented in a structured or planned way, through one or more media, with the goal of having learners achieve prespecified behaviors.

Instructional analysis The procedures applied to an instructional goal in order to identify the relevant skills and their subordinate skills and information required for a student to achieve the goal.

Instructional materials Print or other mediated instruction used by a student to achieve an instructional goal.

Instructional strategy An overall plan of activities to achieve an instructional goal. The strategy includes the sequence of intermediate objectives and the learning activities leading to the instructional goal.

Instructor's manual The collection of written materials given to instructors to facilitate their use of the instructional materials. The manual should include: an overview of the materials, tests with answers, and any supplementary information thought to be useful to the instructors.

Intellectual skill A skill that requires some unique cognitive activity; involves manipulating cognitive symbols, as opposed to simply retrieving previously learned information.

Item analysis table A means of presenting evaluation data that show the percentage of learners who correctly answered each item on a test.

Job aid A device, often in paper or computer form, that is used to relieve the learner's reliance on memory during the performance of a complex task.

Learner analysis The determination of pertinent characteristics of members of the target population. Often includes prior knowledge and attitudes toward the content to be taught, as well as attitudes toward the organization and work environment.

Learner performance data Information about the degree to which learners achieved the objectives following a unit of instruction.

Learner specialist A person knowledgeable about a particular population of learners.

Learning context The actual physical location (or locations) in which the instruction that is under development will be used.

Mastery level A prespecified level of task performance, with no gradations below it, that defines satisfactory achievement of an objective.

Media The physical means of conveying instructional content. Examples include drawings, slides, audiotape, computer, person, model, and so on.

Model A simplified representation of a system, often in picture or flowchart form, showing selected features of the system.

Module An instructional package with a single integrated theme that provides the information needed to develop mastery of specified knowledge and skills, and serves as one component of a total course or curriculum.

Need A discrepancy between what should be and the current status of a situation.

Needs assessment The formal process of identifying discrepancies between current outcomes and desired outcomes for an organization.

Noninstructional solution Means of reducing performance discrepancies other than the imparting of knowledge; includes motivational, environmental, and equipment factors.

Objective A statement of what the learners will be expected to do when they have completed a specified course of instruction, stated in terms of observable performances. Also known as performance objective; behavioral objective; instructional objective.

One-to-one evaluation The first stage in formative evaluation, referring to direct interaction between the designer and individual tryout student.

Performance context The setting in which it is hoped that learners will successfully use the skills they are learning; includes both the physical and social aspects of the setting.

Posttest A criterion-referenced test designed to measure performance on objectives taught during a unit of instruction; given after the instruction. Typically does not include items on entry behaviors.

Preinstructional activities Techniques used to provide the following three events prior to delivering instructional content:

- Get the learners' attention
- Advise them of the prerequisite skills for the unit
- Tell them what they will be able to do after the instruction

Pretest A criterion-referenced test designed to measure performance on objectives to be taught during a unit of instruction and/or performance on entry behaviors; given before instruction begins.

Problem, Ill-structured Situation in which neither the exact rules to be applied nor the exact nature of the solution is identified in the problem statement. Multiple solutions may be acceptable.

Problem, Well-structured Situation in which the nature of the solution is well understood, and there is a generally preferred set of rules to follow to determine the solution.

Psychomotor skill Execution of a sequence of major or subtle physical actions to achieve a specified result. All skills employ some type of physical action; the physical action in a psychomotor skill is the focus of the *new* learning, and is not merely the vehicle for expressing an intellectual skill.

Reliability The consistency or dependability of a measure.

Research An investigation conducted to identify knowledge that is generalized to many students at various times.

Revision The process of producing an amended, improved, or up-to-date version of a set of instructional materials.

Skill An ability to perform an action or group of actions; involves overt performance.

Small-group evaluation The second stage of formative evaluation, referring to the use of a small number of tryout students who study an instructional program without intervention from the designer and are tested to assess the effectiveness of the instruction.

Step One skill identified in the analysis of an instructional goal. Describes a complete task or behavior, or decision, that must be completed when someone performs the instructional goal. Most goals include five or more steps (see sub-step).

Subject-matter expert (SME) See Subject-matter specialist.

Subject-matter specialist A person knowledgeable about a particular content area. Also known as content specialist; subject-matter expert (SME).

Subordinate objective An objective that must be attained in order to accomplish a terminal objective. Also known as enabling objective; intermediate objective.

Subordinate skill A skill that must be achieved in order to learn a higher-level skill. Also known as subskill or enabling skill.

Sub-step One component of a major step in a goal. There must be two or more sub-steps to justify a sub-step analysis. Performing each of the sub-steps in sequence is equivalent to performing the step from which they were derived.

Summative evaluation Evaluation designed and used after an instructional program has been implemented and formative evaluation completed. The purpose is to present conclusions about the worth of the program or product and make recommendations about its adoption or retention.

Superordinate skill Higher-level competency that is composed of and achieved by learning subordinate skills.

System A set of interrelated parts working together toward a defined goal.

Systems approach Procedure used by instructional designers to create instruction. Each step requires input from prior steps and provides input to the next step. Evaluation provides feedback that is used to revise instruction until it meets the original need or specification.

Target population The total collection of possible users of a given instructional program.

Terminal objective An objective the learners will be expected to accomplish when they have completed a course of instruction, made up of subordinate objectives. Often, a more specific statement of the instructional goal.

Training A prespecified and planned experience that enables a person to do something that he or she couldn't do before.

Transfer of learning The process whereby the learner applies skills learned in one context to another, similar context. Also referred to as transfer of training.

Tryout students A representative sample of the target population; may be used to test an instructional program prior to final implementation.

Validity The degree to which a measuring instrument actually measures what it is intended to measure.

Verbal information Requirement to provide a specific response to relatively specific stimuli; involves recall of information.

APPENDIXES

Many readers of this textbook are educators. The examples in this section relate to school curriculum to aid applying the Dick and Carey model to school learning. Many of you are also using this textbook as a resource for developing your own instruction. We thought it would be helpful for you to see abbreviated example products from each step in the design model collected together in one place. It should benefit those of you who are required to document your design process and develop materials as a course project. The following list will help you locate materials in the Appendixes.

APPENDIX A

Description of Problem (Need), Purpose of Instruction, Target Group, and Delivery System

PROBLEM (NEED)

During a middle school faculty meeting called to discuss problems of students' written composition, teachers decided to conduct a needs assessment study. Each teacher assigned a short essay for his or her students, to be written on a common topic. A newly formed evaluation team of teachers reviewed the themes to identify possible common problems. They reported that, generally, students use one type of sentence—namely, declarative, simple sentences—to communicate their thoughts rather than varying their sentence structure by purpose or complexity. Additionally, punctuation other than periods and commas was absent from students' work, and commas were rare.

PURPOSE

Teachers decided to design special instruction that focused students on (1) writing a variety of sentence types based upon sentence purpose, (2) writing using a variety of sentence structures that vary in complexity, and (3) using a variety of punctuation to match sentence type and complexity. Through instruction focused directly on the problems, they hoped to change the current pattern of simplistic similarity found in students' compositions. They decided to create two units of instruction with the following goals:

1. In written composition, students will use a variety of sentence types and accompanying punctuation based on the purpose and mood of the sentence.

2. In written composition, students will use a variety of sentence types and accompanying punctuation based on the complexity or structure of the sentence.

TARGET GROUP

The composition units with their special emphasis on sentence variety were judged most appropriate for sixth-grade classes that contain students presently achieving at average and above average levels of language expression. These groups will be very heterogeneous in their current writing skill; therefore, instruction on writing sentence types as well as on using sentence types in compositions should be included in the materials.

DELIVERY SYSTEM

For this unit on writing skills, the assumption is made at the outset of the design process that instruction will be delivered by a teacher in a traditional elementary or middle school classroom.

APPENDIX B

Goal Analysis of the Instructional Goal on Story Writing

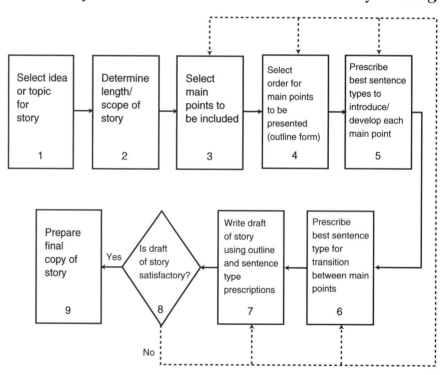

GOAL

In writing short stories, use a variety of sentence types based upon sentence purpose and the idea or mood being communicated.

APPENDIX C

Hierarchical Analysis of Declarative Sentence Portion of Story-Writing Goal with Entry Behavior Lines

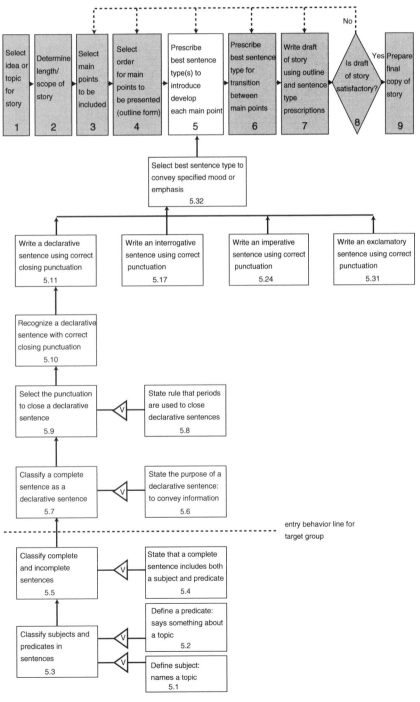

APPENDIX D

Design Evaluation Chart Containing Subskills, Performance Objectives, and Parallel Test Items

Subordinate Skills	Performance Objectives	Parallel Test Items
5.1 Define subject.	5.1 Given the term *subject*, define the term. The definition must include that the subject names a topic.	1. Define the *subject* part of a sentence. 2. What does the *subject* part of a sentence do? 3. The *subject* part of a sentence names the _____.
5.2 Define predicate.	5.2 Given the term *predicate*, define the term. The definition must include that the predicate says something about the subject or topic.	1. Define the *predicate* part of a sentence. 2. What does the *predicate* part of a sentence do? 3. The *predicate* part of a sentence tells something about the _____.
5.3 Classify subjects and predicates in complete sentences.	5.3 Given several complete, simple declarative sentences, locate all the subjects and predicates.	Directions: Locate the *subjects* and the *predicates* in the following sentences. Draw *one* line under the subject and *two* lines under the *predicate* in each sentence. 1. The carnival was a roaring success. 2. The soccer team was victorious this season. 3. Susan got an after-school job weeding flower beds. 4. George's father was pleased with his report card.
5.4 State that a complete statement includes both a subject and a predicate.	5.4 Given the term *complete sentence*, define the concept. The definition must name both the subject and the predicate.	1. Define a *complete sentence*. 2. What elements does a *complete sentence* contain? 3. A complete sentence contains both a(n)_____ and a(n) _____.
5.5 Classify complete and incomplete sentences.	5.5.1 Given several complete and incomplete declarative sentences, locate all those that are complete.	Directions: Locate complete sentences. Place an X in the space before each complete sentence. _____1. John closely followed the directions.

Subordinate Skills	Performance Objectives	Parallel Test Items
		_____2. The team that was most excited.
		_____3. The dogsled jolted and bumped over the frozen land.
		_____4. Found the lost friends happy to see her.
		_____5. The plants in the garden.
	5.5.2 Given several complete and incomplete declarative sentences, locate all those missing subjects and all those missing predicates.	Directions: Locate missing subjects and predicates. Place a P before all of the items that are *missing a predicate*. Place an S before all items that are *missing a subject*.
		_____1. John closely followed the directions.
		_____2. The team that was most excited.
		_____3. The dogsled jolted and bumped over the frozen land.
		_____4. Found the lost friends happy to see her.
		_____5. The plants in the garden.
		_____6. Played on the beach all day.
5.6 State the purpose of a declarative sentence.	5.6 Given the terms *declarative sentence* and *purpose*, state the purpose of a declarative sentence. The purpose should include to convey/tell information.	1. What *purpose* does a *declarative sentence* serve? 2. The *purpose* of a *declarative sentence* is to _____.
5.7 Classify a complete sentence as a declarative sentence.	5.7 Given several complete simple sentences that include declarative, interrogative, and exclamatory sentences that are correctly or incorrectly closed using a period, locate all those that are declarative.	Directions: Locate declarative sentences. Place the letter D in the space before the sentences that are *declarative*.
		_____1. Place the stamp in the upper right corner of the envelope.
		_____2. Are you hungry.
		_____3. Sarah selected a mystery book.
		_____4. The woods looked quiet and peaceful.
		_____5. Wow, look at that fire.
		_____6. Some birds do not migrate.
		_____7. Which of the birds migrate.
5.8 State that periods are used to close declarative sentences.	5.8 Given the terms *declarative sentence* and *closing punctuation*, name the period as the closing punctuation. The term *period* must be spelled correctly.	1. The closing punctuation used with a declarative sentence is called a _____. 2. Declarative sentences are closed using what punctuation mark?
5.9 Select the punctuation used to close a declarative sentence.	5.9 Given illustrations of a period, comma, exclamation point, and a question mark; the terms *declarative sentence* and *closing punctuation*, select the period.	1. Circle the closing punctuation used to end a declarative sentence. , ! . ?

Subordinate Skills	Performance Objectives	Parallel Test Items
5.10 Recognize a declarative sentence with correct closing punctuation.	5.10 Given several simple declarative sentences with correct and incorrect punctuation, select all the declarative sentences with correct closing punctuation.	Directions: Locate correct punctuation for a declarative sentence. Place the letter D in the space before all the *declarative sentences* that *end* with the *correct punctuation mark.* _____1. John likes to read space stories? _____2. I ride two miles to school on the bus. _____3. I got an A on the spelling test! _____4. Juanita is traveling with her parents.
5.11 Write declarative sentences with correct closing punctuation.	5.11 Write declarative sentences on: (1) selected topics and (2) topics of student choice. Sentences must be complete and closed with a period.	1. Directions: Write five declarative sentences that describe today's assembly. 2. Directions: Write five declarative sentences on topics of your own choice.

APPENDIX E

Instructional Strategy for Objective Sequence and Clusters, Preinstructional Activities, and Assessment Activities

Objective Clusters (One Hour for Each)

1	2	3	4	5	6
5.6	5.12	5.18	5.25	5.11	5.32
5.7	5.13	5.19	5.26	5.17	
5.8	5.14	5.20	5.27	5.24	
5.9	5.15	5.21	5.28	5.31	
5.10	5.16	5.22	5.29		
5.11	5.17	5.23	5.30		
		5.24	5.31		

PREINSTRUCTIONAL ACTIVITIES FOR UNIT ON WRITING COMPOSITIONS

PREINSTRUCTIONAL ACTIVITIES

MOTIVATION: A brief story will be used as an introduction. It will be on a topic of *high interest* to sixth graders, and it will contain all four sentence types to illustrate the point of variety and increased interest through varying sentence type.

OBJECTIVES: Each of the four types of sentences in the sample story will be highlighted and described in the introduction. The purpose of the unit, learning to write stories that contain a variety of sentence types, will be included.

ENTRY BEHAVIORS: Since there are several entry behaviors noted in the instructional analysis, a test including entry behaviors will be developed and administered to determine whether students have the required prerequisite skills.

ASSESSMENT ACTIVITIES FOR UNIT ON WRITING COMPOSITIONS

ASSESSMENT

PRETESTS: Administer a brief test of entry behaviors for subskills 5.1, 5.2, 5.3, 5.4, and 5.5. The test will be a short, paper-and-pencil test. If learners do not have prerequisites, then a lesson covering these subskills will be inserted as the first lesson in the unit. Two pretests will be administered after the first lesson, which will be used to motivate learners, inform them of the objectives, and provide example stories. For the pretests, students will be asked to write a brief story using all four sentence types as well as to complete objective questions on subordinate skills.

POSTTESTS: Two different types of posttest will be administered. An objective test will be administered following instruction on Objective 5 to facilitate diagnosis of problems students may be having with these subordinate skills. A second posttest, story writing, will be administered following all instruction in the unit.

STUDENT GROUPINGS AND MEDIA SELECTIONS FOR UNIT ON WRITING COMPOSITIONS

Students will work individually, but will also convene as needed in small work groups with the teacher for question/answer, extra practice, customized feedback, and to maintain pacing. The primary medium will be illustrated text, but the teacher will be prepared with extra examples, nonexamples, and practice to support small group work if needed.

APPENDIX F

Instructional Strategy for the Content Presentation and Student Participation Components and the Lesson Time Allocation Based on the Strategy

Objective 5.6 State Purpose of Declarative Sentence	Objective 5.7 Classify a Complete Sentence As Declarative
Content Presentation	*Content Presentation*
CONTENT: Declarative sentences are used to convey information, to tell the reader something.	CONTENT: Declarative sentences are used to convey information, to tell the reader something.
EXAMPLES: Joan likes to roller skate. It rained the day of the picnic. Fire drills are important. The roller coaster makes my stomach flutter.	EXAMPLES: 1. Tom enjoys space stories. 2. The kittens are all sold. 3. Mr. Jones is very tall. NONEXAMPLES: (Point out why each is not an example.) 1. What does Tom like to read? 2. Are the kittens still for sale? 3. How does Mr. Jones look?
Student Participation	*Student Participation*
PRACTICE ITEMS: What does a declarative sentence do? What does Joan like to do? How does a roller coaster make me feel? FEEDBACK: State that a declarative sentence is used to convey information. Point out what each sentence tells us.	PRACTICE ITEMS: Choose the declarative sentences: 1. How did the flowers smell? 2. Where was Julie going? 3. The traffic is noisy. 4. The sailboat is fun to ride. 5. This dog is very, very thin. FEEDBACK: State why declaratives 3, 4, and 5 are sentences, and 1 and 2 are not.
Objective 5.8 State Periods Used to Close Declarative Sentence	**Objective 5.9 Select Punctuation to Close Declarative Sentence**
Content Presentation	*Content Presentation*
CONTENT: Periods are used to close declarative sentences.	CONTENT: Periods are used to close declarative sentences.
EXAMPLES: The story is exciting. The bear slinked through the campground.	EXAMPLES: The windows had cobwebs in them. The zebra sounded like a horse.

NONEXAMPLES:
The poppies were red and orange?
The sunset was red and orange!

Student Participation	**Student Participation**
PRACTICE ITEMS: What punctuation mark is used to close declarative sentences? FEEDBACK: Restate that the period is used to close declarative sentences.	PRACTICE ITEMS: Select the punctuation mark—period (.), question mark (?), or exclamation mark (!)—to close these declarative sentences: 1. The frost covered the ground 2. Snow was piled along the road 3. The pond was covered with ice FEEDBACK: State that periods should be used to close all the declarative sentences.

Objective 5.10 Recognize Declarative Sentence with Correct Punctuation	**Objective 5.11 Write a Declarative Sentence with Correct Punctuation**
Content Presentation	**Content Presentation**
CONTENT: Only periods are used to close declarative sentences. EXAMPLES: 1. The store had many different bicycles. 2. The store had several types of trains. NONEXAMPLES: What types of trains did the store have? Put your trains away! I feel so happy!	CONTENT: Declarative sentences convey information and are closed using a period. EXAMPLES: 1. The classroom was sunny and bright. 2. Everyone came to the party. NONEXAMPLES: 1. Did John come to the party? 2. John, look out!
Student Participation	**Student Participation**

PRACTICE ITEMS: Which of the following are declarative sentences with correct punctuation?
1. Place your hands on the desk!
2. Begin on page one!
3. Where should we stop?
4. Camping can be fun.
5. Surfing is good exercise.
 	
FEEDBACK: Indicate why 4 and 5 are declarative, and 1, 2, and 3 are not.
	PRACTICE ITEMS:
	1. Write five declarative sentences.
	2. Change the following sentences to declarative.
	  a. How did John look?
	  b. Where did Billie go?
	  c. The sky was very dark!
	
	FEEDBACK: Provide students with list of criteria they can use to evaluate their sentences, e.g., has subject, has predicate, conveys information, and is closed with a period. Give examples of how 2a, b, and c could be rewritten as declarative sentences.

Lesson Time Allocation Based Upon Instructional Strategy

Activity	Time Planned	Activity	Time Planned
Session 1		**Session 5**	
1. Introductory, motivational materials	1 hour	1. Pretest on objectives 5.18–5.24	15 min.
		2. Instruction on objectives 5.18–5.11	40 min.
2. Entry behaviors pretest			
Session 2		**Session 6**	
1. Theme writing pretest	1 hour	1. Pretest on objectives 5.25–5.31	15 min.
		2. Instruction on objectives 5.25–5.31 40 min.	
Session 3		**Session 7**	
1. Pretest on objectives 5.6–5.11	15 min.	1. Review of objectives 5.11, 5.17, 5.24, and 5.31	1 hour
2. Instruction on objectives 5.6–5.11	40 min.		
Session 4		**Session 8**	
1. Pretest on objectives 5.12–5.17	15 min.	1. Pretest on objective 5.32	15 min.
2. Instruction on objectives 5.12–5.17	40 min.	2. Instruction on objective 5.32	40 min.
		Session 9	
		1. Posttest on objectives 5.6–5.32	1 hour

APPENDIX G

Session 1: Motivational Materials, Unit Objectives, and Assessment of Entry Behaviors

Component	Subskill	Text
Introduction/ Motivation (Strategy Appendix E)		We can make stories we write more interesting by using different types of sentences when we write them. Using different types of sentences in our stories does not change the message, it only changes the way we tell it. Different kinds of sentences help the readers know what we want to say and how we feel about exactly what we have said. It involves them in what they are reading because it helps the story come alive.

To show you how using several different kinds of sentences makes a story more interesting, we have written the same story two ways. Story A has all the same kind of sentences in it, while Story B has four different kinds of sentences in it. Read both stories and compare them.

Story A

(1) Yesterday, my Uncle Frank bought a present for me. (2) It was large, wrapped in fancy blue paper, and it had model cars on the ribbon. (3) The card said not to open it until my birthday. (4) I wondered what was inside the box. (5) I held the package, shook it, and turned it upside down. (6) My mother told me to stop playing with the package. (7) Later when she saw me holding the present, she took it and put it away. (8) I would like to find it.

Story B

(1) Yesterday, my Uncle Frank bought a present for me! (2) It was large, wrapped in fancy blue paper, and had model cars on the ribbon. (3) "Do not open until your birthday!" was written on the card. (4) What could be inside the box? (5) I held the package, shook it, and turned it upside down. (6) "Stop playing with your package," said Mother. (7) Later, when she saw me holding the present, she took it and put it away. (8) Where could she have hidden it?

Story B simply tells the same story in a more interesting way. When we write our own stories, we should remember that using several different kinds of sentences in them will make any story more interesting.

Objectives (Strategy Appendix E)		During this unit you are going to learn to write stories that have different kinds of sentences in them. You will focus on four different kinds of sentences including: 1. Declarative sentences that tell the reader something 2. Interrogative sentences that ask questions 3. Imperative sentences that command, direct or request something 4. Exclamatory sentences that show emotion or excitement.

Of course, writing stories that have all four kinds of sentences will require some instruction and lots of practice. The lessons that follow will teach you about each of the sentences and allow you to practice writing each one. After learning to write all four sentence types, you will use them together to create interesting short stories.

Prerequisites (Strategy Appendix E)		Before learning to write different types of sentences, it is important for you to remember facts about complete and incomplete sentences. To help you remember these facts, answer the questions on the short quiz that follows. When you have finished the quiz, close your booklet and read quietly at your desk until your teacher tells you what to do next. REMEMBER TO PUT YOUR NAME ON YOUR QUIZ PAPER

Pretest on Entry Behaviors (Strategy Appendix E)	5.1 5.2	Define the following terms related to sentences. 1. A subject_____ _____ 2. A predicate_____ _____

Locate subjects and predicates. In the following statements, draw *one line under the subjects* and *two lines under the predicates.*

5.3	3. The carnival was a roaring success. 4. The soccer team was victorious this season. 5. Susan got an after-school job weeding flower beds.
5.4	6. Define a complete sentence. _____ _____

Locate complete and incomplete sentences. Place a C before all the following sentences that are *complete.* If the sentence is not complete, write an S to indicate that the *subject* is missing. Write a P to indicate that the *predicate* is missing.

5.5	_____7. John closely followed the directions. _____8. The team that was most excited. _____9. The dogsled jolted and bumped over the frozen land. _____10. Found the lost friends happy to see her.

APPENDIX H

Session 2: Pretest Story and Rubric to Evaluate Stories

Component	Subskill	Text
Pretest Theme (Strategy Appendix E)	Instructional Goal	Write a short, one-page story using a variety of sentence types to hold the interest of the reader and to strengthen the idea or mood of your story. In your story you should:

1. Use at least *two* of each of the following types of sentences: declarative, interrogative, imperative, and exclamatory.
2. Use only *complete* sentences.
3. Use the *correct punctuation* based on sentence type and *mood*.
4. Select the best type of sentence to convey the idea you wish.

Select one of the following titles for your theme.*

1. I Really Didn't Expect That!
2. He/She/You Shouldn't Have Done It!
3. I Will Think Twice Before I Do That Again!

*The title does not count as one of your exclamatory sentences.

TOTAL
ERRORS

TOTAL
ERRORS

_____ I. Declarative Sentences
    _____ 1. Number of declarative sentences
    _____ 2. Sentences complete
        _____ a. number of subjects incomplete
        _____ b. number of predicates incomplete
    _____ 3. Number of periods used to close sentences
    _____ 4. Sentence type appropriate for idea/mood conveyed
        _____ a. number appropriate
        _____ b. number inappropriate
    _____ 5. Transition smooth

_____ III. Imperative Sentences
    _____ 1. Number of imperative sentences
    _____ 2. Sentences complete
        _____ a. number of subjects incomplete
        _____ b. number of predicates incomplete
    _____ 3. Number of exclamation points used for strong requests, instructions
    _____ 4. Number of periods used for mild directions, requests
    _____ 5. Sentence type appropriate for idea/mood conveyed
        _____ a. number appropriate

TOTAL

ERRORS _____

TOTAL

ERRORS _____

_____ II. Interrogative Sentences

_____ 1. Number of interrogative
sentences

_____ 2. Sentences complete

_____ a. number of subjects
incomplete

_____ b. number of predi-
cates incomplete

_____ 3. Question marks used to
close sentences

_____ 4. Number of questions appropriate to lead reader

_____ 5. Number of questions appropriate to seek information

_____ 6. Sentence type appropriate
for idea/mood conveyed

_____ a. number appropriate

_____ b. number inappropriate

_____ 7. Transition smooth

_____ IV. Exclamatory Sentences

_____ 1. Number of exclamatory
sentences

_____ 2. Sentences complete

_____ a. number of sub-
jects incomplete

_____ b. number of predi-
cates incomplete

_____ 3. Number of exclamation
points used to close
sentences

_____ 4. Sentence type appropriate
for idea/mood conveyed

_____ a. number appropriate

_____ b. number inappro-
priate

_____ 5. Transition smooth

APPENDIX I

Session 3: Pretest and Instruction in Subordinate Skills 5.6 Through 5.11

Component	Subskill	Text
Objective Pretest (Strategy Appendix E) Instructions	5.6–5.11	The following short quiz has questions about declarative sentences on it. Put your name and the date on the top before you begin. Answer each question. If you are not sure of the answer, guess what the answer might be. Do not be upset if you do not know some of the answers, since you may not have had instruction on declarative sentences yet. When you finish the quiz, raise your hand and it will be collected. You may begin the lesson when you finish the quiz.
	5.6	1. The purpose of a declarative sentence is to _____.
	5.7	Determine whether the following sentences are declarative. If a sentence is declarative, mark a *D* in the space before the sentence.
		2. _____ Wow look at that fire
		3. _____ Sarah selected a mystery book
		4. _____ Did Sarah select a mystery book
		5. _____ The woods look quiet and peaceful
		6. _____ Are you hungry
	5.8	7. The punctuation mark used to close a declarative sentence is called a(an) _____.
	5.9	Place the punctuation mark that should follow these sentences in the blank to the left of the sentence.
		8. _____ Gina did not get a bike for her birthday
		9. _____ Sam worked in the yard after school
	5.10	Identify declarative sentences with correct ending punctuation. Place a D beside each correct sentence.
		10. _____ Did George get many presents.
		11. _____ The air was warm and balmy?
		12. _____ Jenny was late for class.
		13. _____ Ken was happy when they arrived.
		14. _____ What is the first day of winter.
	5.11	Write two declarative sentences with correct punctuation that describe today's class.
		15.
		16.
	5.11	Write two declarative sentences, with correct punctuation, on topics of your choice.

Component	Subskill	Text

17.

18.

Declarative Sentences

Content Presentation (Appendix F) — 5.6

A declarative sentence is used to convey information, to tell the reader something, or describe something. When you want to state a fact or describe something in a direct manner, you write a declarative sentence.

Here are some declarative sentences used to state facts.

Examples

1. Joan likes to roller skate.
2. Fire drills are important.

The first sentence tells us what Joan likes to do. The second sentence tells us that fire drills are an important activity.

Content

Declarative sentences can also be used to describe something. The following sentences are descriptions.

Examples

1. It rained the day of the picnic.
2. The roller coaster makes my stomach flutter.

The first sentence describes the day as rainy and the second one describes how a roller coaster makes the writer's stomach feel.

5.7

Look at the next two sentences. One is a declarative sentence and one is not.

Nonexamples

1. Tom enjoys reading space stories.
2. What does Tom want to read?

The first sentence is declarative since it tells us what kind of stories Tom likes to read. The second sentence is not declarative. After reading this sentence, we do not know what Tom likes to read. Since the second sentence cannot give the reader information, it is *not* a declarative sentence.

Practice — 5.6 5.7

Read the following pairs of sentences. Which of the sentences are declarative and why?

Are the kittens still for sale?
The kittens are all sold.
Mr. Jones is very tall.
How did Mr. Jones look?

Feedback

In the first pair of sentences the declarative sentence tells us that the kittens are all sold. The other sentence does not tell us whether they are sold or not. Likewise, the declarative sentence tells us that Mr. Jones is very tall, but the other sentence does not provide any clues about how Mr. Jones looks.

Embedded Questions — 5.6 5.7

1. What does a declarative sentence do? _____

_____

2. Which of the following sentences are declarative? Place a *D* beside the declarative ones.

_____a. How did the flowers smell
_____b. Where was Julie going
_____c. The traffic is noisy
_____d. How do you do it
_____e. The sailboat is fun to ride

Content Presentation (Appendix F) — 5.8

Punctuation marks are used to close complete sentences. The period (.) is the punctuation mark that is always used to close a declarative sentence. When you see a period at the end of a sentence, it is a clue that the sentence *may* be a declarative one. Other types of sentences may use a period, but a sentence that (1) conveys information and (2) is closed with a period is always a declarative sentence.

Here are some declarative sentences that are correctly punctuated.

1. The story is exciting.
2. The bear slinked through the campground.

We know the first sentence is declarative because it describes the story and is closed using a period. The second sentence is declarative because it tells what the bear did, and it is closed with a period.

Content Presentation	5.9	If a sentence appears to be declarative because it tells something or describes something, yet the punctuation mark at the end of the sentence is not a period, then the sentence is not a declarative one.

Some sentences tell the reader something, and this is a clue that they might be declarative. However, a period is not used to close the sentence. This means that they are *not* declarative. Look at these examples.

Nonexamples	1. He is huge! 2. My shoes are gone!

Neither of these sentences is declarative because periods are not used to close them.

Practice	5.8 5.9	Remember, to be a declarative sentence, it must tell the reader something, and it must close with a period. Consider these sentences. Which are declarative?

_____1. The frost covered the ground!
_____2. The frost covered the ground.
_____3. What covered the ground?

Feedback	The first sentence is *not* declarative. Although it tells us about frost on the ground, it does not end with a *period*. The second sentence is declarative. It tells about frost on the ground and it ends with a period. The third sentence is *not* declarative because it does not convey information and it does not end with a period.

Embedded Questions	5.8	3. What punctuation mark is used to close a declarative sentence? _____ _____
	5.9	4. Place the *correct punctuation mark* at the end of these sentences. a. The sunset is red and orange_____ b. The snow was piled along the road_____ c. The pond is covered with ice_____
	5.10	5. Which of the following sentences are declarative? Place a *D* beside the declarative ones. _____a. The poppies were red and orange. _____b. Did the zebra sound like a horse? _____c. The zebra sounded like a horse! _____d. The windows had cobwebs in them. _____e. I lost my key!
Content Presentation	5.11	You can write your own declarative sentences. To write correct declarative sentences, you should write them *to tell or describe something,* and you should always *close them with periods.*

For each of the topics listed below, a declarative sentence has been written. Write a sentence of your own on each topic that is different from the one shown.

	Topic	Sentence
Examples and Embedded Test	5.11 Oranges	1. Oranges grow on trees. 2.
	Mother	1. My mother is a teacher. 2.
	School	1. I like to go to school. 2.

Friends	1. My friends come to my house to play.
	2.
The Ocean	1. Fish live in the ocean.
	2.

Embedded Test 5.11

Write four declarative sentences on topics of your own choice.

1.
2.
3.
4.

Answers to embedded questions 5.6, 5.7, 5.8, 5.9, 5.10, and 5.11 (These are not for students during field trials, but may be inserted in finished instruction for use as feedback.)

1. A declarative sentence tells us something or conveys information.
2. _____ a. How did the flowers smell
   _____ b. Where was Julie going
   __D__ c. The traffic is noisy
   _____ d. How do you do it
   __D__ e. The sailboat is fun to ride
3. Period
4. a. The sunset is red and orange.
   b. The snow was piled along the road.
   c. The pond is covered with ice.
5. __D__ a. The poppies were red and orange.
   _____ b. Did the zebra sound like a horse?
   _____ c. The zebra sounded like a horse!
   __D__ d. The windows had cobwebs in them.
   _____ e. I lost my key!

Topic	Sentence
Oranges	1. Oranges grow on trees.
	2. Oranges grow in Florida and California.
Mother	3. My mother is a teacher.
	4. Mother goes to practice with me.
School	5. I like to go to school.
	6. School can be fun and boring.
Friends	7. My friends come to my house to play.
	8. I play games with my friends.
The ocean	9. Fish live in the ocean.
	10. The ocean is very deep.

APPENDIX J

Group's and Individuals' Achievement of Objectives and Attitudes About Instruction

Student Responses by Item Within Objective on the Entry Behaviors Section of the Pretest

Objectives:	5.1	5.2		5.3		5.4		5.5						
Items	1	2	3	4	5	6	7	8	9	10	Score	%	Obj.	%
Students ↓ 1							X		X		2	20	0	0
2			X	X	X		X		X		5	50	1	20
3			X	X	X		X		X		5	50	1	20
4	X		X	X	X		X		X		6	60	2	40
5	X	X	X	X	X		X	X	X	X	9	90	4	80
6	X	X	X	X	X	X	X	X	X	X	10	100	5	100
7	X	X	X	X	X	X	X	X	X	X	10	100	5	100
8	X	X	X	X	X	X	X	X	X	X	10	100	5	100
9	X	X	X	X	X	X	X	X	X	X	10	100	5	100
10	X	X	X	X	X	X	X	X	X	X	10	100	5	100
11	X	X	X	X	X	X	X	X	X	X	10	100	5	100
12	X	X	X	X	X	X	X	X	X	X	10	100	5	100
13	X	X	X	X	X	X	X	X	X	X	10	100	5	100
14	X	X	X	X	X	X	X	X	X	X	10	100	5	100
15	X	X	X	X	X	X	X	X	X	X	10	100	5	100
Total Right	12	11	14	14	14	10	15	11	15	11				
% Right	80	73	93	93	93	66	100	73	100	73				
% Object.	80	73		93		66		73						

Note: X = correct response; blank = incorrect response.

Pretest for Declarative Sentences: Student Performance by Item within Objective

Objective	5.6	5.7					5.8	5.9		5.10					5.11				#		#	
Item	1	2	3	4	5	6	7	8	9	10	11	12	13	14	15	16	17	18	Score	%	Obj.	%
1			X		X		X	X	X		X	X	X						8	44	2	33
2			X		X		X	X	X		X	X	X						8	44	2	33
3			X		X		X	X	X		X	X	X						8	44	2	33
4			X		X		X	X	X		X	X	X						8	44	2	33
5			X		X		X	X	X		X	X	X			X	X	X	11	61	2	33
6			X		X		X	X	X		X	X	X			X	X	X	11	61	2	33
7			X		X		X	X	X		X	X	X			X	X	X	11	61	2	33
8			X		X		X	X	X		X	X	X			X	X	X	11	61	2	33
9			X		X		X	X	X		X	X	X		X			X	10	55	2	33
10	X		X	X	X	X	X	X	X		X	X	X		X	X	X	X	15	83	4	66
11	X	X	X	X	X	X	X	X	X	X	X	X	X	X	X	X	X	X	18	100	6	100
12	X	X	X	X	X	X	X	X	X	X	X	X	X	X	X	X	X	X	18	100	6	100
13	X	X	X	X	X	X	X	X	X	X	X	X	X	X	X	X	X	X	18	100	6	100
14	X	X	X	X	X	X	X	X	X	X	X	X	X	X	X	X	X	X	18	100	6	100
15	X	X	X	X	X	X	X	X	X	X	X	X	X	X	X	X	X	X	18	100	6	100
# Right	6	5	15	6	15	6	15	15	15	5	15	15	15	5	7	10	10	11				
% Right	40	33	100	40	100	40	100	100	100	33	100	100	100	33	46	66	66	73				
% Mastering	40			26			100	100				33					40					

Student Performance by Item within Objective on Embedded Questions for Declarative Sentences

Objective	5.6	5.7					5.8	5.9			5.10					5.11									Raw	Percent	#	%
Item	1	A	B	C	D	E	3	A	B	C	A	B	C	D	E	1	2	3	4	5	6	7	8	9	Score (24)	Correct	obj (6)	obj
1	X	X	X	X	X	X	X	X	X	X		X	X	X	X		X			X		X	X	X	19	88	4	66
2	X	X	X	X	X	X	X	X	X	X	X	X	X	X	X		X		X	X	X	X	X	X	22	92	5	83
3	X	X	X	X	X	X	X	X	X	X	X	X	X	X	X	X	X	X	X	X	X	X	X	X	24	100	6	100
4	X	X	X	X	X	X	X	X	X	X	X	X	X	X	X	X	X	X	X	X	X	X	X	X	24	100	6	100
5	X	X	X	X	X	X	X	X	X	X	X	X	X	X	X	X	X	X	X	X	X	X	X	X	24	100	6	100
6	X	X	X	X	X	X	X	X	X	X	X	X	X	X	X	X	X	X	X	X	X	X	X	X	24	100	6	100
7	X	X	X	X	X	X	X	X	X	X	X	X	X	X	X	X	X	X	X	X	X	X	X	X	24	100	6	100
8	X	X	X	X	X	X	X	X	X	X	X	X	X	X	X	X	X	X	X	X	X	X	X	X	24	100	6	100
9	X	X	X	X	X	X	X	X	X	X	X	X	X	X	X	X	X	X	X	X	X	X	X	X	24	100	6	100
10	X	X	X	X	X	X	X	X	X	X	X	X	X	X	X	X	X	X	X	X	X	X	X	X	24	100	6	100
11	X	X	X	X	X	X	X	X	X	X	X	X	X	X	X	X	X	X	X	X	X	X	X	X	24	100	6	100
12	X	X	X	X	X	X	X	X	X	X	X	X	X	X	X	X	X	X	X	X	X	X	X	X	24	100	6	100
13	X	X	X	X	X	X	X	X	X	X	X	X	X	X	X	X	X	X	X	X	X	X	X	X	24	100	6	100
14	X	X	X	X	X	X	X	X	X	X	X	X	X	X	X	X	X	X	X	X	X	X	X	X	24	100	6	100
15	X	X	X	X	X	X	X	X	X	X	X	X	X	X	X	X	X	X	X	X	X	X	X	X	24	100	6	100
Number of students	15	15	15	15	15	15	15	15	15	15	14	15	15	15	15	13	15	13	14	15	14	15	15	15				x̄ = 17.8
Percent of students correct	100	100	100	100	100	100	100	100	100	100	93	100	100	100	100	86	100	86	93	100	93	100	100	100				

X = Correct
A blank space reflects an incorrect response

Student Performance on Objectives on the Pretest, Embedded Test Items, and Posttest

Objective	5.6			5.7			5.8			5.9			5.10			5.11		
Content	Purpose			Identify			Name Punctuation			Punctuate			Recognize			Write		
Test	Pre	Emb	Post	Pre	Emb	Post	Pre	Emb	Post	Pre	Emb	Post	Pre	Emb	Post	Pre	Emb	Post
1		X	X		X	X	X	X	X	X	X	X		X				
2		X	X		X	X	X	X	X	X	X	X		X			X	
3		X	X		X	X	X	X	X	X	X	X		X	X		X	
4		X	X		X	X	X	X	X	X	X	X		X			X	
5		X	X		X	X	X	X	X	X	X	X		X	X		X	
6		X	X		X	X	X	X	X	X	X	X		X	X	X	X	X
7		X	X		X	X	X	X	X	X	X	X		X	X	X	X	X
8		X	X		X	X	X	X	X	X	X	X		X	X	X	X	X
9		X	X		X	X	X	X	X	X	X	X		X	X		X	X
10	X	X	X		X	X	X	X	X	X	X	X		X	X	X	X	X
11	X	X	X	X	X	X	X	X	X	X	X	X	X	X	X	X	X	X
12	X	X	X		X	X	X	X	X	X	X	X	X	X	X		X	X
13	X	X	X	X	X	X	X	X	X	X	X	X	X	X	X	X	X	X
14	X	X	X	X	X	X	X	X	X	X	X	X	X	X	X	X	X	X
15	X	X	X	X	X	X	X	X	X	X	X	X	X	X	X	X	X	X
Number of students passing	6	15	15	4	15	15	15	15	15	15	15	15	5	15	12	8	14	10
Percent of students passing	40	100	100	27	100	100	100	100	100	100	100	100	33	100	80	53	93	66
Differences	+60		0	+73		0	0		0	0		0	+67		−20	+40		−27

X = Objective passed

Entry Behavior Items, Pretest, Embedded Test, and Posttest by Percentage of Possible Items and by Percentage of Possible Objectives

	Percentage of Total Items					Percentage of Total Objectives			
Student	Entry behavior	Pretest	Embedded test	Posttest	Student	Entry behavior	Pretest	Embedded test	Posttest
1	20	44	79	80	1	0	33	66	66
2	50	44	92	80	2	20	33	83	66
3	50	44	100	85	3	20	33	100	83
4	60	44	100	80	4	40	33	100	66
5	90	61	100	85	5	80	33	100	83
6	100	61	100	100	6	100	33	100	100
7	100	61	100	100	7	100	33	100	100
8	100	61	100	100	8	100	33	100	100
9	100	55	100	100	9	100	83	100	100
10	100	83	100	100	10	100	66	100	100
11	100	100	100	100	11	100	100	100	100
12	100	100	100	100	12	100	100	100	100
13	100	100	100	100	13	100	100	100	100
14	100	100	100	100	14	100	100	100	100
15	100	100	100	100	15	100	100	100	100
# items	10	18	24	24	# obj	5	6	6	6

Students' Performance
Plotted by Objective on
Pretest, Embedded Test
Items, and Posttest

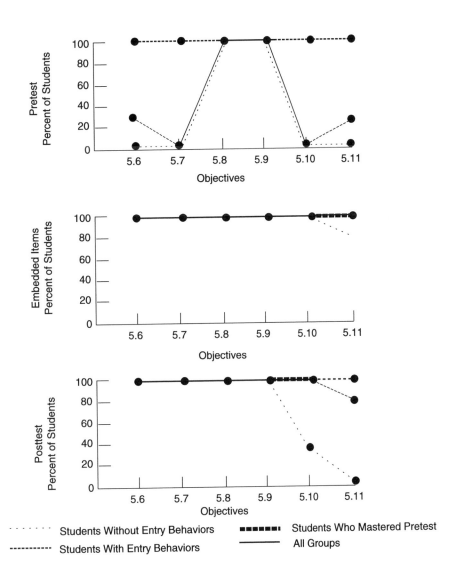

**SUMMARY OF STUDENTS' RESPONSES ON ATTITUDE
QUESTIONNAIRE BY GROUP**

Name *Summary*   Date *1-6*   Class *Small Group*

Attitude Questionnaire

Please answer the following questions to help us understand what you thought about the lessons on writing different kinds of sentences. Your opinions will help us make better lessons for you.

A. Motivation

   1. Did you enjoy the story about the birthday present?

     __15__   Yes //// -HH- / -HH-

     _____   No

   2. Did you think the version of the story that had all types of sentences included (B) was more interesting than the first (A)?

     __15__   Yes //// -HH- / -HH-

     _____   No

   3. Did reading the story make you want to write more interesting stories yourself?

     __15__   Yes //// -HH- / -HH-

     _____   No

   4. What type of stories do you most like to read? *horses, pets, space, sports, nature, cars, mysteries*

B. Objectives

   1. Did you understand that you were going to learn to write stories that were more interesting?

     __15__   Yes //// -HH- / -HH-

     _____   No

   2. Did you understand that you were going to learn to use four different kinds of sentences in your stories?

     __15__   Yes //// -HH- / -HH-

     _____   No

   3. Did you want to write different types of sentences?

     __15__   Yes //// -HH- / -HH-

     _____   No

C. Entry Behaviors

   1. Were the questions about subjects, predicates, and complete sentences clear to you?

     __15__   Yes //// -HH- / -HH-

     _____   No

   2. Did you already know about subjects, predicates, and complete sentences before you started?

     __14__   Yes /// -HH- / -HH-

     __1__   No /

   3. Do you wish information about subjects, predicates, and complete sentences had been included in the lesson?

     _____   Yes

     __15__   No //// -HH- / -HH-

D. Tests

   1. Did you think the questions on the pretest were clear?

     __8__   Yes /// -HH-   *Didn't know the answers*

     __7__   No //// //   *Vocabulary clear*

   2. Did you think you knew most of the answers on the pretest?

     __9__   Yes //// -HH-

     __6__   No /// ///

   3. Were the questions on the posttest clear or confusing?

     __15__   Clear //// -HH- / -HH-

     _____   Confusing

   4. Did you think questions within the lesson were clear or confusing?

     __15__   Clear //// -HH- / -HH-

     _____   Confusing

E. Instruction

   1. Was the instruction interesting?

     __15__   Yes //// -HH- / -HH-

     _____   No

2. Was the instruction clear?

___15___ Yes /// ///// / /////

_____ No

If not, what wasn't clear? ____*Where were the stories ?*____

3. Were the example questions helpful?

___10___ Yes //// ///// /

___5___ No /////

4. Were there too many examples? Too Few?

___5___ Yes ___3___ Yes

___10___ No ___4___ No

5. Did the practice questions in the instruction help you?

___10___ Yes //// ///// /

___5___ No /////

If not, why not? _____

6. Did the feedback exercises in the instruction help you?

___10___ Yes /// ///// /

___5___ No /////

If not, why not? _____

B. Objectives

1. Generally, did you like the lesson?

___15___ Yes //// ///// / /////

_____ No

2. Did you learn to do things you couldn't do before?

___10___ Yes //// ///// /

___5___ No /////

3. What do you think would improve the lesson most?
More example stories to see; pick out declarative sentences in stories;
the lesson wasn't about writing stories

APPENDIX K

Materials Revision Analysis Form

Component	Problem	Change	Evidence and Source
Motivational introductory material	None	Perhaps add another example story to the material	Students reported enjoying illustrative story and understanding the purpose for the unit (attitude questionnaire). All groups reported wanting to read more example stories on the questionnaire and in the debriefing session.
Entry behaviors items	None	None	1. Items did identify students who would have difficulty with first lesson (comparison of entry behavior scores and posttest scores). 2. Test fits time frame. 3. Students under stood vocabulary used and question structure.
Pretest on instructional objectives	None	None	1. Pretest did separate students who knew the materials from those who did not. 2. Vocabulary level OK. 3. Time frame OK. 4. Question format OK.
Materials content	1. Instruction on punctuation (5.8 and 5.9) not needed by any students	Potential removal of punctuation objectives from lesson	Observe problems with periods used to close imperative and exclamatory sentences in subsequent lesson—may provide foundation here.

Component	Problem	Change	Evidence and Source
	2. Entire lesson not needed by students who mastered pretest	Possibly have high ability students begin with lesson two	Five students did not need lesson (pretest, embedded test, postest, attitude questionnaire).
	3. Entry behaviors skills and sentence writing skills not mastered by some members of the group	Develop a set of remedial materials for these students to cover entry behaviors as well as provide more practice in writing sentences	1. Four students had difficulty recognizing complete sentences, subjects, and predicates (pretest). 2. Four students had difficulty writing sentence (posttest, objective 5.11).
	4. Students lost focus on story writing in lesson on sentences	Add stories from which students can classify declarative sentences. Have students write declarative sentences for given stories	Debriefing session and questionnaire.
Embedded tests	Predictive validity (embedded items did not indicate eventual problems on posttest for same items)	Insert embedded test items on recognizing complete sentences and writing sentences in materials a distance from instruction and examples	Embedded test items functioned well in the materials, *but* they did not predict students who would have difficulty on the posttest. This may be related to students' ability to mimic sentences in the embedded tests (embedded and posttest scores).
Posttest	None	None	1. Test did identify students having difficulty with objectives 5.10 and 5.11. 2. Time OK. 3. Question format OK. 4. Vocabulary OK (posttest data).
Attitude questionnaire	None	None	1. Did detect dissatisfaction of high-ability students with lesson. 2. Information corroborated correct level of difficulty for students with prerequisite skills. 3. Information from students without the prerequisites (guessing) was corroborated with test data.

INDEX

as criterion-referenced test, 159–161
developing, 160–161
to evaluate stories, 392–393
for evaluating elaborated goals, terminal objectives and performance, 141
for evaluating material completeness and accuracy, 361–362
for evaluating materials learning and instructional strategies on materials, 362–367
for evaluating motor skills, 167–170
for evaluating test items, 165–166
for examining instructional characteristics, 365–367
for expert judgment perceptions, 368–369
frequency count on, 161
rating scale as, 160–161
Clark, R., 206
Cluster analysis, 65–66
for verbal information, 90–91, *93*
for verbal information subordinate skills, 77–79
of verbal information task for leading group discussion, *79*
Clustering, in instructional strategy, 188–189, 214–215
Cognitive psychology, 5
Cognitive views of learning, 5
Concepts, 38–42
Conditions, derivation of, 126–128
Conditions of Learning, The (Gagné), 5, 189
Confidence, of learners, 190
Congruence analysis, 352–353
Congruence in instructional design, 163–164
evaluating test design and, 171–172
Constructivist approach, 5
to developing instructional strategy, 209
Content, learner attitudes toward, 97, 104
Content analysis, 353
Content presentation, 193, 213, 216–221, 260
for checking account instructional goals, 274–278
Content sequence, for instructional strategy, 187–188
Context, of skill uses, 23
Context analysis
data for analysis in learning environment, 102
in formative evaluation, 302–303
of learning environment, 100–102, 107–108

of performance setting, 99–100
public school contexts, 102–103
Context-centered criteria, for evaluating materials, 246–247
Course management information, accompanying instructional materials, 245–246
Criteria-centered tests, examples of, 165
Criterion
definition of, 146
derivation of, 128–129
in testing of mastery levels, 150
Criterion-referenced tests, 5, 146, 194
assessment-centered criteria for, 153
design elements for conducting design evaluation, *181*
designing, 149–150
developing, 157–162
directions on, 156, 158
evaluating, 156–157, 171–172
for evaluating behaviors relating to attitudes, 170
goal-centered criteria for, 151–152
learner-centered criteria for, 152–153
mastery criteria for, 153–154
response format for, 159
scoring of, 161–162
types of, 146–148, 149
writing, 151–153
Cronbach, L. J., 283
Cues, for learners, 126
Current user analysis, 354
Customer service, instructional goals for providing, 27–30

Data. *See also* Formative evaluation
analysis across tests, 336–337
analysis of, 324–331
for context analysis in learning environment, 102
for context analysis in performance setting, 100
entry behaviors and, 330
in formative evaluation, 297–300
for learner analysis, 99
in one-to-one evaluation, 287–288, 324–325
for selected materials and instructor-led instruction, 302
sequence for examining, 330
in small-group evaluation, 325–331
summary of congruence analysis, 361
types of, 330
Data interpretation, in one-to-one evaluation, 291
Delivery system, 185–186, 187, 248, 378. *See also* Learning
confirming, 221–224

Motor skills. *See* Psychomotor skills
MSDS (materials safety data sheet), 51

Nathenson, 194
Needs assessment, 16–30, 25–26, 378
Neighborhood Crime Watch (NCW)
    organizations. *See* specific topics
    and examples
Newby, T., 209
Newstrom, J. W., 196

Objective(s)
    strategy for, 391
    of tests, 149–150
Objective-referenced tests, 146
Objective-style tests, 149
    students answering items correctly
        on checking account pretest and
        posttest, *344*
One-to-one evaluation, 8, 286–291, 359
    analyzing data from, 324–325
    assessments and questionnaires in,
        289–290
    data collection for, 287–288
    data interpretation and, 291
    learning time and, 290
    procedure of, 288–289
Open university model, 243–245
Outcomes analysis, 351
Output, of learner analysis, 99

Paraphrasing, in criterion-referenced
    test development, 158–159
Participation. *See* Students
Pedagogical theory, of Moore and
    Kearsley, 197–198
Performance
    graphing of, *329*, 329–330
    pretest/posttest graph showing, *329*
    as test, 149, 150
Performance analysis, 19–22
Performance by objective, 341
Performance context
    analysis of, 99–100
    data collection for context analysis in,
        100
    formative evaluation in, 295–297
    for instructional goal, 117–118
    for NCW leaders, 107
    sample form for analyzing, 113
Performance objectives, 7
    behaviors for, 125
    checklist of criteria for evaluating
        elaborated goals, terminal objec-
        tives and performance, 141
    components of, 124–125
    conditions for, 126–128
    criteria for, 128–129
    defined, 123

evaluation of, 130–131
examples of, 132–138
function of, 131–132
for subskills in banking goal, *80, 81,*
    140, 175
writing, 120–142
Performance technology approach, 17,
    18–19
Portfolio assessments, 162–163
Posttest, 148, 149, 200
    performance by objective, 328, 341
    purpose of, 148
    students answering objective-based
        items correctly on, *344*
    summary for instructional analysis,
        329
Practice
    of psychomotor skills, 201
    of verbal information, 201
Practice tests, 148, 149
Preinstructional activities, 190–193,
    192–197, 213, 215–216, 257–259
    for banking instructional goal, 227,
        228–237
    for group leadership instructional
        goal, 256
    for unit on leading group discussion,
        216
    for writing compositions unit, 385
Preinstructional text, converting to
    graphics, *257*
Prerequisites. *See also* Subordinate skills
    informing learner of, 192–193
    strategy for, 391
Prescriptive approach, to developing
    instructional strategy, 209
Pretest. *See also* Preinstructional activi-
    ties
    for checking account instructional
        goals, 273–274
    on entry behaviors, 391
    in formative evaluation field trial,
        300
    graph showing learner performance,
        329
    for group leadership instructional
        goal, 258–259
    performance by objective on, 328
    purpose of, 147
    story and evaluation checklist,
        392–393
    students answering objective-based
        items correctly on, *344*
    in subordinate skills, 394–397
    summary for instructional analysis,
        329
    for unit on leading group discussion,
        216
Prior knowledge, 97, 104